# Enfield L

**ENFIELD CENTR...**
**CECIL ROAD**
**ENFIELD EN2 6TW**
Lending: 020 8379 8...
Reference: 020 8379 8
Music: 020 8379 839

| | field STW | | |
|---|---|---|---|
| | | | 10. SEP 0 |
| | | 19. JUL 03 | 1 OCT 2004 |
| 04 DEC | | | 21. JAN 05 |
| | 30. DEC | 8070 28-8-03 | |
| 19. JUN 01 | 02. AUG 01 | 04 OCT 03 | 26. FEB 05 |
| FEB 2001 | 22. | (M) 23.9.03 | 05. APR |
| | 09. MAR 02 | 18. OCT 03 | 26 Apr 4050 |
| 09. | 23. MAY 02 | 27. NOV 03 | 7 June 5071 |
| 19. APR 01 | 13.6.02 | | 28 June 6070 |
| 10. MAY | 18. AUG 02 | 12. JAN 04 | 01. 04 |
| 05. JUL 01 | 28 SEP 02 | 17. APR 04 | 09. MAY 06 |

Please remember that this item will attract overdue charges if not returned by the latest date stamped above. You may renew it in person, by telephone or by post quoting the barcode number and your library card number.

19 DEC 2006
23 SEP 2007

30126  01052510 0

# FIFTY YEARS PLUS
# 1924–1974
*A Family in the Licensed Trade*

Stanley W. Standbrook

MINERVA PRESS
LONDON
ATLANTA MONTREUX SYDNEY

FIFTY YEARS PLUS 1924–1974: *A Family in the Licensed Trade*
Copyright © Stanley W. Standbrook 1998

All Rights Reserved

No part of this book may be reproduced in any form
by photocopying or by any electronic or mechanical means,
including information storage or retrieval systems,
without permission in writing from both the copyright
owner and the publisher of this book.

ISBN 0 75410 138 X

First Published 1997 by
MINERVA PRESS
195 Knightsbridge
London SW7 1RE

Printed in Great Britain for Minerva Press

# FIFTY YEARS PLUS
## 1924–1974
*A Family in the Licensed Trade*

*I dedicate this book to my dear
and understanding wife, Audrey,
together with all my family, also to
everyone who does not let wealth override
kindness and care to others*

Please note – all comparative prices quoted refer to the period in which the book was completed in 1973, also when stating facts at that period regarding owners and names or properties, many of which have been demolished.

*National Price Index 1974: 25.3*
*National Price Index 1998: 159.5*
*Increase approximately 6.5 times*

# Contents

|      | Foreword                            | xi  |
|------|-------------------------------------|-----|
| I    | The Old George Inn & Plague         | 19  |
| II   | Enfield in the Seventeenth Century  | 25  |
| III  | The Old Palace & St Andrew's Church | 36  |
| IV   | Old Enfield Properties              | 47  |
| V    | The New River                       | 53  |
| VI   | Owners of The George Inn            | 56  |
| VII  | Dick Turpin                         | 64  |
| VIII | The Lamentable Gin Era              | 69  |
| IX   | Licensees and the Enfield Fly       | 75  |
| X    | Enfield Chase – Charles Lamb        | 78  |
| XI   | The Coach Revival                   | 85  |
| XII  | The George Rebuilt                  | 91  |
| XIII | The Petrol Motor                    | 103 |
| XIV  | A.J.S. and The Railway Tavern       | 111 |
| XV   | A.J.S. Billiards & Tom Newman       | 128 |
| XVI  | Grandparents Standbrook             | 138 |

| | | |
|---|---|---|
| XVII | Grandparents Plucks & Allens | 147 |
| XVIII | The George & Enfield 1924 | 156 |
| XIX | Enfield Pubs & Landlords in the Twenties | 175 |
| XX | Working at The Rogat Tool & Stamping Company | 196 |
| XXI | James Neilson's Estate Office | 218 |
| XXII | Strike 1926 and Alterations at The George | 242 |
| XXIII | The Tudor Room and Gunpowder Plot | 255 |
| XXIV | A.J.S. Arm Amputated – Amateur and Professional Boxing | 269 |
| XXV | Charlie Boy – Flying 1927 | 280 |
| XXVI | Our Wedding. The Cuffley Hotel | 294 |
| XXVII | King George Died. Golf & Bowls | 309 |
| XXVIII | Brian is Born and Opening of Cuffley Hotel | 319 |
| XXIX | Coronation George VI. Theobalds Sale | 327 |
| XXX | Preparing for War | 343 |
| XXXI | By Air to Arundel – Cricket | 351 |
| XXXII | War – Extracts from Diary | 364 |
| XXXIII | Royal Artillery | 423 |
| XXXIV | Released after Five Years | 458 |

| | | |
|---|---|---|
| XXXV | The Cuffley Hotel and a New Restaurant | 464 |
| XXXVI | Back to The George | 485 |
| XXXVII | Walk across Wales | 499 |
| XXXVIII | Coronation Elizabeth II | 513 |
| XXXIX | Diary – Happenings in the Kitchen | 524 |
| XL | Elizabethan 53 Club – Presentation of Gavel | 532 |
| XLI | Function – House of Commons, Rt. Hon. Iain Macleod – A.J. Standbrook – His Demise and Tributes | 550 |
| | Epilogue | 565 |

# Foreword

I conceived the thought of compiling a factual book a long while back; in fact it was following the death of Mother (Jennie) in 1967 that the urge was accelerated. My thoughts were continually relating the past with the present, and, to say the least, confusion resulted when I realised the relationship was primarily in context only with the prevailing mood. How easily one could justify their argument either way, especially if the subject be in the category of 'then and now'. For instance – 'Are people generally better off now compared with any previous period?' We can measure or compare commodities but we cannot in any way measure feelings, thoughts, impressions, contentment, pressures and numerous other considerations that would be applicable. The majority of people have to be hooked on today's 'time and money' relationship, tending to make them mindful of the present, forgetting that today is simply the outcome of yesterday which so quickly combines with tomorrow transiently to become today again, and so through the process of life time flows into memories. But what of memories – are we not prone to manipulate words, maybe to harmonise with the circumstances at the time, and subconsciously to be encouraged by the fading accuracy of the interpretation that weeks, months and years induce. I quickly appreciated that nebulous memories were quite easily exchanged for the spoken word, but not so when attempted in the written word. Following the compilation of numerous notes with a deal more unfilled parenthesis than writing, I realised the impossible task I had undertaken, and so my records were filed and forgotten.

After moving from Cuffley to Winchmore Hill I was delighted to enjoy the luxury of a study which allowed me to sort the many papers I had collected over a period of fifty years, many of which I had not looked at since popping them into one of the many box files. My original intention was to launch the book on behalf of charity on 24th June, 1974 when celebrating fifty years from the date when my father (A.J.S.) acquired the license of The George in 1924.

Having made a file for each year of this period plus many more, I actually commenced writing in February 1973. Because the book is now twenty-five years behind schedule, the references to comparisons of 'then and now', 'now' will imply the year 1974 unless other information be quoted in parenthesis.

I appreciated and took full advantage of having an extremely efficient and office-trained wife; seldom laying pen to paper – my letters if not crudely dictated were written in diary note form, knowing they would be manipulated and when typed be ready for me to sign without reading. This, of course, is in no way an advantage for me now, plus the fact time never allowed me to indulge in and relish the pleasure of reading commendable literature (which is regrettable) and so I viewed the project as a go-as-you-please exercise, thinking more of compiling a chronological record than a story. Never did it occur to me to have the effrontery to make capital gain from the undertaking, therefore I resolved enthusiastically to let charity benefit if the sales exceeded the cost of production.

Because the book basically portrays the licensed trade I considered it equitable, should the sales prove sufficiently remunerative, that half of the proceeds be donated to the Licensed Victuallers Charitable Funds. The remaining half to be given to Enfield charities, in which my family have been interested, including the Mentally and Physically Handicapped, help for the aged, the Enfield and Chesunt League of Hospital Friends, The Western Enfield Samaritans, and on the broader scale the Red Cross and St John's Ambulance Brigade, both of whom are so often taken for granted – always there, wherever, whatever and without recompense!

The initial programme was to contain the book in some eighty thousand words embodying the history of The George plus every licensee since 1716, together with such of Enfield history that came within my experience or is applicable to the story. In addition to characterising a few local pubs and landlords (my apologies for not portraying more) and a general report on the Standbrook family, plus the fifty years at The George, I also contemplated additional concise chapters on alcohol and excise; licensees and their persecution in respect of some laws; violence and the ludicrous inadequacy of punishment administered; also my views on charity (a word I dislike) or rather help or thought for others.

The period of compiling and writing this manual has been subjected to extreme changes, creating long and short periods of suppression; this has obviously not been conducive to extracting the best from my inexperience, nor in making the continuity effective. I found it difficult to estimate the number of words required to complete such an indecisive collection of rambling thoughts. I was constantly told not to wander from the subject but this was the area I really proved to be efficient in: as a matter of fact the eighty thousand words were swallowed up when I had completed the year 1940. I continued hopefully, thinking perhaps with a few deletions the intended programme could still be more or less adhered to, but when writing 1952 and 1953 I knew the objective had failed and so very reluctantly I decided to terminate this book at the end of 1954 when my respects could be extended to A.J.S. who died that year. However, should sufficient copies of the book be sold enabling charity to benefit by a reasonable amount, I intend to complete the fifty years by recording the years from 1955 to 1974 in another volume.

I sincerely hope that readers whose knowledge of my various subjects surpasses my own will bear with me and excuse any inaccuracies, misleading descriptions or mistakes.

A high percentage of success in writing is due to the precision and enthusiasm of the author's research, and in this field I have certainly failed my intentions – again the culprit is 'time!' The only visits made for information or research were on two occasions at Charrington's Mile End Brewery where Frank Richardson, the company secretary, and Frederick Convoy, the office manager looked after my companion, Leo Eastwick, and myself so warmly and courteously that our somewhat cheerless chore of examining the old deeds was made a refreshing pleasure. We also made two calls at Tottenham magistrates court where again our very old friend and widely respected Charlie Rowe made us so much at home and attended to all our requirements. I also visited the Enfield Gazette offices where the kindness of David Paul and his staff made my two visits searching the records a pleasure and a less burdensome task.

One other visit was made to St Andrew's Parish Church through the kindness of Mr Westaway, arranging for our very old friend Bert Attwood, the verger, to let me have access to the whole of the parish registers the first one he placed in front of me was my own signature – our wedding June 1934 – what a shaky signature! A whole week is required at least, to glean any real knowledge or benefit.

I was very fortunate and comforted in the knowledge of having such a remarkable friend as Leo Eastwick to inject sufficient confidence into my system to complete the maiden folio which he reviewed and corrected (some early pages looked as if a moronic doodler had been performing) and so it continued.

Leo, after completing fifty years with the *Enfield Gazette* retired, but still maintained his 'Townsman' column which had been a feature for twenty-three years. The all too commonly quoted phrase 'nobody is indispensable' is perhaps correct, but not always are the expended replaced with quite the same level of talent or depth of mind, and it is doubtful if anyone will equal Leo for his comprehensive knowledge of Enfield, including the town's personalities, sport and history; but above all this, it was his projection of thought that was so disturbingly transformed into such descriptive and expressive phrasing that always made his writing a delight to read. Sadly, Leo passed away on 31st January, 1976. On that day I wrote in my diary the following:

*Brian phoned early evening to say poor Leo died at 2 p.m. this afternoon (Don, his brother, phoned The George not having my number).*

*Words cannot describe my feelings; the forty-five years I have known Leo have been without change; never have I heard him say anything derogatory or bear animosity against anyone. I feel half my book has been torn up – two more folios to be completed and checked! How I was looking forward to him being the main guest if the book is ever launched – and so the inevitable turn-over of life proceeds with its toll. Phoned Ron Renvoize (president of the Enfield Cricket Club) to let others know.*

My grateful thanks to Derek Jones BA, for checking the final folios, reading the book and conveying to me his advice and encouragement without which this book may never have been completed.

I would also like to express my appreciation to David Pam, the Borough of Enfield history and museums officer who has so sympathetically contributed additional authoritative historical facts regarding The George Inn and other respective references.

My intention was to thank, by name, the numerous persons I have contacted for information or confirmation in connection with the various subjects enumerated in this book, but if everyone who has been involved one way or another, was included, several hundred names would have to be mentioned. Many were unsuccessful in supplying information but their efforts were nonetheless appreciated. Therefore, would everybody, no matter how trivial the contribution in the context of importance, kindly accept my warm appreciation and grateful thanks for assisting and encouraging this well-intentioned and benevolent undertaking.

The last year of Enfield as an urban district council was fittingly the year that terminates the first part of this book. The integration, with Edmonton and Southgate making a single Borough, did not materialise until 1965 and I would therefore like readers to understand that the information or material depicting the London Borough of Enfield as a whole is minimal, and historically the references are only intended to reflect a glimpse of Enfield's long association with Britain's history in context with the book's contents.

My apologies for the many names of persons who should have but have not been mentioned, also the numerous incidents of which one or many may be recalled by some readers that may have them wondering why there has been no mention?

In depth my temperament and ego were humbly content with the thought that there would not be any personal monetary gain, especially in these 'hungry for money' times. Proudly but with humility I am conscious of introducing a modicum of charitable blackmail here, but I shall not be sensitive about my effort should I know of anyone attempting to read this book and muttering 'rubbish' (only providing the book has been purchased and not borrowed) since the difference between the cost and selling price will be a donation to charity.

I shall be delighted to hear from any reader who may wish to correct any mis-statement, false impression, misconception or indeed enlighten me further regarding any subject matter quoted herein; should the reference or observation appear sufficiently interesting perhaps the corrections or additions may be incorporated in the second volume. D.V.

'Judge not the past too harshly; consider the stupidity of the present, and the frightening uncertainty of the future.'

The financial aspect relating to the production of the book, receipts, charitable awards and audit will be very kindly undertaken by Lodge Parker & Co., Chartered Accountants, 182 Gloucester Place, London NW1 6DS. Tel: 0171 706 4345.

# Chapter I

The early George Inn and owners – hearth and window taxes – the Great Plague in Enfield and London

The earliest information relating to The George has recently been passed to me by David Pam (local history and museums officer). This refers to some particulars regarding the sale of cottages and chantries on 8th June, 1548. The reference has been translated as follows: parcels of the lands and possessions of St Leonards Church in Shoreditch. Rent of one tenement there *cumomnibus sellar ac solar,* meaning 'with all the cellar and upstairs parlour'.

The second reference is in 1572: 'The heirs of William Budder holdeth a house in Enfield called The George and divers parcels of land there unto belonging which belonged to St Leonards Church, Shoreditch'.

The next reference indicates that his son owned the premises and was a student at the grammar school (William Budder having died the previous year). In a survey of Enfield 1572 the following is listed under the heading. 'In Enfield Green where the church standeth – moving from west to east – the site of the manor or Mansion house of Enfield' – the cottage and yard then the tenement of William Budder, which would obviously be the house referred to earlier as The George, and the present site of the inn today, and so was within the grounds of the ancient Manorial Palace of Enfield that included the palace and ground of Elizabeth I and known as Enfield Green.

After these had been alienated by the Crown in 1629 parts of the freehold adjoining the road were sold to various individuals for building purposes.

The following diminished extract of an indenture dated 22nd June, 1666 presents proof again of the property being then known as The George Inn:

> Between Edward Heath, citizen and fishmonger of London of the one part and Thomas Taylor of Enfield, Middlesex of the other part. Witness that the said Edward Heath in consideration of one hundred and seventy four pounds of lawful English money paid and sold to Thomas Taylor all that messuage, tenement or inn commonly called or known by the name or sign of The George – situate and being at Enfield aforesaid.

Apparently Thomas Taylor who acquired The George Inn from Edward Heath in 1666 for £174, died in 1684, leaving the property to his two sons – William and Christopher, both of London. One was a haberdasher and the other a milliner.

They sold the inn to a member of an old and well known Enfield family who had resided in the parish from at least the fifteenth century, one John Wilburd, tallow chandler of London. By the indenture dated 28th and 29th August, 1684 the premises were conveyed to him for £250. These deeds are now in the possession of Bass-Charrington and were acquired when the freehold property was conveyed to Charrington & Co. in 1925 from Savilles Brewery.

It was generally and obviously thought that the inn was not named The George until after the accession of King

George I in 1714 but there is little doubt that the name is an abbreviation of Saint George. An inn so named in Glastonbury bore a figure of 'The Saint', and Stow's Survey of London, first printed in 1598, mentions two inns of that name in London.

The Hearth Tax returns of 1664 for Enfield Green mention a Thomas Taylor as being the owner of two empty houses but do not mention Edward Heath. The George was described as a substantial house having nine hearths. This tax was levied from 1662 until 1689. Its records are very important for local historians as they provide an indication of the size of the houses at that time. Those in receipt of poor relief or in houses worth less than twenty shillings per annum not paying parish rates were exempt, but otherwise residents were required to pay two shillings per hearth. The parish constable compiled lists of householders and numbers of hearths and gave those to the justices of the peace in quarter sessions. The tax was collected twice a year at Michaelmas and Ladyday.

This tax was replaced by the Window Tax and imposed by parliament in 1696 to help meet the cost of re-minting damaged coinage. After 1792 houses with between seven and nine windows were taxed at two shillings, and from ten to nineteen windows at four shillings. In 1825 houses with less than eight windows were exempt. The tax was abolished in 1851, Scotland was exempt altogether in 1707.

A terrier or rental of the Manor of Enfield within the Duchy of Lancaster for the years 1656 to 1777 mentions The George Inn in 1686. Three tenements near The George Inn. (A terrier lists the possessions and rights of a manor or church).

*The Historical Notices of Enfield* by J. Tuff (1858) says that The George Inn by tradition was the last house attacked by the Plague when it visited Enfield.

Be this legendary or not, many inns suffered this dreaded disease. The George being one of the most remorselessly attacked. The landlord, Francis Ross, lost his servant Richard Meade in September, followed by the two maid servants, his daughters Mary and Jane, then the baby, and lastly his wife, Mary.

The first and worst recorded outbreak of the disease affecting Enfield occurred in the year 1603, the first year of the reign of James I, when 180 persons died; this number would have been very serious indeed even in 1965 before the integration of Enfield with Southgate and Edmonton with a population of approximately one hundred and fifteen thousand; but when we consider that the population of Enfield in the early seventeenth century was only one thousand five hundred to two thousand the outcome must have been appalling. In 1626 a further out-break occurred which caused a further sixty-seven deaths.

The great Plague of 1665 which accounted for between seventy and a hundred thousand deaths in London was less severe in Enfield than elsewhere. The number of deaths recorded was sixty-six, out of a probable population of about two thousand eight hundred.

It is on record that the first persons seized with the Plague in London were two men, said to have been Frenchmen, who were members of a family living near the top of Drury Lane in the parish of St Giles. The parish suffered the loss of three thousand two hundred and sixteen of the inhabitants. An interesting reference to the Plague years is presented on p. 311 of Ford & Hodson's *History of Enfield*. In a survey of the Chase made in 1658 a site (now known as Chase Side) on the north-east corner of the Green is marked as the Pest House and in the presentment to the jury of the Manor in 1636 described as a cottage erected 'by the appointment of His Majesty's Justice of the Peace for the harbouring of infected people during the last great infection'.

This house was demolished in 1911 and now a row of houses occupies this site and that of a pond to the north of the house, believed to mark the site of the 'Plague Pit'. The main pest house was set up by the parish on the marshes near Enfield Lock, well away from the populated part of the village. (Chase Side, in 1700 was known as Little Woodside. A map issued in 1770 shows Baker Street as the only road going northwards. The name Chase Side first appears in 1800.)

During the fourteenth century this bubonic plague, known as the Black Death, was responsible for no fewer than twenty-five million deaths in Europe, almost a quarter of the population. If only the majority of people today would offer thanks for bewildering but comparatively safe and easy times!

The Great Fire which followed the Plague and, perhaps mercifully, swept across London, starting on Saturday 1st September, 1666, could have been a blessing in disguise. John Evelyn, the celebrated diarist, describes the scene on 3rd September, with the north of the City aflame, the sky alight for ten miles around and the scaffolds around St Paul's catching fire. The next day he records seeing the stones of the great cathedral being catapulted through the air; the bells melting and the molten lead running in streams down the streets, with the pavements too hot for feet.

On 7th September he reports the building's total destruction and the six acres of lead on the cathedral roof melted. The only piece not consumed by the fire was over the altar at the east end.

The fire could have created the basis, or have been the forerunner, to the present astronomical cost of land. Sir Richard Ford, after a court case involving compensation regarding Kings Street, that was to be made from Guildhall down to Cheapside, declared 'by this means that which was not fourpence a foot afore, will now, when houses are built, be worth fifteen shillings a foot!'

Parliament appointed a committee to look into the cause of the fire because religious intolerance raged so violently and the Roman Catholics were widely accused of starting the fire. An Enfield schoolmaster named John Chisshull came forward with evidence of an Enfield family named St George who had two days before the fire started, forecast 'the burning of the City' to a Mrs Eves. The committee absolved the Catholic family from any implication in the fire, much to the disappointment of John Chisshull. The St George family left the neighbourhood soon afterwards. Enfield must have been buzzing with the exciting tales coming in from the city by word of mouth; and we all know, with a few exchanges, how distorted a short report may finish up. How the rumours must have been mulled over by the locals quaffing their pots of ale in the candlelit inns and taverns.

# Chapter II

Enfield Town in the seventeenth and other centuries – brewers of Enfield including Edward Heath the owner of The George – coffee and tea in England – The Cottager and general hygiene

The first photograph in the photo section depicts a picture of Enfield about the early sixteenth century.

The sleepy, contented, mellow, unhurried atmosphere this picture projects is surely the absolute answer to the present veneered, noisy, money-crazed and too quickly advanced world we now exist in. The only thing in common with our present town is that the traffic is going the same way, if not so fast. Most of us would no doubt like to go back in time to experience for a spell the simplicity of this period, but very few would wish to stay without a few of our present advanced amenities, nowadays taken for granted.

One has little difficulty in imagining the scene on a summer's evening with the sun sinking low in the sky and shedding liquid gold on to the mellow tiled roofs, as if they had been draped in a blanket to keep warmth in for the cooling night. The almost luminous effect of the sun's rays on the painted wooden and rustic brick buildings on the north side are contrasted with the creeping, deepening shadows overtaking the sidewalks and displaying a rich hardened surface worn by continuous trampling over the last century or so. A light warm breeze, laden with delicate aromas carried in from surrounding farmland and the heavily wooded Chase, summons every little puff, attempting to unhinge the first of those parchment tinted leaves that appear reluctant to fall. Ripples are put into motion by the drinking deer (in earlier years they may well have been slaughtered by the hungry locals), otherwise the breeze fails to disturb the silver flecked surface of the rivulet winding through the town, so lazily it gives the impression of battling to reverse its flow. Interviewed in 1899 three inhabitants, each of whom had been in Enfield for more than seventy years, all said they had heard that a stream had existed in Enfield Town around the end of the 1700s. Mr Bilton, a Parish Church bellringer in the year 1851, when he was eighty-four years of age, told another old inhabitant that he remembered the stream, and that one winter he had also seen a herd of deer in the town during severe weather.

Alternatively it could be different if one's imagination registers the same picture on a winter's night! The wind howling and screaming through lofty trees and around the roofs and gables, catching the nigh frozen rain and driving it horizontally against the windows, almost snuffing out the only light created by flickering candles and yellow rays emitted from oil lamps, occasionally strengthened by the dancing flames of a log fire. The roads and sidewalks having greedily soaked up the relentless rain sufficiently to turn them into squelching muddy pools.

With no drainage, and no street lighting, the only comfortable place to go to would be the village inn, but, unless one was living very close to the local, it would be an intolerable effort to make the journey, and after a few pots of the strongest ale it would be well nigh impossible to evade the worst hazards going home. Even in the middle of the last century pedestrians carried lanterns on winter evenings.

An appropriate time to say a few favourable words relating to alcohol. There can be little doubt of the value of ale or other alcoholic beverages at this period. Apart from its importance as a considerable proportion of the people's diet it must have been generally the safest available beverage from an hygienic viewpoint; the water in those days would have been most unreliable. Tea, coffee and the like had only just been introduced into England, and it is extremely unlikely that any of these beverages would have been available to the general public outside London; the price also would have been prohibitive.

The following has been extracted from the *Occasional Paper* No. 33 titled 'The Rude Multitude' by David Pam (Enfield and the Civil War) and covers some of the changes in the district between the years 1620 and 1660.

> There were three common brewers active in Enfield. Christopher Hill had been brought up in the trade but had been established on his own only about two years. He brewed four and a half quarters of malt a week. Edward Heath, his main rival, had long since served an apprenticeship to the trade. He lived at the inn on Enfield Green called The George where he brewed four quarters of malt each week. His household was a large one consisting of a wife, three sons, three men and two maids. He farmed about thirty-six acres of arable. The third brewer was Edward Moss who was in a smaller way of business brewing only a quarter of malt at a time.
>
> There are no fewer than thirty-nine victuallers or ale-house keepers, seven of whom were widows, in

the town. Two of them, Robert Rash and John Garman, brewed their own beer. Robert Rash was the landlord of The White Hart, Ponders End; a photograph taken in the early years of this century shows the brewery still there; it was undoubtedly a thriving hostelry. He lived with his wife, two children and four servants. The word servant must not be given its Victorian connotation for these would have been engaged in brewing and serving, and perhaps also on the land, though his arable holding was less than twenty acres. He was another of those who expressed dissatisfaction with the King's unparliamentary taxation in 1627. Forty shillings had been demanded of him; the collector reported 'that he could not yet be spoken to' but he expected an answer the following week. Nine months later that answer had still not been received. Many years subsequently, in 1643, the county committee decided that he was worth £200 and he was charged £10 tax of which he paid £3 and was discharged. The White Hart was one of the many houses in Enfield where parliamentary troops were quartered that year. John Garman's appears to have been a less thriving establishment. He died in 1633, left everything to his wife except a small gift of ten shillings, 'to be paid by my wife as she is able'. The remainder of the victuallers would have been supplied no doubt by either Edward Heath serving the ale-houses around Enfield Green, along Chase Side, Parsonage Street and Baker Street or by Christopher Hill supplying the ale-houses from Ponders End to Horsepoolstones. (Enfield Wash).

The majority of the ale-house keepers also farmed land and many were engaged in other trades. William Stanborough was licensed to trade in meal, Michael Kirby, who kept a house jointly with his widowed mother on Enfield Green, was a glazier, William Barnes was the sexton, Richard Heydon and William Coverley were bricklayers, Andrew Heydon a gardener, Jeffrey Bissiter a joiner, three of the victuallers were also tailors.

The following are some further notes on Edward Heath (then licensee The George Inn): in 1644 he quartered two Parliamentary troopers for forty-nine days, a Francis Nuans and Thomas Worsly for which he was reimbursed for the following account:

|            | £  | s  | d |
|------------|----|----|---|
| Men's diet | 3  | 5  | 4 |
| Hay        | 1  | 12 | 8 |
|            | £4 | 18s | 0d |

Also in 1642 one bay horse was given as part of his tax to Parliament which was listed and valued at £13 by the commissioners. There were several other taxes during this period – 'Coat & Conduct money' (imposed by Charles I government) of which Edward Heath was warned of but apparently did not pay his assessed four shillings. (This tax was to pay for the war in Scotland.) Then there was the 'ship money' which he paid twenty shillings out of the assessed forty shillings in 1627 stating that he was willing to pay but pleaded he was poor.

London's first coffee house was established in St Michael's Alley, Cornhill, about the year 1652 by a

Mr Bowman, former coachman to Mr Hodges, who was a Turkish merchant. The new drink was naturally very unpopular with the local vintners who, in the early stages, saw the drinking of the 'sooty drink' as it was then known, as very competitive. Garraway's, London's most celebrated coffee house in Exchange Alley, Cornhill (demolished in the latter half of the nineteenth century) issued the following notice or shop-bill about the turn of the 1660s:

> Tea in England hath been sold in the leaf for six pounds and sometimes for ten pounds the pound weight, and in respect of its former scarceness and dearness it hath only been used as a regalia in high treatments and entertainments, and presents made thereof to princes and grandees. The said Thomas Garraway did purchase a quantity thereof and first publicly sold the said tea in leaf, and drink made according to the directions of the most knowing merchants and travellers into those eastern countries: and upon knowledge and experience of the said Garraway's continued care and industry in obtaining the best tea, and making drink thereof, very many noblemen, physicians, merchants, and gentlemen of quality, have ever since sent to him for the said leaf, and daily resort to his home, in Exchange Alley aforesaid, to drink the drink thereof.
>
> These are to give notice that the said Thomas Garraway hath tea to sell from 16s to 50s a pound.

Samuel Pepys records in his diary that on 28th September, 1660, 'I did send for a cup of tea (a China drink) of which I had never drank before'.

At the same period the Earl of Arlington brought a parcel of tea home from Holland at a cost of sixty shillings. His home was Arlington House, which was demolished in 1703. The site was purchased by the Duke of Buckingham, who built a mansion of red brick on the site. George III purchased the house in 1762 for £21,000. In 1775 the mansion was settled on Queen Charlotte (in exchange for Somerset House) and the property was after referred to as 'The Queen's House' – and later, of course, as Buckingham Palace. So in all probability the first cup of tea made in England was made on the site of the palace! I am sure there are recordings of earlier reports about tea, but it is a pleasant thought!

The roads at this period were, indeed, in a poor state, and in inclement weather almost impassable. An act was passed in 1662 giving Surveyors the authority, in conjunction with local justices of the peace, to levy a rate not to exceed sixpence in the pound for repairing and improving the common highways, but the system was anything but progressive. Public transport was almost non-existent; the first 'stage coaches' carrying goods and passengers between towns were promoted in the 1640s. The latter half of the seventeenth century saw a great development in coach building, and in 1677 the Coach and Coach Harness Makers' Company was founded by Charles II. The coach builders were taking the bulk and clumsiness out of the previous design and creating much smaller and lighter carriages. After seeing his coach-builders, Pepys notes in his diary for 5th November, 1668 – 'Did pitch upon a little chariot who's body was framed but not cornered, it being very light, and will be very genteel and sober.'

Little do we hear of ordinary everyday things essential to the survival of the normal individual, so few in fact that we may suppose that not many, if any, items were worthy of future inheritance. An example of the period in question would be an ordinary bottle, and other similar containers, a rare sight in a humble home. So much are they a part of modern living today that without them it would be doubtful if society could function.

There are of course many inventories that refer to the more prosperous households around this period that contain many of these luxuries.

Glass bottles were still novel in the middle of the seventeenth century, and presumably wine played a great part in introducing them to this country. Stoneware jugs or, in the more affluent homes, white pottery (Delft) were used to bring wine to the table. Wine was not stored unless the household was large enough to take a whole cask, in which case it would be tapped and drawn as and when required. The early 1670s saw the glass bottle superseding the jug. At this period they were made with a squat wide body, wide base and a proportionately long neck. In the main these bottles belonged to the wine merchant or the tavern owner who had their own initials and date incorporated in the seal. One of these bottles dated 1699 was auctioned at Christie's early in 1973 for two hundred and eighty guineas.

Pepys recorded in his diary in 1663 that he visited the 'Mitre' to see new wine put into his crested bottles.

The luxuries of a normal working family at the end of the seventeenth century, and indeed up to the nineteenth century, must have been almost non-existent; a fact extremely difficult for any of us living in this sophisticated age to grasp. A television breakdown today is almost in the category of a major disaster! Obviously there was no gas, electricity, or hot water laid on and the local pump was the only source of water supply. There was no bath or toilet convenience inside, and probably only an outside privy which would not be connected to any sewer or even a cesspit. The only washing facilities would be a hewn stone sink.

Normal house coal, now almost banned from burning in fireplaces, was plentiful towards the end of the sixteenth century and the people were using it instead of wood under pressure of necessity, but I very much doubt if the average cottager existing close to such places as the Chase would substitute coal when wood was there for the collecting, especially as the London price was between 15s 0d (75p) and £1 per ton. Among the mining areas the price for coal was only 5s 0d (25p) to 7s 0d (35p) per ton.

Coal once banished because of the grimy filthy smoke, found its way back to the furnaces of the London brewers in 1578 as we learn from a petition presented to the council by the Company of Brewers, wherein they offer to revert to burning wood only in the brewhouses nearest Westminster Palace as they understood that the Queen 'findeth hersealfe greately greved and anoyed with the taste and smoke of the sea coales' (then known as sea coals due to the products close proximity to the sea). Up to this period the supplies of coal had been obtained without the miners penetrating far below the surface.

Perhaps the following appears a little irrelevant but I wonder sometimes if many of us completely appreciate our modern living conditions. It really is difficult to conceive that less than one hundred years ago an average of only about one third of the houses had a WC and almost half had to be content with pail privies! The septic tank was not developed until 1896 and the ball valve for cisterns, the forerunner of today's system, came into being less than one hundred years ago. Until the end of the First World War the marble topped wash stand, with its typically Victorian coloured water jugs and basins of flowered design were in use in almost all houses.

The average kitchen then had only the hot grate for both cooking and heating. This piece of equipment was then recessed in the wall and on one side was the roasting oven and on the other side a boiler. The fire was set high in the centre and had horizontal fire bars. The top had a lift-off boiling and cooking plate over the fire and another over the oven. This was manufactured in cast iron and made to sparkle by continuous cleaning with blacklead.

Over three thousand years ago any Egyptian house belonging to the prosperous had a bathroom and lavatory basin.

Waste water ran through a channel into a vase sunk in the ground which formed a soakaway. The 'closet' had a stone seat and the output fell into a removable vase in a pit below.

In 1400 BC 'closets' were quite common to the Greeks and Romans and the inhabitants of Crete; these were built over a conduit of running water.

During the middle ages, and for long after, latrines or privies were placed over large pits, straddled by wooden seats which were known to rot, and one may well imagine the unhappy results.

London in the fifteenth century could boast of twelve recorded public latrines; there were probably a lot more. 'Public' privies were also common and, wherever possible, were built over rivers or streams.

The Romans were responsible for bringing the bath to Britain; these were centrally heated by hot air cavities. Oil was used in place of soap and this was taken off with a skin scraper called a 'strigil'.

The medieval monasteries seemed to be the only section of Britain which took sanitation and ablution seriously. Up to the eighteenth century washing was not looked upon kindly, and bathing was out of the question.

It seems quite unbelievable that even in my time bathrooms in ordinary houses were almost unknown; the first private house the family lived in (1910–1912) had no bathroom and the normal routine was to bath in the scullery in what was called a 'hip bath', which was portable and had to be filled and emptied by hand. My goodness, mums had their hands full then!

# Chapter III

The George known as The Pineapple – the old palace, the cedar tree and Dr Robert Uvedale – the market place – St Andrew's Church and the Sunday meat market

To continue with the picture of Enfield Town and the buildings in this sketch. The old George Inn is near the centre of the picture. The inn sign appears to be standing in exactly the same position as it is today.

The following is an interesting and unsolved report that appeared as part of 'Townman's' notes in the *Enfield Gazette & Observer* some time ago. It concerns the proceedings of the Stamford Hill Turnpike Trust. Does it refer to The George and the former Ebben's Bakery? 'In April 1773 the Surveyor, Charles Brown, was ordered to remove the Sign Post and Sign belonging to the ale house known by the sign of The Pineapple in Enfield Town, kept by John Scott, and the rails set before the house of William Axton, baker, in the said town, the same being great annoyances to the public road'.

It is the first time I have ever heard of an inn named The Pineapple. In the eighteenth century Enfieldians were doubtless being introduced to exotic fruits from tropical America, just as our own junior population has become familiar with the delights of Coca Cola from the same continent.

In 1791 a certain John Scott was the town Beadle as well as nurseryman. Did he keep The Pineapple in 1773?

It is now idle to speculate, but one cannot help wondering whether the present George Inn did not once offer its hospitality as The Pineapple. If Ebben's Bakery, now out of business but believed to have been at least as old as the late 1700s, was once owned by Mr Axton. The sign and rails of the two premises may well have formed a joint impediment to passengers.

The corner building to the left of The George and one of the last remaining relics of the Old Town (now Harris Carpet Store) was, prior to the complete restoration of the building in 1956, the bakery in question. It was last kept by Mr Alfred Ebben, a well known character whose family purchased the business in the 1830s from a man named Jelly, who, incidentally ran the town's post office from this shop. The property adjoining was occupied until 1976 by Dr Alice Lloyd, who had practised there since the early Twenties.

When the fences which formerly enclosed the gardens in front of the shops and The George Inn became decayed, the gardens suffered encroachment by the public to such an extent that eventually the area became part of the roadway.

The property to the right of The George would have been erected when the grounds of the old palace was sold off in 1629 for building purposes. At the end of these buildings was a lane which is now Sydney Road, previously known as Gashouse Lane so called after the Enfield Gas Company formed in 1849 with their headquarters there. Prior to this it was called Slaughterhouse Lane, both names being anything but romantic.

The next building on the right is as yet unidentified. Behind and towering above the building will be seen the old palace which was the manor house of Enfield; or more probably rebuilt in 1552 by Edward VI for his sister

Princess Elizabeth (records indicate that in 1339 the original building was the home of Humphrey De Bohum). He also settled the Manor of Enfield and Worcesters on her for life. The first real interest in Enfield by the royal family occurred in 1540 when Lord Rutland gave the Manor of Worcesters, together with a mansion known as Elsynge Hall, to Henry VIII. His children Prince Edward and Princess Elizabeth spent a large part of their early life there. The site of Elsynge Hall was between Forty Hall and Maidens Brook on the left of the avenue of trees. It was later demolished by Sir Nicholas Raynton.

There is no record of Queen Elizabeth ever residing at the old palace in Enfield town. About the year 1665 the palace was leased to Doctor Robert Uvedale who, on his own account, maintained a private boarding school for the sons of the nobility. He was one of the leading botanists of the day and the grounds of the palace blossomed into one of the most exotic gardens in and around London. The famous cedar tree he planted in the grounds somewhere between the years 1665 and 1670, and local legend holds that it was the first cedar to be grown in England. The shoots were brought from Mount Libanus, Lebanon, by one of his former students. The sweet pea was also introduced into England from Sicily by him.

When the Great Plague was at its peak in 1665, the doctor devised his own method of seeking immunity by placing a brick into the fire before the family retired each night. In the morning the red hot brick was placed in the middle of the hall floor and a quart of vinegar poured on to it. Grouped around the brick the family inhaled the fumes and then went to prayers. The house was then locked up, after which they walked to Winchmore Hill and back, following which the doctor attended to his duties as head of the grammar school. They all remained completely free from infection.

The property continued as a school but gradually declined through neglect and eventually parts of the old mansion were pulled down. It was acquired for use as the post office in 1906, after which it became the home of the Enfield Town Constitutional Club until 1928, when the old place was demolished.

Had The Rising Sun been included in the picture the rather low elongated building would have been fifty yards or so on from the palace, roughly where now stands the Eastern Electricity Board showrooms. It was an old inn dating back from the middle of the seventeenth century. The Baptists held their first service in a room over the bars in March, 1867; they later built a tabernacle in London Road which was sold to Woolworth's for £5,750 in 1925. The brewers in 1880 were Christie & Company and later the Cannon Brewery Company. The inn was taken over by Taylor Walker & Company (now integrated with the Ind Coope consortium). The Rising Sun was pulled down in 1933 and the license then held by Freddie Frost was transferred to the new Rising Sun at Edmonton. The present licensees are Ted and Mary Green.

Opposite the palace the sign post of The Kings Head is seen standing in much the same position as it does today.

The inn was kept by David Walker in 1791 and its position alongside the parish church suggests that there was probably an inn here from much earlier times. Regular coach services to London ran from the Kings Head in Charles Lamb's day. Stage coaches became active around 1640, travelling between towns carrying goods and passengers, of which some of the latter travelled at a cheap rate sitting outside in a basket placed between the hind wheels. The inn was rebuilt in 1899.

The market place came into existence in 1304, when Edward I granted to Humphrey de Bohun, Lord of the Manor, a license to hold a weekly market on Mondays, and two annual fairs. In 1632 the trustees purchased from Francis Saunders a property with adjoining grounds known as the 'Vine', which they converted into a market place, and erected a market house.

In 1619 James I granted a charter for a weekly market, the trustees to administer the proceeds in trust for the poor of Enfield. It unfortunately ceased to function early in the eighteenth century, but was revived in 1826, when the lessee, Mr John Hill, arranged for a new market cross to be erected through public subscription. The information recorded on the cross was almost indecipherable caused by the weather together with a fair share of vandalism administered by the local boys.

The cross was removed in 1904 and replaced by the present structure which commemorates the coronation of Edward VII, the cost again being borne by public subscription. The old Gothic style cross was re-erected in the grounds of Myddelton House, Forty Hill, the home of the late Mr E.A. Bowles, affectionately known as 'Gussy'. His brother, the late Sir Henry F. Bowles who resided at Forty Hall (once the manor house of Worcesters and built by Sir Nicolas Raynton about 1630) adjoined the grounds of Myddelton House. The leaden market pump, a portable pillory, and an old milestone stood in the market place until 1805, and the stocks removed, it is believed, in 1820.

St Andrew's Parish Church, standing majestically at the rear of the market place, is proudly the town's only building left offering reminders of Enfield's great antiquity. The

Festival of St Andrew was instituted in AD 350 and it may be assumed that a church stood there in the late Saxon period. The Domesday book records a church on the existing site.

The Domesday book is the record of the economic survey of England made under William the Conqueror, 1085–1086. It was the people of England who gave it this name (domesday – judgement day) because no one could escape the enquiry into his land holdings, and because there was no appeal against its decision. This register shows exactly how much land the church held, and that these very large holdings had been acquired by free grants from Saxon kings. In 1086 the Church possessed more than a quarter of all the cultivated land in England. Much of this property was held by the Church under a royal lease, often on condition that some service should be rendered, such as saying masses for the King weekly or even more often. The original book can be seen in the Public Record Office in London.

Reconstructed somewhere between AD 1200 and 1300, only the east and south walls of the sanctuary, with lancet window, now remain. The tower was built in the fourteenth century, as was St John's Chapel now the present Royal Artillery Memorial Chapel that was dedicated in 1962. Successive additions and alterations were made in the fifteenth, sixteenth and seventeenth centuries.

The Church possesses monuments of great interest, including some fine brasses, one of which is presumed to be one of the two finest in England. This is in memorium to Jocosa, wife of Sir John Tiptoft, who died at the age of forty-two on 22nd September, 1446. Sir John was Lord of the Manor of Worcesters and at that time residing at Elsynge Hall (known then as Wroth's Place). In 1350 the

Lord of the Manor was John de Enfield and John Wroth married his widow, through whom it descended to Sir John Tiptoft, whose son became Earl of Worcester – hence the name of the manor.

The belfry contains a peal of eight bells which were installed in 1724. A ninth bell called 'Ting Tang', which rings five minutes before service, was placed there in 1680.

Since 1190, or in the period of seven hundred and eighty-four years, the Parish Church has been patronised by no less than fifty vicars, and the longest serving was the first one appointed; Robertus, described as 'Vicarius de Enefielde'.

The last six vicars whom our family have had the pleasure to meet, are the Rev. Richard Howel Brown (1905–1928), Rev. Geoffrey William Daisley (until 1939), Rev. J.B. Harington Evans (until 1955), Rev. Graham Buston (until 1965), Rev. Eric Franklin Tinker (until 1969) when the present vicar, the Rev. Peter Burkett Morgan was installed.

One has to study the parish church records to appreciate the meritorious part St Andrew's played in the past in all matters relating to the community's well-being. It would not be amiss to say the whole village or town revolved around the church, and to a great extent the complete story of the neighbourhood unfolds in these records.

The register of the churchwardens, Overseers of the Poor, 1777 to 1796, showed that the levy on William Hobirk, licensee of The George in 1792, was £1 7s 6d.

Another entry from a register reads as follows: Elizabeth, wife of Mathew Head, buried 31st July, 1679. Affidavit was made delivered to Mr Benjamin Younge, Vicar, within eight days according to the late act of parliament for burying in woollen. The 'Wool Act' was passed by parliament in the reign of Charles II and was instituted to help the declining wool trade. The dead shall be buried wrapped in a woollen shroud subject to a penalty of £5. Many chose to pay the fine. It would be difficult to conceive a more regular and secure source of revenue.

Another interesting extract relating to the Church is taken from the MSS of the Marquis of Salisbury, Lord Burleigh of the Manor of Theobalds and dated 1604. Lord Burleigh died in 1598 and the estate passed to his second son, Sir Robert Cecil, who was now in residence.

*A plumber named Christopher Greene had contracted with the Parish for the repairs to the Church roof. The new casting and laying of the leads, and in preparation had already stripped the roof when he was forced to work for the King (James I) who had succeeded Elizabeth in 1603.*

*Now by the practice of some London plumbers, he is forced by the warrant of the Sergeant Plumber to attend the King's service at Eltham; a practice among the Londoners, and likely to be an unreasonable charge to the parishioners. They beg Greene will be released and the Church now uncovered, finished with expedition.*

The following is an impassioned happening connected with the Church. For fear of losing some of the story's significance the article has been printed as recorded. The paper was written by David Pam and presented to the Edmonton Hundred Historical Society:

### *The Sunday Meat Market in Enfield Town*

Precisely when the practice of holding a market for the sale of meat outside the church gates originated in Edmonton and Enfield, I do not know. It had ceased in Edmonton by 1560, for John Sadler in his will of that date speaks of the road, Church Street, Edmonton, 'from the churche yarde door where the butcher used to stand', and since he expected his executors to know the place he meant, we must assume that they had stood there until only a short time earlier. In Enfield the market lasted longer and was to cause much controversy between the ministers and their congregation. The Vicar from 1579, Leonard Chambers, and his Minister, or Curate, as we should now say, Leonard Thickpenny, were constantly preaching against the Sunday market and making violent attacks from the pulpit against those whom they accused of supporting it. After one particularly bitter sermon some of the parishioners wrote, in a petition to the Lord Treasurer, 'to be plain we have many of these sermons in a year... every Sunday and Holyday, we have quarrellings and brawlings, little or much, what for one thing and what for another, they the said Leonard Chambers our Vicar, and Leonard Thickpenny our Minister being the originals and authors thereof'.

David Pam

The vicar maintained a vociferous campaign against the market. John Aylmer, Bishop of London, intervened on his behalf. The vicar invited his allies down from Cambridge. Dr Perne, Master of Peterhouse, on 13th October, 1583, not only preached against the market but afterwards publicly, in every man's hearing in Enfield Market Place, threatened the laws of the realm against the supporters of the market, and called upon Mr Wroth, as justice of the peace, to see the laws obeyed. Mr Wroth, it was alleged, 'then gave out great speeches, but nothing done'. Two years later, on 25th November, 1585, Doctor Good, of King's College, from the pulpit called upon the parishioners to see the error of their ways. Whereupon, Mr Wroth, with the same alacrity as on the previous occasion, forbade the butchers to use the market, in which injunction he was followed by the churchwardens, and the curate, but all to no avail. Robert Wroth, though a strong Puritan, as a member of parliament seems to have played a double game in all this, for when Lord Burleigh, involved in everything as usual, sent for the vicar at Wroth's house – Durants – Robert Wroth met the vicar in the outer courtyard to try to persuade him to relent his opposition, but this to no avail, the vicar only demanding him 'to continue anew that man he was at the last parliament, and not to be a labourer for the market'.

The climax was reached on the morning of Sunday, 12th June, 1586 when there came from Tottenham to the market square at Enfield a strange butcher with an ox ready dressed for sale, and the magistrate (being presumably the aforenamed Mr Wroth) seeing him 'did rather permit him than forbid'. It was then that the Minister, Leonard Thickpenny, his exasperation no longer to be contained, and set on by the vicar, did 'in a very outrageous manner, very evil be-seeming a man of the Church, or one of his calling, in a maddened mood, most ruffian-like, came to the butcher, where violently he pulled from him most part of his meat and threw it on the ground, most pitiful to behold, and not contented with that violence and outrage offered to us all by casting the meat upon the ground, which we the poorest sort determined to have bought that same day for our dinners, but there, in the presence of a great many honest poore men, threatened the aforesaid butcher, to beat him, yea, and also used these speeches, that he would kill him if he were hanged for the same within half an hour after he had done it.'

All this is contained in the petition sent to Lord Burleigh over the names of Thomas Banks, the head constable (whose name has been subsequently crossed out) Edmund Alcock, Thomas Brent, a labourer, and Robert Cox, a carpenter. The petition throws some light on the literacy, or more appropriately, the illiteracy within our parish in 1586, despite the fact that a school had probably been in existence for some eighty years. The petition took the form of names listed under that quarter of the parish where each man had his home. The list had been sent to each house and the head of the family was expected to indicate his approval with a signature or mark; the names of those who did not approve were marked with a letter 'D'. Of the 393 names on the list only thirty-two thus disapproved, five names were crossed out for reasons unknown and twenty-four apparently took the precaution to be out when the collector called, for there is no indication against these names. Parishioners to the number of 332 indicated their support for the continuance of their meat market. The illiteracy is indicated by the fact that 305 out of the 332 could so indicate only with a mark. Of the remaining twenty-seven, seventeen could signify with one letter only, three could manage two letters and two wrote their Christian names, one John and one Wyllam. There were five apparently able to make a signature. Another minor by-product of the petition is an indication of the geographical distribution of the population. We find an equal number of households east and west of the line now drawn by the Great Cambridge road.

# Chapter IV

The grammar school – The Greyhound Inn – Logsden's Yard – Enfield Court – The Rummer

The Enfield grammar school snugly nestling a few yards from the Church is to most of us a normal modern institution, but its primeval inheritance must not be overlooked. Although the incised stone over the north door bears the date 1557 it could well be that the correct date is 1558; this doubt was brought about by a change of calendar formality in 1752.

Until that year, the New Year began on 25th March, thus the prolonged dating of two deeds in 1557 and 1558 created this discrepancy; albeit the stone stays at 1557 and the date between the two deeds is only a matter of four months.

In actual fact the foundation of the school may trace its origin back to 1418, when Robert Blossom by his will charged his estate with the maintenance of a charity, which was transferred to Enfield through his widow marrying a John Hadfield, of Enfield. Trustees (then known as feoffees) administered the estate, and, in fact, one of them was John Tiptoft (see *Brasses, St Andrews Church*, page 11).

These free grammar schools appeared to be the only means of education that existed for the masses at that period, and as free schools they were the forerunner of the present educational system. During their early years the emphasis was more on spiritual than general education –

understandably when one considers the sources of income for maintaining these 'free' schools. Benefactors would endow land, buildings or a small or large part of their estate to one or more priests (not to the religious establishments) who in return would say daily mass and offer prayers for the donor, or for any other persons he may have named, 'for the goodness of their soul and life hereafter'. These endowments of services were intended to last for all time and were known as 'chantries'. The chantry-priests, apart from serving as assistant curates, occasionally acted as schoolmasters for the poor.

The establishment allowance in 1558 for running the free school was £6 13s 4d. In 1621 a new deed of trust was made whereby the present school was endowed with £20 per annum 'for a learned, neat and competent Master', to teach the children of all the inhabitants the cross row or alphabetical letters, reading, writing, arithmetic and grammar. In these free schools it was usual to make a small levy for candles, brooms and birches.

Dr Robert Uvedale (or Udall) became the master in 1664 and proved to be one of the most capable, talented and colourful heads of the school. A person of his drive and ability would obviously not be satisfied for long with an annual salary of £20 and it resulted in him leasing the old palace.

Later he was accused of neglecting the children of the free school by giving too much of his time and concentration to the boarding school he was promoting in the mansion opposite.

His son, Robert Uvedale (Doctor of Divinity was Vicar of Enfield from 1721 to 1731.

The Rev. J. Milne in 1793 commenced with an annual salary of £55 and the school flourished so well that with an average attendance of one hundred-odd pupils he managed to raise the salary to £100 and furthermore was assisted by two ushers, one with a salary of £40 and another at £10 per annum. Through the Benflect Estate (Poynett's) becoming enriched by a new purchase and increased rents the master eventually, in 1825, contrived a salary of £130 which was subject to conditions as to the number of pupils attending. Mr Milne also took in boarders, as had been the custom of his predecessors, but the practise had to be discontinued because of dissension and disputes between the 'private' and 'free' boys. Boys at this period were admitted from the age of seven.

Fees were started in 1874 and the rate was £6 per annum with the maximum of ten per cent 'free places'.

The school was built circa 1590 and today the original part remains built with those delightful Tudor bricks that have mellowed to a soft, warm, rustic red which only time can fashion. At the close of the last century the school was enlarged when the lease of The Kings Head terminated, and the large assembly rooms were taken over, together with the bowling green in front and the kitchen garden with its fine old barn.

The lower school which was previously Enfield Court (referred to on page 51) was acquired by the educational authorities in the early Twenties and is now fully integrated in the new comprehensive system. New extensions have recently been made at the back of the old or upper school.

The Greyhound, the sign of which in the picture is partly covering that of The Kings Head, was an old inn dating from the seventeenth century, later to be known as the Old Court House, and used as the town's public offices until late in the 1800s. Charles Cowden Clarke, scholar, and friend of the leading literary figures of that time, spent his honeymoon there after marrying Mary Victoria Novello in 1828. Clarke, son of the proprietor of the Enfield school, was friend and tutor to the poet John Keats. The old house in which the school was conducted was designed by Edward Helder, master mason to Wren and built about the middle of the seventeenth century. The facade is displayed in the Victoria and Albert Museum. It was almost certainly the birthplace in 1766 of Isaac Disraeli; the father of Benjamin Disraeli, who was prime minister in 1868 and again in 1874 until 1880. This delightful house met an inevitable fate at the hands of a demolition squad after temporary use as the Enfield town (Great Eastern) railway station from 1849 to 1872.

The old Greyhound was pulled down in 1897 and the present building erected and occupied by the London & Provincial Bank. It was acquired in 1918 by Barclays, the present owners. A copy of the frontispiece picture has been presented to the present manager, Mr Leslie Pym, in recognition of the service and general kindness extended to our family by all the managers since 1924.

Little is known of the buildings on the right of The Greyhound but it may be safely assumed they were demolished during the early part of the eighteenth century to make way for the new buildings. One of these was a Hanoverian House, occupied for many years by the Logsden family, who were coach builders. In a sizeable area at the rear, known as 'Logsden's Yard', there was a chapel in which services were held until 1864. The congregation at certain periods of the year was swelled by a hundred or more extra persons – temporary harvesters who contracted to gather the local farmer's crops. These gangs of harvesters tramped the countryside, mainly sleeping rough, for little more than their food. One particular farmer in Green

Street would allow up to one hundred and fifty workers to sleep in his barns. Often these roving workers were entertained to tea after the service by Mr and Mrs Ebenezer Gibbons, of Fir Tree House, their home in Silver Street, which was recently demolished. The chapel was demolished in 1923 when the property was developed on Logsden's site. The property was then in the possession of Fountains, who took over the coach building business until it was overtaken by the motor age. The local Tradesman's Ball was held at Enfield Court, built about 1690, on the west side of Baker Street. Enfield Court, now the lower grammar school was the residence of Col. Sir Alfred Somerset, KCB, DL, JP. Guests would leave their coaches at Logsden's and the ladies would dress upstairs by candlelight. Sir Alfred was the godson of General Martin, who died in 1852. During the battle of Waterloo Lord John Somerset, son of the fifth Duke of Beaufort, saved the life of General Martin, who ultimately, in gratitude, bequeathed the property to the son of his preserver.

The old inn on the extreme right of the picture was named The Rummer, so called after the name of a traditional English glass of the eighteenth century, with a large bowl and a squat stem which was used for holding 'punch'. The inn was noted for its stabling and post horses.

In 1839 the landlord, Mr William Camfield, was also listed as a horse dealer. The place was renamed The Railway Inn after the railway came to Enfield in 1849, and in 1870 extensive alterations were carried out by L. & W.D. Patman. The Patman family, prominent local residents for the past two hundred years or more, was known so well to Enfieldians through Sydney Patman who died in 1959, sadly the last of a long line. He was a prominent member of the Enfield Cricket Club and was in the process of writing the club's history before he passed away. The club's past president Mr Merle Gaunt, is continuing with the project. I have been privileged to see Sydney Patman's very fine collection of his own drawings, etchings and prints together with his notes and information on old Enfield. The inn was rebuilt in the early Thirties and renamed The Beaconsfield and finally underwent more extensive alterations after the property was leased to Henekeys by Whitbreads Brewery in 1934. The business is now directly managed by the brewers.

On the further side of the market place, and in spacious grounds, stood Burleigh House a large gaunt-looking place probably built during the seventeenth century, and pulled down in 1913 to make way for the Rialto cinema and the shops fronting Church Street. The old house is reputed to have contained a 'powder closet' for the ladies, who popped their heads through a curtain so that their elaborate hair arrangements could be sprinkled with powder by a servant.

# Chapter V

The New River – mansion on Enfield Green – elm trees in centre of town

Although the New River may not be seen in the picture a mention must be made of its historical importance and especially of its connection with Enfield. How many thousands – no millions – of people have crossed the bridge at the further end of the town without any knowledge of its real significance or why there has to be a bridge there at all? Very understandable. Who wants to know about yesterday when faced with today's confused and noisy juggernaut town – yet one can, within four or five minutes, turn off at the bridge and walk along the bank to the next bridge. Every yard, every second, diminishes the confused noises, and the disturbed mind returns again to tranquillity and composure conducive to more congenial thoughts.

For seven miles this man-made river curls its way through the town's territory, but today, instead of the energetic flow that was attempting to keep pace with the Londoner's requirements the stream is now at a standstill, having been handed over to the local authority in 1938 on amenity grounds. Almost unbelievable that this ribbon of water, starting from the springs at Chadwell, near Ware, then wound for thirty-nine miles and gave London the major part of its water supply.

This gigantic undertaking and great engineering feat was launched in 1609 by Sir Hugh Myddelton; against strong opposition and in extremely adverse conditions. The project cost half a million pounds, and there is little doubt that without the encouragement and financial support provided by James I (who was then in residence at Theobalds Palace) the whole enterprise would have collapsed.

Little did the king know he was to suffer the fate of being thrown from his horse into the New River when it was iced over in the depth of winter. It would have gone ill with him that day if Sir Richard Young, seeing the accident, had not gone quickly to the rescue. The following I quote from *The Palace of Theobalds*, by John Charles Earle. From an original letter dated 1622:

> *The ice broke and in plunged his august Majesty head foremost, while nothing but his boots remained visible. His attendants had to empty him, like an inverted cask, of the river water he had drunk so freely against his will.*

Horsemanship was not one of the king's strong points. After his favourite huntsman had been killed, he vowed he would never hunt again in the Royal Chase. King James died at Theobalds on the 27th March, 1625. This, sadly, brought the termination of Royal Enfield, that much closer.

In 1613 the four years of trials and tribulations culminated in a public ceremony which was presided over by Sir Hugh's brother, Sir Thomas Myddelton, who was then Lord Mayor of London. With great pomp and ceremony the water was released into new cisterns called the 'New River Head' at Islington. The minimum number of workmen at any one time was six hundred and a goodly representation attended this triumphant termination.

The shares brought no wealth to its founders, but the New River Company later became one of the world's richest. A single share in 1897 was sold for £125,000.

Whilst supervising the project Sir Hugh lived at Bush Hill House, Bush Hill Road which afterwards became his country residence. The house, re-named 'Halliwick', was later the home of Sir Samuel Cunard, founder of the Cunard Steamship Company. It is now a school for physically handicapped children, and many local people donate generously to the children's welfare.

A map dated 1658 shows a house on the site where the Central Library now stands; this is thought to have been the house of Sir Robert Jason, who had a mansion on Enfield Green in 1686.

Two great elm trees dominated the centre of the town where the island triangle is now situated; one was burnt down during the bonfire night celebrations early in the eighteen hundreds, and the other was blown down in a raging gale in 1836.

# Chapter VI

The house of Hanover – owners and licensees of The George Inn 1716–1888 – furnishings – Hannah Sell – licensees from 1716 to 1725 – jobs and wages, early 1700s

The house of Hanover was established with the arrival of George I on 18th September, 1714: a king who was perhaps, understandably, difficult for English people to accept; the son of Princess Sophia, Electress of Hanover and granddaughter of James I. He was of sombre disposition, expressionless, shy, hating pomp and large gatherings where he was the subject of attention, but he was inspired by hunting, racing with perhaps a generous affinity for the ladies. He did have a shrewd perception of reasoning which betokened good judgement and basic common sense. His knowledge of the English language was so sparse that the man regarded as England's first prime minister, Robert Walpole, presided over the cabinet.

I wonder how different life would have been, and how the course of history may have developed had the Jacobite uprising in 1715 won the day against the Whigs who had put George I on the throne of England. The Jacobites, followers of the House of Stuart, rebelled against the Hanoverian accession but were defeated in Scotland and the North of England. The insurrection lost its momentum and fizzled out in 1716 and was followed by numerous trials for treason, which resulted in about thirty executions.

John Wilburd (now spelt with an i in place of y), of Shoreditch, now the owner of The George Inn, made his will on the 1st December, 1715 and the following has been extracted: 'And my mind and will is that if the said messuage or Inn called the George Inn should at any time hereafter happen to be burnt down or destroyed by fire (as God forbid) and the value thereof sunk and lessened, then and in such case I do hereby order and direct that my said Grandson Samuel Wilburd *shall be and out of the said farm lands and houses to him hereby given, give and pay unto my said* Grandson Eleazer and his heirs the sum of £300'. He died very soon after this will was made.

There is no evidence of the owner ever being in residence or of his being the licensee of the inn. The earliest Licensed Victuallers Register for the Edmonton Division names Hannah Sell as the licensee in 1716.

*The History of Enfield* by Cuthbert Whitaker (1911) says: 'The George Inn, built early in the eighteenth century on the site of an older house has given place to the present modern but effective structure'. There is no reference whatever in any of the deeds or indentures to the inn being rebuilt, nor is there such reference in the many leases. The elevation of the building clearly suggests early Georgian, somewhere between 1710 and 1740.

Referring to the picture of the old inn, the front elevation, except perhaps for the fascia board, would have been almost the same, as it was when built, but the rear of the building was constructed mainly of wooden weathered board, suggesting an earlier period. The property was demolished in 1895 and I am annoyed to think that I had every opportunity of finding out all about the interior and general layout from personal friends of the family and also from customers.

After all, in 1924 a person had only to be forty-five years old to have been actually working on the demolition of the old structure or on the rebuilding of the present house; even in 1929, when I first worked full time there, many of the customers would tell me tales of the old house – unfortunately not one of these were noted.

Glasses would have been used only on rare occasions, for serving punch and the like; the predominating utensils would have been made of pewter, in all sizes but mainly pints and quarts, with and without pouring lips. Brass and copper were probably much in evidence. The furniture was possibly country made, consisting mainly of benches and settles; floors could have been either left in the natural wood or possibly covered in a coloured or patterned oil cloth. The walls may have been panelled but were more likely covered with a printed paper; flock paper was also obtainable at this time, as was printed calico. The beer or ale was served only from the 'wood'; perhaps not always at the correct temperature, but who cared! The customers then had not been conned into the belief that 'life is impossible and unjust if this and that is not iced'. Only a few years ago it would have been sacrilege to serve a Guinness cold; today advertisements will advise it to be drunk 'chilled'. I personally always enjoyed a Guinness after a white hot poker had been plunged in it, of course in very cold weather.

Beer drawn straight from the cask by tap is now almost non-existent; but the music of a burbling tap as the golden brown liquid hit the pewter stays in the ears, changing its harmonious tinkling tune as the pot filled and was lowered and raised to maximise the head consistent with filling without any overspill. Then, unlike today, the almost empty silence would only be broken perhaps by a passing squeaky cart wheel or the neigh of a horse in the stable. Except for the human voice, and maybe a crackle and splatter from the log fire, these homely sounds would soothe the ear of the fatigued traveller unhindered.

Let our imagination wander back to 1716 when Hannah Sell supposedly takes over the newly rebuilt George Inn. I find it intriguing to think a woman held a license at this period, although it was apparently quite common, in fact the female brewers known as brewsters go back to the fifteenth century and those that brewed the liquor on the premises of the inns and taverns were commonly referred to as 'ale wives'. It was quite feasible that Hannah was brewing some or all of the beer she retailed at The George Inn as did Edward Heath up to the time he disposed of the property.

Hannah held The George on a yearly lease at a rent of £30 16s 8d (£30.83) which was paid to John Wilburd's widow. Whether or not the brewhouse on the north side of the road leading from Shoreditch to Hackney, owned by her husband, was still functioning in her name is uncertain; if so, as the lessee it is probable Hannah was made to buy a quantity of her stock from the owner brewer which could have been an early example of the development of the controversial brewery 'tie'.

There is little doubt that the business was a flourishing concern. I would roughly estimate her takings including alcoholic and non-alcoholic drinks, food, stabling, lettings and incidentals appertaining to the trade at approximately £40 per week. The approximate weekly expense including rent which was 12s 0d (60p), wages, poor rate and general overheads would have been in the region of £8 2s 6d (£8.12½). Assuming the profit margin was in the order of thirty-three point three per cent Hannah would have had a fairly prosperous return of something between £5 and £6 per week, especially with all of her living expenses covered.

Around this period beer was retailing at 3d (1.25p) per quart giving the publican an average 13s 0d (65p) profit on a barrel (36 gallons). Better quality beer was 4d (1.66p) a quart pot these prices remained unchanged until 1761 when the beer duty was raised from 5s 0d to 8s 0d per barrel.

Hannah Sell, whom I can only imagine as an interesting and great character, was probably the most wealthy of all the hosts that ever held the license of The George Inn. When she died in 1725 she held the leases on four London properties apart from The George. In the cellar stood ten butts of beer (equivalent to three barrels or 108 gallons each) valued at £45.

The spirits then referred to as strong water were purchased from the distiller, Mr Puleston and her wine from Mr Allen, the vintner. She also sold arrack, an eastern spirit made mainly from dates.

Superfluous to her income from the normal trading of the Inn, Hannah had some flourishing sidelines such as acting as the village banker-cum-pawnbroker and money loans. In the final settlement of her affairs Mr John Ballet's overdraft 'by book and by bond' amounted with interest due to £165 17s 0d. Two other loans amounted to £76 10s 0d and innumerable small debts 'upon goods pledged'.

The inn must have catered widely, proved by the large outstanding settlements made to the bakers, grocers, butchers, corn chandlers and for oats for the stables.

She had £500 invested in the East India Company and £50 in the South Sea Company later to collapse involving the government in grave scandal as the notorious 'South Sea Bubble'.

Philip Baron, the undertaker, received the handsome sum of £33 expenses for her funeral which suggests the occasion was carried out in great style.

The business was taken over by her son, William Sells, who could have found his mother's activities difficult to follow because the licensing register records a James Dugden (sometimes spelt Dugdell) holding the license in 1726.

Prices of materials, goods for sale, and wages, at this period, would have altered little, and the following information has been extracted from David and Charles's reprints of *Neves-City and Country Purchases* (first printed in 1703 and again in 1736) also *The London Tradesman* (1747). Building bricks were anything from nine shillings to eighteen shillings per thousand depending upon whether they were collected or delivered.

The 1974 prices for the ordinary Fletton Bricks would be approximately £26 per thousand delivered, and the better grade as much as £35 per thousand. Regarding bricklayers' wages I quote: 'A journeyman bricklayer has commonly half a crown a day, and the foreman of the work may have three shillings or perhaps a guinea a week, and a labourer one shilling and eight pence a day. But they say they are out of business for five if not six months of the year; and in and about London drink more than one third of the other six'.

Plasterers would receive twopence three-farthings per yard, including sizing.

House painters' wages were from two shillings and sixpence to three shillings per day, and they were idle from four to five months of the year. If not in robust health their lungs and nerves were often affected by the white lead in the paint.

The following quote is amusing:

> The journeymen of this branch are the dirtiest, laziest and most debauched set of fellows that are of any trade in and about London; therefore I think no parent ought to be so mad as to bind his child apprentice for seven years to a branch that may be learned in as many hours, in which he cannot earn a subsistence when he has got it; runs the risk of breaking his neck every day and in the end turns out a mere blackguard.

Lead was commonly used in those days, and the cost of laying, including workmanship, was sixteen to seventeen shillings per hundredweight. Piping cost one shilling and fourpence a yard for half-inch bore and three shillings and sixpence a yard for one-and-a-half inch bore.

Another interesting entry, that if applied today would grind our building industry to an immediate halt, concerns an act passed by parliament after the Fire of London 'that all roofs, window frames and cellar floors to be made of *oak*'!

The average hours worked then were from 6 a.m. until 8 p.m. An assistant in a snuffshop was on duty from 7 a.m. until 10 p.m. – fifteen hours! The woollen draper appears to have had the easiest time, especially during the winter months, working from 8 a.m. until dark.

The average working man's wages were ten to fifteen shillings per week. An engraver earned thirty shillings per week, while a copper plate engraver could earn three pounds per week (today approximately £120). I quote another example of the state of sanitation only two hundred and twenty-three years ago:

> In Architecture, are Conduits or Conveyances for the Suillage and Filth of a House; which, how base so

ever they are in use, yet for the health of the inhabitants, they are as necessary and considerable as (perhaps) anything about a house.

Concerning these, I find in our authors, this Counsel, that art should imitate nature in these ignoble conveyances, and separate them from sight (where there wants a running water) into the most remote and lowest and thickest part of the foundation, with secret vents passing up through the walls (like a tunnel) to the wide air aloft; which all Italian Artisans comment for the discharge of noisome vapours, though elsewhere (to my knowledge) little practised.

# Chapter VII

Dick Turpin

During this period there was a desperate villain commencing to make his living as a butcher, as a cattle thief, robber, highwayman, and finally a murderer. The notorious Dick Turpin was in the early stages of his career of crime. Unfortunately he was portrayed glamorously by Ainsworth in *Rookwood* and from then on he was misrepresented and projected as another 'Robin Hood'. Born at Hempstead, near Dunmow, Essex, in 1705 he was, at an early age, apprenticed to a butcher at Whitechapel, and the evidence suggests he was a vicious and very quarrelsome lad, determined to live by his wits rather than by work. After he had served his apprenticeship the butcher was extremely glad to be rid of him. Later he was reported to have married Hester Palmer, whose father was landlord of The Rose & Crown, Clay Hill, Enfield. He was then reputed to have opened a butcher's shop in Sewardstone, near Waltham Abbey, augmenting his takings by rustling cattle from the local farmers and selling the hides to a tanner at Waltham Abbey. Eventually he was found out by a farmer who recognised his own hides, and a warrant was issued for his arrest. When the representatives of the law called at the shop, Turpin, sensing trouble, clambered out of a rear window and fled. He next fell in with a gang of smugglers which was broken up by the revenue officers, but Turpin was one of the few who evaded capture. After this episode he joined a mob of deer-stealers concentrating on Epping Forest and neighbouring parks; this was not very remunerative, so they turned to housebreaking. Most of their exploits were recorded, and many roguish and unsavoury tales were reported. A reward of £100 was offered after the robbing of a farmer named Francis near Marylebone; the whole plot having been concocted at The White Bear Inn, Drury Lane, on 7th February, 1735.

The reward offered succeeded in bringing one of the gang forward to inform on the others, resulting in a number being arrested, but again Turpin escaped. Whilst riding towards Cambridge he fell in with a notorious highwayman called King, and together they committed so many plunderings on the highway that they were known to every innkeeper in Essex, who refused to give them shelter. They then retreated to a cave known to Turpin at High Beech, in Epping Forest, between The Kings Oak and the Loughton Road; later to be marked by a pub called Turpin's Cave which was demolished by Bass Charrington in January 1972. The pair were victualled and provided with other necessities by Turpin's wife.

An assistant keeper of Epping Forest named Thomas Morris, with an assistant, approached the cave on 4th June, 1737, with the intention of arresting the highwayman but he was tricked into complacency by friendly gestures, allowing Turpin to snatch his gun and shoot him dead. Notices were now posted up with the reward raised to £200 and with the following description of the wanted man, 'About 5'9" high, very marked with the Smallpox, his cheek bones broad, his face thinner towards the bottom, his visage short, pretty upright, and broad about the shoulders.'

After meeting his wife at an inn in Hertford, Turpin was recognised by a butcher to whom Turpin was in debt and, saying he would get the money from his wife in the next room, he slipped out of a window and rode hard to meet his companion King. As they approached The Green Man, in Epping Forest, they overtook a man riding a fine thoroughbred horse. Turpin's mount was weary and spent after his arduous ride, and so at pistol point he ordered the man, named Major, to change mounts. Major went on to The Green Man and related the story to Bayes, the landlord, who immediately formed the opinion that Turpin was the culprit. Enquiries followed and on the Monday following Saturday's crime, information was received that the stolen horse had been left at The Red Lion, in Whitechapel. Bayes and others waited for Turpin to collect the horse, which he duly did late at night. He was seized, taken into the inn and questioned by a constable. Promised release if he told all the facts he stated that a stout man in a white coat was waiting for the horse in Red Lion Street, and so he was accompanied by constables to the place where King was waiting. King, seeing the game was up, pulled a pistol, but it misfired; desperately he attempted to draw the other pistol but this became fastened in his pocket. He shouted to Turpin, 'Shoot or we are taken!' Turpin did just that, but instead of shooting the law he shot his companion. King collapsed, saying, 'Dick, you have killed me.' Turpin flung himself on his horse and raced away.

King lived for a week, in which time he confessed the crimes he and Turpin had committed.

After being hunted in Epping Forest, suffering continual terror of capture, Turpin decided to go north to Yorkshire. At Long Sutton, Lincolnshire, he stole some horses and very soon afterwards was captured, but yet again escaped while being escorted to a magistrate. Arriving at Welton in

Yorkshire, he assumed the name of John Palmer (after his wife).

Whilst living the life of a country gentleman, but still carrying on with his crimes, an incident happened that created suspicion and led to his arrest. Charged with everything that in those days carried the extreme penalty, he was condemned to be hanged, and the sentence was duly carried out on 10th April, 1739.

There were numerous stories and legends concerning Turpin's association with The Rose and Crown, Clay Hill, Enfield; one being that he married Betty Millington, the daughter of the landlord and actually took the inn over but, quickly tiring of the business, left to open the butcher's at Sewardstone, in Essex.

The general story is that Turpin's grandfather – Samuel Nott – was the owner of The Rose and Crown, but this account has little support in view of his father's name being Turpin and his mother's maiden name Palmer; without a doubt a relationship exists somewhere in the controversial tales and legends.

Arthur Wm. Fish took over a butcher's shop, opposite The Hop Poles, Baker Street, in 1894 and in 1901 acquired the freehold of the Rose and Crown from Whitbread's – as a 'free house' – meaning that the beers sold were not tied to any particular brewer. Len, his son, was then three years old and well remembers the many happenings and tales during the following few years before his father sold the property to Mann and Crossman in 1908.

Len assures me that Dick Turpin spent a period hiding in the loft (now the new restaurant), the landlord tending to his wants. His horse was stabled at the rear, but whether it was the legendary Black Bess or not we shall never know. Len also remembers being ushered to this loft when the brook that wanders down from White Webbs overflowed in 1908 and flooded the inn, the water rising above the counters.

Len Fish took over the butcher's shop in 1919 on the death of his father, and retired from the business in 1966; well-known and respected in the district and in the 'horsey' world. Under his chairmanship the Enfield and District Horse Society's show at Forty Hall has grown into one of the major events in the show jumping calendar.

# Chapter VIII

Owners and licensees from 1734 – prize fighting 1719 to 1750 – Lord Derby introduces The Oaks – yard of ale – the lamentable gin era

The next indenture is dated 15th July, 1734, between Eleazer Wilburd (John Wilburd's grandson) and Thomas Powell. An interesting extract from the document shows that Eleazer

> in consideration of £250 of Lawful money of Great Britain, did bargain, sell, assign transfer and set over unto the said Thomas Powell all and singular one annuity or yearly rent charge of £48 issuing and payable out of all that Messuage Tenement or Inn situate and being in Enfield in the County of Middlesex called or known by the name or sign of The George and in the tenure or occupation of James Dugdell his assigns or undertenants and all those two messuages or tenements situate and being at a certain place called Horsepool Stones (near The Bell Enfield Highway) and were situated and called or known by the name of The Red Lion Ragged Inn in the several Tenures or occupation of George Blackwell and John Dyer to hold unto the said Thomas Powell his executors etc, etc from the date hereof for a term of ninety-nine years.

The name of James Dugdell (or Dugden) certainly establishes the fact he was the licensee then. Horsepool Stones is marked on an old map but The Red Lion Ragged Inn or The Red Lion and The Ragged Inn so far remains unidentified but obviously the properties came within the tenure of The George Inn.

There are two other documents relating to the first deed, the first is a sale of Wilburd to Powell for £600 and the second is a mortgage on a loan to Powell of £500.

No register was preserved from 1733 to 1750 but we may assume that Dugdell or Thomas Dunball could have been the licensee for all or part of this period; the latter is recorded in the register from 1751 until 1759 but he is also quoted as being the occupier in an indenture dated 3rd and 4th October, 1765 when, by the register, Mary Ford held the license.

John Shipman was the next license holder, appearing only in 1760. He was followed by Peter Ford, landlord for only two years (1761/2) then Mary Ford until 1766, followed by William Briggs from 1767 until 1761.

It appears Peter and Mary Ford were either husband and wife or brother and sister, or a more obvious conclusion is that they were married whilst Mary was holding the license, after which it was transferred to Peter and later in 1762 he died; the license again returning to Mary, since it was in her name until 1766.

A court book of the Manor of Durants and Gartons dated 1791 quotes a will dated 1762 in which a Mr John Gay (brewer) leaves all his property including The George Inn to his two daughters, Mary Ostliffe and Sarah Brough. The deeds connected with the ownership have so far not appeared in evidence of this, and we can only assume that

John Gay purchased the freehold sometime after the mid-eighteenth century.

To digress for a while and refer to other interests from the period would be a welcome rest from the dull and laborious task of attempting to condense and understand the complicated repetitive legal jargon contained in the Abstract of Deeds and Indentures.

In 1719 James Figg, the first acknowledged English champion of the prize ring, opened his school of arms, teaching broadsword and single stick exercises and the art of combat with fists. Patronised by royalty the school was known as Figg's Amphitheatre and was situated in Oxford Road, London. Challenged three times by Ned Sutton, the principal contender, Figg remained champion by beating him on each of three occasions and retired undefeated in 1734. Figg discovered the 'Father of Boxing', Jack Broughton, who became champion of England by beating George Taylor in twenty minutes at the booth, run by Taylor himself at Tottenham Court Road; the probable date was 1740, but could have been later. He remained champion until 1750 when he was beaten by Jack Slack, a very much younger man. The prize was for £600 and the Duke of Cumberland backed him for £10,000; during the contest the Duke remarked, 'What are you at Broughton?' and the battered fighter, with both eyes closed, protested gamely, 'I'm blind, I'm not beat.' The same year an act of parliament was passed banning boxing, but the 'noble art' still went on, in fact we see on 3rd May 1786, when Humphries beat Sam Martin in one hundred and five minutes for 320 guineas at Newmarket, that the nobility were taking a keen interest; this match was attended by the Prince of Wales and the Duke of York, together with some of the French nobility, who mingled with the 'fancy', as the young gallants were then known.

Broughton created the first boxing gloves known as mufflers, and also wrote the first code of rules governing boxing in 1743, and these regulations were adhered to until they were superseded by the London Prize Ring Rules in 1838. Broughton died a rich man at the fine old age of eighty-five.

From 1730 onwards regular horse race meetings were held on Epsom Downs and in 1779 Lord Derby introduced the first 'Oaks' race meeting; winning the event with his own filly – Bridget.

The middle of the eighteenth century saw the birth of the 'Yard of Ale' glass, or Yard glass, as well as many other varied trick glasses that were designed to pour contents in any direction except where the would-be consumer intended. They were very popular in the inns and taverns. The genuine Yard glass holds approximately two and a half to three pints and to consume this at all demands an extreme effort, let alone emptying a two and a half pint, three-feet long funnel-mouthed glass in six and a half seconds as Lawrence Hill, of Bolton, did on 17th December, 1964 at the age of twenty-two. A three pint Yard was downed in 10.15 seconds by Jack Boyle at The Bay Horse, Ormsgill, Barrow-in-Furness. These details are quoted from the *Guiness Book of Records*. When one considers the boisterous rough handling the early glasses must have received it is understandable that so few of the original specimens were salvaged.

Justice during this era, and indeed for many years to follow, proved its distressing toughness as the following examples demonstrate. In 1762 John Batt of Potters Bar, was committed to the Bridewell (Fleet Street) for cutting down trees in Enfield Chase, and sentenced to be whipped publicly in the market place of Enfield once a month during his imprisonment.

For the same offence a woman was publicly whipped at the cart's tail from the Bridewell prison to Enfield, and the record stated, 'she to undergo the same discipline twice more'.

George Barrington of Enfield stole a gold watch from a Henry Townsend resulting in his transportation to Botany Bay, Australia. He ultimately became an influential and affluent settler.

An interesting report from the book dated 1753, called *The Universal Magazine of Knowledge & Pleasure* I thought sufficiently interesting to record, particularly as the first Penny Post was not instituted until the issue of the Penny Black in 1840! (I now have the pleasure of owning one).

> The Penny-Post mail was robbed of his watch, and afterwards shot by two highwaymen at Winchmore Hill, near Southgate, died of his wounds on Monday evening, at six o'clock at The King's Head, Winchmore Hill, about four hours after that barbarous act was committed.
>
> Yesterday Christopher Johnson and John Stockdale were committed to Newgate by Henry Fielding Esq; being charged with the above-mentioned robbery and murder. When before the Justice, each charged the other with murder. The former is twenty-two years of age, the latter but seventeen and clerk to the attorney.

21st June

For this crime it is certain one or both would have been hanged.

The King's Head which stands in the Green at Winchmore Hill is one of the Borough of Enfield's well-known pubs. The hosts are now Henry and Janet Duffield who took over in 1969.

The early middle of the eighteenth century unfortunately established an appalling era during which cheap gin was introduced to England after the excise duty on French wines and brandy had been increased. In London a great proportion of the population succumbed to the nauseating dope-like effect it produced, and a wave of debauchery swept the capital. In 'Gin Lane' Hogarth depicts a vendor's and pawnbroker's paradise, in which the denizens sunk to the horrible depths of depravity. Some retailers set up notices inviting the people to be drunk for one penny or for tuppence they would supply straw for nothing, on which to lay their bodies in a drunken stupor.

Gin, especially Holland Gin has certain medicinal qualities, mainly derived from the juniper berries and the aromatic oil which they produce. Otherwise it is distilled from grain, mainly maize, and unlike most other spirits it is not necessary to allow any time for maturing after distillation. There is little doubt of the popularity of gin which is mainly due to its quality of blending pleasantly with so many other ingredients.

# Chapter IX

Owners and Licensees from 1765 – William Hobkirk and The Enfield Fly – Examples of Justice – Fisticuffs

Back to The George Inn again. An indenture dated 3rd and 4th October, 1765, declares that William Powell, only son and heir of James Powell, died and willed the inn to his wife, who conveyed the premises and business to a Joseph Allvey for £900. The deed shows Thomas Dunball as the tenant and occupier but, as previously referred to, he was not then the license holder. There is also a reference to Allvey acquiring the title of three cottages, a barn, seven stables and an orchard, as well as three gardens for a further £300.

Joseph Allvey in his will dated 17th February, 1766, conveyed The George and all its appurtenances to George Hoffman and Charles Hunter in trust for Elizabeth Chivers for life, and for her to have the option of transferring the property to her name if she so wished.

William Hobkirk became the licensee in 1772, and according to the Land Tax books he held the property as occupier from the proprietors Beckett and Ostlife (now spelt with only one f) the granddaughters of John Gay. Hobkirk appears to be one of the few innkeepers to have produced any worthwhile information. In 1783 he put into operation a public vehicle service to London from The George Inn to Aldersgate Street, and as far as can be ascertained this was the earliest Enfield-to-London passenger service on record. The following is a copy of the original notice advertising the pioneer 'Enfield Fly':

### ENFIELD FLY

Upon springs, to carry five inside passengers only

Will set out on Monday, 31st March, 1783, and every following day (Tuesdays excepted) at eight o'clock in the morning during the summer season from The George Inn, Enfield, to The Castle and Falcon Inn in Aldersgate Street, where places and parcels are taken at Mr Dupont's Bar for the same, returns from there at four in the afternoon to Enfield. And for better accommodation for ladies and gentlemen whose business may call them to that part of the town the Fly will stop at Cameron's, Grocer, No 106 opposite Bow Church, Cheapside, every afternoon between four and five o'clock. On Sundays the same will call at Mr Snaggs, book-seller, No 89 Bishopsgate at five o'clock in the afternoon. Places and parcels to go by the said Fly are taken every day in the week at Mr Snaggs aforesaid, also Mr Fearn's, shopkeeper, near The Fighting Cocks in Baker Street, Enfield.

| | |
|---|---|
| To and from Bishopsgate Street | 2s 0d each |
| To and from The Castle and Falcon Inn | 2s 3d each |

William Hobkirk, proprietor of the said Fly, thanks the public in general for the encouragement he has hitherto received and will endeavour to merit a continuance of the same by unremitted endeavours to oblige.

NB Ladies and gentlemen who choose to be fetched from or carried to their own houses at the several places in Enfield hereinafter mentioned shall be waited on upon paying additionally, namely to Bulls Cross, Turkey Street and the further part of Clay Hill – one shilling (1s 0d), Forty Hill – sixpence (6d) and Chase Side – threepence (3d).

During this period no celebrated fisticuff contests are known to have taken place in Enfield, but George Ingleston, known to the fraternity as 'The Brewer' ended his sporting days peacefully working for his patron Captain Brailsford, who owned the Cannon Brewery opposite The Hop Poles in Baker Street. Ingleston once beat the celebrated 'gentleman' Jackson, a tremendous athlete who later defeated Daniel Mendoza for the championship of England, which he held from 1795 to 1803. Jackson had to retire with an injured ankle in the fight against Ingleston. In 1788 William Ward, a bruiser of ill-fame, who was on his way to see a fight between Mendoza and Richard Humphreys, dismounted when his party's coach halted at Ponders End, provoked a drunken blacksmith, named Edwin Swain, to challenge him and savagely beat the Enfield man to death. This assault earned him a stay of three months in Newgate.

# Chapter X

Licenses 1796 – Enfield Chase – seventeen changes in twenty-eight years – Robert Mathison 1828 – The Stag – Charles Lamb and The Crown and Horseshoes – the Mathison family

The license was in the family name of Hobkirk for twenty-eight years. Letitia, his wife, took over in 1796, I presume after the death of her husband, and held the license until 1800, when her daughter Mary was registered as the licensee. According to the Land Tax Assessment books it was Mary and Sarah Hobkirk in possession.

In 1801 Thomas Game held the license and would have been host to the commissioners who had been appointed by parliament to enquire into the rights of the commoners of the parish of Enfield when its commons, marshes and waste lands were enclosed. They were all accommodated and victualled at The George. The commoners' claim was for compensation for the loss of the ancient rights whereby, regardless of their standing, or however humble, they were allowed to pasture their animals or cut bushes, turves, peat, and to enjoy other amenities on large tracts of the Chase. A survey of Enfield proved there were nine hundred and twenty inhabited dwellings in the parish with a population of 5,881, and the number of cattle on common ground was 1,614. Mr Abraham Wilkinson, who had purchased White Webbs, wrote to John Middleton (author of the Agricultural Survey) complaining as follows: 'I bought this estate and thought to make a great profit from the Chase, but the commoners turn so many beast on it that there is no room for mine'. Unfortunately the records and notes of the commissioners' enquiry no longer exist, but it is known that the first step taken was to secure their pay, by exercising their powers and selling off ninety acres under the hammer at £27 per acre (Wilkinson reports the cheapest land was selling at £34 per acre). The bulk of the land was sold off to interested parties of which the largest beneficiary was Trinity College, Cambridge, who were the owners of almost all the parish tithes. This means they received one tenth in kind of the produce of the land annually.

The farmers and landowners benefited immensely by this act now that they were free of this encumbrance of the tithe. The cottagers and peasants derived little or no benefit from this because they had few, if any, tithable possessions, but they still retained the same rights of common.

Thomas Game held the license for one year only, for in 1802 we see Thomas Howell installed, who again was the license holder for only one year. He was replaced by William Pritchard, who managed to stay for two years (1803 and 1804) as 'Mine Host'.

Following the four licensees mentioned since 1800 were William Markhall (1805–1807), Robert Lake (1808), William Markhall (again in 1809), Samuel Odell (1810), Thomas Judd (1811), Samuel Coomes (1812–1814), Patrick Rowney (1815), Henry Porter (1816–1820), Augustus Aves (1821–1822), William Keen (1823), Charles Dickenson (1824–1825), George Abbott (1826) and Robert Mathison, who settled down for a long family period in 1828.

There appears little reason for the extraordinary succession of landlords during this period; no fewer than seventeen changes of license in twenty-eight years. The steady population growth of Enfield during these years from 5,881 in 1801 to 8,812 in 1831 must surely have been conducive to the promotion of trade – perhaps the ghost 'Old George' had been at work? In the thirty-two years during which time I lived there many peculiar things happened, but I do not recall any confrontation with the apparition so much talked about now. Charles Dickenson, the licensee aforementioned was convicted in 1824 for breach of recognisance: 'For that the said Charles Dickenson, being an Alehouse keeper, victualler and retailer of Ale, Beer or other excisable liquors did at the Parish of Enfield... on Sunday the first day of August now last past in his house known by the sign of The George permit and suffer drinking during the usual hours of Divine Service, whereby he hath forfeited the sum of One Pound, this being his first offence...'

The register stops at 1829 after George Abbott became the license holder in 1826.

Fortunately the record continues among the indentures and documents held at the Mile End Brewery offices of Charrington & Co, and from information contributed by Ken Mathison, great grandson of the next licensee in 1828 Robert Mathison. There is an indenture of that year of Robert being granted a fourteen year lease at £70 per annum, including stables and trees etc, from Mrs Beckett who still held the freehold.

In 1844, apart from making his will, this Mathison apprenticed his son Robert on 10th August to Jack Logsden, coachmaker of Enfield, for six years. The indenture says that in consideration of £13 received from Robert Mathison he Jack Logsden will learn and teach his son the art of coach-building. The reward – one shilling per week for the first year and an advance of another shilling per week in each succeeding year.

Whilst in this period of time, and again to provide a brief diversion for the reader, we will revert to The Stag, at the western end of the town. Surprisingly, the two cottages which Sir Edward Jeynes sold to George Smith in 1803 for £210 did not become licensed until 1843, when Elizabeth Smith sold them to Samuel Richards for £200 and they became known as The Stag. There appeared little need for a Capital Gains Tax in those days.

In 1896 a Mr C. Coventry leased the premises to West & Co, brewers, for eighty years at £50 per annum with a covenant for the lessor to rebuild within seven years at an approximate cost of £600. The brewery must have acquired the freehold at a later date as the Licensed Register shows that the owners then were Gripper Bros., who at one time and another had owned a large percentage of the Enfield Hostelries.

On 22nd September, 1898, West's granted a fourteen-year lease at £25 per annum of the rear part of The Stag to the National Telephone Co Ltd, and so these premises may have been Enfield's first telephone exchange.

The brewery was taken over by Hoare & Co in 1926 (famous for their Toby Ale) who, in turn, were absorbed by Charrington & Co.

Reg West, who was a director in his family's brewery, was living in Enfield until 1938, later moving to St Margaret's Bay. The brewery celebrated their centenary by brewing a very strong beer early this century, and I am fortunate in still possessing two bottles, now about sixty years old; it was extremely mellow when the last bottle was sampled, some twenty-five years ago!

Charles Lamb lived in Enfield from 1827 until 1833. In 1832 an incident occurred involving him which implicates the well-known and unusually situated inn called The

Crown & Horseshoes, off Chase Side. At the time the essayist had given up his own house, and was in lodgings with friends, the Westwoods, in the house now known as Westwood Cottage. Being very close to the inn it became a favourite haunt of Lamb and he was always pleased to introduce his many literary friends to it, including the rigid and imposing Wordsworth. On 19th December, Lamb visited The Crown & Horseshoes to obtain an extra pint of porter for a friend named Moxon who had paid him a late visit. On arriving in the parlour he found four men playing dominoes; one of whom, named Danby, had recently returned from India and was carrying a fair amount of money. The other three were named Johnson, Fare and Cooper. Fare invited Lamb to join in the game which he did. At the terminal hour Johnson took Danby up Holtwhites Hill and ruthlessly murdered him. The three were tried at the Old Bailey. Fare was acquitted, and Cooper turned king's evidence, whilst Johnson was convicted and received the death penalty. Lamb was summoned to appear before Dr Cresswell the following morning to offer information as to what happened in the bar parlour on the evening in question.

The old inn's hosts are now Ray and Sue Williamson who took over the license from Vic and Joan Groves in November 1974. Vic played for Arsenal FC for almost ten years, leaving the club in 1964.

In addition to Enfield's association with the many well-known literary personalities, it is pleasing to record that Thomas Hardy married his second wife Florence Dugdale in February 1914 in Enfield, her home town following the death of his first wife née Emma Gifford.

Robert Mathison died in 1864 leaving the whole of his estate to his wife Jane, who carried on the business for only eighteen months when she also died, making her son Robert the sole executor and leaving one-third of the estate to him and two-thirds to her daughters Francis and Ann.

I have in my possession a receipt dated 7th March, 1866, for a quarter's rent due Christmas, 1865, for £11 5s 0d less property tax of 3s 9d. The penny Inland Revenue stamp is signed by Edward Beckett who, we must assume, was the son of Mary Beckett, descendant of John Gay. The probate value of The George Inn then was £1,800.

Francis and Ann stayed out of the business, but granted a twenty-one year lease to Robert at a rent of £53 6s 8d.

In 1868 Beckett sold The George to Robert and his two sisters for £1,100. The old photograph I possess showing The George Inn with Robert Mathison displayed as the licensee, verifying the date as not later than 1888 and possibly very much earlier, produces a conundrum in that the signpost exhibits the brewers as being Truman, Hanbury & Buxton. I can only suggest that Mathison negotiated some sort of a 'tie' for their beer; for which a remuneration would have been granted in return.

Robert succeeded to all the property on the death of Francis in 1884 and Ann in 1886. The George was then valued at £1,200 in addition there was one house in Silver Street let at £30 per annum to Eleanor Pepper and valued at £400, and another in Silver Street let at £25 per annum in the occupancy of Alfred Horlock (Blake & Horlock), Funeral Directors, also valued at £400. In 1888 Robert Mathison sold the freehold of The George to Ebenezer Saville, of Hatton Garden, and Phillip Saville, of Stratford (Saville's Brewery) for £5,550. During the last year at The George as licensee Robert must have witnessed Queen Victoria's Jubilee in 1887, also the demolition of Sir Walter Raleigh's cottage which was situated at the corner of

Gordon Road and Chase Side. The contents including the oak panelling were sold by auction at an earlier date. Following the sale on 1st October, Robert with his large family of eight daughters and one son, moved to Budleigh Salterton in Devon. Ken Mathison, referred to earlier, is the son of the only son of Robert; and we were privileged to have him and his wife as our guests at The George for the opening of the new Elizabeth Bar in March, 1970. Ken informs me that he has in his possession the family bible of 1823 and in this year his great grandfather was 'Mine Host' of the old Nags Head on the corner of Southbury Road. This inn was rebuilt in 1882 and again in 1933 only to be finally demolished in 1960.

# Chapter XI

The coach revival from The George – the old police station and its establishment – auction at The George 1887 – breach of the Licensing Act 1887 – a sleepy driver 1887 – Meyers Enfield Observer

This era, or the latter period of the long reign by the Mathison family as host's of The George was romanticised by a brief revival of the old coaching days. Col. A.P. Somerset (later Sir Alfred), of Enfield Court, was a keen supporter of the movement, and a member of The Coaching Club. He was a cousin of the Duke of Beaufort, who himself maintained the Brighton run with the famous 'Age' coach long after its rivals had all been put out of business by the ever-spreading network of railways. On the first day of June 1875 the Hirondelle, Sir Alfred's four-horse coach, left The George Inn on its first journey to St Albans, and the journey was repeated on each Tuesday and Saturday during the summer season. The route was extended to Luton, and later to Hitchin, where the rendezvous was The Sun Inn. Horses were changed at South Mimms and again at St Albans, which was reached in about one and a half hours. The coach left The George about 11 a.m. and soon after 6 p.m. the team would be seen galloping back into town. The fare to Luton was five shillings or eight shillings and sixpence return. St Albans was three shillings single fare or five shillings return (approximately seven pounds now).

Leo Eastwick to whom I refer in the foreword was always so proud of the picture of the Four in Hand. His grandfather Charles Matthew Eastwick was coachman and guard to Sir Alfred and is seen holding the Hirondelle coach door, before starting on their journey from the old George.

The Sun at Hitchin displayed an original notice advertising the coach service from The George. I obtained permission to copy it, but, unfortunately, after having made arrangements with the photographer I phoned to confirm my visit only to be told that the hotel had been sold to Crest Hotels (Charrington & Co), and no information whatever was available regarding the notice.

One cannot help but think that the thought behind the Coaching enterprise was a backlash of the pressures created at that period. The fast expanding town had an enormous growth rate, and industrial expansion was in progress, while the extension of the railway from Wood Green to Enfield Chase in 1871 would be adding to the noise, smoke and confusion. To those of this present age the scene conjured up is that of a country village ideally tranquil, but Enfield's citizens must have regretted the passing of the peacefulness of earlier times, much as we today look back wistfully to the Seventies. (Steam vehicles, while feasible, were at the time banned by the famous 'Red Flag' Law.)

The old vestry offices on the right of the key picture almost adjoining Barclays Bank were then the town's police station, in charge of which was a dominating character weighing sixteen stone; the hearty and robust Inspector Robert Gould, who was assisted by four sergeants and thirty-six constables, of whom one sergeant and two constables were mounted. It would be a pleasant sight indeed today to witness a charging steed in pursuit of a horse and cart with a 'one over the top' driver careering through the town somewhat out of control only to be finally arrested – as was once the case. The accused pleaded that his horse was not capable of going fast, and that he had been driving some electors home from the poll (probably having had a little 'quicky' at each elector's house?). He was fined five shillings plus costs. The outstanding crimes appearing on the charge lists were for poaching, begging, picking pockets, cruelty to horses and passing counterfeit coins. A divisional detective was also stationed in Enfield. The vestry offices have been occupied since 1937 by the solicitors Trefor R. James.

The police headquarters was transferred to new premises at the corner of London Road and Cecil Road in 1873 (now awaiting demolition) and finally moved to the modern establishment in Baker Street in 1965.

The following three reports relating to this period and extracted from the *Meyers' Observer* appear sufficiently interesting to reprint.

### AUCTION SALES

On Monday evening last Messrs. Humbert Son & Flint offered for sale by public auction, at The George Inn, sixty plots of freehold land, situate near Brimsdown railway station, and forming part of the Oatland's Estate. The attendance was moderately large, but only one plot was knocked down – the price being £22 – as the reserve was not reached in any of the subsequent bids!

4th November, 1887

## BREACH OF THE LICENSING ACT

Phineas Mardle, New Road, South Street, Ponders End, was summoned for unlawfully obtaining intoxicating liquor at The Stag beerhouse by falsely representing himself to be a traveller on the 14th August, and he was further charged with obtaining liquor during the hours when the house should have been closed; and George Passmore, New Road, South Street, Ponders End, was charged for like offences at the same time and place. Inspector Brown deposed that on Sunday the 10th ult., at 11.30 a.m. he visited The Stag Inn. He saw two defendants sitting down in the front of the bar. The landlady was just in the act of bringing a pewter pot of beer to them, when he asked if they were *bona fide* travellers. The landlady said 'Yes, they say they are'. He asked the defendants, and they said they came from Tottenham, but they seemed confused. When asked to give the name of the street they then admitted they came from Ponders End. When they were charged the proprietor returned them a shilling which they had paid on the beer and took the pewter pot away from them. The distance which they lived from the house was two and a half miles at the outside. Both defendants pleaded guilty, and were fined ten shillings each and costs or, in default, fourteen days' imprisonment.

2nd September, 1887

## A SLEEPY DRIVER

George Burgess, Crouch Lane, Cheshunt, was summoned for riding on a cart without having or holding the reins on the 10th September. Inspector Deacon said he saw the defendant in a cart coming at an early hour in the morning along Enfield Wash. He was on the wrong side of the road. The reins were tied to the cart, and he was lying down asleep. That night two street lamps were knocked down and broken, doubtless by sleeping teamsters. The Chairman; If the horses were not more intelligent than the men there would be more lamps broken. A fine of five shillings was imposed, or three days' imprisonment.

7th October, 1887

On 1st October, 1887 Mr J.H. Meyers sold the local newspaper *Meyers' Enfield Observer* which he launched in 1859 to Captain H.F. Bowles (later Colonel Sir Henry). The paper had a difficult period until Mr Cuthbert Whitaker, son of the founder of *Whitakers Almanack* was appointed as manager and editor in 1908. The position of secretary was given to an old apprentice of the firm, Mr Ambrose (Bert) Wiseman who, two years later, was appointed secretary and manager. In 1922 Mr Charles Maunder became the editor having joined the company in the late 1880s. He retired in 1949 having completed sixty years with the firm of Meyers Brooks, twenty-seven as editor of the *Gazette* and was succeeded by his son Mr C.R. (Reg) Maunder who retired in 1973, having completed fifty years' service of which twenty-three were in the capacity of editor. His sister, Marjorie, also managed for thirty-four years, retiring as manageress of the office staff. Mr Wiseman was later appointed managing director and in 1939 the office was shared with his son Mr Cyril (Bob)

Wiseman. At the death of Sir Henry Bowles in 1944, Mr A.R. Wiseman succeeded him as chairman and also held the office of managing director until he died in 1959 the year in which he saw *The Gazette* celebrate its centenary. His son followed in the footsteps of his father by taking over the office of managing director. An extraordinary record for the two families; the Maunders, who occupied the editorial chair for fifty years and for the Wisemans whose association ended only in 1975 – altogether well over two hundred and fifty years.

The present editor is H.W. (Bert) Huggins who joined *The Gazette* straight from school, taking over from David Paul who left after four years editorship to take up an appointment with the National Council for the Training of Journalists.

# Chapter XII

Owners and licensees from 1888 – The George rebuilt 1896 and opening night – comparisons and prices of the period – The Pauper's Christmas beer – Bowyer's sale at The George 1896 – Enfield Football Club – collection following a fatal accident

Savill Bros, brewers of Stratford, acquired The George and installed Ernest Jones as the Licensee in 1888. There is no information as to whether Mr Jones was a tenant or lessee. In October 1895 John Hermann Ernst took the license from him, after which he negotiated a fifty year lease from 1896 with Savill Bros, at a yearly rental of £120. The George was completely rebuilt (only parts of the old cellar remain) in 1896 and was re-opened in June, which makes it obvious why the enormous price of £10,000 was paid for the lease. The money was loaned to Ernst by the brewery at five per cent. The following report was published in the issue of *Meyers' Observer* dated Friday 26th June, 1896.

### THE GEORGE HOTEL

On Wednesday evening a large company attended by invitation of Mr Ernst to celebrate the opening of this house after the re-building. About one hundred and fifty guests were entertained at dinner, Mr Gomm being in the chair. After the removal of the cloth the usual loyal and patriotic toasts were given, followed by the toast of the evening, 'Health and Prosperity to the Host', which was enthusiastically received and suitably acknowledged by Mr Ernst. Mrs Louise Taylor, Mr Jones (violinist), Mr Nickolds, Mr Nicholson, Mr Franks (Barnet), and numerous others took part in an excellent programme of vocal and instrumental music. During the evening the Enfield Foresters Band played selections of popular music in front of the house. The new building forms an attractive feature in the town, and its arrangements are such as to meet all the requirements of the business of a suburban hotel, including a magnificent apartment primarily intended for the Masonic functions which have long been held at this house, a spacious and well ventilated billiard room, fitted with a Thurston billiard table, and other conveniently arranged apartments. The ground floor is occupied by saloon and other bars, which are handsomely fitted and furnished.

The extraordinary outcome is that the Wednesday quoted is the 24th June which happens to coincide with the day A.J. Standbrook took over the license in 1924!

However low the cost of all the necessities required to live at this period it still appears amazing how the essentials were purchased from such meagre wages as prevailed towards the end of the nineteenth century, though, when one spoke of one pound sterling it was 240 pennies – and a penny was worth something. Today (1974) our penny is considered almost a nuisance and yet its worth is 2.4 times the old penny with only one hundred to the pound – this was unwittingly the greatest psychological confidence trick of the century when on Monday 15th February, 1971, our money was decimalised! In the era of which we are speaking the wage for a 'lockie' at the Royal Small Arms

Factory was twenty-four shillings a week. The joint wage for a porter and porteress (man and wife) at Chace Farm School was raised from £45 to £53 per annum, with no allowance for beer or uniform, as was normal in other districts. A cook-housemaid was paid around £18 per annum but, of course, her home was provided. Incidentally a license had to be acquired if one wished to employ a servant; one employer was fined twenty shillings and costs for employing a gardener without having a license. Post Office workers had their hours reduced from nine hours a day to eight hours, making a forty-eight hour week, and it was recorded that a very noticeable improvement had been effected in appearance and behaviour!

To offset those relatively low wages a six-roomed house could be rented for seven shillings and sixpence per week; coal was one shilling a cwt, potatoes averaged four shillings a cwt, cucumbers one penny and marrows twopence each, but tea was still quite expensive at one shilling and fourpence to two shillings a lb. For the men a striped flannel tennis jacket could be bought for seven shillings and elevenpence, and ladies French woven corsets cost one shilling to one shilling and sixpence three farthings, knickers or drawers one shilling threepence halfpenny to one shilling and elevenpence, and nightdresses, fully trimmed, one shilling and elevenpence to two shillings and elevenpence. Bonnets ranged from fourpence three farthings to one shilling and a halfpenny.

Enfield Grammar School fees were two pounds per term. A day out to Hitchin on the Hirondelle four-in-hand (booking office at The George) cost nine shillings return.

Beer and spirits had little or no change in the retail price during the last quarter of the nineteenth century, but for the record I quote the following from price lists dated 1896 of the Victoria Wine Company who commenced operating in 1865 and by 1896 possessed one thousand wine shops.

|  | Per bottle |  |
|---|---|---|
| Canadian Club Whisky (seven years old) | 4s 0d | (20p) |
| Scotch Whisky – not branded | 1s 8½d | (8½p) |
| Scotch Whisky – branded six–seven years old | 3s 6d | (17½p) |
| Scotch Whisky – branded ten years old | 3s 10d | (19.1p) |
| Gins (sweetened or unsweetened according to strength) | 1s 6½d | (7.7p) |
|  | 2s 1d | (14.6p) |
| Brandy (according to strength and age) | 1s 8½d | (8½p) |
|  | 5s 1d | (25½p) |
| Brandy Cognac (fourteen years old) | 6s 1d | 30.4p) |
| Brandy Cognac (eighteen years old) | 7s 1d | (35½p) |
| Brandy Cognac Martells XXX | 5s 4d | (27.7p) |
| Benedictine D.O.M | 3s 6d | (17½p) |
| Spanish Ports | 1s 0d | (5p) |
| Port – Oporto (fifteen types) from | 1s 6d (7½p) to |  |
|  | 5s 10d | (29.2p) |
| Sherry from | 1s 3d | 6.3p) |
| Sauterne from | 1s 1d | (5½p) |
| Burgundy from | 1s 2d | (6p) |
| Champagne – |  |  |

| | | |
|---|---|---|
| Roper Freres 1889 | 2s 4½d | (11.8p) |
| Champagne – | | |
| G.H. Mumm | 3s 6½d | (17.7p) |
| Stones Ginger Wine | 1s 0d | (5p) |
| Rose's Lime Juice Cordial | 1s 1d | (5.4p) |
| Ind Coope's Bitter | | |
| Ale XK Per Pin | | |
| (Per Pin = 4½ Gallons) | 6s 3d | (31.4p) |
| Ind Coope's Bitter Ale AK | 5s 3d | (26.2p) |
| Guinness – | | |
| Dublin Stout – ½ pint | 2d | (0.83p) |
| Tottenham Lager beer | | |
| in corked bottles ½ pint | 2d | (0.83p) |
| Tea per pound | 1s 4d | (6.6p) |
| Tea per pound (Ceylon) | 1s 0d | (9.2p) |
| | 2s 4d | (11.7p) |

NB Where prices in the book are quoted in old pence only, convert by multiplying by 100 and dividing by 240.

The old melancholy story of balance of payments prevailed. Imports up from £170,000 to £38,473,856 and exports – although up by £3 million, were £21,127,168 – a cool deficit of £17,346,488. If this was all too depressing one could escape to Australia by steamship by booking with Sewell and Crowther, Cockspur Street, London for £11 11s 0d!

Coursing was still being organised in the grounds adjoining The Cock Inn Palmers Green. Ladies' stakes for fox terriers of 15 lbs or under offered a £4 prize to the winner.

Beer and spirits had little or no change in the wholesale or retail price during the last quarter of the nineteenth century.

### WORTHING (WEST END)
### BURLINGTON HOUSE HOTEL

Delightfully situated, facing the sea, sheltered from North and East winds. Spacious Coffee, Smoking, Drawing and Billiards room. Combined Hotel and Rail Tickets are issued; Saturday to Monday – First Class Rail 36s 0d, 2nd Class Rail 31s 6d. Friday to Tuesday – First Class Rail 57s 6d, 2nd Class Rail 53s 0d. They include Bed, Breakfast, Luncheon, Table d'Hote and attendance. The express leaves London 5.05 p.m., leaves Worthing 9.40 a.m. Apply to Messrs. Jakins & Co Ltd., 99 Leadenhall Street EC4 and branches.

> Advertisement in the local paper dated
> 20th November, 1886

The following letter to *The Enfield Gazette* from a reader was published in the 4th December, 1896 issue.

### THE PAUPERS' CHRISTMAS BEER

Dear Sir,

I venture to think that the majority of the ratepayers are surprised to hear that the Guardians of the Edmonton Union have decided to deprive the unfortunate inmates of the workhouse of their annual pint of beer on Christmas Day. Last year they passed a resolution 'That in future ginger ale or other temperance drinks should be supplied to the inmates instead of porter'. Several ratepayers then expressed, through the local newspapers, their indignation at such a course being adopted; and as one of the Guardians (Mr Tydeman) very liberally offered to provide the beer at his own expense, the matter was again discussed at a meeting of the Guardians, who then decided to accept Mr Tydeman's offer, thus proving that it was a question of economy rather than the furtherance of the temperance cause. I am sure there will be no difficulty in raising amongst kindly-disposed people a sufficient sum to pay for the cost of the beer; and I, for one, shall be very pleased to subscribe towards the fund. I was not present at the paupers' Christmas dinner last year, but can quite understand the opinion expressed by Mr Tydeman as to 'the joy which the old people in the workhouse learnt that they were not to be debarred from having their drop of beer'. The chief argument used by two of the members against allowing the usual refreshment, appeared to be that hitherto the 'stuff' which had been supplied was so bad that the Guardians could not drink it themselves. If such has been the case, why did they so far neglect their duty in not seeing that beer of good quality was provided. One of the Guardians treated his co-members to an account of his experience amongst the working class, and went so far as to say that some of his own workmen 'spent their money at the public-house week after week'.

If this gentleman is so desirous of furthering the cause of total abstinence it seems rather strange that he should number amongst his own employees (as he says he does) those who so freely partake of that of which he seeks to deprive the poor and old at the coming festive season. I am, dear sir,

Yours truly

A LARGE RATEPAYER

## BYCULLAH PARK, ENFIELD

Enfield Operatic Society was inaugurated in 1896 and promoted its first performance at the Athenaeum, Windmill Hill, on the 4th and 5th February of *H.M.S. Pinafore* or *The Lass That Loved a Sailor.*

The 2nd April, 1896 saw the sale of the effects of the old George by Alfred Bowyer, Principal of the firm now trading as Messrs. Bowyer and Bowyer, the well-known estate agents and auctioneers. *Meyers' Observer* displayed the following advertisement:

> Nineteen Years' Local Experience
> MR ALFRED BOWYER
> Surveyor, Auctioneer
> GEORGE INN, Enfield Town

SURPLUS HOUSEHOLD FURNITURE and effects comprising bedroom appointments, six feet mahogany sideboard, bagatelle board, one hundred chairs, Sutherland Loo [*No! Nothing to do with a 'loo' but could have been a Victorian table on which the card game of Loo was played and previously known as Lanter-Loo*] and other tables, COTTAGE PIANOFORTE and other useful effects, relics of the old George for sale by auction by

> MR ALFRED BOWYER

Upon the new premises as above, on Thursday next, 2nd April, 1896 at 12 o'clock precisely by order of Messrs. Savill Bros Ltd. View morning of sale. Catalogues of the Auctioneer, Enfield Town.

John Hermann Ernst appeared to be quite a popular landlord, being interested in many of Enfield's sporting activities and supporting local charities, including the Enfield Bonfire Boys, of which he was a committee member. The annual procession and fancy dress carnival of this body was one of the outstanding events of the year, and a considerable sum of money was raised for the Enfield Cottage Hospital. The following notice *(Meyers' Observer,* 1896) would no doubt have resulted in benefit to some charity.

'GREEN DRAGON'
Winchmore Hill
Proprietor Frank Parkin
A BILLIARD MATCH
500 up, will be played
On Thursday, 19th March, 1896
at 7 o'clock, between
MR ERNST, of THE GEORGE, Enfield
and
MR MAYERS, of THE COCK, Palmers Green.
A supper will be held in connection with the above on the following Thursday, 26th March. Tickets two shillings and sixpence each

The last meeting of the Enfield Football Club to be held at the old George was on Saturday 18th April, 1896 and was reported as follows:

ENFIELD FC GENERAL MEETING
THE ENGLISH CUP TO BE ENTERED FOR

A large gathering of members was present at the annual meeting of the above club, which was held at

The George Hotel on Saturday evening last. The election of officers resulted as follows: Captain, Mr E. E. Dashper; vice-captain, Mr E.R. Crickmer: captain, reserves, Mr W. Coleman; vice-captain, reserves, Mr E.G. Lough. Committee: Messrs. Cooper, Cranfield, Duce, Harrower, Jennings, Jun, Vanderpump, Rogers and C.W. Whitaker. Hon. secretary, Mr J.J. Jarvis; (later Sir John) hon. treasurer Mr A.H.D. Collyer. After giving a report of the season's doings, the secretary (Mr J.J. Jarvis) gave the club's programme for next season. It was intended he said, to compete in the English, Amateur, Middlesex and London Senior Cup competitions, besides a strong league (to be decided upon) whilst 'friendlies' with the Casuals, Old Foresters, Vampires, Cheshunt, Ealing, Idlers and probably Uxbridge, would figure on the match list. An effort would also be made to increase the accommodation on the ground by erecting a grand stand and effecting many other improvements. It was decided to award club caps to Messrs. E.E. and F.C. Dashper, P.R. Harrower, B.J. Asbury and H.E. Elliott. Hearty votes of thanks to the hon. sec and the chairman concluded the proceedings.

The club certainly 'went to town' with their annual dinner, held in the Dukes Salon at the Holborn Restaurant, which had the pleasure of accommodating the club on Saturday 25th April, 1896. Elaborately printed menus displayed a seven course meal and coffee. There were thirteen toasts, and eleven artistes included the great W.H. Berry; whose fee for two spots was five shillings.

We had the pleasure of his company at least once a week almost until he died in the late Fifties.

The George was used by the team for the changing rooms from this period until the outbreak of the 1914 War.

After selling the lease back to Savill's in 1899 Ernst became the Licensee of The Four Swans, Waltham Cross, on the 30th April, 1900.

In January 1896 Enfield pubs figured generously following a fatal accident when a carpenter named J.P. Clarke fell from a window whilst working on a building in Little Park. The following list bears testimony to the kindness and thought shown in response to an appeal for aid on behalf of the man's widow and five children.

*Collecting Boxes*

|  | £ | s | d |
|---|---|---|---|
| Golf Club |  | 9 | 0 |
| Mr Collins Wheatsheaf | 3 | 17 | 2½ |
| Mr Arberry, Nag's Head |  | 4 | 10 |
| Mr Waller, Ridgeway Tavern |  | 19 | 7 |
| Mr Cooper, Wheatsheaf, Baker Street | 1 | 7 | 0 |
| Mr Baldwin, Railway Inn |  | 17 | 0½ |
| Mrs Watts, Windmill Tavern |  | 10 | 6 |
| Mr Frost, George Inn |  | 9 | 11 |
| Mr Willis, Rising Sun |  | 18 | 11 |
| St James Lodge | 1 | 0 | 0 |
| Enfield Chapter, £1 1s 0d | 2 | 19 | 11½ |
| Mr Wren, King's Head |  | 15 | 0¾ |
| Mr Chandler, Holly Bush |  | 5 | 1 |
| Mr W. Smith, Stag | 2 | 4 | 3 |
| Mr Ball, Horse Shoes | 2 | 11 | 9 |

| | | | |
|---|---|---|---|
| Mr Broadbridge, Six Bells | 1 | 12 | 5¼ |
| Mr Stribling, Chase Side | | 10 | 1 |
| Mr Capp, Baker Street | | 8 | 10½ |
| Mr Wackett | | 6 | 8½ |
| Mr Jones, Hop Poles | | 6 | 2 |
| Mr Palmer, Railway Tavern | | 11 | 1 |
| Mr Horlock, Bell Inn | | 7 | 9½ |

*Subscription Lists*

| | | | |
|---|---|---|---|
| George Hotel | 6 | 7 | 3 |
| Mr Watts | 1 | 4 | 6 |
| Mr R. Upton, assisted by Messrs. Clarkson and Wright | 9 | 16 | 0 |
| Mr R. Finch | 2 | 11 | 0 |
| Parker Bros | 9 | 10 | 0 |
| Gibson Bros | 12 | 2 | 6 |
| Lloyd's Bank | 9 | 16 | 0 |
| Mr P. Rumney (per Parker Bros) | 5 | 5 | 0 |
| | £78 | 6s | 7½d |

It would be doubtful whether any town in England projected more of the village atmosphere than Enfield did then, considering the size of the town and a population topping forty thousand, in fact this attitude prevailed until the start of the Second World War when the population had increased to well over one hundred thousand.

# Chapter XIII

Licensees from 1899 – the petrol motor arrives – the passing of Queen Victoria – The first tramcar – stable times – prices of food and drink – farewell to Steve Lambert 1924

Richard Marner acquired the license in 1899 but remained for only two years. One cannot but surmise that the volume of business was inadequate in relation to the size of the new building. With its six bars and function hall a large staff would have to be employed regardless of the amount of trade and the general overheads would obviously be high. Enfield was expanding very fast and although widespread the population in 1900 was approximately forty-two thousand – a sevenfold increase in one hundred years. It is not improbable that the change to a modern hotel type establishment from a mellow inn had been a little too sudden.

George W. Moore, the next licensee, was the first to be installed as a tenant at The George under the brewers. The conditions of the agreement appear more severe than the one A. J. Standbrook signed in 1924; Mr Moore was tied to Savill's for all beers, and to Taplows for wines spirits, cordials and sweets. It appears quite obvious the business was not very lucrative, whatever the cause, for George reigned only for little over one year.

The potential of Enfield at this time must have offered considerable scope for employment; all types of new manufacturing projects were being introduced. The building enterprises alone should have contributed to the town's advancement, and the beginning of a new era marked the introduction of the petrol engine.

Imagine the quietude of the town, in which nothing faster than the horse had disturbed the dusty streets, and notes little louder than the rumble and squeaks of laden carts had awakened the nights. All this was broken by an awesome sound around 1899, when the controversial period was ushered in by Albert Olley's newfangled motorcar – a high, open two-seater Benz with its large slender carriage-like wheels, solid tyres and gleaming brass headlamps. Albert and his brother Victor were trading as cycle manufacturers and electrical engineers in the town. They later attempted to get a J.A.P. engine powered flying machine into the air in the grounds of Myddelton House, but without success. The pilot was 'Boy' Seamer, of Seamer & Middleton (currently specialising in Land Rovers) from whom in later years Alfred Standbrook, otherwise known as A.J.S., purchased several cars.

Another pair of engineering brothers interested in producing cycles were Bill and Syd Graham, who were later to establish the well-known Graham Bros Garage and showrooms in the town (acquired later by Arlington). They are reputed to have designed and built the first motorcycle sidecar.

There was every sign that the horse was on the way out when in 1903 the speed limit for cars was raised to 20 mph making derisory the 1865 law which forbade speeds higher than 4 mph in the country and 2 mph in towns – attributable to the 'Red Flag' law.

Alas, today the quality of life is seriously threatened by the ever-increasing flood of motor cars and the accompanying monster vehicles, and like it or not everyone must be caught up in this race to nowhere. Given time for a little thought most normal people must look back longingly to the days when the horse stood harnessed by the kerb munching in his nosebag and snorting contentedly, so that the chaff rose like a wispy tiny cloud in the sunshine. Basketwork 'haybottles' stood outside The George at this period – they contained fodder for the horses whilst the drivers were consoling themselves with a pot of ale inside.

Edward VII came to the throne in 1901 after the passing of his mother, Queen Victoria, following her long and illustrious reign of sixty-four years. On 13th January her signature was put to state papers with great effort, and the last entry was made in her personal journal, which had been methodically kept for sixty-nine years. Perhaps the present Queen's Christmas message to the Commonwealth was in some way attributable to her great grandmother's message to the Empire at her Diamond Jubilee in June 1897, when from Buckingham Palace, the Queen pressed a button which telegraphed a message throughout the Empire.

Charles T. Andrews became 'mine host' in 1902 and settled down for ten years. His son Cecil and daughter Gladys Altham are still living in Enfield. Charles was known to everyone as 'Happy Days'. The reason for this nickname was that when offered a drink he would never propose an orthodox toast, such as 'Good Health' or 'Cheers', but always 'Happy Days' – after all, a pleasant enough toast for anyone.

Perhaps the army officer who requested accommodation for his men and was refused didn't think the 'Happy Days' touch very applicable, for we see in a newspaper account of local court proceedings that Charles was fined £2 plus seven shillings costs for refusing to billet soldiers!

There are still a number of friends or old patrons of The George around who remember 'Happy Days'. One in particular is Dick Clark, who would sneak in with his friend and play billiards in the rear bar when he was attending the grammar school, only to be chased out by the ostler, Bill Ewer. About 1960 Mr Ewer returned for his first visit to England after emigrating to Canada and visited The George. Having made himself known to me I introduced Dick Clark to him and sure enough they both remembered the frequent incidents. When I took him around The George he recalled exactly how it was before the many alterations, and named the regular visitors who stabled their horses at the inn, as well as the names of the horses which he tethered to the many rings in the stable. But now unfortunately this is due for demolition under the new development scheme.

Enfield must be thankful to the far-sighted persons who were responsible for purchasing the land for our parks and open spaces; they have helped considerably to keep the rural atmosphere in such a commercialised town. The town park was acquired after Phillip Twells – banker and MP for the City of London, left his estate to his widow on his death in 1880. After twenty-one years she also died, and the council bought twenty-three acres of the grounds at £570 per acre – approximately £13,000. Altogether six parks and open spaces were purchased from 1903 to 1911 comprising one hundred and sixty-six acres at a cost of £51,932 – some £312 per acre. Today's price (1974) as building land, would be in between £6 and £10 million. Following the integration with Edmonton and Southgate in 1965, the London Borough of Enfield had a higher proportion of green space than any other London Borough. The first supply of electricity arrived in 1906 and during the following year the North-Met power station was opened at Brimsdown. Electricity, without doubt, must have helped to change the people's lives more quickly than any other discovery, and more sophisticatedly, mainly owing to vast power being produced almost without sound, but so little credit or appreciation is given to this giant commercial project that is responsible for so many of our personal comforts.

On 3rd July, 1909 the first tramcar arrived at the terminus outside The George – two years after the opening of the power station. The cheap day fare to Wood Green return was twopence – remember that is less than one penny in today's coinage! To ease the acuteness of the bend at Freeman's corner some picturesque old buildings were torn down, including Savill Bros (brewers) Depot, as well as a major part of the premises of Mrs Schmidt confectioner, pastry cook and restaurant proprietor, behind which The George grounds then extended. George Wimpey, the contractor responsible for laying the tramcar track, entertained his staff and workmen to a dinner at The George on the same evening.

The Great Northern Railway extended the line from Enfield Chase to Cuffley in 1910. One would have thought this would have developed Crews Hill and Cuffley really quickly, but it was not until 1924 that any progress was made.

Edward VII passed away in 1910 and was succeeded by his second son George V, at whose Coronation in 1911 the enormous number of five hundred and fifty orphanage children were given a special treat at Chase Farm School (now the hospital) to mark this auspicious occasion.

The George again changed landlords in 1911; the incoming tenant being William R. Freeman, who stayed for less than two years. He was followed by another Freeman (Thomas G.) – there is no information to say if the latter was the son or brother of the former. He was there as licensee for less than one year, leaving in December 1914.

The period following Queen Victoria's death, terminating at the outbreak of the First World War, was still tinged with the Victorian era, seemingly awaiting some form of liberation, but it was a period when respect and discipline appeared naturally inbuilt – a necessary quality considering the hard and difficult times the majority of people were experiencing.

One major and very important factor was the general stabilisation of the prices of all commodities – this was partly due to the lack of change in taxation and, of course, there was no specific rate of growth as is demanded by requirements of the modern world. Excise duty remained steady, if there was any change at all it was infinitesimal, and so the following prices quoted below for January 1914, had remained very little more than they were in 1885.

SAVILL BROS STRATFORD Enfield Office.
'October Brewings are now in splendid condition'
(Just think – three months mellowly maturing)

| | |
|---|---|
| Mild Ale and Light Bitter Ale 18 gals (kilderkin) | 18s 0d |
| IPA 18 gals (kilderkin) | 30s 0d |
| Stout 18 gals (kilderkin) | 24s 0d |
| Double Stout 18 gals (kilderkin) | 30s 0d |

Also obtained in nine gals (firkin) and four and a half gals (pin) at proportionate prices.

Whisky obtainable from three shillings to three shillings and sixpence per bottle.

Although dining out was not 'the thing' as it is today, there was a fair amount of necessary eating out and the prices quoted would have been fairly normal in an ordinary dining room:

Soup twopence, fish fourpence, entrees and roasts sixpence, steak sixpence to eightpence, vegetables one penny, new peas twopence, salads one penny to twopence, sweets twopence, cheese one penny, serviette and ring one penny. Port, sherry, burgundy, claret threepence a glass. Whisky, gin, rum twopence a glass. Brandy twopence halfpenny a glass. Beer one penny halfpenny.

Arthur G. Rata acquired the license from Thomas Freeman in November 1914, four months after the outbreak of War. He became well-known locally and was a frequent visitor to The George after A.J. Standbrook took possession. Mr Rata later purchased the Queens Hall Cinema (renamed the Florida and closed in 1976). His wife was the daughter of Alan Fairhead, the very respected and well-known local builders who went into liquidation in 1963, Fairhead's premises were demolished to make way for the car park at the rear of The George, which in turn will also be developed.

Steven (Steve) Lambert was installed as 'mine host' during the closing stages of the war in 1918. He was a very popular character, very kind-hearted, so much so that his popularity and good nature perhaps in great measure resulted in his departure in 1924. A farewell dinner and concert was held in Mr and Mrs Lambert's honour on 18th June, six days before their departure from The George. Mr Sydney Fussell presided over a gathering of over sixty friends, including many well-known Enfield personalities of which the following were to be quite closely linked one way or another with our family; Ben Chandler (my brother George married his daughter Phyllis); Archie Fairlie, C. Fairlie senior, Bob Laing, Jimmy Albon, George Holdsworth, Jack Skinner, Tommy Brain, Bill Carter, Reuben Baines.

Many of their ladies joined them later for the concert. Presentations were made to Mr and Mrs Lambert and several very complimentary speeches were made in their honour.

# Chapter XIV

Alfred J. Standbrook – The Railway Tavern Buckhurst Hill – the First World War – the times before and after

The most likeable and amiable person in my life and the one who did most to influence my character and way of thinking was my father Alfred James Standbrook. Of course, we had our differences but the few serious confrontations were created mainly by considerations not directly attributable to either of us.

A.J.S. was a licensee who reflected all the qualities of the complete 'Mine host'. Born at Addlestone, Surrey in 1886, his early life was greatly dominated by the game of billiards, and he became the boy champion of England at the age of sixteen. He played Miss Fairweather, the lady champion, twice (it may have been three times), and the following is an extract from the *Evening News* dated 13th March, 1901:

> Billiards is generally looked upon as a game for 'mere men' only to indulge in, and the fact that a lady, Miss Fairweather, was going to play accounted for the large attendance at Alf Standbrook's establishment in Rouell Road, Bermondsey, last evening. The fact, too, that the lady is champion of her sex was also another attraction. She was opposed by Master Alf Standbrook in a game of 500 up. The latter played very well indeed for a youngster, and reached double figures upon many occasions, but the lady champion,

although playing much below her form, led from start to finish, and won a very interesting game by 27 points.

The other match was played at The Castle at Woodford, where A.J.S. worked as a billiard 'marker' from the age of sixteen, cycling from Bermondsey each day! In this game I believe he beat the lady champion.

He later played as a professional under his father's wing. This, unfortunately, put an end to his amateur status when he was requested to play in matches on his arrival at Enfield.

At this period, 1902, at the tender age of sixteen he must have met Jennie Pluck, his wife-to-be, and I gather that in the next two years Fred Pluck 'mine host' of The Castle and his future father-in-law, was rather indifferent to this East End boy gallivanting about with his daughter! The outcome of this romance, to the rage of the bride's dignified parents, was that Alf and Jennie departed in great haste to the Isle of Wight, where they were married. Father was eighteen and Mother seventeen. They worked at Daishes Hotel, Shanklin, which they later managed. Brother Alf was born there in 1906.

There is no record of when or why they left the Isle of Wight, but it is probable that they came back to the mainland when brother George was on the way; for he was born in November, 1907, at Abbott Road, Poplar – a true Cockney born within the sound of Bow Bells of the church of St Mary-le-Bow. This church was built on the site of one of the earliest churches built by William the Conqueror.

The young couple's first license was acquired in 1908, when A.J.S. became 'mine host' of The Railway Tavern at

Queens Road, Buckhurst Hill on 2nd July. I was born there the following year.

I have the original statement of settlement by J.J. Hill & Weaver, Auctioneers and Valuers, 28 Theobalds Road, London WC. It is interesting to note that the valuation of the complete inventory was £61 2s 0d and the liquor stock supplied by Ind Coope and Company was as follows: Wines and Spirits £11 11s 0d and beer and ale £4 6s 5d; a total of only £15 17s 5d – the equivalent of four or five bottles of Champagne today (1974)!

The most outstanding item on the statement of settlement appears to be the total expenses relative to the cost of the ingoing: £16 5s 0d on £56 0s 2d or approximately twenty-nine per cent. The expenses today on an ingoing, say, of £6,000, would be somewhere in the region of £600 which would be only ten per cent of the total.

It appears quite ludicrous now that a pub could possibly continue business with such a low liquor stock as £15 17s 5d but the value in goods could have represented in stock the following:

|  | £ | s | d |
|---|---|---|---|
| 42 bottles of port, sherry and wine @ 2s 0d | 4 | 4 | 0 |
| 49 bottles of spirits @ 3s 0d | 7 | 7 | 0 |
|  | 11 | 11 | 0 |
| 2 barrels low gravity beer (72 gals @ 1s 0d) | 3 | 12 | 0 |
| 1 Firkin high gravity beer (nine gals @ 1s 6d) |  | 13 | 6 |

Almost every small community invariably had one, or maybe two, simple-minded souls prone to be fair prey for the local jokers. A.J.S. loved to tell the story of how he came off second best playing the part of the joker when he and other licensees tricked local Joe into taking a long walk for nothing. Calling at The Railway Joe asked for the new hand barrow to collect some goods at a neighbouring pub for A.J.S. but on arriving he was given a drink and sent on another call, and so on until he was finally sent back to The Railway. Going into the bar he called for a pint and then amazed A.J.S. by saying, 'Have one yourself Guv!' 'I'll have a small beer,' Father replied, wondering what the catch was. 'Cheers' A.J.S. said, and went on 'You've put the barrow away Joe?' In an unusually contented manner Joe replied, 'Luv us Guv, don't be stupid – I've sold that!'

Tancy Lee the clever little feather and flyweight boxer with the devastating right swing, from Leith, Edinburgh, trained for periods at The Railway Tavern in his early days. He took the British and European fly-weight title from Jimmy Wilde at the National Sporting Club on 25th January, 1915, referee stopping the contest in the seventeenth round. This was Wilde's first defeat in an important contest. He regained the title by knocking out Joe Symonds in twelve rounds at the NSC in 1916 after Symonds had stopped Lee in sixteen rounds in 1915. Lee later became the British featherweight champion by knocking out Charlie Hardcastle in four rounds at the NSC in 1917 and went on to win a Lonsdale belt outright by defeating Joe Conn and Danny Morgan. He relinquished the title in 1919, when he was in his mid-thirties.

In later years when taken to The Railway Tavern on a nostalgic visit by A.J.S., and again in recent years with friends, I was always fascinated by the old brass till or

National Cash Register, and would try to recapture the scene in 1908 with my parents performing their role of 'mine hosts' behind the bar. Alf would have been four and George two years old then and, I should imagine, a sprightly handful.

On my last visit to The Tavern I had a long chat with Mrs Claude Attlee (who with her husband were the hosts) in which I indicated my keen desire to acquire the till. It was a difficult proposition to make an offer for it because the value was only £5, and that was an allowance on purchasing a new National Cash Register – now reduced to £1 – but to replace it with a new one would have cost £160 or thereabouts. In the early Seventies, however, after the business was taken over by Ronald and Beryl Carter in 1968, the representative for NCR negotiated the purchase of this dignified piece of equipment for £3 10s 0d.

This particular cash register, model 346DD, now completely overhauled by National's, was manufactured between the years 1905 and 1908 and retailed at fifty-five guineas, but the majority were sold under a special offer at forty-five guineas. Even so, the depreciation must have been enormous when one considered that the complete inventory at The Railway was only £56 0s 2d!

The family left The Railway Tavern in 1910 and moved to Kimberley Avenue, Seven Kings. I remember little of our stay there, except quite a striking scene of the doctor calling, and meeting us boys whilst we were all munching raw potatoes, and the doctor remarking how good they were for us. I have always been under the impression that the visit was connected with my sister's birth, but Peggy assures me that her birth certificate states that she was born in Wetherden Street, Leyton on 18th October, 1912. I have never heard this address mentioned by any of the family before, I can only assume Mother slipped away with friends to have Peggy in peace and quiet away from the noisy trio!

After about two years we moved to 125 St Albans Road, Seven Kings, and just before the first war, for reasons unknown, we moved almost opposite to number 144. I am not certain of the purchase price of this house, but think it was around £275; and it was sold for between £300 and £350 after the war.

On 4th May, 1910, King Edward VII died and the country mourned a sovereign who, by his very charm and humble dignity, had enhanced the popularity of the royal family. Fortunately his oldest son Prince George was equipped in every way to project the image set by his father, whom he idolised. King George and Queen Mary were crowned at Westminster Abbey on the 22nd June, 1911, and in no small way they gave the necessary stability to this turbulent period. The populace in general were enduring general living conditions so sordid and ignoble that it was reflected in strikes, marches and a general bitter discontent. The foundation of these perplexities still seem to be the cause of today's misunderstanding – 'inflation', the purchasing power of the pound versus wages! In 1911 (from 1900) the pound dropped in value by twenty-five per cent and in the average weekly wage had risen by only tuppence farthing! (Today little less than one penny).

Apart from the cost of new houses and land, as well as the inflationary high interest rates, most people should today be content with their lot but, of course, affluence is a greater moral disturber than danger of starvation. In the latter case everybody will, from necessity, pull together, and in the former case everything and everybody is inclined to be pulled apart.

Father drove a bus for a period prior to the war; they were real old bone rattlers, but an absolute boon for shortish journeys. We heard many grumbles regarding the vehicles and their spasmodic behaviour. The first time I recall A.J.S. using undignified language was when he talked of the bloody brakes not working. On given duties; George and I would meet Father at one of his stops on the Romford Road and hand him his sandwich lunch.

I only just remember seeing the horse tram – the last one to run was in London 1915.

Then came the declaration of war, that fateful day Tuesday 4th August, 1914. The outbreak continued for four long miserable, heartbreaking years – with little left but desolation, and all seemingly for little gain. The cost in loss of life and in human suffering cannot be assessed in ordinary terms and no one person will ever totally appreciate the full significance of those sad and sorrowful years, to say nothing of the astronomical cost financially.

A.J.S. enlisted in the Royal Naval Air services, later to become the Royal Flying Corps. Mother naturally thought the whole exercise dreadful, having four young children, but A.J.S. was comparatively lucky in that, apart from being away when on long distance driving, he was stationed near home.

The daylight air raid on Saturday 7th July, 1917, was an outstanding incident that I vividly remember. No fewer than twenty-two Gothas flew across London dropping bombs in the heart of London, one quite close to St Paul's Cathedral (mark 2 on photograph) Liverpool Street Station and The General Post Office were among several other places hit.

From Meads Lane the gang and I were watching, as we thought, a flight of birds, when 'Podgy' Pogson, the butcher, dressed in his blue striped apron and the inevitable straw hat, ushered us children home, explaining it was a German raid. On arriving back home we found poor Mother had swooned; the reason being that Alf and George had taken a picnic lunch to the aerodrome and Father was loose in London with his lorry. The reasons appear inadequate enough now, but in 1917 it was a grave occurrence. I was completely fascinated watching the scene through binoculars. Flying very high, the machines appeared to resemble a swarm of gnats, twisting, diving and gyrating in what appeared such a small space. Little puffs of smoke dotted the sky and there was the delayed pop-pop and splutter of machine gun fire among the fading and growing buzz of aircraft.

Those heroic young pilots who joined the RFC, long since forgotten by most, must have won the admiration of everybody. The whole operation of flying was then so novel, and the technical knowledge of heavier-than-air machines so limited, it seemed hardly feasible that flying should play such a momentous part in the years to follow. Winston Churchill was one of the few in Britain to see the enormous potential, but unfortunately his policies were not adhered to when he left the Admiralty. In 1914 our total air force consisted of only sixty-two planes, which included twelve naval, and twenty seaplanes.

The Zeppelin raids were, or seemed to be, a sinister adjunct to war in the air. The monsters were awe-inspiring and yet caught in the searchlights they possessed a solemn beauty. Powered by six 240 hp engines, mounting a crew of about twenty-two, achieving a speed of between fifty-five and sixty mph and carrying a bomb load of up to 5,000 lbs – or one hundred 50 lb bombs – having a greater range than aircraft.

I saw the Billericay Zeppelin plunge in flames to its doom, an inglorious and ghastly spectacle. A.J.S. was detailed to clear the wreckage, and arrived at St Albans Road with a lorry loaded to absolute capacity with twisted and charred aluminium from the wreck. Needless to say the load was slightly lighter on leaving. Most of the neighbours took some of the metal as souvenirs and half a propeller was sawn up and distributed later. I still have a piece of the aluminium as another tragic reminder of the utter stupidity of war, which the world seems to find so difficult to admit.

Referring back to Enfield which was an important target for the raiders, added to which surplus bombs were jettisoned over the area by the raiders when returning to Germany; residents witnessed their full share of action and many could confirm the welcome but tragic end of two Schutte-Lanz airships that were brought down at Cuffley and Potters Bar. The Cuffley victim was the first to be downed on British soil and the feat was accomplished on 3rd September, 1916 by Lieut. William Leefe Robinson who received the VC. This Schutte-Lanz was 500 ft long with three gondolas and a forward navigating cabin, carrying a crew of sixteen. The Potters Bar airship was brought down by 2nd Lieut. Tempest. Both pilots were of the RFC.

Each evening an empty tramcar moved on to the terminus at Southbury Road, opposite the present Metropolitan Water Board offices, with a searchlight mounted on its top deck. There was no ack-ack defence as such until later in the war, and early defences against air attack were one-pounder pom poms, and six-pounder Hotchkiss guns mounted on elevated points in London. Later thirteen-pounder guns, three-inch guns and some

French 75 mm guns were brought into use. The hill on the Ridgeway, upon which the former Country Club stood, was known as Gun Hill because a gun was mounted thereabouts. There was also 'Moaning Minnie' firing from Theobalds; the nickname was acquired from the continuous thump-thump when expending its shells in the numerous raids. Referring to the French 75 mm gun I had my gun crew training on this in the last war – the gun with the big kick. By comparison with the Second World War the 1914–1918 conflict appears almost insignificant, but considering the fear of the unknown when the first high explosive bombs were dropped, the talk of the Germans using poisonous gas, and the huge ghostly-looking Zeppelins that moved stealthily and almost silently across the skies, citizens' fears were nonetheless comparable with those caused by the parachuted land mines, rockets, and buzz bombs of the last war.

The total of two hundred and forty bombs were dropped on Enfield during the air raids resulting in six hundred houses suffering severe and moderate damage.

Air raid warnings were conveyed by policemen touring the roads on bicycles displaying a notice to 'Take Cover' and a whistle would also be blown. At night the 'Take Cover' warning would also be called. The 'All Clear' message was similarly notified and at night Boy Scouts and Boys Brigade sounded the message on bugles. Mother would herd us all into the corner of a downstairs room, where in complete silence we would await the drone of German planes. Being very close to Fairlop aerodrome we had a fair share of bombs, and seemed surrounded by ack-ack guns. I remember, more than once shrapnel finding its way down the chimney and hitting the high fender or fire guard with a sharp metallic ping.

Fairlop aerodrome and its neighbourhood was a favourite haunt of us boys; we were so fascinated by the aeroplanes. Often we witnessed the fatal plunge of a training plane when practising aerobatics required for aerial combat.

One incident that occurred in a night raid has never ceased to excite me. The raiding planes had passed over; peace and quiet reigned once more, when suddenly the distant throb of one then another plane broke the silence. Noone spoke, but a tenseness prevailed suggesting delayed action of some kind; the engine of one of the planes seemed to roar above the others, then followed the sharp crackle of machine gun fire, first from one then the other as they each manoeuvred into striking position – so low at times it was a wonder the chimney pots were not torn off. The fighter planes were fitted with static machine guns synchronised to fire through the propellers – a principle later copied by the Germans. How they battled this out in the inky blackness and with the then antiquated equipment, only the flyers could have told. There was again a long burst of gunfire, and silence as both planes appeared to fade out. Then one of the engines spluttered and spat like a mistimed two stroke engine, and again purred out an even beat only to be followed once more by complete silence except for the fading distant purring of the other's engine. Suddenly there was a dull thud, and the whole neighbourhood seemed to be alive with people outside their houses shouting, 'He's got him – the Jerry is down' etc. How the devil anyone knew who shot down whom I shall never know, but sure enough the result was confirmed next morning.

Another wartime memory gave me my first perception of grief at the age of six. It was one of those early summer days, perfected by the stillness of the warm air in which everything seemed to buzz lazily with life. Mother and our neighbour, Mrs Hammond, were happily having a little musical session at the piano when the telegram boy arrived. I naturally thought the message was for Mother and when I heard hysterical screams ran frantically into the drawing room only to find poor Mrs Hammond in a state of collapse, with Mother doing her best to comfort her. The tragic telegram told her that her husband had been drowned at sea whilst in action. Poor soul, she was completely demented, a worse degree of distress would be difficult to imagine. The shock resulted in her mind becoming unbalanced but, fortunately, after a long period away, she eventually returned to normal.

Tim, my father's brother and not more than eleven years my senior, was a favourite with me – full of kindness and cheerfulness. In my last memory of him he was standing with his back to the fireplace at St Albans Road, legs apart, his new uniform on and, as ever, with that bland, perpetual smile. The visit was to say 'goodbye' as he was soon off to France. Sadly, that 'goodbye' was forever – he was killed in action in September, 1915. His was such a short life, and so many thousands of teenagers were so served.

It was customary at this period to wear a wide black armband for at least six weeks when in mourning. How well I remember my own being referred to by the teacher in a very compassionate manner on my first day at school and to my embarrassment when forbiddingly the teacher remonstrated with another boy who was apparently playing up.

The years I remember between 1912 and 1918 were extremely lean ones, but so many families were very much worse off than ours. On the face of it in those times life was just an existence, and yet in comparison with today it had something more purposeful and real. I never remember my parents grumbling. We were of course lucky in having a father with a sense of humour, and in any circumstances he could quote funny things in a funny way. I can visualise him now singing the songs that were then all the rage, and it wasn't the song that had one laughing, it was that melodious tone of voice that harmonised with his funny expressions. Nearly always the song would end with a little tap dance that would not have disgraced a music hall star.

Mother experienced little trouble in getting any of us to fetch the bread ration because of the invariable extra piece called 'overweight'. Whether we had permission to 'nick' this or not I cannot remember, but it seldom arrived home.

Cleanliness and tidiness, with a system, were essential features of household life, in fact it was an absolute necessity. There were none of the 'everything does it for you' gimmicks that prevail today, and so all was accomplished the hard way – all steps and hearths were hearth stoned, stoves and grates were blackleaded, scrubbing and washing executed by hand.

The pantry being the only store, food would so easily deteriorate, and yet I remember few stomach upsets. I think these are more prevalent today owing to the misuse or lack of knowledge of the use of the 'Deep Freeze'. Hygiene then was a must; hygiene in its modern form is handed to everyone on a plate, and its basic principles are not thought necessary in a great many cases. The housewife with a family had an arduous life, and the making and mending of clothes was almost a full-time job. Most families mended their own boots and shoes and few were without a hobbing foot, which was the essential piece of equipment for the job. The boy's boots were studded with steel Blakeys which trebled the life of the leather sole.

Although children had no mechanical or sophisticated playthings then, boredom or inactivity were unknown, there was always plenty with which to occupy ourselves, mentally and physically. I never remember gazing into a shop window and seeing toys until we left Seven Kings – so far as I was concerned they were non-existent – but we did ingeniously create some working models for which all the materials were free. My speciality was a model submarine, requiring wood for the hull; metal, preferably lead, for the keel; tin can for the propeller and fins (and Mother's scissors – no mention of use!) and elastic for the drive (always obtainable from old bloomers or the like). Amazing results! With the correct buoyancy found by trimming or loading the keel, and the correct angle of the fins for diving, the model would submerge and surface perfectly.

The children's games and pastimes were so different then. For instance everybody played marbles. Fancy playing 'leg-a-long' today – marbles in the gutter, all the way home from Downshall School. If the game was played today there would be little need for the Pill to keep the population down! The intricately coloured glass marbles, or 'glarnies' as they were known, fascinated me. The largest I remember was about the size of a golf ball. This was a 'forty-eighter'. When they eventually became badly chipped they were known as being 'poxy' and many a 'punch-up' would be the result of a switch on winning. What would the girls of today think of the iron hoop with its hooked iron skimmer? The noise of the latter running over the uneven surface of the hoop created a hard, high-pitched note; lower, then higher, according to the speed of the wheel on the skimmer. The sound is registering in my ears now.

The roads then were so different – those in built up areas were normally grit surfaced and in hot weather regularly watered by a horse drawn vehicle which would spray half the road at a time to lay the dust. Apart from the main road most secondary roads were just flint, which in time would crumble and throw up largish lumps of flint causing any type of vehicle to produce clouds of fine whiteish dust. (When visiting New Zealand in 1962 we found many such roads).

Milk delivery floats were always an object of remembrance; the horse-drawn two wheel lightly built cart was always immaculate with its yellowing paint lightly edged with thin lines of red and, to enhance the spotless image, the milkman's highly polished gleaming brass measures and the service containers were also edged and banded in brass and were replenished with milk from the churns.

The visits to The Clay Hall Tavern, Bow, were always enjoyable, and there was the excitement of meeting many of the fighters of that day. The 4 oz fine black leather boxing gloves which we used were presented to Father after one of Jimmy Wilde's contests. I possessed the gloves until 1940, leaving them in store at The George, but, like so many other items, they were missing on my return. At my age I must be one of very few who saw Jimmy Wilde fight, he was probably the greatest timer of punches and the heaviest puncher pound for pound that ever graced a boxing ring.

The Sunday ritual of going three times to church was adhered to religiously. Whether this really was for our benefit or for that of our parents will always be a subject tinged with doubt, but I enjoyed the choir and invariably executed my duties incorrectly, nearly always turning the wrong way after paying my respects at the altar, or I would have to be awakened after a prayer!

Sometimes we were bundled off to our parents' relations at Addlestone, in Surrey, and it was here I regret starting to smoke cigarettes at the age of seven, and was possibly the youngest in the outfit, the oldest being fourteen. When the horse and cart went to market to collect goods, driven by young Cannon the farmer's son, everyone on board was puffing away as if a prize awaited the first to finish. I must have become an addict, for on arriving home I found myself smoking large cigars with my friend Vincent Charlton – mind you I could have been eight by then. The grand finale had to arrive, and it did when we lit up very strong cigars in the house with little time before Vincent's parents arrived back. We puffed until that dreadful sickly, green feeling crept over us and, heads whirling, we sat on the kerb, and were so ill that life seemed unimportant. That finished my addiction for many years, and it's a pity it was not for life.

One thing I dreaded whilst at Addlestone was visiting the outside loo, especially after dark, the flickering, murky light of the candle would throw distorted shadows on or off the creeping, crawling and flying creatures; and particularly of the Daddy Long Legs which appeared to me like an instrument of the Devil.

One important difference between those days and the present era is dominant in my mind. The natural discipline and respect that appeared then to prevail in all classes of society is sadly and slowly diminishing now. Without any doubt whatsoever this state has been brought about by lack of discipline in schools and homes, for diverse reasons. Teachers are comparatively underpaid and schools therefore understaffed, also we have the attitude of mind created by the psychologists' view point regarding discipline and indoctrinating a certain type of the student sect with the word 'freedom' – which is completely misrepresented! Also in the home there are many cases where households have been blessed with affluence too easily, too quickly.

The war finally came to its end with the signing of an armistice on 11th November, 1918. The body of the Unknown Warrior was brought from somewhere in the neighbourhood of Ypres or Boulogne in an Army ambulance on 9th November, 1920, and lay for the night in a chateau. The next day the coffin was taken across the Channel on the deck of the destroyer Verdun and draped in the Union Jack which had covered the coffins of Nurse Cavell and Captain Fryatt. Exactly two years afterwards, on 11th November, the coffin was taken into Westminster Abbey followed by King George V, the Prince of Wales and the Duke of York. 'Buried among Kings' – a glorious tribute to all who died.

# Chapter XV

The Royal, Leytonstone Road – A.J.S. plays Tom Newman – Cecil Griffiths, 880 yards champion 1923/5 – the crazy gang – Steve Donoghue – the changes – early Twenties

A.J.S. was quickly demobbed. There was no money and precious little work, but the family got by until early in 1919, when Fred Pluck, Mother's father asked A.J.S. to manage The Royal Hotel, Leytonstone Road, Maryland Point, Stratford, of which he had been offered the tenancy, and Father naturally grasped the opportunity of getting back into the trade. The takeover date was quickly settled, and on the morning of the change the joint license was transferred from Percy Reynolds to Fred Pluck and A.J.S. What a 'Fred Karno's' turnout! Mrs Reynolds, the outgoing licensee's wife, was so inebriated that she ranted and swore at everything and everybody, flourishing her hairbrush while in a half-dressed condition, and frightening the life out of me.

The Royal was a Saville's brewery house and was known as The Tap House, being situated directly opposite the brewery. The premises were burnt out by incendiaries during the last war. Laurie Saville thought a great deal of A.J.S., and it was almost a weekly ritual for him to be invited to the brewery for a chat and a drink. In little time the pub was transformed and, with Father's personality and Mother's backing, a thriving business developed. One of the great attractions was the full size billiard table, and although A.J.S. had not played billiards for some twelve or more years he quickly retrieved some of his old skills and would often make a break topping the three figures.

Tommy Newman, the World Champion billiards player (1921–1922 and 1924–1927) and a great friend of A.J.S. from boyhood days, accepted a challenge to play in a charity match of one thousand up and agreed to give A.J.S. five hundred start. George and I with friends watched the game from above, our heads stuck through the fanlights directly over the table – a perfect viewpoint. Tommy Newman was unsettled and just could not produce his form whilst everything ran favourably for A.J.S., who topped up his luck with a break of eighty-four, leaving his opponent in a precarious position at the interval. When I entered the office Father was apologising and commiserating with Tommy. The second half, fortunately, went as Father desired and the game finished with a spectacular three hundred break unfinished which won the match for Tommy Newman.

Joe Davies, one of the world's greatest billiards and snooker players, also a natural sportsman, took the worlds Professional Billiard title from Tom Newman in 1928 and held it until 1933 when Walter Lindrum won it, and after narrowly beating Joe Davis again for the title in 1934 the Worlds Billiard Championship lapsed. The following is a quote from *The Breaks Came My Way* the seventh book by Joe Davis:

> Tom Newman was a very gentlemanly player and a great sportsman in every sense of the word. It was a deep loss to the game when he died in 1943 at the early age of forty-nine, after a long illness and much suffering caused by cancer of the throat. It was a

particularly sad day for me since I had come to the fore when Tom and Willie Smith were kings of the game, and Tom continued to do battle with me during the Thirties when I was a leading player myself. In fact, I think that I was privileged to play more games against Tom than against anyone else.

The game gave us a great deal of fun and, with every chance to practise, we all became quite proficient. From the age of twelve onwards Father gave me serious lessons which were to me more like work than fun, for I would spend half an hour perfecting, perhaps, the 'losing hazard'.

One of my most satisfying operations was preparing the billiard table for play by brushing the nap of the cloth towards the top of the table after which it was ironed the same way with a large iron, oblong in shape, until the delicate nap of the fine, almost sacred, cloth lay the same from end to end and almost glistening with a silk-like sheen.

The balls then were made of ivory, but after 1928 were replaced by composition balls such as benzoline, vitalite or crystallated. I wonder how many poor elephants gave their lives to the cause of billiards at an average of five balls per tusk?

Alf was a pupil at Clark's College in 1920, and George and myself were attending Water Lane Boys' School. Sport prevailed as first priority at school, with art leading from an academic viewpoint! George was on the short list and had several trials for West Ham's schoolboy team and I for the under-14s in The Sun team. In the boys' teams such famous names were included as Jim Barratt, who later captained West Ham United and who also played for England, and 'Ginger' Barton, who played for Clapton. Syd

Puddefoot was then playing for West Ham, and often I played with and against his younger brother.

I well remember George arriving home from a training session with Nightingale, the schoolboy boxing champion of England, and trying to look happy through his bloodied and slightly misshapen face. Volunteers for this job were non-existent.

George was in most things very dedicated and had a much more professional approach than myself. After he had won a scholarship to West Ham Polytechnic I saw him in the school sports competing against Jim Barratt, who was referred to earlier. They were neck and neck on the bend when George collapsed. He just went down like a log. The report from hospital, to which he had been taken by ambulance, was that a piece of his hip bone had been torn away when under excessive strain, and the doctor diagnosed the fracture as an old one that had healed itself. It was without doubt the result of his fall some years earlier from nearly top to bottom of the cliffs at Westcliff.

Although at twelve I was the fastest runner in the school over 100 yards and went on to win the school championships of West Ham when thirteen, I was never confident and lacked faith in myself – maybe because I always seemed to be competing against older boys. Perhaps too, being the youngest of my brothers, I developed an inferiority complex.

Cecil Griffiths, the 880-yards champion of England in 1923 and 1925 and a regular customer at The Royal became a personal friend of Father and, being a member of Surrey Athletic Club, suggested to A.J.S. that I joined, which I did. For normal training he would take me to the GER Athletic Club's cinder track at Stratford. I always enjoyed the free and light atmosphere of these sessions and, although I was only thirteen, training always with seniors, I found myself holding my own when getting off the mark. Cecil would love to have me out in front over one lap, and would shout instructions whether to increase my pace or not and about 100 yards from home he could call for me to go 'full out'. He gauged it so that he had to race to pass me before the mark was reached – with me struggling and exhausted he would fly past like a perfect machine. An amazing characteristic of Cecil was his love for beer. He would take me to a pub in Stratford Broadway immediately after training, call for a shandy for me and a pint of Burton for himself, then the perpetual cigarette – always 'Gold Flake'. This was his regular custom at The Royal and the argument is a two way one. 'Look what can be done on pints and cigarettes!' some might say, but what faster times might he have achieved and how much longer would he have held the championship had he not so indulged? He was happy, so who cared!

Father purchased his first car in 1920 or 1921, and the thing was called an RMC (the boys knew it as Rotten Made Car). They were built by the Canadian Regal Motor Co and only about two hundred of these cars were produced – probably just as well. I recall one occasion when Alf and George were proudly sitting up in the 'dicky' seat, and Father preparing for an easy take off, clutch out, in first gear, clutch slowly in, brake off – and so was the car! It made a fierce leap forward, and before the next start and stop, there were two passengers missing! Alf and George were still in part of the dicky, only it was in the road!

This was a period when I thought nobody else could possibly have parents like mine, and it gave me a fair excuse to take home the odd boy from the orphans home, and request a penny or so for them. Once when taking home a boy named Skilton, of whom I made a great friend, I called to Mother, 'Can I have sixpence, please, Mother?' She replied 'Whatever for?' When I told her, the money was immediately forthcoming. My pocket money then was, I believe, threepence; George had sixpence, but he worked for the extra.

I remember the early act of 'Nervo and Knox' in the 'Cabbage Dance' at the Stratford Empire in 1922 or 1923. They were later joined by Caryll and Munday, then by Eddie Gray and finally by Flanagan and Allen in 1932. They made up the craziest, happiest, fruitiest gang shows to catch the people's imagination of that time; so much so that it is difficult to imagine a promotion to surpass it. Shows such as *Round about Regent Street, London Rhapsody,* about six in all played to packed houses and, including the early monthly shows, they dominated the Palladium for eight years until 1940. Their last performance in the *Crazy Gang* was in 1962.

There were several efficient, respected and eager licensees around the area then, including Tom Croft, in The Essex Arms, later to become a well-known officer in the trade.

Another local well-known personality in the licensed trade was Chris Slennett, who, with his wife Elizabeth, were then the hosts of The Buxton Arms, Buxton Road. Their son, Chris, with whom I became very friendly also entered the licensed trade and retired with his wife, Cis, in 1972 from The Lord Raglan, Walthamstow after some thirty-eight full and enthusiastic years in the business and are now enjoying the comfort of living in a redundant pub called The Two Swans at Birds Green, Beauchamp Roding, Essex now called Two Swans.

His wife's name was Johnson and her father, Dave Johnson, took the license of The Green Gate, High Street, Stratford in 1877, the license continuing with his son and daughter for almost a hundred years; the family relinquished the license in 1975. An amazing innings considering his first day's takings amounted to five pence – apparently the customers who patronised the pub were so undesirable they were all barred! The Brewers, Furze & Co helped T.J. on his way by granting the tenancy free of rent for six months together with a mighty allocation of free beer!

Another licensee family that characterised a typical happy carefree slap-stick family of this era; with their three children Olly, Len and Eileen were Olly and Flo Binks of The Falmouth Arms. Eileen was a sweet demure little child (in fact one of my early childish sweethearts), but what little monsters we boys were.

For the sake of our parents' nerves we were frequently bundled off to a country pub in Rickmansworth, (the Red House or some such name) or to a delightful old timber bakery near Epping – Oh! for some of that early morning bread and buns straight from the ovens! They, or rather we were continually told at both places that we would be sent home if there was no improvement in our almost wicked behaviour!

I do not give much thought to the supernatural but, at some time or other, almost everyone experiences something that leaves them wondering, and I seem not to be an exception. When about eleven years old I was extremely interested in collecting moths and butterflies, and one night, in a vivid dream, I was told of a tree that was swarming with caterpillars of the 'Buff-tipped Hawk Moth' species. The next day I went with a friend to the spot where

I had been directed in the dream, the third tree on the lefthand side of a road leading on to Wanstead Flats, with concrete posts across to stop the access of any vehicles. On arriving at that tree I saw a sight never to be witnessed again. The caterpillars were there in their thousands. Even the pavement was littered with the squashed ones that had fallen and been trodden on, and they were of the species quoted. Was it coincidence or some kind of unknown telepathy? My only other experience of a dream coming true was when I dreamt My Love would win the Derby, which it did in 1948 at odds of 100–9. I naturally backed it, and I also drew this horse in three sweeps!

Race meetings, especially the classics, have always been sportively and justly popular as the object of outings from pubs and centres of relaxation or pleasure. A.J.S., and not forgetting Mother, who invariably finished up with most of the catering chores, ran many of these extremely successful outings.

I was particularly fortunate in attending the three consecutive Derbys which culminated in Steve Donoghue doing the 'hat trick' and being presented with Gold Spurs, to mark this very unique occasion. This record has never been beaten and no wonder the stock phrase then was 'Come on Steve'. These three Derby winners were:

1921 Humorist, 6–1. Trainer C. Morton. Owner Jack Joel. Time 2m 36/5s.

1922 Captain Cuttle, 10–1. Trainer Fred Darling. Owner Lord Woolavington. Time 2m 34.3/5s.

1923 Papyrus, 100–15. Trainer B. Jarvis. Owner B. Irish. Time 2m 38s.

Steve Donoghue (1884–1945) rode fourteen classic winners, and was placed twenty-one times over a period of twenty-eight seasons. He was also champion jockey for ten consecutive years from 1914 until 1923.

I shall never regret attending these early race meetings. Although many may disagree with me I am firmly convinced that later life benefited and was enriched by those experiences. The code of the racecourse in its activities are beyond reproach, and the code of racegoers, together with the bookmaking fraternity, is one of respect and dignified trust. Of course there are exceptions – life without opposites would be so colourless and empty. One of the exceptions is the bookmaker who lays over the odds for any particular horse or horses, taking a lot of money and then 'welching' (departs before the pay-out). This happened with the bookie almost adjoining our bus at one Derby. I put on a considerable number of last-minute bets with him for our party and, just prior to the off, everyone climbed to the top of the bus to watch the race. The excitable babble rose to a crescendo, when the pulsating proverbial declaration 'They're off,' issued from a million throats. Then came the eerie hushed silence that follows until the race gets under way sufficiently to clarify the positions of the leading horses and the jockeys. In those delirious seconds of magical concentration someone else answered to the call 'They're off' – our bookie! He left all behind, except satchel and money!

An entirely new era was born from 1920 onwards. Although they did not seem significant at the time many changes were taking place. More colour was being introduced into life, and a slight improvement in independence and freedom was noticeable. An element of foppishness was distinctly apparent; evident in more colourful clothes. Yellow waistcoats were being worn, silver knobbed walking sticks were popular and the average person was becoming more conscious of clothes and dressing, as well as hair styles. The forerunner to the modern beat music was established with the introduction of the New Dixieland Craze.

Wireless prefaced the world of change. Established in 1922 with '2LO Calling', it created a sweeping craze for do-it-yourself participation. Home-made crystal sets, which obviously were only adapted for the use of earphones, were the acme of simplicity; the main features being a large lacquered coil with a sliding terminal for tuning; a piece of crystal Galena (lead sulphide) which acted as a valve, and a small piece of wire that looked like one coil of a spring (known as the cat's whisker) which was manoeuvred to make the correct contact on the crystal, so finding a sensitive spot. Provided nobody accidentally or cussedly knocked the table the programme came over loud and clear.

# Chapter XVI

Grandparents – Standbrook's – The Clayhall Tavern – Bow – The National Sporting Club

Grandparents on both sides of my family were connected with the licensing trade, and I feel this book would be incomplete without recording some general information about them. Alfred Henry Standbrook, born in 1864 married Blanche Maud Martin, of Addlestone, Surrey in 1885. He was then working as head lift boy at The Hotel Metropole, west London. The then fashionable large family followed – five boys and four girls of whom only the girls are alive.

Entering the licensed trade in 1895 the couple became 'mine hosts' of The Elephant and Castle, Orchard Street, Westminster. After a few years they moved to The Dover Castle at Greenwich, then to The Woodman, Greenwich, and on to The Roull Tavern, Bermondsey, after which they took the license of The Prendergast Arms, Poplar, before finally settling in 1907, at The Clayhall Tavern, Old Ford Road, Bow. Alfred Standbrook's sporting promotions and almost unique ability to create an atmosphere of easy friendliness made him one of the East End's most popular licensees.

A.H.S. was one of the early promoters of Sunday morning football competitions. He would never do anything by halves, and if the prize were to be a cup, or perhaps a shield, it had to be as large as his heart, and that suggested a little ornateness and even, perhaps, an element of showmanship. The date of the illustration coincides with the following story of the 'Missing Cup', but the cup in question is not shown.

A Mr Hawkins, of The Salway Arms, Stratford called at The Bugle Horn at Stone near Aylesbury, early in 1969 and, noticing my brother's name on the licensing strip, inquired whether he was any relative of Alf Standbrook, who promoted football years ago. Apparently, when he and his wife took possession of The Salway Arms, they found the cup in a cupboard, together with other articles that had not been included in the inventory. After cleaning nearly sixty years of grime from it, the following inscription came to light: 'Presented by Alf Standbrook – Sunday morning Football League'. Apparently The Salway Arms won the trophy in 1910 and failed to return it! Mr Hawkins visited The Cambridge after I had telephoned him to confirm the existence of the cup. He appeared so elated at our subsequent meeting, especially in view of our mutual interest in sport, that I was sure at one stage that he was about to present it to me. I arranged to meet him at his establishment, which in due course I did together with my son Brian. The visit brought us little satisfaction. He had earlier intimated that his health had been failing, and thought it wise to sign everything over to his wife; including the cup! I used the utmost diplomacy when asking for just a peep at the inscription but nothing would induce Mrs Hawkins to take the cup from the cabinet. She promised to phone after the cup had been cleaned on Sunday morning and give me a note of the full inscription, but failed to do so.

The Salway Arms has since been demolished, and the whereabouts of the former licensees are unknown.

Grandfather's greatest love was boxing and he promoted many successful shows at the Harrow Football Ground, as well as at the Drill Hall, and Bow Baths, Roman Road. A copy of one of the posters of a promotion in 1915 is illustrated. Note the cost of the ringside seats – three shillings including war tax! Two well-known middleweight boxers whom he sponsored were Harry Paddon and Fred Newberry. One old-timer I must mention who boxed on his promotion is Charlie Ward – if only for the example he set and the credit he gave to the noble art. (He later became a prominent member of the Sportsmans' 68 Club which I founded in 1968, the proceeds of which are donated to charity.) He was never a champion, but always displayed an aggressive non-stop attitude that gave the patrons their money's worth. Among his opponents were Joe Bowker, Harry Mason, Seaman Arthur Hayes, Walter Ross and Sid Shields, bantamweight champion of Scotland. The fifteen round contest between Charlie Ward and the Scottish Champion Sid Shields, was promoted by Alf Standbrook at the Harrow Football Ground in 1917; the referee was J.T. Hulls, the boxing correspondent of the *Sporting Life*.

Charlie Ward, at the age of eighty, is still perky and enjoying life as chairman of his son's company Autoprints International at Deal, from where he frequently drives to and from Woodford covering some 500 miles per week. He has not long returned from America where he covered some 20,000 miles. Whilst there he called on Jack Dempsey, who kindly sent a message and signed a book for me, also a picture of the old National Sporting Club. This, when the requisite numbers of signatures are obtained, will be auctioned for charity.

Another poster announcing contests between Harry Paddon and Sam Simmonds and between Charlie Ward and Private H. Gorman to be held on 11th December, 1915 at The Ring, Blackfriars declares that 'Taxi drivers (in uniform only) will be admitted half price at 9 p.m.' The poster also says that in the interests of public health this building is disinfected with Jeyes Fluid!

Copied from the issue of *Boxing* dated 21st June, 1916:

### STRATFORD
### *Newberry beat Paddon*

Alf Standbrook backed another winner at the Harrow F.C. Grounds on Saturday afternoon. The weather was ideal for outdoor sport, and a big crowd rolled up to see what promised to be a cyclonic disturbance between Fred Newberry and Harry Paddon. Both are tremendous hitters, but in the matter of endurance Newberry triumphed, and thus secured the verdict. He weathered Paddon's hardest punches – and these were quite a few – in a great style, whereas Paddon visibly weakened under the strain, and in the eighth round fell to the floor during a hard rally. When he rose he fought back with all sincerity but bad direction, and at the end of the fifteen rounds Newberry secured a well-earned verdict.

It was with these two gentlemen of the boxing fraternity that I went hand in hand to see Jimmy Wilde box.

After Jimmy Wilde became the British flyweight champion he established his unsurpassed boxing ability by defeating the American champion, Italian born, Young Zulu Kid at the Holborn Stadium, London by knocking him out in the eleventh round for the World

Championship. This diminutive supremo was only seven stone, and conceded weight in most of his bouts which numbered considerably more than seven hundred, of which almost seventy-five per cent he won by knocking his opponent out. He eventually lost when well past his best to the Filipino, Pancho Villa, in June 1923 after which he rightly retired.

My visits to The Clayhall Tavern between the ages of five and eight left strong impressions on me that can never be erased. The East End then captivated my very immature mind and left me with affection and respect for its people. Kindness and thoughtfulness somehow blended with the toughness and uncertainty of life, that certainly created and generated a feeling of trust, respect and togetherness.

How my grandmother kept so cheerful and helpful must be beyond normal comprehension, especially as she had been a country girl and had never previously visited London. She brought up a family of nine, and suffered six changes to different pubs in twelve years, as well as two short periods 'in private'. On top of that she must have been working for a minimum of ninety hours a week. That's how it was in those days – one had to be strong in mind and body, tough and dedicated.

There was a gymnasium at The Tavern which was used by a number of well-known personalities, including Pedlar Palmer, Matt Wells, Jack Hart, Nat Simmons, Kid Olds, Johnny Summers and Sam Russell. A.H.S. organised the London General Omnibus Championship at The Ring by kind permission of Dick Burge. J.T. Hulls was the referee and Dan Sullivan the boxing manager.

The following is a cutting from the *Sporting Life* issue of 23rd July, 1966, dealing with the sport *fifty years ago*.

The generosity of boxers and those who look on the sport, which is proverbial, was strikingly demonstrated at Mr Alf Standbrook's tournament at the Harrow F.C. Ground, Stratford, yesterday. One of the principals in a six-round contest should have been Bert Hicks, of Walthamstow, but on Wednesday last he met with an unfortunate accident which has deprived him of the sight of an eye. When Hicks was introduced from the ring there was an immediate shower of silver and coppers, followed by a demand for a collection which was at once taken up by willing hands. Nor was this all, for one of the ringside patrons offered his watch for auction, an example followed by others. Some gave walking sticks, wrist watches, cigar-holders, and umbrellas, all of which produced brisk bidding and in the end the splendid sum of £34 6s 2d was realised.

Another cutting dated 18th November, 1964, under the heading fifty years ago records that: 'Mr Alf Standbrook has given a punching ball and two sets of boxing gloves for use by our troops at the Front'.

A.H.S. was a member of the old National Sporting Club and was included in the original painting showing Jim Driscoll and Joe Bowker shaking hands in the ring together with three hundred and twenty-seven members and guests of the club, all of whom sat separately for the artist W. Howard Robinson. This amazing picture hangs in the British Boxing Board of Control Office. Commenced in

1912 it took some seven years to complete, the boxers posed only on this occasion.

Bowker won the British Bantamweight Championship in 1902; the world bantamweight title in 1904 and the British Featherweight Championship in 1905. Driscoll beat him twice and on one of these occasions, in 1906, he took the Featherweight title from him.

There were one hundred photographic copies made of the original painting, and a key plan numbering every person portrayed. I am fortunate in possessing one of these photographs together with the key plan.

Several copies of it have been made, which I have presented to interested parties; one of whom is Reg Gutteridge whose grandfather Arthur Gutteridge, father of the famous Gutteridge twins Dick and Jack so well-known in the boxing world, is numbered three hundred and twenty-seven on the picture (bottom of the extreme right hand post). Among others owning copies are Alan Rudkin, Teddy Waltham, Johnny Pritchett, Harry Carpenter, John Stracey, Simon Evan Smith, Cliff Jones, and Sydney Hulls, whose Grandfather is also portrayed in the picture. A larger copy has recently been presented to Jack Powell on behalf of the London Ex-Boxers Association.

The old National Sporting Club probably did more to establish the sport of boxing in this country than any other organisation. This exclusive club, which opened at 43 King Street, Covent Garden, on 5th March, 1891, was a powerful influence for the good of the sport on an international basis. It was founded by John Fleming and A.F. (Peggy) Bettinson as a middle-class sporting club, and the Earl of Lonsdale was its first president.

'Peggy' Bettinson ruled the club with a rod of iron. The boxers and members had to behave themselves. The contests, which took place after dinner before about one thousand three hundred members and guests, were fought in silence, for no talking was allowed during the rounds.

Bettinson's benefit night in January, 1914, saw a star-studded bill when the members were treated to bouts featuring such famous fighters as Jim Driscoll, Jimmy Wilde, Ted 'Kid' Lewis, Digger Stanley, Sam Langford, Billy Wells, George Carpentier and Kid McCoy.

In the Twenties the sport grew too big for the club. Top-class men could draw bigger crowds and so demand bigger purses than the club could afford. In an effort to stave off a threatened closure the NSC opened its doors to the public for the first time in October 1928, but in twelve months they had to put up the shutters at Covent Garden. The Monday night tournaments were kept going at the Stadium Club in Holborn, the first being held on 9th October, 1929, the main event was between Johnny Cuthbert then British Featherweight Champion and young Pat Daly from Wales.

For a while they carried on at the Stadium Club, Holborn, before moving to 21 Soho Square, W1, in January 1930. It was an uphill struggle to keep the club functioning. A new company was formed in 1930, but the NSC was virtually extinct until 1936, when another enthusiast, John Harding, led a new committee which took over the Empress Hall to put on boxing shows.

New headquarters were opened at the Hotel Splendide, Piccadilly in March 1939, but then came the war, and towards the end of 1940 the NSC Ltd went into voluntary liquidation.

A new NSC Ltd was formed in 1947 with a nominal capital of 150,000 in 1,000,000 shilling shares, and they took over the Empress Club in Berkeley Street in September 1951. This club really has no connection with the old NSC, but since it moved to the Cafe Royal, Regent Street in September 1955 under the leadership of Charles Forte and John E. Harding, it has caught something of the atmosphere of its predecessor.

A.H.S. died aged only fifty-seven and the East End extended its respect and sorrow in a sublime way. He had lived a fairly hard and hectic life, and had one of those systems upon which drink had little effect, but alcohol took its toil in other ways. My family had The Royal Hotel in Leytonstone Road then, and in 1921 the cortege stopped outside in silence for a while. The spectacle was awe-inspiring. There were carriages carrying very large black plumes, enormous creations about four feet high. My memory seems to register these depressing bundles, which seemed to override the countless colourful wreaths. I cannot recollect ever seeing them since.

Grandmother kept the flag flying for several years with the help of two daughters, Ivy and Edie, and son Len, before vacating in 1926. Later she managed the off license which Father obtained in 1931 as the forerunner to The Cambridge full license – which was granted in 1934. After reaching the ripe old age of ninety she passed away in 1955.

# Chapter XVII

Grandparents – Pluck's and Allen's – The Castle at Woodford – a councillor in perspective of being a publican – the docks

Mother's side of the family were in general quite different. Her father, Fred Pluck, was born in 1863 and married Elizabeth Allen some twenty years later, while Elizabeth's brother George married Fred's sister, Adelaide Pluck. George Allen, father of Elizabeth and George was born in 1832 at Brampton near Huntingdon and married Annie Stadward. There were two other children named Mary Ann and Sarah. George Allen was then classed as a Journeyman Carpenter; apparently the Allen family were always builders, and apart from undertaking sizeable developments around the Plaistow area, London, the name Allen in Huntingdon is synonymous with builders. I understand that Rebecca Allen of Brampton is mentioned in Pepys Diary.

George Allen, who married my grandfather's sister had four children; George, who died at the age of fifteen; Adelaide, Sarah and Thomas. The last named, whom I have only known as Tommy, has lived at Frinton-on-Sea with his wife, Adelaide (Connie) in a delightful house on the Esplanade since 1933. He was the only Allen not to venture into the building trade and instead made an extremely successful career in the City being a Freeman of the City of

London by 'Virtue of Service'; he was also and still is an underwriter at Lloyds. He was also an extremely well-known philatelist who for many years collected and bought postage stamps for King George V. The following is a report from an issue of national newspaper of the mid-Twenties.

### £4,150 FOR TWO STAMPS.
### HIGHEST AUCTION PRICE – £2,400 FOR ONE.

Two 1847 Mauritius stamps – a 'Penny orange red' and a 'Twopenny blue' – which are among the rarest prizes in philately, were sold at Plumridge's yesterday for £4,150. The highest price ever given at auction in England for a stamp – £2,400 – was paid by Mr Thomas Allen of Wanstead for the orange red. He paid £1,750 for the twopenny stamp.

Mauritius stamps of the late Forties are surrounded with romance. Thirty years ago a boy's copybook revealed one for which the owner was first offered a pound, but which eventually was bought for the King's collection for £1,450. The boy who owned the copybook 'swapped' a cricket ball for the treasure.

I remember so well some of the strange idiosyncrasies of some of the family. My great-grandmother, Annie Allen (née Stadward) who would have been born about 1835, and her two unmarried daughters, Sarah and Mary Ann, lived in a fairly large house at Westcliff at which resort our family often stayed during the years from 1912 to 1918. I now wonder how they managed to put up with four devil-may-care youngsters in such a completely Victorian household.

Water was not allowed to be drunk unless it was first boiled, and one can imagine four gasping unruly kids dashing in for a drink, to find the water was still warm from boiling. All china, including drinking cups, mugs, etc had to be plain white – anything coloured was taboo.

It was whilst staying there that brother George was lucky to survive a nasty accident whilst walking back to the house with Mother, her two brothers, David and Bill, also my sister Peggy, who would then have been about three years old, and myself. Alf and George were walking along the top of the cliffs in line with us when I noticed them start to descend, trotting at first. George broke into a run, going faster and faster until he overran himself and tumbled out of control. The last part of the cliff was obscured by garden shrubs and it was that moment of seeing him disappear from our sight that panic set in. Jennie and one of my uncles couldn't get to him because of the crowd that had gathered. There was a retaining wall at the bottom, and he appeared to have fallen on his face. However, although unconscious for a long period he made a good recovery having sustained some serious facial and other injuries, one of which was apparent some years later.

Fred Pluck, my grandfather, always appeared to me as having a real purpose for living. He loved life in a careful way – quietly frivolous – had a simple sense of humour, was always very objective in his often sound advice and, at seventy-seven, remained stately and youthful, with a young person's comprehension. He was an enthusiastic motorist, but never completely mastered the art of keeping to the right, or rather left, side of the road. Corners were his speciality – a long blast on the horn and it was a case of 'everybody out of the way'. Strangely enough I never remember him having an accident, but perhaps one or two of his passengers may!

He owned some fascinating motor cars, including a Straker Squire and Itala, also a Metallurgique made in Belgium about 1913 – a tourer of 26 hp. Another unique model was the 1923 fast tourer Delage (which I frequently drove). A racing version was produced that year which in 1924 held the world land speed record of 143.31 mph. The majestic Minerva saloon was the aristocrat, made about 1921 with a three litre engine. It was, I believe, one of the first cars to sport front wheel brakes. Another rare contraption he owned was made by the London Engine Company (telephone engineers) of the phonophore works at Southall in 1912/13. It was known as the LEC and was really a cycle car with a 10 hp two cylinder engine with a belt drive and a radiator which was a replica of the Daimlers. Other cars he possessed pre 1914 were an Oldsmobile, Astor, De Dion, Renault, Sharron and a Pipe.

Mr Pluck was a very competent constructional engineer. One of his early engagements was to supervise the erection of an extension jetty at Table Bay Harbour in South Africa. A letter exists guaranteeing eighteen months employment at an agreed wage of £22 per calendar month, and is dated 15th June, 1891. Another letter dated later the same year, seeks his services to supervise the construction of new dock gates in Scotland, and their erection at Tyne docks. He also played a major part in the steel construction of Tower Bridge.

In 1900 he and grandmother entered the licensed trade – becoming hosts of The Golden Cross at Mill Lane, Woodford. Now demolished, the property was situated at the rear of the well-known landmark and Temperance Hotel, The Wilfred Lawson, also recently pulled down.

After a short period they purchased the freehold of The Castle Hotel Woodford Green. The site then occupied well over half an acre, and included a tennis court and a spacious garage with a repair bay in which I well remember, when very young, operating the bellows when the old forge was being used for repair work. Only a few years before it would have been playing a different role – shoeing horses. The garage must have been one of the earliest to operate a car hire service. Bill, one of the sons, was paid the princely sum of two shillings and sixpence (12½p) per week.

Licensing hours at the hotel then were from 6 a.m. until 11 p.m. – seventeen hours.

Fred Pluck put up for the Woodford Council in 1907 and faced very strong opposition from within the council. In those days it appeared quite nauseating to many people to have a publican in their midst.

Mr Wilkin proposed the following resolution, 'That this meeting do its utmost to secure the return of Mr F. Pluck on Saturday next'. In support of this resolution Mr Wilkin said Mr Pluck was the best of the five candidates. The fight was a serious one, as the supporters of the old members were working hard. Some of the old members' following were advising churchmen and non-conformists not to vote for Mr Pluck on the ground that he was a license holder. Perhaps they did not know that the gentleman who was at the head of the old members' committee was a large shareholder in a brewery. He (the speaker) was a non-conformist and was taught at an early age to be charitable to all men (cheers). He was going to take his coat off and work hard for Mr Pluck and fair play. Mr Pluck did not say he could reduce the rates but would see that they would have their money's worth. There has certainly been a very lax method employed in the conduct of affairs in the past, and things must be altered. The council were greedy and wanted all the seats. A certain local newspaper had said in a leading article that all the best people were supporting the old members. This was a libel on the gentlemen present (cheers). He sincerely hoped Mr Pluck would be returned as a protest against such a scandalous statement (cheers).

Mr Taylor briefly seconded the resolution, saying Mr Pluck was an able and practical man and had for several years been an engineer on most important works. He hoped all would support him.

Mr Langman supported the resolution saying he has known Mr Pluck for twenty-five years and had always found him a gentleman. He liked to see fair play. He had been told that there were certain members of the council who were strongly opposed to Mr Pluck because he lived at The Castle. As a lover of fair play he could not vote for the old members (cheers). The resolution was carried unanimously.

A meeting of the Woodford Ratepayers Association was attended by Fred Pluck prior to his election to the council; he was interviewed and explained his views regarding the rates etc. I quote from the local Press: 'Mr Deer (chairman) said if the ratepayers were satisfied with the council's work in the past they should return these members again. If they were dissatisfied he advised them to vote for Mr Pluck.' The chief objections that several people had against Mr Pluck was that he was a licensed victualler (shame). But Mr Pluck was a respectable law abiding citizen, was highly rated, and his character has to bear the strictest investigation by the Bench who granted him his license, and was just as eligible as any other ratepayer. He also conducted his business in a satisfactory manner and was the second largest ratepayer in Woodford.

Mr Pluck gained nine hundred and forty-six votes, the largest number out of six candidates. He continued to be a highly respected council member until he retired in 1913. The hotel was sold to Trust Houses in 1912 and is now owned by Trumans Brewery. The License is in the name of William A.E. Wilson and Geoffrey Buckland Dyer.

On the other side of the newspaper cutting was an advert by J. Jolliffe, builder and decorator, of Wanstead, advertising seven-roomed houses for sale, freehold at £375 and to let at fifty-five shillings per month inclusive. There were eight-roomed houses available at £475, or to rent at £32 per annum.

Another free house nearby was purchased in 1913. It was called The Travellers Friend, now belonging to the well-known Webster family and continuing as a free house.

After disposing of this establishment in 1918 Fred Pluck took the tenancy of The Royal Hotel, Leytonstone Road, which he kept until 1929. The Sun and Whalebone, Harlow, also came under his wing in 1922 at a yearly rent of £41 10s 0d. At some period he held the tenancy of The Wheatsheaf at Loughton.

Although he continued to hold the licenses of the house mentioned, his primary job continued to be engineering, and from about 1912 he was general manager of the Union Lighterage Co., at Cubitt town.

I was so fascinated with the docks that one Saturday morning I unforgivably let my school football team down by accepting an invitation to be on one of the barges designed by Fred Pluck, while it was launched. The excitement was terrific whilst waiting for the great hulk to commence to slide down the runway. It was a stimulating experience, and the fact of being so high up on a narrow ledge with little to hold on to gave me that fearful testing tension that a youngster loves to experience. It is not possible to know when the vessel is completely afloat; one sees the bows begin to rise slowly after that seemingly neverending drop, that appears eventually to submerge the forepart. When the barge finally ended its wallowing it was pulled in to berth at the end of a string of other barges and, of course, the only way back was an exhilarating climb over the other vessels, clambering from one to the other.

Another operation which never failed to fascinate me was the riveting. The pieces of white hot metal went flying high through the air like distant tracer bullets. They were picked up by a workman known as the holder up and inserted in the hole and held in position for the riveter on the opposite side of the steel plate to hammer the head skilfully until it splayed much larger than the hole containing the rivet, so sealing the plates as if welded. It was that musical, empty metallic ring that reverberated through the yard that arose above all the other seemingly muffled and drab noises. A riveter's money would have been in the region of £3.50 per week.

The never to be forgotten trips on the Thames on one of the tugs will always be cherished especially the crew expounding their knowledge of the engine room etc, and projecting much kindness.

Fred Pluck's two cashiers were coshed and robbed of £2,900, being wages for The Union Lighterage Co., in Philpot Lane, – mugging happened then but a different deterrent followed. Ten years penal servitude, fifteen strokes of the cat was the Old Bailey sentence.

Never shall I cease to wonder why Fred Pluck went into the licensed trade; he was as far removed from being a publican as my father would have been as a bargebuilder.

# Chapter XVIII

The George Inn Enfield 1924 – a 'change day' – general information within the Inn – Enfield, wages and prices in the early Twenties – film and stage stars appearing locally during 1924 – pubs commence the great new projection

In April, 1924, A.J.S. heard of The George being on the market, and promptly went to view it. There were no ifs and buts, the tenancy would be his; but the directors tried their utmost to deter him, saying that the place had not paid its way for many years. A.J.S. would not be discouraged and so signed the tenancy agreement and arranged a date for the change.

The change at The George on 24th June, 1924 proceeded quite normally in its exciting and exhausting way, and it was lucky for our parents that Alf junior, being now eighteen, lightened their burden by being eligible to work full-time in the business. There can be hardly any other business transaction to compare with the complexities of taking over a pub, especially if catering is one of its predominating features. The day commences, with the organisation of the removal arrangements, after which an attendance at the magistrates court by 10 a.m. is imperative for transfer of the justices license. In the case of a morning change the new licensee will hasten to his new home in which his wife will already have set things moving. She will have checked on the catering, arranged food for those officiating, and would also have prepared the tills with floats and made sure that sufficient change was available. The home would still be in the removal van, waiting for the outgoing tenant to vacate, a minor detail compared with the rest of the happenings. Stocktakers on behalf of the two licensees would be checking the stocks, together; the bars and draught beer cellar must be completed for a 10.30 a.m. (then 11.30) opening because the stock before then belongs to the outgoing licensee, and afterwards to the ingoing licensee. Spot checks are taken for the correct proof strength of spirits and the gravity and condition of beers.

Brokers on both sides check the inventory and arbitrate for a final settlement. They settle all outstanding accounts and apportion where necessary the rates, telephone account, check gas and electricity meters and equipment on hire, besides dealing with numerous other incidentals.

The brewery officials are also in attendance and, together with the other specialists they culminate the day's proceedings by handing a cheque with the 'Statement of Change' to the outgoing tenant – paid in full. This performance will take anything up to a non-stop twelve hours, obviously depending on the size of the house. Superimposed on all this, albeit the very reason for being in the trade, is the necessary presence in the bars of the new tenants to meet old and, one hopes, new friends. All this is made possible only by tremendous enthusiasm, and invariably an immense contribution of kindness and goodwill from the customers helps to alleviate the stresses of the day. There has been very little alteration in the format of the 'Statement of Change' for one hundred years or more, except for the deletion of the 'abroad cooper'. He was the person who dipped the casks for quantity and examined all beers to ascertain their correct condition for transfer to the incoming licensee. This task was carried out by the brewery manager at a charge of £3 3s 0d to £3 10s 0d according to the time of change, whether morning or evening. The practice was discontinued about 1960. Another peculiar custom that was generally dropped in the late Forties was that the final account had to be paid in cash! This is quite impractical today, with money at least ten times less in value, but still using more or less the same denominations. Furthermore it involved a very much greater risk of attack by the 'cash and grab' fraternity.

It was not an uncommon practice to be introduced to the business by the outgoing licensee, and he would be paid on the side an agreed amount of cash for his introduction or general help; this was known as 'under the table money'.

The total ingoing for The George was approximately £1,120. The inventory was £1,097 12s 0d, stock £57 and expenses £63. Today this would represent between £10,000 and £12,000.

On arriving downstairs on the morning following this hectic day at The George, A.J.S. found a rather small and serious-looking man actually taking all the china ornaments from the plate shelf that surrounded the lounge bar. The tables were full and his pockets stuffed with them. A.J.S. approached him while he was descending the steps with another load, and in no uncertain manner said, 'What are you doing taking those down?' The rather sour and lined face turned slowly, paused and said, 'Strewth! didn't Steve tell you that I'd only loaned them to him?' and had the effrontery to start ascending for another haul. A.J.S. went to make enquiries, but before he had gone far the funster caught him up, put his hand out to shake hands and introduced himself – 'I'm Dicky Bird – just a joke – no hard feelings?' They were good friends from then on.

The George had six bars then, five of which were situated in the front of the house and which now constitutes the Elizabeth Bar. The service for all of these bars was administered from one horseshoe shaped counter, and were in the following order: first the saloon bar; the entrance to which remains the same, opposite the lounge entrance. Adjoining was the Four Ale bar, so named when a quart or pot of ale was fourpence, and quoted in the following old song:

> When the price comes down again,
> And the four ale they'll be swilling,
> It will break my heart to have to
> part with three 'Pots' a shilling.

This bar was known as the Spit and Sawdust bar; the tables and bare floorboards were scrubbed white every day, after which fresh sawdust was put down, the spittoons cleaned and filled with sand. The centre bar with entrance on the frontage was the Bottle and Jug bar, but was used also as a drinking bar. A public bar adjoined the latter on the right, and the final bar was known as the private bar, and had an eight foot by four foot billiard table installed in it. Access to the two latter bars was by way of a typical curved Victorian entrance porch displaying ornate engraved glass panelling. The sixth bar, known then as the lounge, remains as it then was except for two extensive alterations, and two minor ones. It is now known as the 'Raleigh' bar.

One of the strangest contraptions of Victorian pubs were the little 12 inch square revolving windows in engraved frosted glass, framed by wood. These swivelled between two horizontal members set about 18 inches above the counter, so that when all the windows were closed one couldn't see t'other's face. It was quite embarrassing when they were closed in front of you, a hint to go away. Almost every pub had disposed of these screens by the early Thirties. They are still in use on part of the counter in The Windmill, Windmill Hill.

Another amazing feature concerned toilet amenities. The George was not alone in not having any ladies toilet in any of its bars and the single loo on the first floor which was used for banqueting was the only one available. The five bars in front of the house sported a men's urinal outside at the end of the yard, and there was only a single men's WC in the lounge. I cannot recall any grumbles regarding this lack of facilities. It was quite general. If in trouble one had to use the public one that was only 100 yards away!

The top floor had five bedrooms but no bathroom; that being on the first floor. It was the general men's toilet for functions, and meetings etc. It was divided into a bathroom, WC and urinal by an open top wooden partition with no heating whatsoever, and a floor covering of thick lead – not exactly a hot-house, and no time was wasted there! That was one point to its credit.

The following typifies some of the contents of the inventory of a normal bedroom at The George change.

Four foot six inch brass mounted iron bedstead
Feather bed, flock bolster, two feather pillows
Marble top washstand with two chambers in cupboards and raised marble back and shelf
Set toilet fittings – seven pieces (large jugs and wash bowls, etc)
Earthenware slop pail and cover

Four foot by three foot silvered chimney glass in gilt frame
Eight bamboo curtain poles and rings
Green Holland roller blind to window
Brass railed top fender. Venetian ashpan
Iron coal cauldron. Coal Scoop. Brass mounted poker
Brass duplex paraffin lamp with glass chimney and globe

I must mention the Anidjah fire escape that existed for years in number five bedroom. It consisted of a large iron frame on hinges that swung up against the window frame, when about 20 yards of canvas fell to the ground. This canvas was grasped by whoever was below and pulled out away from the building. The bottom part had handling hoops allowing for three persons on either side, and for this distance the top half of the canvas tunnel was cut away so that the person descending could be seen and braked before being shot into the road. There was a rope to ease oneself down if nervous, but I do not recall anyone using it. The fire brigade inspected the apparatus annually, and how the kids (including the family) loved to volunteer to whiz down this chute into pitch darkness and emerge below at a natural speed checked by the open part of the canvas held by the firemen. There would be two or three hundred people watching this performance.

There was no hot water laid on. This was drawn from an old-fashioned copper from The Pot House, so called because all the pewter pots were cleaned there. The 'Potman' as he was known then, and is still so referred to, was invariably a small man with small hands enabling him to clean the inside of the deep pots with silver sand.

Another arduous job, but always giving a sense of accomplishment when complete was the cleaning of the steel cutlery for the luncheons and banquets in the knife machine. The contraption consisted of a circular narrow drum turned manually with a handle after six or eight knives had been inserted up to the handle, the blades being forced in between pads which were well covered in a brown abrasive powder which was poured in periodically and known as 'Oakleys'.

The heating seemed to be adequate, but was far from it by today's standards. Only two coal fires served the five bars in the front of the house and a coal and gas fire in the lounge – as it is today. The first floor sported just two small coal fires in the banqueting hall. With the all-glass front, and perhaps an adverse direction of wind it did demand a might of bodily heat, in addition to the fires, to stop the teeth chattering!

I must say we appeared to be in a better state of health in regard to colds than we are now, due almost certainly to the advent of central heating and the poor ventilation that goes with it. 'Tis one long cough and splutter for so many when summer leaves us!

Life was so much harder then but it was eased by the simplicity of everything. There were no hoists from the cellars or from the hall – only one hand hoist from kitchen to dining room, which displayed a huge speaking tube. No detergents or washing-up powders, just good old soap, soda and boiling water. All the thick pint and half-pint glasses were cleaned every morning in the latter.

One great improvement today is the extremely hygienic pipe system for transferring the beer from a cellar to service. The method used up to the early Thirties, was plain India rubber tubing or short pieces of pewter (later china) pipe some six to eight inches in length joined together with a rubber connector secured with a wireloop which was tightened with a special tool. This gave the movable part of the pipe flexibility. The only drawback was that if it was not thoroughly brushed very regularly a deposit would quickly form at the joints. The system generally failed at the fixed run of lead piping from the ceiling in the cellar to the pump at the service position. This sometimes ran under floor boards, twisting and turning and without any cleaning points, making the cleaning operation an extremely laborious operation. One may well imagine the condition these pipes would be in when neglected!

Beer pumps today, although the working principle is similar, are much more hygienic, each having a metal piston in the pump cylinder, instead of a leather plunger, called the Bucket, which identically resembled an ordinary bicycle pump, only on a larger scale. Methodical cleaning and maintenance was essential since there is always a considerable yeasty deposit with beer. The normal process of cleaning was with boiling soda water, after which strong salt water was pulled through, followed by a thorough cleansing with cold water.

Practical refrigeration was almost unknown then, but ice was nearly always available and made possible by regular calls from the Carlo Gatti ice lorries, from which one would purchase so many shillingsworth; the blocks being wrapped in sacks and stored in the cellar.

Two other pieces of equipment, then in use but rarely seen now were firstly, a 'saveall' – a tray made of hard metal about one inch high with a flat perforated detachable top. The intention was to catch and save all the overspill and drippings of spirits when filling measures for on or off consumption. There was then a large demand for half or quarterns of whisky or gin to take away, especially at one shilling and fourpence a half quartern! in today's money, just over 6½p for three measures; strangely I never remember seeing any appreciable amount of liquid in one of these trays – either we were canny in seeing there was no waste or somebody was having a cocktail at closing time! Another minor essential was a coin tester: a metal strip with four slots cut in it. The doubtful coin was inserted in one of these slots according to its thickness and levered to one side – if it was counterfeit it would bend very easily. False coins were very common, especially the half-crown. This operation may appear rough and ready today but two and sixpence then would now probably represent about £1.75!

Although in the early Twenties Enfield had a population of over sixty thousand its character was not unlike that of a village. Although well-developed and perhaps a little sprawling, it was commencing to show the real growth potential to which the town was inevitably to submit. Industrially Enfield had from early days made its mark nationally. The Royal Small Arms Factory brought fame to Enfield some one hundred and seventy years ago, and in fact, we can go back to John and Henry Wroth, of Enfield, coming to an arrangement with parliament for making gunpowder at 'The Lock' in 1653. Edison Swan Electric Light Company were operating at Ponders End in 1886 and through successive takeovers, has developed into the world-renowned Thorn Industries. This industrial upsurge created a demand for housing and for about ten years from 1924 new estates were popping up everywhere. Today it is difficult to comprehend that, with so much expansion and apparent prosperity, the cost of living remained constant. This was obviously due to the fact that land and general commodities were not subjected to any forced price increases, which automatically kept wages steady as well.

The town was the terminus for all public transport services, which helped to make the shopping area very busy. There were no defined car parks as such; this was hardly necessary since parking for the car was allowed almost anywhere, and commercial transport was comparatively sparse. Horses and band barrows were still being used for local deliveries.

In the main the shops were small private businesses, the proprietors of which displayed the respect and courtesy that then was expected as part of life. Then the proprietors could obtain staff more easily; efficiency was vital because the average person could not afford to buy indiscriminately and the principal and his assistants had to use every legitimate method of selling. In general there was little excuse for being out of stock or of having to declare, 'Sorry, we cannot get delivery' – which is today's password – because supplies were plentiful. Shopkeepers were not subjected to any kind of purchase tax or value added tax, neither was one forced by 'pay as you earn' to act as an unpaid collector of taxes! We were free from many other pressures that everyone must dutifully accept in our 'hurry along' world. To equate the two periods is quite ludicrous simply because there was so much to be said for and against conditions in 1924 as well as in 1974 but I feel my assessment would be on these lines: 'in so much magnificence there is so much ugliness, and I suggest that today there is a wee bit more of the latter.'

So time slips away. The following is an extract from Ebenezer Gibbons *Recollection of Enfield* written in 1910. I quote it as a parallel to the last paragraph bridging a gap of approximately one hundred and twenty-five years

(Ebenezer Gibbons was born in 1834 and is quoting the 1850s).

> What a difference too, the Penny Post has brought about! When I was a boy we had to pay threepence for a letter to be sent to London. I distinctly remember paying that amount in Mr Jelly's (the bakers) shop, now in the occupation of Mr Ebben (later Keith Royale – now Harris Carpets) which was then the Post Office, for a letter to be sent to Bishopsgate. The office was afterwards located on the premises of Mr Leech, the hairdresser, and he was followed by the two Misses Leach and then by Miss Copeland. I remember her coming to Enfield very well. In fact, in those days it was all so different, with only one or two of the same trade in the place – Mr Duffey, in the Market Place, was the other hairdresser. In those days everybody seemed to know each other's business; and there was a much nicer and kindlier feeling one with another. Why, if a tradesman wanted a little help to tide over a bad time or to make a new start, he had only to ask a tradesman to help, and away would go two or three all round to their neighbours, and the gentry as well; and the needful has soon been obtained many a time, as I have known. On one occasion I remember that my father and one or two more collected £100 for a well-known tradesman in the town who was a very respected townsman. Those were days when we really were neighbours, with the right sort of neighbourly spirit; and there was no cutting of prices as we have come to see in recent years.

So often are the pre-war prices of articles and various commodities quoted, and nearly always in a context suggesting 'how much better off we were', but this is misleading unless we consider the relative wages prevailing. The only true comparison with those days and our own is to divide the cost of the article or commodity into the respective wages.

For instance, petrol was one shilling fourpence halfpenny per gallon and a working man's wage averaged approximately £2 8s 0d (£2.40) per week (Royal Small Arms factory employees earned £2 7s 0d to £2 9s 0d, and they were claiming a ten shilling rise). The cost of one gallon would roughly be one thirty-fifth of those wages. Today the salary would be £40 and petrol 55p, the gallon of petrol being thus nearly one seventy-third of today's comparable wage – twice as cheap as it was in 1924! (Petrol later dropped to one shilling and twopence halfpenny per gallon and in one period may have gone as low as one shilling and one penny.) There are, of course, other items that demonstrate an opposite trend, such as land and housing.

The pay of a deputy clerk of the council was between £8 and £9 per week and an ordinary clerk received £2 10s 0d. A certificated woman school teacher earned approximately £6. A maid could be paid something in the region of £30 per annum, with accommodation and food provided. A labourer's pay was one shilling twopence halfpenny per hour, while a council road sweeper's wage was £2 11s 0d.

A council house rent was relatively expensive at 15s 0d per week – at least a quarter of a workman's wages!

Bacon was sevenpence halfpenny per lb, and bread was for an ordinary loaf fivepence, and sevenpence halfpenny per quartern. Eggs averaged 4s 4d a score.

Men's ready-to-wear tweed suits cost 27s 6d. Charlie Berry was pleased to sell a made-to-measure suit for £3 3s 0d (£3.15) and included an extra pair of trousers! Enfield Grammar School fees were £4 4s 0d a term.

A Ford runabout was priced at £110, while a four-seater Rover tourer was £145. The Austin Seven racer was guaranteed to top 75 mph at £185 and a BSA motorcycle cost £47 10s 0d.

Unemployment relief for a family with one child was £1 5s 0d plus up to twelve shillings rent relief, an allowance for one cwt of coal, and the payment of any life insurance.

In 1924 the Great Cambridge Road was opened from Edmonton to Bush Hill Park.

The two following dated reports were copied from the *Enfield Gazette*:

> Profiteering appears in many forms but we are glad to think that so far the Edmonton Guardians have not asked the Council to increase the rateable value of houses where rent profiteering is discovered. Further information revealed the fact that £2 had been charged for two poorly furnished rooms and as much as 16 shillings to 20 shillings for a single furnished room. This is a deplorable state of affairs, yet we know the practice continues. It may not be confined to furnished rooms in Enfield, yet when one is charged 35 shillings to £2 per week for a flat we cannot help thinking that the sooner this practice ceases the better.
>
> Friday, 3rd October, 1924 – It is urged by a certain school of economists that there is no sense in clinging to pre-war ideas of prices and values. These, it is suggested, together with the notion that anything

is dear because it costs double or nearly double the pre-war figure. Present prices should be regarded as normal and permanent and we should base our calculations accordingly. To do so comes easy to the teachers and others whose pay is two or three times what it was in pre-war times, but it is an impossibility for millions of our population, who will be unable to live at all unless prices are brought down. The shipbuilders are getting barely forty per cent more in wages than before the war, and yet there is no work for about a third of their number since it is being done cheaper abroad.

Similar conditions prevail in the iron and steel, engineering and other industries. The miners are hoping by international action to raise the wages and shorten the hours of the coal-getters in Germany, but with little prospect of success. The pay of miners, textile, metal, railway and general factory workers, and builders in Germany ranges from sixpence to eight pence per hour in the new stabilised currency, and the average working hours a week are fifty-four. It is only by the women working that average working class families in Germany can make ends meet. This means competition such as our export trades cannot hope to contend with, unless prices and cost of production are lowered in this country.

Prices must come down, or the trade on which a large proportion of the population depends will disappear.

Friday, 19th September, 1924

The first cigarette machine was installed in the town to give an after 8 p.m. service. (Tobacco could not lawfully be sold anywhere and not excluding licensed houses after 8 p.m.)

Mr J. Spencer-Hill, of The Chantry, on the Ridgeway, recommended that Enfield should receive its proper status and become a borough, especially as the town had a population of over sixty thousand and a rateable value exceeding £346,000. The recommendation was honoured thirty-one years later.

Col. R.V.K. Applin, the Conservative MP was elected to parliament by 2,079 votes from W.W. Henderson (Labour), Tommy Dufton was then the Conservative agent.

The Borough of Islington was advertising locally in the following terms: 'Notice to Farmers – Road sweepings with high percentage of horse manure, if desired may be mixed with a good percentage of vegetable refuse – three shillings and sixpence per ton, loaded free and carriage paid.'

Talk of Enfield becoming a smokeless zone? Eventually the first steps were taken in 1956 under the 'Clean Air Act'; the final order for Enfield began 1975.

The Railway Inn, later known as The Beaconsfield, now Henekeys, had plans for a new lounge and dining room passed at the Licensing Sessions. The application was opposed by The George and The Kings Head. This was a normal act of opposition carried out by all brewers.

The Stag then licensed only for beer was granted a wine license. A full license was granted in 1947.

The inaugural meeting of the Enfield Bowling Club was held on 22nd August, 1924 at The George. Some well-known names were present, including Sydney Fussell, Tommy Scott, Percy Weaver, Jack Skinner, Bob Vernum, Bill Carter, Charlie Maunder, Charlie Simmonds, George Empson and Arthur Briden.

Albany Park Bowling Club opened their green on the 7th June; the first wood being bowled by A. Burrage.

Bernard Fitch, licensee of The Cross Keys, Edmonton, and well-known as a local sportsman, acted as referee at the horse jumping competition held in the town park in September, 1924. Many well-known local personalities helped to promote the show including Major Leggatt, Col. Applin, Major Medcalfe and Bill Graham (of Graham Bros. Garage; now Arlingtons).

I quote the following report dated 1st August, 1924, because A.J.S. became very friendly with James Neilson and his manager Ben Liffen. The outcome was that I myself joined the firm early in 1925, and it was then I met James Neilson's secretary, Audrey Clarke, later my wife.

At the invitation of Admiral Sir Hedworth Meux and Lady Meux, of Theobalds Park, the estate and park staff were entertained at Wembley during that month. The party which numbered seventy-one, were conveyed to the exhibition in charabancs provided by Messrs Meeson Bros. and left the park gates at 8.45 a.m. Lunch and tea were served in the Stadium Hall. Mr J. Neilson, agent to Sir Hedworth Meux, took the chair at the lunch. The toast of the Admiral and Lady Meux was heartily acknowledged by the company. The whole of the expenses were defrayed by Sir Hedworth Meux and it was the unanimous vote of the party that the day had been a real success. Theobalds Park was reached at 9 p.m.

In the week during which the Standbrook family arrived in Enfield The Queens Hall Cinema was showing that great film *Coming Through the Rye* featuring Alma Taylor. The Rialto was presenting Lionel Barrymore in *Unseeing Eyes* and the proprietors were allowing the full benefit of the reduction of the entertainments tax (it happened occasionally in those days).

Sandy Powell and Elsie Carisle were performing at the Wood Green Empire.

Earlier Seymour Hicks played in, produced and presented the play *Broadway Jones.*

So many people so many times find that names escape their memories when the occasion arises. Just to refresh the recollection of some of the old-time stars the following are names which featured in films in Enfield or who were playing at the local Empire during 1924.

| | |
|---|---|
| Will Rogers | Reginald Denny |
| Leslie Henson | Bransbury Williams |
| John Barrymore | Whit Cunliffe |
| Lewis Stone | Fay Compton |
| Tom Mix | Clive Brooks |
| Gloria Swanson | Ramon Novarro |
| Ivor Novello | Lionel Barrymore |
| Jack Holt | Florence Desmond |
| Buster Keaton | George Robey |
| Douglas Fairbanks | Pola Negri |
| Edna Best | Jackie Coogan |
| Betty Compton | George Arliss |
| Rudolph Valentino | Lilian Gish |
| Victor McLagien | Normal Talmadge |
| Ernie Lotings | Richard Talmadge |
| Mary Pickford | Ernie Mayne |
| Matheson Lang | Bebe Daniels |
| Harry Tate | Sandy Powell |
| Owen Nares | Fred Karno |
| George Robey | Constance Talmadge |
| Harold Lloyd | Lon Chaney |

Gracie Fields             Clara Bow
Nellie Wallace            Richard Dix

The early Twenties and late Thirties witnessed a pronounced era of change in licensed houses. The improvement of premises and introduction of a more home-like atmosphere was instrumental in captivating the patronage of the ladies. Billiard rooms were converted into lounges; or two, maybe three rooms were incorporated to form one large bar, introducing the open plan effect. Ceilings were lowered and refurbishing including carpeting, became almost a craze. The sparse old-fashioned lighting, with its inevitable hanging white opal globes, was replaced by more colourful and attractive fittings. Music became an integral part of the general reappraisement, from which the sophisticated background music developed. Another very significant feature was the development of catering in public houses, with ever-increasing demand for quick service and snacks due to the fast-growing popularity of the motor car. 'The start of the race to nowhere'.

This period was without doubt a vintage time for licensees; though in making this statement I do not wish to deprecate the great qualities of present day licensees, who are labouring under the added pressures common to everybody engaged in the trade in these difficult times.

An outstanding feature of those earlier days was the very beneficial licensee–brewer relationship; which, of course, does still exist in some smaller concerns. The whole emphasis then was on producing and selling beer, promoting the sales by absolute goodwill and healthy rivalry. Brewers were basically brewers of beer, property speculating was unknown and rents were fair and comparatively static. All this helped to create a partnership which converted the best of everybody's efforts, to mutual benefit.

Today the brewers, like all other producers are forced into a situation where the 'only-money-matters' outlook is unavoidable. It is caused by world inflation, created primarily by supplies not satisfying demands, which engenders a false affluence. This in turn produces rising prices, high interest rates, and inflation – the aggravation starts somewhere and finishes up everywhere!

# Chapter XIX
Some Enfield pubs and landlords in the Twenties

Enfield in the Twenties was fortunate in having so many licensees who characterised this period. It is possible to mention only a few of the town's pubs, time being the arch enemy to everyone's intended accomplishments. Acquiring information is time-consuming, and I shall quote only those houses of which I already possess some basic information, or with which I am familiar through family connections. So much pleasure could be derived from meeting and chatting with old regular customers who have patronised their own favourite locals for half a century or more, and how much more enriched this book would have been had their tales been recorded. Alas, we must reproach our old adversary – time.

It's amazing to think that by going back only twelve generations one could be listening to magical tales such as could have been handed down from villagers of Elizabeth I's reign. Tavern gossip might have centred round events in 1574, when Alencon, the youngest son of Catherine, consort of Henry II of France, nearly became the consort of Elizabeth I by the connivance of his mother. After he had inherited the title of Duke of Anjou there followed the normal French court celebrations in the course of which Catherine, as alleged by Lord North, the Queen's envoy, insulted Elizabeth by dressing two female dwarfs in English costume. In a written apology Catherine remarked that if Lord North's French had been better the incident would have been interpreted as innocent buffoonery.

Unfortunately Enfield, in common with virtually every town in England, is still undergoing the decline of the brewery–tenant licensee partnership. The few old-established licensees remaining are seeing the conclusion of an age-long partnership which is being replaced, speaking figuratively, by brewery nationalisation.

A family which may claim the longest association with the trade is the Everetts. Anne retained the license of the attractive, typical sixteenth century inn, The Pied Bull at Bulls Cross, following the untimely passing of her husband Denton in 1965. The building was originally part of the Royal Chase and was used as kennels for the hunting dogs during the reign of James I. She is now residing a few doors away in an attractive cottage called The Orchards which, previously The Spotted Cow, was renamed when the brewers, Whitbread & Co, made the premises redundant following the transfer of license to the newly built Isaac Walton at Green Street during 1924. Mr and Mrs Everett, the parents of Denton, were then the license holders of The Spotted Cow and at the inn's closure they moved on to the nearby Pied Bull. Following the death of Denton's father, his mother continued holding the license until Denton took over in 1950. Her mother, Mary Everett, who was born in 1839 and died in 1910 transferred the license to her son in 1906. An agreement dated 1887 between George Gripper of Tottenham, brewer, (eventually taken over by Whitbread's Brewery) and Mary Everett, of The Spotted Cow, states the annual rent was £25, or £50 should liquor be obtained from any other source. Records indicate that Mary Everett's father, Richard Rich, owned the premises originally, and that between the years 1872 and 1887 his stock was being purchased from Christie & Co. Richard was born in 1807 and died in 1878 and there seems little doubt that he was the owner and licensee of the old Wheelwrights Inn in Goff's Lane, Goff's Oak in 1848 before acquiring The Spotted Cow. He was by trade a wheelwright! The little inn ceased to function in 1970, when the license was transferred to the new Wheelwrights which was erected almost directly opposite. The tiny, quaint old inn had atmosphere typical of the countryside and, completely unspoiled by time, was still without a bathroom. The licensees Nigel and Mavis Stamp, must have had heavy hearts when they vacated the premises shortly before the closing of the old inn, especially as Nigel's parents – Harry and Edith – had previously held the license from 1942 until Nigel and Mavis became the hosts in 1957.

Another active licensee whose family can claim a record of nearly one hundred years as hosts of The Windmill Inn, Windmill Hill, is Flossie Oakley. This inn was named after the windmill that was originally erected during the sixteenth century on top of the hill close to the Church of St Mary Magdalene which, incidentally, was built in 1883 at the expense of Georgina Twells in memory of her husband, Philip Twells, the total cost being £32,000. The original mill was later replaced by another but finally pulled down early in the century, having been in the Robinson family for nearly two hundred years. Thomas Gray, grandfather of Flossie, was granted the license of The Windmill on the 11th March, 1881, but sadly, after only a few years as host he suffered a severe fall from his horse resulting in a broken neck from which he later died. After his death, his widow Louise remarried and continued running the inn in the name of Mrs Watts until her death in 1910. The license was then transferred to her son, Ernest Gray. Known to everyone as 'Diamond', he was a great sporting personality, and with a fondness for shooting and racing; together with A.J.S. and Bert Greenall they could have master-minded any panel on horse racing or the music halls. Following his death in 1934, his sister Agnes Oakley, kept the flag flying and held the license until she passed away in 1955 when Flossie continued the sequence. For nearly seventy years, therefore, the inn has been successfully controlled by the fairer sex. Felicitations to Flossie and her mother, and to their customers. Still going strong and looking forward to the 11th March, 1981 to celebrate one hundred years. Flossie still has many of the original pint pewter pots that were being used at the inn nearly one hundred years ago; Brian and I are each the proud possessors of one of them – these were presented to us as a reminder of the long association of the two families. A copy of the original Extension of Licensing Hours to celebrate Queen Victoria's Diamond Jubilee may be seen in the bar.

Jack and Doreen Fairlie are still happily continuing in their role as mine hosts of The Old Sergeant, Parsonage Lane, where Jack has held the license since 1936. I feel justified in saying that it would be difficult to find a licensee more dedicated to his business and, in a broader sense, more devoted to the trade in general. He is involved in all aspects of the Licensed Victuallers Association's activities, local and national, and apart from the burden of many offices in this field he has given his time and endured the responsibilities of office in many other local interests. All this, of course, has again been possible only by the complete compatibility with his wife Doreen. She has also held office in the Ladies Auxiliary and, like so many of her colleagues in all other auxiliaries, has been responsible for thousands of pounds being raised for the Licensed Victuallers' and other charities.

Charles Fairlie, grandfather of Jack, acquired the license of The Hop Poles, Baker Street, on 11th July, 1901. His son, Archie and wife Maud, followed on when Charles died in 1931. Archie, apart from his keen interest in local sports and charity, was also a dedicated worker on behalf of the licensed trade, and in 1959 he had the honour to be President of the Northern Suburban Licensed Victuallers Association, of which he was a past chairman and trustee. In 1951 the family celebrated their fifty years of occupation. Archie became semi-retired in 1958 and was followed by his son Lester and daughter-in-law, Clarice. The license was relinquished in 1958.

Archie passed away in 1967 aged eighty-three, and Lester died when only fifty-four in 1969. The present Hop Poles was rebuilt in 1909. The last licensees who vacated in June were the very popular Boy and Babs Ede, who declared, 'We have enjoyed every minute of the last fourteen years.' So once again another busy, lively, orthodox pub passes to brewery management!

The Chandler family had a long and distinguished record in the trade but unfortunately their reign ceased in Enfield when Ben Chandler passed away on 8th November, 1956, aged eighty-five, while still holding the license of The Enfield Arms which adjoins Enfield town railway station. William Chandler, Ben's father, secured the license of The Holly Bush, Lancaster Road, in 1873. The property was then owned, as were so many in the north of London, by Gripper Brothers. William's son Ben and wife Bessie both left the teaching profession to enter the licensed trade. Commencing their new career as licensees of The

Rose, at Bexley Heath, they took over The Holly Bush on 8th December, 1904, following the retirement of William. The old tavern was replaced by the existing premises in 1927. Ben relinquished the license in 1954. The present licensees are Fred and Glad Beardmore. The Enfield Arms was acquired in 1912 and rebuilt in 1924 by Alan Fairhead at a cost of £8,787.

George and Amy Ives followed on at The Enfield Arms, taking over from Harry and Grace Wilson, an extremely dedicated and likeable couple who had been managing for the late Ben Chandler. George was Chairman of the local LV Association in 1959 and 1960; he and Amy gave much of their time to the protection and charitable side of the LVA at all levels. His son, George, is the secretary of the LV Homes at Denham. Trumans Brewery installed a manager when George and Amy vacated.

Ben Chandler junior and his wife Kitty acquired the license of The Kings Head (rebuilt on the site of The Old Vine Inn) in the market square in May 1931, and after four years of busy light-hearted and lively occupation they vacated and transferred to The Holly Bush, which he managed for his father. Following his period of war service in the Navy, Ben continued his connection with outside bar catering, two of which were concerned with the 'Royalty' Hall, at Southgate, and the Tottenham Palais. The pair retired to Cornwall some twenty years ago to enjoy tranquillity and peacefulness in a fascinating old mill house completely isolated from the hurly-burly of the outer world.

Harry Finn was the licensee at The Kings Head before Ben, having held the license since 1908. He appeared before the local magistrates at court during the Great War in June 1916, charged under the No Treating Act. The indictment read as follows: 'For supplying intoxicating liquor for consumption on the premises, the same not being ordered and paid for by person supplied, on 20th May, 1916.' The penalty incurred was a fine of ten shillings or seven days imprisonment. The following has been extracted from *The Times History of the Great War*: 'By the spring of 1917 38,000,000 of the established population of 41,000,000 in Great Britain were living under orders which cut deeply into one of the most firmly rooted of the national habits. Hours of drinking were stringently reduced, the potency of spirituous liquors greatly weakened and the custom of 'treating' forbidden. The total quantity of drink for distribution was limited and the price of every kind of intoxicant was unlimited.' *The Times* history described this step as little short of a revolution – and with what justification!

The Kings Head followed the normal pattern of brewery policy when managers replaced the last tenants.

In 1924 The Old Wheatsheaf, Windmill Hill, was in the capable hands of Jimmy and Mrs Albon, who acquired the license in 1922. Jimmy was a likeable and friendly character who, in a humble way, prompted a spontaneous and an amicable companionship. In 1936 he transferred to The Stag and Hounds, Bury Street, which he successfully conducted until his retirement in 1947. He was succeeded by Charlie and Daisy Pyle who, in time, created a warmth and welcome that induced the popularity and atmosphere the bars enjoy today. Charlie sustained a grievous loss when his wife passed away in 1965, but the blow was softened by having his daughter Daphne and husband Ken Pink in the business. While they virtually managed The Stag and Hounds I am told that Charlie (in his eighty-fifth year) was for many years very much the 'governor', actively taking part in many aspects of the business. (He died in April 1974 and the license was granted to Ken and Daphne.)

When Jimmy left The Old Wheatsheaf in 1936 his son Fred and daughter-in-law Rose continued with the license. When they moved and took over a pub in Truro in 1953 they were followed by Norman and Betty Fish who have maintained a homely cordiality enjoyed and appreciated by all their patrons.

The old Plough, Crews Hill, was appropriately blessed with licensees well-fitted to preside over the affairs of a rustic hostelry. I well recall my early visits in 1925 and my appreciation of Ted Firmin, and his wife Elsie, who so typified the host of a vintage country inn where beer was quaffed by locals as a part of their diet and by others who met to enjoy the uninhibited chatter of the locals in that mellow atmosphere. The new Plough was opened in 1937, leaving the old inn looking lifeless, sad and dejected, until it was purchased by Arthur Brown & Son and given a complete face lift when the building once more presented a cheerful appearance. Tiggy, Ted's son, came in to the business after being demobbed in 1946 and on the retirement of his father soon afterwards the license was transferred to him. Ted died in 1969. The Plough went to brewery management when Tiggy took an appointment with the owners, McMullen and Co.

In 1924 Harry Miller was the licensee of The Six Bells, Chase Side, but whether or not he purchased the eighteen year lease that year I have no proof. The lease was sold in August for £4,000 with an annual rent of £45. Harry was an unusual character. Previously a chef, he made full use of his qualifications in the preparation of food. In memory I see him leaning or pushing against the counter with a large proportion of his stomach nestling on top! In 1885 the pub had only a six-day license, but enjoyed the full license soon afterwards.

In 1957 Clifford and Peggy Shaw came to The Six Bells, but in 1962 tragedy struck when Clifford fell down the stairs leading from the first floor landing and sustained a fractured skull, an injury from which he later died. Peggy continued holding the license and in 1965 married Dennis Hawkins, Detective Chief Superintendent in command of CID of No. 2 District. Dennis retired from the police on his wedding day, having more than completed the normal years of service. In 1966 Peggy relinquished the license of The Six Bells after which she and Dennis enjoyed a spell of living in private until 1969 when they purchased The Maplin Hotel at Frinton-on-Sea and with the assistance of Peggy's daughter, Lesley, and her husband Robert Darvill, the hotel has developed into an extremely popular rendezvous.

The Six Bells was yet another house to come under brewery management following the departure of the last tenants, Dick and Hilda Rose, in 1972. The present managers, Albert and Eileen Jacobs, were installed in 1973 and Eileen vows that the tills go into action occasionally after the bars are closed and everywhere locked up; she is also positive of having company at various times when working at the books, in fact, she is sure it is Clifford Shaw continuing to watch the pub's progress and accepts the phenomenon as almost an intimate and bewitching acquaintance.

The old Goat, standing on the corner of Goat Lane at Forty Hill, is now a private residence, the license having been transferred to the new premises in 1930 still in the name of Victor and Dorothy Parr, who had held the license of the old Goat since 1919. When Vic died the license was transferred to his wife, who later purchased the historical and fascinating Little Abbey Hotel at Great Missenden. The hotel was recently sold after many years of very successful operation.

The license was then held for several years by Wally and Dora Reid, who relinquished the tenancy to take over stewardship of the North Enfield Conservative Club. They recently retired and are now living at Clacton.

The brewers, Trumans, installed mangers at The Goat when George and Maisie Tozer left to take over the catering at the new Starlight Club which had been created and promoted by Tom Unwin, the chairman of the Enfield Football Club. The present managers are George and Molly Matthews.

One of the quaintest little pubs, before being rebuilt was The Robin Hood at Botany Bay, once a comparatively inaccessible part of the parish. The name of the hamlet seems to be a rural joke implying a remoteness like that of Botany Bay, near Sydney in Australia, which was discovered by Captain Cook in 1770, and so named by John Banks, the botanist in his party, because of the immense variety of its flora. It was proposed to use the place for a convict settlement, but the suggestion was abandoned and the location transferred to Sydney instead. The transportation of convicts ceased in 1840.

Elizabeth Sarah Hine was holding the license at The Robin Hood in 1924 and must have held it for a considerable time, for the records show her attending the magistrates court on the 29th June, 1908, for permitting drunkenness on the premises, the result being a fine of £5 or one month's imprisonment! Harry Williams secured the license in 1928 and for several years the old place remained as it had been for the previous one hundred years or so.

The image is still fresh in my memory of the main bar with its sparse, country-style furnishings and almost patternless lino. The surface of the counter had a mellow, naturally dark, beer-soaked unevenness, worn so by decades of thumping pots and coins, this all made to look so much more characteristic by the yellow flickering oil lamps which emitted a harmonious pungent smell. Dear old Harry Williams would visit the town to bank two or three times a week – I am certain his takings hardly warranted it, but he did so love his large brandy and soda in The George at midday! I visualise him now, neatly groomed, always the gentleman; short and rotund with a distinct absence of neck supporting a rather florid baby face with small twinkling, coquettish eyes that betrayed a sense of mischief! His son, Reg, became the licensee of the new house when it was rebuilt in 1935. How quiet and devoid of character the building appeared at that time; it was quite customary in those days to ring the bell for service, especially at midday.

After the war there was little change until Jerry and Win Baldwin obtained the tenancy, making a brave attempt to put new life into the house, but it was not until John and Pearl Heard, after a short period as proprietors of The Woolpack Inn (previously The New Bridge Inn) at Hertford were installed as hosts on 6th February, 1956, that the great transformation began. The premises, situation and locality seemed to accord entirely with their personalities, this was strongly reflected in the outcome of the numerous developments and improvements that followed over the years, making the establishment one of the most popular rendezvous in the district.

An Enfield inn with an atmosphere similar to that of The Robin Hood in 1924, although not quite so remote, was The Fallow Buck, at Clay Hill. The Fallow Buck proudly and neatly bonded into its surroundings at the top of Clay Hill may well be the oldest original building in Enfield. Part of the Royal Chase, the building was used as a hunting lodge during the reign of Elizabeth I. The license was then held by a well-known character named Frank Jelfs, who was seldom lost for words. With Frank and his wife Gladys one could always pass a jolly session if only to listen to Frank's ready-witted irony. I remember calling in when the brewery collector was leaving after his monthly visit. Frank did not fully appreciate the humorous side of the story as he told it to me because he was so hopping mad. Apparently, when the collector told him what a lucky man he was to be living in such glorious countryside, Frank sarcastically retorted (trade had been slack), 'Well, what about a bit of this b— turf for the brewery instead of that cheque?' His great gimmick was a generations-old cured leg of mutton which he had hanging in the bar, which was reported to have been prepared by the landlord for his son's homecoming from the Crimean War, but alas, the poor lad was killed in action the day before he was due to leave for home.

If still existing, the leg would be now some one hundred and twenty years old; it was certainly in a healthy condition when I last saw it, albeit looking somewhat mummified.

At this period there was a tremendous difference between an inn situated a little way out of town and one located in a built-up area. The weather completely controlled the volume of trade, and the only means of transport in inclement weather was a motor-car which then was popular but the price and running costs of which were not within the budget of the majority of customers, and so Frank vacated The Fallow Buck. He had always vowed never to take on a large licensed house with all the attendant pressures it would entail, but eventually, after gaining experience by managing The Holly Bush, he was offered the tenancy of The Cooks Ferry Inn at Angel Road, Edmonton, which he took over in the late Forties. After several years of apparently successful occupation, the distressed or disillusioned man sadly took his own life. Naturally merry and carefree he descended to wretchedness and sorrow as a result of the change.

The Fallow Buck is now in the energetic and enthusiastic hands of John and Betty Wright who took over the license in 1961. This change was another excellent example of the brewers and licensee promoting a scheme that restored the 'olde worlde' atmosphere, but also retained and improved amenities that are appropriate to present day clientele. John had a very successful career in boxing, winning various junior championships, after which he went on to win the ABA title as middleweight, and was unlucky to lose to Lazzlo Pappe in the 1948 Olympic Games. Pappe turned professional and succeeded in winning the European middleweight championship in 1962. John also joined the professional ranks and, after beating some well-known boxers, commenced suffering from a spinal injury that affected the nerves in one leg, which naturally marred his performance. He retired after losing badly to Rocco King from Randolph Turpin's camp. Silly chap – John should have given up. The leg had failed him and, not being able to make use of the ring he took much unnecessary punishment – but there, that was John, game to the last.

The King & Tinker, snugly nestling in the rural and unspoiled White Webbs Lane, is reputed to be one of Britain's oldest taverns. Nelson Hewitt was the innkeeper in 1924. During this period as host, and for many years to follow, the little inn had suffered few changes and was indeed more or less as it had been over the centuries. The oil lamp lighting blended harmoniously with its rather sparse furnishings and an old world and nostalgic atmosphere which was completely conducive to reminiscing with old friends or listening to the tales of the old timers, especially with the accompaniment of some good old draught beer and a spluttering log fire. The name King & Tinker is derived from the legendary story of James I and the tinker. Whilst hunting in the Chase, King James became detached from his party and on arriving at the tavern, he met the tinker quaffing his pot of ale. When asked if he had seen the King's hunting party he replied, 'I never saw the King, sir, in all my old days.' The King replied with a hearty laugh. 'I tell thee, honest fellow, if thou canst but ride, thou shall get up behind me, and I will take thee to see James, the sovereign King,' and so the tinker bewilderingly clambered on the horse and straddled himself behind the King, saying, 'But, sir, his Lord will be dressed so fine, how shall I know him from the rest.' James replied, 'When thou dost come there, the King will be covered, the nobles all bare.' Meeting up with the huntsmen the nobles gathered around, all bareheaded and the tinker seeing his companion was the only one with his head covered flung himself from the horse. The following verses from the ballad complete the story:

> Like one that was frightened quite out of his wits,
> Then down on his knees he instantly gets,
> Beseeching for mercy – the King to him said,
> 'Thou are a good fellow, so be not afraid;
> Come tell me thy name.' 'It is John of the Vale,

A mender of kettles, and a lover of good ale.'
'Then rise up, Sir John, I will honour thee here,
And create thee a Knight of five hundred a year.'
This was a good thing for the tinker indeed;
Then unto the Court he was sent with all speed,
Where great store of pleasure and pastime was seen
In the royal presence of both King and Queen.

The premises were completely transformed when Peter and Margaret Holliday took the tenancy, in 1952. The brewers Ind Coope provided the necessary money to make the alterations which enhanced the antique appearance of the tavern, and superimposed on these efforts were the ideas of Peter and Margaret with regard to furnishings, and unique candle lighting and many other novel additions that completely blended with the atmosphere of the past. The young and charming hosts gave up the license to take over a 'free'(not tied to the brewers) pub, The White Horse Inn at Priors Dene near Petersfield in Hampshire. They were successfully followed in August 1962 by Cliff and Betty Ryan. Cliff was known world-wide in the tough sport of ice hockey and completed his career with the Wembley Lions. As an international he represented Canada during the late Forties and early Fifties.

The Rose & Crown which, seen from afar, looked markedly like nature herself had been responsible for fashioning and placing this very old English inn at the bottom of the valley at Clay Hill, where the site adjoining an ages old brook was known as 'Bull Beggars Hole'. Samuel Nott, purported to be the grandfather or related to Dick Turpin, and by legend was landlord of the inn at some time – certainly in 1635 he rented a parcel of pasture land adjoining which was later sold in the name of Turpin. The freehold was purchased by the brewers, Mann & Crossman in 1908 from Arthur Fish and let on a long lease to Amelia Kitson, the daughter of the Golding family who were well-known multiple licensees in London. The license was transferred to her husband, George, after Amelia died in 1936. He also held the license of The Chase Side Tavern, Southgate, about this period. The Kitson family were also running the following: The Britannia, Barking, The Brooklands Arms, Lambeth, The Jolly Fisherman, Barking, The Edinburgh Wells, Norfolk, The Patricia, Plaistow and an off license at Peckham named The Gadman Stores.

Sonny and Majorie Jacques managed the business for George Kitson for some years until his death in 1957 after which they continued managing with George's wife, Mary, until the lease expired in 1967 when the license passed to Sonny Jacques.

The building and bars were typical of the seventeenth century inn, but much as most people prefer these monuments of the Tudor or Stuart period to remain unaltered, it has been necessary to make modifications, with the minimum loss of character, to conform in some measure with present day requirements and demands, so this old inn underwent very extensive alterations.

The first major upheaval was in the mid-Sixties, then followed the creation of the Crown Bar followed by numerous other improvements and terminated with the new restaurant named the Highwayman's Retreat which was opened in 1970 – Sonny quotes it as being the most altered pub on record.

The result is an excellent example of how to retain atmosphere and charm whilst blending in the provisions for catering and improved areas with sympathetic furnishings for an increasingly selective clientele. The brewers installed a manager when Sonny and Marjorie relinquished the license in 1972.

Eileen Young, another lady licensee, was hostess of the Whitbread's house The Old Bell, Baker Street, in 1924. In 1916 she also found herself at the magistrates court in connection with the No Treating Act, but with a choice of paying a £5 fine or seven weeks imprisonment. This was very harsh compared with the choice Harry Finn, of The Kings Head, had in the same year – only ten shillings or seven days! Poor ladies, always on the receiving end! The present hosts are Ron and Helen Leader, who took over from Harry Conyard in 1966. Ron was the current hard-working and popular chairman of the Northern Suburban LVA (until 1975 when Spencer Leaver was installed).

The license of The Stag, in Church Street, was held by Violet Oates in 1924, and passed to Annie Knight on 23rd May, 1935. It was then only a beer and wine house, and the full license was not granted until 1947. Everybody knew Annie and had an affectionate regard for her. It was unusual to hear someone say, 'I'll see you at The Stag'; it was always, 'See you at Annie's!' She always conveyed the feeling of explosive energy, with a voice that one was compelled to listen to – sharp, clear and melodious. A great character who attracted almost as much news to her pub as the local press gathered! After only two long tenancies covering a period of over fifty years, the house went over to brewery management when Annie left in November 1971.

The Jolly Farmers, Enfield Road, was another typical country inn until it was rebuilt in 1935. Albert Slade, himself a farmer, was the licensee in 1883 and in 1924 the property passed to his son Algernon, but the license was held by Emily Slade, probably his sister. The license until the early Thirties only permitted the sale of beer and wine. This applied to most of the smaller country pubs.

The brewers, McMullens, purchased the property in the late Twenties and Bill and Lottie Smith acquired the license in 1934, and after some ten years of successful and busy trading his cousin Bert with his wife Doll continued successfully until 1954 when they relinquished the license to go into retirement.

The house, very surprisingly, went to brewery management, the commencement of an entirely new era in the tied house system. Avery, Son and Fairbairn were appointed to act for the transfer of the license, and it was not uncommon at this period for the licensing bench to actually contest and refuse the change from tenant licensee to brewery management. Ernie Fairbairn, the senior partner, saw me after the proceedings and explained in all sincerity the extenuating circumstances making it an isolated case, but most licensees thought this act was the foundation for the changing pattern of pubs.

Bert Smith died in February 1960. His wife Doll (still hail and hearty at eighty-six) now lives with her daughter Doris and son-in-law George Smith who held the license of The Black Bull at Fyfield, Ongar.

(The family retired in October 1976 to Writtle in Essex, but the license happily continued in the family when Alan and Margaret, son and daughter-in-law of George and Doris became mine hosts.)

Many old English inns and taverns have disappeared over the years. One such pub was The Vine beer house with Jimmy Doon as the tenant in the middle of the last century. Standing at the corner of Trinity Street, Chase Side, it was described as an old-fashioned bow-windowed place. The licensee later obtained the license of The Little

Wonder, Batley Road, currently in the very capable hands of Gordon and Marion Todd, who took over the license from Dick Deadman on 17th June, 1964.

There was the little White Horse beerhouse in Silver Street almost adjoining Lloyds Bank. The licensee in the 1850s was named Petty whose rent was £14 per annum. The premises were later to become a tobacconists shop run by Jack Tranter.

Another beerhouse quoted in the following advertisement of 27th November, 1896, has long since disappeared:

SEE THIS – Genuine BEERHOUSE, good living and something to spare, ENFIELD TOWN. £200 cash, doing five barrels per week proof, no rent or taxes, all let off, large yard and stabling; only changed hands once in many years, held under large brewers. This only wants to be seen by a working couple – Apply at the Woodman, Baker Street, Enfield Town or to Mr Charles Massina, 46 Park Ridings, Wood Green, Hornsey.

November 27, 1896

The old Nags Head, which has been previously mentioned, was in the hands of the Cherry family for forty-one years. Bert, together with his wife Alice became mine hosts in 1912. Unfortunately Bert suffered a long illness and died in 1920. Alice very ably managed the business during this period and continued holding the license after his death. She was a credit to the licensed trade in every way – popular but strict and extremely exacting, a typical kindly person reminiscent of earlier times with her upright

Victorian carriage; and invariably wearing a white blouse with a high neckline. Her face was so fastidiously groomed that her features gave the appearance of delicate bone china and she was so very precise in words, manner and meaning.

The old Nags Head was demolished during the early Thirties and rebuilt with a more modern theme. Shortly after the license was again operating a lorry crashed through the front wall, finally coming to rest near the bar counter – a miracle there were no casualties. Alice retired in 1939 and the license was taken over by Gilbert, her late husband's brother who with his wife Hilda were the hosts until 1953. They both gave a great deal of their time to the Northern Suburban Licensed Victuallers Association serving on various committees. Their daughter Joan was sister-in-law to Flossie Oakley of The Windmill.

There was always an element of keen competition prevailing between The Nags Head and The George with regard to the 'give away' morning counter snacks, in fact competition became so tough that a canny customer could have quite a satisfactory meal between the two houses with a half of 'bitter beer' in each – cost approximately eightpence (3.3p). Harry and Mrs Conyard, extremely popular hosts, acquired the license in 1953 and had the unhappy experience of closing the doors of The Nags Head to the public for the last time before its conversion to business premises in 1960. (Now Wendy's Dress Shop.) They moved to The Old Bell in Baker Street, having taken the license from Jack Hayden, another well-known and popular licensee.

The landlord of The Alma, Nags Head Road, in 1876 was Robert Vernum whose son Bob presented my wife with an old Toby jug that came from The Alma over a century ago. The original Toby jugs were made early in the nineteenth century for dispensing beer, and portrayed the face of Toby Philpott, a Yorkshire farmer described as a mighty drinker. The water jug in question is modelled on the face of Toby and is advertising old Irish whisky by Mitchells of Belfast. Bob Vernum, who passed away in 1973 in his eighty-second year, was one of Enfield's very likeable and well-known residents.

I well remember my early family visits in the middle and late Twenties, to The Rose and Crown, Edmonton, when Edith Gosling was holding the license. Her charming and attractive daughter Queenie was invariably there and her presence alone would influence a sense of liveliness that encouraged the spirited conversation that enhanced the genial atmosphere. After the sadness of her mother's death in 1927 Queenie continued with the license (much to her horror) until her brother Ronnie was of age to hold it and take over. Queenie later married John Shaw, the doctor who officiated at her birth. What an immensely dynamic and delightful character he was! His decisive, gruff, vibrating voice was attractive and, mingled with his Scottish accent, made all other noises appear to fade in the background. He died on 19th July, 1962 in his ninetieth year. A very affectionate friendship existed between them and A.J.S. and Jennie.

# Chapter XX

Some Enfield clubs and members associated with The George – athletic AAA records of 1924 and 1974 – sports notes 1924 – working at the Rogat Tool and Stamping Co. – voluntary fire service – alterations – prices and comparisons

A.J.S. very quickly found himself involved in local affairs, especially sport. He became a great friend of the Enfield Football Club which then had a team abounding in local characters such as Bert Hird, headmaster of the Chase Side Boys School, who later became a founder member and afterwards secretary of the Enfield Standbrook Bowls Tournament until illness compelled him to retire. Bert passed away on 7th April, 1970. I continue to have the pleasure of taking a little present to his wife, Doris, on behalf of the bowlers a day or two before the annual presentation of prizes. Another player well-known to everybody was Harry Ruskin who, incidentally, became the licensee of The Clay Hall Tavern, grandfather's old pub. An exciting performer was little Wally Green, the will o' the wisp of the team.

One of the best-loved figures was Syd Crowl, a great character who served the club from the early 1900s until after the Great War, during which he played with Tottenham Hotspur. Syd was also one of the Enfield Cricket Club's leading batsmen and its former captain. Jimmy Dyson, still living locally, was a long serving full-back who played many times for his County.

Major Percy W. Leggatt was then president of the club. His family had the welfare of Enfield deeply at heart and in return were held in the highest esteem. The Major or his brother Dudley were associated with most of the town's social and sporting bodies and it was a heartening spectacle to see them riding through the town on their immaculately groomed horses. Later in the day a second progression was made on bicycles. The patron of the Enfield Football Club was W.W. Henderson, MB. Other officials were Jack Skinner, Bob Vernum, Cyril Lea, Reuben Baines, Billy Stear, Bill Newport, Bill Malone, Ernie Tidmarsh (only known to me as Tiddy) and Cecil Pilbeam, a model chairman.

I remember Jennie kicking off a charity match at the Enfield ground in Cherry Orchard Lane, and I possess a photograph of both teams with some of the officials showing Alf and Jennie together with R.G. Porter in the centre of the group. The players look familiar enough with their jerseys and longish shorts, but the others! With their flat caps, skimped jackets, wide brimmed trilbies they look most strange. One little character whose name escapes me has his bowler perched dead centre on a head topping a face that could well belong to a member of the Crazy Gang! I mustn't be too unfair to Jennie as she was the only female there, but how everybody conformed to the fashion of those days, with the men condoning them, is now beyond comprehension.

The Enfield Cricket Club has always had a friendly relationship with The George and the club too was fortunate in having so many conspicuous characters who contributed immensely to its well-being. I recall among those who were members during this period: Stan

Edwards, Ernie Yeomans, Eddie Tong, Billie Finch, Wally Wilson, Bob Vernum, 'Cauker' Boundy, Frank Vanderpump, Don Ellis, Gordon Parr, Reg Allen, Viga Larsson, Cecil Pilbeam, Freddie Slieldrake, Mick Chinn, Harry Walton, Ralph King, Arthur Rosewell, Charles Marshall, Sidney Patman and Stuart Roach. The club, during part of the mid-nineteenth century, played their home matches in a meadow at the rear of The George grounds which then faced part of London Road, formerly known as London Lane. The ground is now occupied by Woolworth's store and The Enfield Highway Co-operative Society's premises. The entrance was adjacent to some cottages where The Duke of Abercorn is now sited in Sydney Road. (The present licensees, Len and Dolly Franks, are now awaiting the date for the premises to be demolished as part of the forthcoming development scheme. They came to Enfield after suffering a similar experience in 1961 when their previous pub The Crown at Southgate was scheduled for re-development.) Onlookers would have made their way there flanked on one side by fruit trees and on the other by a market garden. The land before the development of Sydney, Cecil and Raleigh Roads was known as 'Broomfields' (fields of broom).

Robert Mathison, of The George, catered for the teams on match days. The groundsman was Nat Kingsbury who would drive the team to away matches in a coach and four. One may readily imagine the spirit of conviviality that must have prevailed after partaking of a little refreshment at a wayside tavern when homeward bound. An interesting copy of an account rendered to the Enfield Cricket Club in 1813 was as follows:

*The Gentlemen of the Enfield Cricket Club, 24th August 1813*

|  | £ | s | d |
|---|---|---|---|
| Luncheons served |  | 10 | 6 |
| Dinner for twenty-five @ 3s 0d | 3 | 15 | 0 |
| Beer for twenty-five |  | 12 | 6 |
| Beer during the day |  | 10 | 0 |
| Lemonade during the day | 1 | 6 | 0 |
| Soda water and brandy |  | 14 | 0 |
| Bottles of porter |  | 14 | 0 |
| Bottles of cider |  | 4 | 6 |
| Bottles of ale |  | 2 | 6 |
| Brandy and gin |  | 12 | 0 |
| Eight bottles of wine | 2 | 8 | 0 |
| Supper for six | 6 | 10 | 6 |
| Eating for boy and? |  | 2 | 6 |
| Mr Smith's bill | 1 | 0 | 8 |
| Mr Cuffley's bill | 1 | 13 | 10 |
|  | £14 | 16s | 6d |

Incidentally, present day sufferers from apparently never-ending development schemes may note that such activity was not entirely escapable even in 1813 for this was the year in which Lords (named after the Yorkshireman Thomas Lord) had to change its venue owing to the inevitable building process.

The town's Constitutional Club, which was housed in the Old Palace, had a very close link with The George, and A.J.S. made a host of friends when he became a member. The following townspeople I met through Father then or in later years (quoted for record only and would advise readers to elude unless interested): Frank Robbins, Bill Carter, Bert

Greenall, Stan Edwards, Jim Neilson, Ben Liffen, Sydney Fussell, Dick Clark, Ernie Carter, Stan Simmonds, Jack Skinner, Jack Dafforne, Sid Brown, Dicky Bird, Fred Fielding, Yen Skinner, Alf Maxwell, Billy Finch, Bob Vernum, Lewis Dixon, Dick Spratly, Charlie Berry, Sydney Collier, Harry Rettig, Reg Allen, Tommy Dufton, Bob Laing, Jack Tranter, Bob Fish, Ernie Yeomans, Viga Larssen, Bert Hinkins, Alf Wright, Charlie Maunder, Taffy Lewis, Stan King, Charlie Marshall, Tommy Prudames, Tommy Roach, Arthur Bridger, Tommy Ives, Sid Crowl, Major (later Colonel) Medcalf, Colonel Aplin, Cauker Boundy, Ron Fouracres, Tommy Scott, Bill Carter and family, Harry Postans, Bill Perry, Ernie Winterflood, Bert Bowyer and George Monk.

Another club with whom a close and respected companionship developed was the Bush Hill Park Social Club. Unlike the majority of clubs it attracted the younger element, since one of its main attractions was a first-class tennis section, apart from the extremely enthusiastic bowls section, which could then boast of having some of the youngest members in Enfield. The club held a dinner at The George in 1924 and, although it was held before A.J.S. took over, the names quoted were for years known and respected by our family. Coincidentally we lived in the house in Bazile Road, which was then occupied by Mr Warner Jones, the chairman of the club who presided at that evening's function. Included in the company were: Freddie Hodgkinson, W.J. Gomm, Percy Weaver, H.R. and A. Seymour, Billy Bales, C. Stiles, Alex Watson, Percy Dashwood, Cuthbert Brown, W. Davey, Arthur Goodwin, D.B. Drake, Harry Watson, Rupert Sage, J. Parker, J.B. Jacobs, Al Stiles, J. Flockton, Harry Brown, R. Campbell, E. Edwards, F. Warner Jones, Freddie Briggs, the Taverner family, Edgar Dipple, Frank Newton, the Oxley family and the Scott family.

The North Enfield Conservative Club had its share of local characters headed by their president, Col. H.F. Bowles, supported by R.G. Porter and Dudley Leggatt. Some of the members our family had pleasure in knowing were: Charlie Maunder, Tom Harrington, Harry Beadman, Yen Skinner, Tommy Dufton, Lewis Hill, Alf Lyne, G.V. Fletcher, W. Sweeting, Col. H.F. Bowles, R.G. Porter, H. Jackson, George Empson, Major P.W. Leggatt, George Monk, A. Westwood, W.F. Cunliffe, G. Price, A. Moody, W.J. Biggs and Ernie Tidmarsh (Tiddy).

The old Enfield Athletic Club, now known as the Enfield Harriers following its integration with the Ponders End Athletic Club in 1965, has for fifty years had a gratifying friendly association with The George and our family. In perusing the early records one fully appreciates the tremendous efforts and fortitude required to develop an athletic club to the standard it attained in such a short time.

Their first meeting was convened at Lancaster Hall in Silver Street on 1st September, 1920. For the record I quote the names of those attending: Norman Easlea, Lindley Armitage, Jack Skinner, Fred Blunt, Tommy Dufton, Bill Newport, Bob Vernum, Charlie Maunder, Bert Hird, A.A. Brooks, W.J. Fawley, W.C. Taylor, C.A.T. Harrison, W.A. Hope, A.J. Carnell, A. Scott, A.C. Briggs, W.H. Manning, H. Barwick, L.A. Austin.

John J. Jarvis (later Sir John) accepted the presidency and commendably held this honour for thirty years. On his death in 1950 this office was passed on to his son, Sir Adrian.

The first committee meeting was held at 45 Silver Street on the 3rd November, and the club's initial promotion was an open seven mile walk from Chase Side School (of which Bert Hird was then headmaster) the prizes being in value £3, £2 and £1 – extremely good in those days.

Enfield Football Club accommodated the club for their first annual sports meeting at Cherry Orchard Lane. This was held on Saturday, 23rd July, 1921. This ground was also used from May to August for training at a fee of £5.

The first year's balance sheet at the end of September produced a loss of £16 17s 2d but in 1922 the deficit had been erased, and the club had 15s 6½d in hand. From then on they grew in strength, always expanding and always searching and scheming for ways to raise more money, in common with all other clubs and associations in Enfield who have always been so appreciative of any help given to them, financially or otherwise.

In June 1922 the ladies competed in the annual sports events by virtue of a very gentlemanly action on the part of the committee – an invitation to an egg and spoon race, but in 1924 the ladies section was officially formed and they have since more than proved their prowess in representing Enfield. Their section had its fiftieth anniversary in 1974.

The first dinner and concert was held at The George on 20th January, 1923. The menu, costing 5s 6d, would have been as follows:

Hors d'oeuvres
Soup
Fish
Poultry
Sweet
Cheese and Biscuits
Coffee

The AGM was also held at this venue that year.

Enfield War Memorial Hospital received half the proceeds derived from the sports and fete held in the town park in 1923. This share amounted to the agreeable sum of £26 7s 5d.

In 1925 the sports were held in Durants Park and the hospital benefited by the sum of nearly £50. This praiseworthy effort continued for many years.

Afterwards the event, together with a fair, was promoted in the town park until almost the outbreak of the second world war.

Some more well-known and respected names reinforced the club in those early years, among them Nick Wootton, J.F. Miller, Wally Nunn, Fred Blunt, Cecil Grint, Reg Lunnon, Phil Gale, Stan Blumner, Bill Cook, Mary Amies (later the Ladies Olympic Team manager and eventually president of the club – she died in 1975) and Ernie and Sid Oliver.

Although the boxing section was created, and affiliation to the Amateur Boxing Association applied for in 1921, it was eight years before the first show was promoted. This was held in the Assembly Rooms (Athenaeum) on 6th March, 1929. The enthusiastic members responsible for this section were Ernie and Sid Oliver, Bill Walker and Fred Blunt.

From the profit of £6 the local hospital benefited by £2 and the Ponders End Nurses Fund by £1. The last show under the auspices of the Enfield Athletic Club was held in 1938.

One of the most well remembered active members of the athletic section was C.W. (Sticker) Hyde, who won the AAA championship for the seven mile walking event in

1928, 1929 and 1930 – tremendous feat! When training I found it a problem to pass him while running.

Well do I remember The George as the starting point for the many road walks, the number of entries being anything up to eighty. Little imagination is necessary to appreciate the turmoil and repugnant odours that impregnated every niche in the building from body sweat and embrocation. Everybody at the start and finish went in parties into the only bathroom in the house and never have I witnessed so many knobbly knees and furry legs in one place!

We are glad to report a meeting of a similar nature which is held every boxing morning, the only difference is that in addition to walking there are now races for men, boys and ladies.

Lindley Armitage appears to be the only remaining member of the club who was present at the inaugural meeting held in 1920. He served as a committee member from 1920–1969 and was treasurer for the latter thirty-nine years. In 1929 he was made a vice-president and for outstanding service to the club was made a life member in 1953. He was awarded the Billy Hope Memorial Trophy in 1967. Although no longer a committee member he is still active in coaching, in which he has taken an absorbing interest since before the 1948 Olympics. In recent years he has been associated with UK coaching at national level in the throwing events. It was at his instigation that Jan Kopyto, a former Polish national coach, came to Enfield and was appointed UK national javelin coach. He is a vice-patron of the Women's Amateur Athletic Association and its honorary auditor for many years. His wife Isobel has for many years been an extremely keen supporter of the ladies section, acting as secretary for several years, and she was also responsible in instigating the two major annual meetings.

Norman Easlea, who died in 1972, was another founder member who gave fifty-two years of unselfish and vigorous service at all levels to the club and to athletics in general. He was president of the Race Walking Association and their representative to the AAA, as well as chairman of the Middlesex County AAA and the Southern Counties AAA on a two year term. Norman had the honour of being the senior vice-president of the AAA. A proud outstanding performance or record between Lindley and Norman, so many years of dedication to athletics!

Ken Easlea, Norman's son, is continuing with the club in an extremely active capacity as a veteran walker, having been twenty-nine years with it and was recently honoured with a life membership for completing twenty-eight years of competitive walking. This all began with an accident in a coal mine when a cable wound off a pulley and fell on him, seriously injuring his thigh. While recovering the doctor suggested lots of exercise and that is when Ken realised his challenge.

He has won the Middlesex two mile track walk four times over twenty-one years; the Southern Counties ten mile walk in 1962, was first reserve for Britain against America in the ten kilometres event and was then a veteran. He holds the first class national standard at all distances and has won at every distance, including the London to Brighton walk.

Other important names in the walking section were: Fred Morgan, Johnny Johnson, Jesse Haywood, 'Tich' Marler and Stan Mantor.

The first Enfield athlete to represent Enfield in the Olympic Games was Paul Valla at Wembley in 1948.

The Sir John Jarvis Trophy which was awarded in his memory in 1951 for the club's best championship performance was won that year by Doreen Lee. The following are the winners of the trophy in date order:

| | | | |
|---|---|---|---|
| 1951 | Doreen Lee | 1962 | C.W. Fogg |
| 1952 | W. Ingoe | 1963 | D. Peggs |
| 1953 | S.R. Mantor | 1964/5 | S. Turpin |
| 1954 | J.H. Hassell | 1966 | S. Turpin |
| 1955 | A.R. Ayien | 1967 | P. Pinnington |
| 1956 | C.W. Fogg | 1968 | R. Jones |
| 1957 | P.J. Mellor | 1969 | P. Pinnington |
| 1958 | P. Alsford | 1970 | L. Peck |
| 1959 | J.H. Hassell | 1971 | C. Mathers |
| 1960 | S.R. Mantor | 1972 | C. Mathers |
| 1961 | Helen Claxton | 1973 | C. Mathers shared T. Paice |

Finally in 1974 this coveted trophy was won by Jill Duffield and in 1975 and 1976 this honour was held by Geoff Capes.

The very debatable question of comparisons then and now of records in sport that may be timed or measured, also other sports that cannot, will forever remain a subject to be disputed; so many issues are involved such as equipment, conditions of tracks or ground, also the modern training techniques which in many sports today may be controversial. I quote some of the results from the 1924 and 1974 AAA games. Today the track races are all quoted in metres but they have been converted accordingly:

NOTE: BR represents the AAA National Record and WR the World Record standing then.

|  |  | BR | WR |
|---|---|---|---|
| 1924 | 100 Yards | | |
| | Harold Abrahams 9.9 | 9.7 | 9.6 |
| | (Equivalent 100 metres 10.83) | | |
| | 1 Mile | | |
| | W. R. Seagrave 4.21.2 | 4.13.8 | 4.10.4 |
| | (Equivalent 1500 metres 4.33) | | |
| | High Jump | | |
| | L. Stanley 6'1½" | 6'4" | 6'8¼" |
| | Long Jump | | |
| | H. Abrahams 22'8½" | 23'9" | 25'5¾" |
| | Triple Jump | | |
| | J. Higginson 45'11" | 46'9¾" | 50'11¾" |
| | Putting the Weight | | |
| | R.S. Woods 43'10" | 47'10" | 52'7½" |
| | Throwing the Hammer | | |
| | M.C. Nokes 167'8½" | 172'3½" | 189'6½" |
| 1974 | 100 Metres | | |
| | Steve Williams 10.2 | 10.3 | 9.9 |
| | (Equivalent 100 Yards 9.32) | | |
| | 1500 Metres | | |
| | Tony Waldrop 3.41.9 | 3.38.5 | 3.32.2 |
| | (Equivalent 1 Mile 3.58.2) | | |
| | High Jump | | |
| | Dwight Jones 7'0½" | 6'10" | 7'6½" |
| | Long Jump | | |
| | Alan Lerwill 25'6" | 26'7¾" | 29'2½" |

| | | | |
|---|---|---|---|
| Triple Jump | | | |
| Toshiaki Inque | 52'10¾" | 53'7¼" | 57'2¾" |
| Putting the Shot | | | |
| A. Feverback | 70'1½" | 68'7" | 71'7" |
| (shot weights 16 lbs) | | | |
| The Hammer | | | |
| A. Barnard | 231'8" | 233'7" | 250'8" |

$$100 \text{ metres} = 109.3 \text{ yards}$$
$$1500 \text{ metres} = 1{,}640.2 \text{ yards}$$

The lounge bar of The George then had a country atmosphere; everybody appeared to know one another and this atmosphere prevailed more or less until the outbreak of the second war. A few of the regulars who patronised The George in 1924 were characterised by Day (Arthur Skinner) the *Enfield Gazette* cartoonist. The individual called Ernie was the waiter and his very attitude and posture were typical of the butler seen in a well-known advertisement captioned, 'Your Kensitas, Sir'.

Many of the 1924 Spurs football team patronised The George, especially following the home games, including Jimmy Seed, Tommy Clay, Stan Bliss, Arthur Grimsdell, Bert Smith and Jimmy Dimmock. I was in constant touch with Jimmy until he died in 1972. He played for Tottenham from 1919 until 1931 and of course scored that great goal in 1921 against Wolverhampton that brought the FA Cup back south again after twenty years. The game was played at Stamford Bridge and watched by seventy two thousand paying a record £13,000 for their pleasure. The FA final went to Wembley in 1923.

The Tottenham Football Club incurred a loss of £1,476 in the 1923/24 season and finished fifteenth with thirty-eight points. A season ticket then cost £5 – fifty years on £27.60 and in 1977 £42.75 and unfortunately relegated.

The 1924 Derby winner was the favourite Sansovino. Ridden by Tommy Weston it gave Lord Derby his first Derby winner and the first in the family for over a century. What a diabolical day that was. A.J.S. had organised the usual outing, this time by charabanc, and again I was privileged to be included. Never have I seen such persistently torrential rain. Tractors had to be employed to extricate thousands of vehicles, some of which had sunk in the sodden turf up to the axles. At first we attempted to push our vehicle, but it went deeper and deeper in, and we gave up after several of our party were coated completely in mud. I believe Father paid five pounds to have our charabanc extracted!

Enfield could quite possibly boast promoting the first known race course in Britain which was sited on Bycullah Park and was in operation when James I was in residence at Theobalds. The races were then called Bell Courses because the prize was a silver bell, later altered into a cup; the origin of the phrase 'to beat the bell'. Many residents were pleased when the course was built on around the 1870s since the races attracted an element of rowdyism.

Jack Dempsey was heavyweight champion of the world (1919–1926). Tommy Milligan won the British welterweight championship by beating Ted (Kid) Lewis (my guest in later years) over twenty rounds at Edinburgh (after holding the championship since 1920) and Walter Hagen won the British Open Championship at Holylake with a score of 301 (seventy-two holes).

Borotra became the Wimbledon men's singles champion by beating Rene Lacoste, and Miss Kitty McKane beat Miss Helen Wills (later Mrs Moody) for the ladies' championship. The latter went on to win the championship in 1927. She won it in all eight times between that year and 1938 – a record which still stands.

The early years at The George kept A.J.S. and Jennie very busy. The period offered little to the inactive or to those not prepared to work, but the future appeared inviting to enterprising and adventurous people, and so all obstacles were brushed aside in their abounding enthusiasm and dedication.

As I have mentioned before A.J.S. abhorred lazy, or dilatory people, and as the move to Enfield had terminated my schooling at only fourteen years of age he quickly put a curb on my freedom! After a little conniving with the customers I was under orders to report to the Rogat Tool and Stamping Co, at Queensway, Ponders End. How Father detested clock watchers! Little did he know his son would be doing just that – not exactly because I wished to watch the clock – it just couldn't be helped. The drab, melancholy-looking contraption was magnetically caught in my vision whichever way I gazed. Maybe I would have tolerated it if its hands were attempting to work like my own – from 8 a.m. until 6.30 p.m. nine-and-a-half working hours a day, and all on small repetitive jobs, of which most were manual. The pay appears somewhat crazy now, but for me as a boy to draw approximately 12s 0d (60p) per week, representing fifty-four hours at 23s 4d (1.35p), per hour was reasonable. In 1974 this would represent approximately £61 after taking into account the basic rate calculated on a forty hour week. My goodness, society should be a little more satisfied and civilised than it is now!

The lunch break was divided into three parts – cycling, eating and football. The latter game was played in the fields opposite the factory, where also any altercations, which were few, were settled in a manly way with a good old-fashioned punch-up.

Considering the wages then paid one encountered little militancy, and heard few grumbles other than such as would be expected in a healthy 'freedom-of-speech' barrack room. My recollections were of working with honest-to-goodness chaps who were obviously all mentally geared to the prevailing difficult times. There was certainly no animosity created by failure to belong to the union then. Nothing will ever replace the healthy freedom of the past – so unappreciated today. Why? With affluence should freedom diminish?

Unions are essential and commendable if their aims are conducted correctly, but in so many instances they appear nowadays to be governed by a minority of the tiresome and troublesome extremists who abuse their immense freedom and sap the vitality of the enterprising.

Wally Ball, the foreman for whom I had much respect, was responsible for twenty or more of the personnel for which his pay was £2 10s 0d (£2.50) per week.

I became particularly friendly with two of my colleagues working there – Leslie Myddleton and Stan Statham. Leslie and I set up a small workshop on one of The George's pot-houses and later moved to a room above the old stable. How we would dream of acquiring finance to start our own engineering company! The first customer to suffer was my mother. I conned her into buying the first article produced: an inlaid tray for seven shillings and sixpence (37½p)! I visualise Father now standing at the bottom of the stairs underneath the workshop, in a furious rage and shouting,

'You up there, Stan? – you've fused all the bloody lights again!' I did have some strange antiquated pieces of equipment and I should never have run it all off the lighting supply! Les went on to promote the 'Myddleton Tool Co.' which developed into a sizeable concern. He sold the company during the early Sixties.

The name Rogat was derived from the names of the directors Rogerson and Attwood. Cyril Attwood was later to play in The George 1937 charity golf tournament.

In July 1924 A.J.S. purchased a Douglas motor cycle, which gave endless fun to his sons. I applied for my license immediately and was fortunate in being issued with one which allowed me also to drive motor vehicles as from 31st July. This machine was completely trouble-free. The engine was 2¾ horsepower with horizontal twin cylinders, and the flywheel of polished steel was unprotected. The gears were operated by a lever on top of the petrol tank, having similar action to the old electric tram or train controller lever, and was belt driven. The method of lighting was by carbide lamp, the carbide being a compound, calcium carbide which, when moistened, would yield acetylene gas producing, when ignited, a very fine white light. The gas gave off a diabolical smell, and in earlier years a piece in teacher's ink well would be good for a laugh, always providing one was not found out! I can see it now all bubbling over the desk!

One astonishing feature of this period was that practically the whole country relied upon a voluntary fire service, not until 1935 were steps taken to introduce the professional brigade in Enfield. Brother Alf joined. This necessitated the installation of bells under the bed, and even the unimaginative may easily visualise the commotion and frustration resulting from an alarm. It appears now almost beyond comprehension that Enfield and other large towns managed so efficiently with a voluntary service, and just think of the saving of rates!

A sizeable alteration was carried out at The George during 1925. The small 'still' room in the back lounge was demolished and the service counter continued through to the flank wall that divided the premises from 'Ebbens'. One of the pot-houses was included in the bar space but still no ladies' loo. Evidently the number of ladies using the bar, or the quantity of liquor ladies consumed, was not sufficient to warrant the installation!

In general, the trade was much more simple then and one can scarcely imagine a pub today without the sales gimmicks, and with only manual pumps for the draught beer – uncluttered with the keg points displaying highly coloured lighted points of sale. There were only very few fancy made-up drinks. Bottled shandy, snowballs and dozens of similar mixtures had yet to become popular. Bianco's were almost unheard of – the only really popular vermouths were Martini (sweet) and that was used only for 'gin and it', and Noilly Prat (dry) for 'gin and French'. Today if one asked for a dry Martini one would be served with just that – plain Martini (dry). Until about 1940 the request would have been interpreted as a cocktail with the following ingredients: gin, French vermouth, and a dash of orange bitters served with a twist of lemon. A trinity was gin and mixed vermouths – sweet and dry. A gin and orange would have meant gin and orange bitters and not squash. There was comparatively little bottled beer in the early Twenties while crown corks were generally unknown. Corks had to be drawn by a cork drawer which was clamped to the counter, and opening a bottle of Bass then was as exciting as opening a bottle of champagne today!

A bottle of whisky retailed at 12s 6d (62½p) of which 8s 5½d (42.29p) was excise duty. A bottle of ordinary port was 3s 6d (17½p). A pint of ale in the public bar was 5d (2.08p), bitter in the lounge was 8d (3.33p) pint. Whisky, gin, port, sherry and gin and vermouth were all 8d (3.33p).

In 1925 the number of bulk barrels of beer produced in the United Kingdom was nearly twenty-seven million, and the average strength or gravity was almost 1,043. The excise duty paid was nearly £76 million, and the average cost per pint was 6d (2½p). The total brewing industry profits for the year 1924–1925 was £25½ million. This represents approximately 0.787 old pence or 0.327 new pence profit on a pint of beer at retail prices which then averaged 6d (2½p). We must remember this includes all ancillary profits or income such as rents, investments, by-products and so on. However concerned the consumer was then about profits or the prospect of beer being reduced in price, it was obviously not possible.

The beer output for 1974–1975 exceeded thirty-seven million barrels but the average gravity had dropped to 1,037.26 which reduced the excise duty to a mere £3,043.2 million – enough to make a beer drinker either proud of his enormous contribution to the country's coffers or to have another one to take away his despondency. The average cost per pint then was approximately 3s 7d (18p). The gross profit per pint on these considerably increased approximate calculations would be five old pence or 2.1 new pence. Taking all this into consideration, how many other commodities can show only just over sixfold increase in profits and selling price over the period of fifty years?

Maybe these figures convey little comfort to the anti-tippling fraternity and I can well sympathise with those that under given circumstances have been motivated through personal or known suffering created by excess drinking. My personal interpretation of alcohol is in the context of moderation, in which case imbibing, without a doubt, can be the greatest stabiliser, health contributor, characteriser and social medium known, but I repeat 'in moderation'. If the level of alcohol slightly exceeds a moderate intake the resulting effect could be projected in a thousand different moods letting escape his or her level of degree of charm, humour, reliability, kindness, thought for others and benevolent inspirations! The pity of it unfortunately, as in every other aspect of life, is an insignificant but important number of persons may and do reverse all these pleasures when alcohol is indulged in too freely. Nevertheless I am certain the majority of people do realise that the excessive taxation applied to the licensed trade together with the tax on tobacco have undoubtedly been one of the largest contributions to the country's incomprehensible treasure trove.

Clara and Alice were two of the staff I remember most. The former came with A.J.S. from The Royal to The George and it would be difficult to match her for reliability, honesty and all those perfections that must accompany the ideal bartender. Poor Clara how she suffered the awful embarrassment in such a dignified attitude when Edgar Dipple's poodle nipped behind the counter and tiddled up against her leg! Alice was the housemaid, so typical of the times. Such a little thing but often in trouble. Either she was without her little white lace head-piece, or her stockings were falling down; she was a character in her natural way who could have played a part in any film.

The Eastern Enfield Tradesmen's Association held a dinner and concert at The George in January, 1925. The menu comprised: tomato soup, turbot with hollandaise sauce, roast ribs of beef or saddle of lamb, castle pudding and wine sauce or peach melba, cheese, coffee. The cost would have been around 4s 6d (22½p). The chairman was Owen Feltham, and speakers were Councillor F.J. Spackman, Colonel R.V.K. Applin, MP, C. Sweeting, and E.W. Cottage (press).

Woolworth's opened their first British store in Liverpool during 1909. The Enfield branch opened in 1925 – this extraordinary enterprise of stores projecting sales with a limit of 3d or 6d (2½p) continued until those price levels were progressively phased out through the war years. The reference to 3d and 6d stores was removed in the immediate post-war era but continued in some areas until the early Fifties.

There are, for various reasons, some things that escape the wind of change. For instance over fifty years ago the annual meeting of the Channel Tunnel Company was held at The Cannon Street Hotel. The chairman reported that the prime minister, Mr Bonar Law, stated that if adequate guarantees were forthcoming the money would be made available, and the question was referred to parliament. The engineer, Mr Tempest, gave assurances that the British portion could be constructed for £1¼ million, an equal sum being required for the French half. The project is still in the pipeline, but at a slightly different estimate of approaching £1,000 million!

Again, fifty years ago, the chancellor of the Exchequer refused to introduce the proposal that a charge for admission to the British Museum should be made on the grounds of cost. It was estimated that the cost of installing turnstiles would be at least £5,000 and another employee would have to be engaged at 32s 6d (£1.67½) to operate them. Charges were introduced by the Chancellor in 1974 and rapidly abolished after a change of government.

# Chapter XXI

At the estate office of James Neilson – Theobalds Park Estate – Lady Meux and the 1901 Derby winner – The old Rectory Manor – rent collecting

Early 1925 I left the Rogat Engineering Co and joined the well-known surveyors and estate agents James Neilson with whom I spent four agreeable and rewarding years. I shall always appreciate the opportunities I had of acquiring so much knowledge offered through a variety of subjects and experiences.

Apart from the respected and dignified boss Jim Neilson, and the turbulent but big-hearted manager, Ben Liffen, there was only Miss Audrey Brett-Clarke and Jim Rogers employed at the office in Church Street. Jack Pulling, who joined the firm in 1920, had been transferred to Bulls Cross Farm, the home of Jim and Lillian Neilson, expressly for the county agricultural returns. Few will come better than Jack Pulling, now a partner with fifty-five years meritorious service behind him.

In those days the duties of an employee of a firm of surveyors and auctioneers, especially those firms which undertook agricultural work, were many and diverse. Demarcation lines were unknown, and one had to be willing to do anything, regardless of bad weather or spoiled clothing.

Certain disciplines had to be observed, and we were always conscious that another job might be hard to get! Jim

Neilson was a stickler for time observance, and it was no use telling him you had missed a bus or tram. His answer was that you should have been there in time to catch an earlier one! My own duties ranged from surveying to selling houses and licking stamps. At Bulls Cross Farm Jack Pulling's job covered book-keeping and general clerical work, keeping pedigree records of cattle and pigs, tattooing the ears of cattle and pigs with pedigree numbers and even, after tuition by the local vet, castrating calves and piglets. As a relaxation he did a bit of bird scaring with a 12 bore gun. A herd of pedigree Red Poll cattle and of Middle White pigs were kept at the farm, and a number of show successes were achieved in the Thirties.

I commenced operation by preparing and witnessing a sale of goods and chattels at Arnolds Farm, known as The Paddocks, Crews Hill. With Jim Rogers I entered into the exciting job of finding the articles entered in the catalogue and sticking on to them the respective lot numbers. I well remember my first encounter with Ben Liffen. He arrived on his Douglas motor cycle, sporting his brown leggings, to see how we were getting along at a time when we had been searching for a Venetian ashtray. When this was reported to B.J. he blew his top. 'You, you tell me neither of you know what a Venetian ashtray is – look behind you, there's the b— thing in the fire grate – good Gawd!' Well, you live and learn – the only difference was that the tray caught a different kind of ash.

My starting wage was 10s 0d (50p) per week. I am sure that for the first month or so I was overpaid and could have been little more than an hindrance, although Ben appreciated the little errands I could run, especially for his packet of St Julien tobacco. I was so naïve that when quoting the depth of a plot of land I thought it was the depth downwards. However, it was not long before I had mastered the typewriter, and was conversant with office duties and routine. Although at this stage my knowledge of architecture and surveying was nil, I quickly found myself at home on the drawing board, being forcefully instructed through Ben's long experience.

On the advice of Ben I attended the Tottenham polytechnic for a course of building construction. I was pleased to have a colleague with me from Enfield named Jack Garey whose father was a well-known local builder, and who is now carrying on the business with his son, Hugh. After fifty years it is gratifying to see Jack the chairman of the Enfield Society of Mentally Handicapped Children and working with such a deep sense of purpose. To so many people this charity means little, due to the dated and true saying, 'What the eye does not see, the heart does not grieve', but if any charity is worthy of consideration, this one must justify the thought, if only to consider momentarily those wonderful people who care for these tragically stricken persons.

I would often cycle to the poly, and on one occasion when late I was making up time by following a tram – full speed with no wind resistance! Suddenly, I was plunged into blackness. the flight through the air stopped with a crunch as I hit the other end of a deep gaping hole. As I lay huddled and semi-conscious, someone looked down on me and shouted, 'What the b— hell are you doing down there?' The road was under repair and the night watchman had taken away the rope to let the tram through, and me!

Neilson's managed the Theobalds Park Estate comprising some three thousand acres and stretching over Crews Hill, Cuffley and Cheshunt. The estate is still managed by James Neilson but the area has dwindled to only 2,000 acres, the majority of which is divided into seven farms.

The following is a brief historical report of this once royal estate.

About 1559 Sir William Cecil, secretary of state to Edward VI and Queen Elizabeth and the throne's leading counsellor for over fifty years, chose the Manor of Theobalds (then known as Tibbalds or Thebaudes; the name of the previous owner) as the spot where he might erect a small mansion as a residence for his younger son. After a visit from Queen Elizabeth in 1564 he planned to enlarge the house so that he could entertain her with the magnificence becoming his queen. Labour was provided for the poor in the gardens, and it is said he scattered pleasure around him like a fountain that could not be exhausted, and that he made the palace dance with delight. In 1571 he was created Baron Burleigh by Elizabeth, who took great interest in the estate and repaired to the palace fifteen times with her court between the years 1564 and 1597, enjoying Burleigh's sumptuous entertaining and staying from three to six weeks at a time. His second wife, Mildred, died after forty-three years of companionship that was happy and affectionate, and the loneliness and despondency that followed in his advancing years hastened his end and in 1598, when his seventy-eighth year, he passed away.

On Lord Burleigh's death, Theobalds passed into the hands of his second son Sir Robert Cecil, who later became Earl of Salisbury. He also assumed the highest offices of state, becoming chief minister to Queen Elizabeth, and after her death in 1603 he was confirmed in office by King James.

Extracts from the MSS of the Marquis of Salisbury (Theobalds Park):

## The Confession of Joseph Calton, Parson, for Hunting in the Old Park of Enfield

*Examined in the Gate-house at Westminster he confesseth that John Rice and William, servants to one Wilde of Edmonton, farmer, and John Humphrey of Edmonton, labourer, were in his company at the Old Park of Enfield. The said Rice, William and Humphrey met him between examinates house and Wilde's house, and brought a dog with them, and examinate brought another dog of his brother-in-law, Nicholas Rodesby.*

*They came from Edmonton through the common field called the Hyde and so the next way to the Old Park, and not within the Chase, and there put on the said dogs whether they killed anything or nothing he knows not, and after seeking for their dogs and not finding them they departed altogether, thinking their dogs to be taken up by the keeper. No more dogs or persons were in their company. Denieth that he ever heretofore was at any time hunting in the Chase or Park.*

27th May, 1578

The examination of John Humphrey, taken by Sir Thomas Barrington – 25th July, 1578:

*Examinate saith that between Easter and Whitsuntide last, being at one Wilde's house at Edmonton as a labouring man, Thomas Wray came to see Wilde's dog on a Sunday, with John Rice, his servant. They persuaded examinate to go with them to hunt in the Great Park of Enfield. At the time appointed they went to the Park and put on the dogs, but whether they killed or no examinate knoweth not, for they lost their dogs. Joseph Claton brought a staff to Wray's house, and Wray willed him to leave his staff and take a long bow and arrows, which he did.*

25th July, 1582 – Earl of Warwick (Hatfield House) to Lord Burleigh (Theobalds Park):

*Albeit – I have otherwise diversely made myself beholding to your Lordship yet in respect I have not much troubled your game at Enfield I would hartely request you to bestow a Buck of this season upon me ther. The deere thrive so badly at Hatfield as I am not for this year able to pleasure neither myself nor any friend I have with a Buck ther.*

Henry Middlemore (Tenant – Enfield Palace) to Lord Burleigh (Theobalds Park):

*Craves Burleigh's resolution with regard to the purchase by him of some part of Mr Abington's lands. Would have waited upon his Lordship himself but his lameness would not suffer him. His grief which was hitherto in his hip is now fallen with greater extremity of rage in his foot, and he lives in great torment of pain, but in greater fear of the gout.*

An interesting entry referring to barges on the River Lea dated 8th September, 1588:

*Richard Broke of Ware hath two barges. The Great Blue Lion, the burden whereof is 42 quarters and worketh with five men, and the Little Blue Lion of 28 quarters with three.*

*Robert Doe of Enfield hath one barge, The Maltesacke, the burden whereof is 38 quarters and worketh with four men.*

*The masters of the barges are in number 44, the servants working in them are seven score and odd.*

*Appended are Lord Burleigh's notes, as follows: The burdens of the barges 1m 1c (1,100 quarters). The numbers of men occupied 1c xxiii (123). A great barge costeth 40 marks (£40) with all the furniture. Greatest barge laden draweth xvj (six inches). Least also draweth XVj.*

*They laid on Saturday and Monday go down to the Boo (Bow) Bridge to carry the tyde. From ye Boo with the tyde they will pass in four hours if they roo (row) away. They came on to London with fludd (flood tide) and return at an ebb to the creke mouth and then with a flood. The lock at ye Bow do open at the first beginning of flow. They shut it at the highest of the flood. They come from the Bow to Waltham in six hours, and from Waltham to Ware in another six hours.*

*Examination of John Pennyfather of Cheston in the County of Hertfordshire, taken at Enfield the 8th October, 1595.*

*The said examinate being met in a place called Balstocker in Enfield, going to London with a close basket and seven partridges some alive and some dead, confesseth he took them on Tuesday the 7th of this month a little after sunset and was carrying them to London to one Mr Stapleford, one of the Queen's purveyors, at whose request he took them for the Queen's use and service, as he saith, and should have of him for every quick partridge 10d. Being demanded how long he hath used this trade and how often he had taken the partridges in this manner will not confess but this only time.*

*Being further demanded of whom he had learned to take partridges, he saith he hath seen divers take them, and nameth one, Vale belonging to the Lord Chamberlain or to some of his gentlemen and saith that Vale is an ordinary taker of partridges and dwells at Hadley.*

*12th October, 1595. Sir H. Cocke to Sir Robert Cecil – has this day received his letters touching one Pennyfather and son who he perceives have lately offended in taking of partridges – an old occupation of the fathers for which he had heretofore been punished. The son many other ways is a very lewd fellow, and ran away above two years past with another man's wife from Cheshunt, for whom the writer has often sent forth his warrant. God willing, will, with all convenient speed do what is possible against them. From Punsbourne the 12th October, 1595.*

*U. Skynner to Sir Robert Cecil. Relative to one brought before him at Enfield by Mr Hayes whom Mr Hayes met going to London with partridges taken against the Statute and Who's examination he sends herewith.*

*He has since brought as his surety, Mr Stapleford, a purveyor for Her Majesty's household, mentioned in the examination, who affirmed, as much as is contained therein denied that he had ever any partridges on him but three and those for Her Majesty's diet, and these were pretended to be, but misliked much the taking of any so near Lord Burleigh's house (Theobalds) where Her Majesty so often resorted and had cause to have them preserved for her own disport, beside Burleigh's pleasure, and Cecil's resorting also more frequently. Westminster 11th October, 1595.*

James stayed four days at Theobalds on his way to London from Scotland to take possession of the crown. It was reported that the Scots who accompanied him to his new Dominions brought with them their dirt as well as their poverty. The Countess of Dorset registered her surprise at the change which had taken place at Theobalds since the preceding reign in regard to the want of cleanliness. Soon after quitting the palace she found her retinue swarming with those tiny adherents which in our day seldom infest a countess's train.

In 1607 Robert Cecil then Earl of Salisbury exchanged by royal request Theobalds mansion with the far more valuable palace and manor of Hatfield known as Hatfield House, which, of course, is still in the possession of the Cecil family the sixth Marquis of Salisbury being in residence. This majestic Elizabethan House is open to the public during the summer months.

King James died in 1625 and his son Charles was proclaimed king. He spent much less time at Theobalds than his father. He ruled the country without parliament from 1629 to 1640 and then came the Civil War. He set out from Theobalds on the 3rd March, 1643, to raise his standard at Nottingham, and after seven years of intrigue and bloody civil conflict Charles, after a questionable trial held in the medieval Westminster Hall, was executed in front of Whitehall Palace on 30th January, 1649.

Although the survey of Theobalds by the commissioners appointed by the Cromwellian parliament reported the majestic building in excellent repair and recommended it not to be demolished, parliament decided to do so; but it appears the deciding factor was money, because the building was estimated to be worth £200 a year exclusive of the park, but razed to the ground the materials would realise £8,275 11s 0d! This period unfortunately witnessed the end of so many of Britain's fine buildings which we should be enjoying today.

Later the site, the park and the manor were granted by Charles II to George Monck, the Duke of Albemarle. On his death in 1670 the estate passed to his son Christopher the second Duke of Albemarle at whose death the property lapsed to the crown again.

William III of Orange in 1689 presented the grounds and park and what little remained of the palace to William Bentinck, Earl of Portland, which later was possessed by his son Henry, Duke of Portland.

The manor was separated from the park and house, and towards the end of the eighteenth century was inherited by Oliver Cromwell the last male descendant of Henry, the Protector's son – ironical that the estate, once the residence of King Charles I, should finally be in the possession of the descendant of the one who had undermined his authority!

In 1762 the estate was sold to one of the Prescott family, after which the remains of the palace completely disappeared and in 1765 the present mansion was erected, some distance away.

The Prescott family leased Theobalds to Sir Henry Meux, the brewer, in 1820 and after his death in 1860 the estate was purchased by his son, Sir Henry Bruce Meux. In 1878 he married Valerie Susie Langdon who later was responsible for the lavish entertainment so frequently enjoyed by famous people. Shooting and hunting parties including the young members of the aristocracy were constant during the seasons, Edward VII and George V were regular visitors for the shooting. The novel additions Lady Meux had installed were a great attraction to her guests and included an indoor real tennis court and swimming pool, a roller skating rink, gymnasium, Turkish baths etc. There were numerous other attractions such as a museum which included an outstanding collection of Egyptian antiquities as well as the mummy and coffin of Les-Asmu.

The Turkish baths were well padded steam rooms with varying degrees of temperature; I remember one was called The Trepidariam, and the gymnasium had a number of unique electric-powered mechanical exercising machines, one of which reproduced the exact action of the movement of a horse when walking and trotting either fast or slow. Another similar machine simulated the effects of a moving camel. Many a happy hour did I spend in this miniature sports complex.

Sir Henry died in 1900, leaving his wife one of the richest women in the country. Dame Valerie Susie Meux died in 1910 and the estate passed to Hedworth Lambton, the third son of the second Earl of Durham. He married the daughter of Lord Arlington, the widow of Viscount Chelsea. The name Meux was assumed in 1911. As beneficiary under the will of Dame Valerie the estate was left to him on condition he assumed the name Meux in preference to his surname of Lambton. He was a former MP for Portsmouth and later became Sir Hedworth Meux, Admiral of the Fleet. Following the demise of Lady Meux (née Chelsea) Sir Hedworth married Lady Charles Montagu (the Lady Meux we would have dealt with during my period with James Neilson 1925–1929).

The house continued to witness some great social occasions, but nothing comparable with Dame Valerie in her younger days, although one long twenty-first birthday party in the Twenties lasted some four weeks and was attended by many important persons of the period including the Prince of Wales.

Admiral Sir Hedworth Meux was also a racing enthusiast and bloodstock breeder. He owned and ran Glasgow Stud Farm at Crews Hill as a racing and breeding establishment from about 1912 until the farm was sold to the British Bloodstock Agency in 1928.

The Admiral had little or no interest in betting, but was a great sportsman.

When he died in 1929 nothing at all of his considerable wealth was left to his wife who had no issue. The estate and his fortune was instead left to the youngest daughter of Lady Chelsea, his first wife the Rt. Hon. Victoria Gilmour, who would have been the beneficiary had he not changed his name to Meux. Her son Sir Ian Gilmour MP, now owns the estate through trustees.

A large oil painting which hung in the Elizabeth bar at The George for nearly fifty years has now been loaned by the Standbrook family to be displayed at its original home – Theobalds Park College. The picture was executed by Lutyen at Theobalds and depicts Lady Meux (Dame Valerie) with Volodyovski, the horse she bred to win the Derby in 1901. She was the first woman to play any decisive part in the history of the Derby. The horse was known by the name of 'Voly' or 'Bottle o' Whisky'. Lady Meux leased him as a yearling to Lord William Beresford, VC, who sent him to be trained by the American, John Huggins, at Newmarket. Unfortunately Lord Beresford died in the December and his widow and executor, Lilian, Duchess of Marlborough, maintained that the lease of the horse automatically continued, but Lady Meux thought otherwise, and a law-suit resulted. Mr Justice Grantham decided the lease was personal and terminated with the death of his Lordship.

Lady Meux then leased the horse to the American sportsman W.C. Whitney, who continued the colt's training with Huggins. There were twenty-five runners in the 1901 Derby and 'Voly', ridden by the American jockey Lester Reiff, was made favourite at 5–2. Winning by three-quarters of a length Voly set a new record time of 2m 40 4/55. An all American effort with the owner-breeder producing the goods but gaining no credit – how this typifies our complacent England!

The Beresford Trust was founded in 1903 by William Whitney in memory of Lord William, and to create the fund he gave the equivalent of the Derby prize, which was £5,670, in investments and securities. The beneficiaries were stable and stud employees or those unable to work through old age or ill-health. The trust is still functioning.

I also possess a catalogue of the eight day sale held at Theobalds from 15th–26th May, 1911, by order of the executors of the late Lady Meux. The auctioneers were Waring & Gillows and the catalogue displays 1,670 lots including 10,000 ounces of fine antique silver, a large percentage of this dating from Elizabeth to George I. This alone would have been a fine investment; today worth something over three million pounds, and probably sold for something under eight thousand pounds. The catering at the sale was arranged by Mr Gargine of The White Hart Hotel, Buckingham; the luncheon being two shillings (10p) and two shillings and sixpence (12½p) per head.

Lady Meux would regularly phone the office from her London residence, number 10 Portman Square, and request the farm to deliver some eggs, farm butter, and a chicken or two. Jack Pulling would take them from the farm to London on his motor cycle. He also delivered similarly to Mrs Gilmour's flat off Park Lane.

Neilson's office was then situated next to the gates of the old palace, about the centre of where Pearsons stands now. It was comparatively antiquated but on entering one was responsive to the quietude and the almost drowsy atmosphere that was superimposed upon and strengthened by the mellow, pungent odour thrown off from old papers and old books.

A shelf around the office supported an array of large steel deed boxes displaying the names of some of the important clients, such as Admiral Sir Hedworth Meux, Sir Henry Bowles, Sir Duncan Orr-Lewis, Major Bosanquet, Alfred Bath, Col. Somerset and Alfred Maxwell.

Well do I recall Ben requesting me to repair the large circular swivel chair in the inner office. I was always quite brilliant at dismantling anything, but not quite so competent rebuilding. However, in this instance I was more than satisfied with my efforts – ball bearings were all cleaned and greased and as I whirled around on them I was a little proud. Ben arrived back from lunch soon after 2 p.m. and within ten seconds there was the most awful confused sound of bangs and crashes that I could only identify with the complete collapse of the office. Bewildered I went to see what had happened – one second's glance and I had the answer. The rotating seat was in two pieces and poor Ben had one half of the seat on his head, his sacred pipe was broken, his legs poked out the other side of the desk and he was so excited he couldn't speak. In the complicated exercise of disentanglement I never did know what he called me. I was so pleased it was not the boss; he was such a big man!

Sir Henry Bowles, then Col. H.F. Bowles, was MP for Enfield from 1889 until 1906, and until his death in 1944 he was very active in all aspects of Enfield life. I always had that sense of awe when I was sent to hand over papers or documents at his dignified residence Forty Hall at the top of Forty Hill. This stately mansion set in delightful grounds is open to the public as a museum with emphasis on local history. Part is used for exhibitions, and facilities are provided for banqueting and other functions. It was built by Sir Nicholas Raynton (Lord Mayor of London 1640) in

1629. He purchased the estate from William Lord Cecil, Earl of Salisbury, in 1616, and added Elsinge Hall to his estate in 1635, but haplessly for Enfield this great house, steeped in royal history, was pulled down soon after its purchase. The manor house of John de Enefielde in 1350, and the manor of Worcesters as well as a one time residence of the children of Henry VIII, represented a part of Enfield's history that has never really been related or exploited in any detail.

Miss Audrey Brett-Clarke, now my wife, was well-established at the office when I arrived. She was very precise and proper, as was befitting in a young woman of that day and age, with a first-class secretarial training. Moreover I did feel slightly inadequate and humble, but one day I was lotting up a farm sale when I was sent back to the office for labels to be placed on the hindquarters of horses. Well, I made a bit of a muck of the request, and I cannot think what I called that rear part of the horse, but Audrey saw the funny side of it, and from then on the barrier was swept away. We became good friends, so much so that I invited Audrey to an evening out, and thinking only the best would do, I hired a limousine which I left in the next road before walking to the house, scared I might give the wrong impression. What excitement when we were ushered into a box at the Wood Green Empire with a pound box of chocolates. As a final act of conceit and extravagance I produced two programmes – one each! The sequel is that about a month afterwards we were attending Wood Green Empire with free passes by public transport, with no chocolates – and only one programme.

Neilson's had an office at Cuffley, just a wooden structure resembling a garden shed but adequate at that time, as the land for sale was then being released from the

Meux estate. During the summer I attended two days a week and how noticeable was the placid undisturbed emptiness. I would walk up the short, steep Plough Hill where perched on the top was the old Plough Inn. Dear old Lizzie Rideout would cook and serve my lunch – all for one shilling and sixpence (7½p) including a shandy.

Her husband was a tall, gaunt-looking man, happier, I am sure, tending the animals than being fettered to a stuffy pub. I never went in or out without my eyes being attracted to the many pictures illustrating macabre scenes which occurred during the great war when the Zeppelin shot down by Leefe Robinson, crashed near The Plough. The monument commemorating this episode is but a few yards away.

Little did I think when I sketched Lower Hanyards Farm from the office that, a decade later A.J.S. would have obtained the license for the pub and that my view afterwards would be obscured. When I look at the pen drawing now it appears quite a ramshackle place; the Wombwells were farming it then. Next to the office were a pair of delightful thatched cottages. The one nearest was then a tea shop which, in fine weather, was extremely busy catering for trippers. What a rum old customer the proprietor; fantastic tales he unwound to me. The land towards Northaw Road was free of any buildings. Opposite and next to The Cuffley Hotel were two wooden cottages erected during the first war and which later I owned. They were recently demolished to make way for new flats. On the opposite corner was the station master's house.

Cuffley was then so devoid of life during the week that if, having shut the office for any reason, a couple were seen to be walking my way, I would double back and open up, so as not to miss the enquiry should that be their purpose.

How I implored A.J.S. to buy land at Cuffley; the average price was £2 10s 0d to £3 per foot with a depth of 200 ft. Cuffley Hill was completely virgin on the North side, and the woods with their dense undergrowth seemed to resist the immoral attack of survey and development! Ben was an extremely talented person at his job of surveying and architecture but in addition his vast store of general knowledge seemed infinite. I must record that basically the whole development of Cuffley was due to Ben with, of course, my uncertain and doubtful help, although I must admit he did have me to unleash his feelings on when things went wrong. This reminds me of an incident which again involves his beloved pipe. We were taking a measurement on Cuffley Hill – billhooking our way through the tangled undergrowth. My finger was in the end loop and I was attempting to control a 66 ft measuring tape, with surveying pins in the other hand, while Ben was tugging and snatching at the tape so much that I really feared the end of my finger would be severed at the top joint, so with the next big tug I let go. What a relief, but where was Ben? He had completely vanished. I had walked forward some ten paces when I saw a flushed face, slightly distorted with fury, pop up out of the ground – Oh, good heavens, he had fallen into a ditch. The appalling, or rather frightening thing was that the end of his pipe was missing again! Imagination only can convey the violence of his language.

As one wanders back in memory, life seems more and more a cocktail of 'ifs, buts, whys and ups and downs'. I am reminded of another side of Ben. His wife Nellie, who already had a daughter named Joan, gave birth to a boy, whom they named John, but after only one month the baby died. Ben asked me if I would go back to the flat over the office and help him move some furniture around. On arrival I found a distraught Ben who beckoned me to follow him upstairs – no speaking, just actions never since can I remember such complete and utterly devout silence. Ben led me straight to the baby lying in the pram in the centre of the room so pathetic, only a little lily on the baby's chest and it was difficult to believe that life had been extinguished. Poor Ben; perspiration was pouring from him. The whole time I was there Ben tip-toed, and I naturally did likewise. We moved things with extreme care, as if it would have been blasphemous to have made any sound.

William Neilson (Bill) joined the firm in 1927/28 having attended Merchant Taylors School and completing his education at the College of Estate Management where he had the honour of being the first president of the students' association. He certainly livened the office up even if he did operate at times in an unorthodox way. He could, and would, bluster his way through anything, but he was always an extremely deep thinker, easily diagnosed by looking at his finger nails, of which there was little left! We became great friends, for he was a very philosophical character with whom it was impossible to disagree. How sorry I was that A.J.S. never fully took the advice given by the Neilson family with regard to hotels and sites. Lack of funds was the major reason, but four of the sites were passed on by A.J.S. to Charrington's Brewery, one of which was The Cuffley Hotel site.

I well remember one of Bill's crazy exploits when he purchased an old 'T' type Ford for £3. The car had been in the open for a considerable time and after inspection he decided the thing was too far gone even to consider on-the-spot repairs for driving it home. So off he hurried to the farm, later returning with a great farm horse and cart together with pick axes and shovels with which we dug it out of the stoney soil. To think only another three feet and we could have buried it! However we roped the contraption to the rear of the cart and trundled it away to Bulls Cross Farm. I cannot ever remember feeling more stupid. If only this enormous horse would break into a gallop, I was thinking. Bill was relaxed, he had something to do, at least the reins had to be held. As for me I was sitting bolt upright – no other way of sitting in a 'T' Ford with hands clutching the steering wheel while attempting to look intelligent, which was not possible and I was aware of it! Bill quickly repaired this captivating conglomeration of old iron and had endless fun driving it on the private estate roads. He was under age for a car license.

The Westmore Land estate off Green Street was developed by Neilsons, and I remember going to check some land measurements with Bill, taking an unused new steel 66 ft tape and ten new survey pins, presented to me by Ben with such solemnity as if he were handing me the crown jewels for safe keeping. Well, a little tug here and a little snatch there soon made two separate tapes of it! Alas, Bill was not a little bit perturbed when returning to see Ben – I think he slid off for a cup of tea and so did not witness the explosion. This is one of the estates upon which, when developed, I would spend the weekend. I have a copy letter which was sent to the office enclosing ten shillings as a deposit on number 12 Westmoor Road. The houses were selling for £600.

Another important building development projected by James Neilson was the old Rectory Estate in 1926, the houses of which front Parsonage Lane and Baker Street. The old manor house, called the Rectory, unfortunately had to be demolished, and only the exquisite wrought iron entrance gates were saved; these were sent to South Kensington to be exhibited in the Victoria and Albert Museum.

I spent a considerable time in the old manor measuring and taking stock of this and that just before it met its sad fate. One cannot help feeling a measure of sorrow in witnessing the end of any building, especially one mellowed with age. The old Rectory had endured the weathering of four centuries if only the sadness could be compensated by the exhilarating thought that such a building could unfold its complete story before destruction came. One could wander back in time listening to all of the strange happenings, the intrigues, the merriment, the grief, the hatred, the kindness, the pride, with scenes of haughtiness or humbleness and, above all with the characters playing their lurid turbulent, and hilarious parts?

The old Rectory Manor, which was formerly known as the Manor of Surlowes, was no doubt granted out of the Manor of Enfield after William of Normandy had defeated Harold at Hastings and bestowed on his first war lord, Geoffrey de Mandeville, the lands and lordships of Enfield. These were previously held by the Dane named Asgar who, under Edward the Confessor and Harold, held the exalted military rank of the 'King's Staller' or 'Master of the Horse'. He was wounded whilst fighting with the London contingent at Senlac, after which he was carried back to London where he conducted the defence against William. His fate seems to be unknown.

The Domesday Book, in the year 1086, quotes the Manor of Enfield as belonging to de Mandeville and valued at £50 with an approximate area of something over 5,000 acres, one hundred and fourteen households and an estimated three hundred and fifty to four hundred inhabitants.

This Rectory Manor was granted to Lord Audley in 1538 by Henry VIII and after reverting to the crown it was assigned by Henry in 1548 to Trinity College, Cambridge.

Still impressed deeply on my memory are the surveys of this proposed housing estate, the marking out, the sets of plans for the council and my tracings of them. I see Ben working himself up in a frenzy when the very quiet and likeable Arthur Harston, the well-known local builder, would arrive ten minutes late for the appointment at 9 a.m.!

Monastery Gardens, the new road through the estate was named by Ben Liffen's wife Nellie after being chosen from the many names suggested by the staff.

The houses were offered at £825 to £875 freehold, or £700 to £750 leasehold, and could be purchased from £100 down with the balance spread over fourteen to eighteen years.

When I think of the choice and extravagant things for amusement offered today compared with the meagre entertainment then – my mind flits back to the Old Queen's Hall (referred to previously) in 1924 – the flickering hazy pictures all brought to life with Nellie Liffen (Ben's wife) reading the film as music and transferring the moods, the excitement and laughter to the keyboard of her sharply-tuned tinkling piano. I see the cowboys galloping into hell with the baddies waiting t'other side of the hill, and Nellie giving it her all. The twinkling fingers crash on the keyboard as if hell was descending, the tempo and crescendo has arrived at such a furious and terrifying pitch that the audience are gasping surely they must all be doomed, then silence. The whole scene changes, the hero has the baddies covered from the rear and they release his lover – the rest must be imagined, but only with the piano in mind and Nellie now tinkling cunningly to awaken and stimulate the senses of the patrons watching the touching love scenes.

One of my big-hearted deeds at the office was to look after Joan (Ben's daughter) whilst everyone was away; sweet little Joan who was not six years old wanted to play something more exciting than hide and seek so we settled for Cowboys and Indians for a little more action. Well! She must have worked up a little paddy – perhaps she thought I was having the best of it, so unbeknown to me she collected a great round ebony ruler, and the next time I stealthily popped my head around the door and murmured some silly remark like 'Boo' or 'Gotcher' she had me, wallop! with all her revengeful might right across the eye. Never since have I witnessed a black eye so perfectly complete. I told Ben the door slammed in my face. When I meet Joan now she continues to remind me with so much laughter that almost says, 'I won that game'.

What a jovial character Jim Neilson was – and what happy memories I have of parties at the lovely old eighteenth century Bulls Cross Farm. Bill and I would spend an evening there whilst Jim and Lillian, with Agatha (I only knew her as Aunt Agatha) would go out for the evening and Agatha would slip back and give Bill and me a cigarette each! Jim died in 1942 aged sixty-nine and Lillian died in 1970. Bill is semi-retired; and now drives every week from his home at Porlock, Somerset, to visit the office, and to attend the Enfield Rotary Meeting. Jack Pulling's son, Stephen, is a partner with the firm and the consultant architect is John Neilson.

Monday morning rent collections always had an air of mild excitement about them, whether brought about by the time factor or by wondering as to what would impede my progress. There were excuses as to why no rent was forthcoming, complaints regarding repairs and requests to see the landlord. It was an extremely busy morning but to anybody who thought a little deeper than the mere collection of money there were object lessons in human life. Here one witnessed right and wrong priorities and encountered the crafty, the open and honest, the moaners, the clean, the grubby, the filthy (only one), those poor, who yet had pride and those who were better off but without any. There was a difference in the smells which came forth when the front door opened, from the sweet fragrance of an early Monday morning wash to the sour airless odour of decay. Of course, the majority, say ninety per cent, nice, clean living people and, as with all minorities, a few to make things bad for the rest. The normal rents then ranged from about 8s 0d (40p) to 15s 0d (75p) and apart from the tenants, the landlords were finding it extremely difficult in those days to maintain their property, and efforts to sell this type of property for investment met with a very poor response. As a typical example Neilsons sold Colchester Cottages adjoining The George, four in all, to Charringtons in 1926 for £930, the rents being 7s 8d (38.33p) to 8s 4d (41.66p) per week inclusive of rates. This was not much of an investment an average income of 32s 0d (£1.60) per week out of which the rates, cost of decorating and all repairs were paid. These cottages abutted on to the annexe or old stables at The George and were demolished in 1972 in connection with the new development programme. The annexe was also to be included in the scheme.

Vine Lane, a passage leading from the town and adjoining Pearsons' original shop on the corner of Sydney Road, was on the market by Neilson's at £100 a foot (there is doubt as to the eventual sale), the frontage being about eleven feet. This showed the crazy property explosion – it was an astonishingly inflationary price! As for the large corner site, now occupied by Howard's, it was on the books for some twelve months at £5,000 – when offering the property to a proposed purchaser at that price the vendor was usually confronted with a look of antagonistic indignation. One could almost hear his thoughts, 'He should be inside'. How things change!

To arrive at the value of The Falcon, Waltham Cross, I was detailed to make a plan, find the cubic capacity and arrive at the price by estimating at so much a cubic foot. Billy Scott, the licensee, was very accommodating and held the tape when taking diagonal measurements. It was sold to Meux Brewery in 1927 for £10,000. Incidentally I had an extraordinary and lucky skid while on my way there. Cycling in top gear, with a following wind of gale force my brakes locked and when I came to a halt without falling off I looked back and saw a thin black line. I waved a motor-cyclist down and asked him to hold the end of a tape to help measure the line – it was an amazing 106 ft 6 ins. The act would create a little fun today – if one had lived to tell the tale?

With great support from the Neilson family and firm, and with enthusiastic help from Bob Beadman I organised my first charity promotion at The George. It took the form of a buffet dance in 1927, and the proceeds were donated to the Enfield War Memorial Hospital.

# Chapter XXII

The beginning of the 'strike new look' – clothes and music – brother George at Standard Telephones and the fish shop – strike of 1926 – the motorist – roads and cars – The Crown Inn, Elsenham and rough cider – alterations and some old music hall stars – Alf marries Edna Tyrie and takes over The Lord Brooke – Walthamstow – George replaces Alf at The George – George and A.J.S. in a clash – my first car and motorcycle at the displeasure of A.J.S. – the early 'dirt-track' racing and Reg Pointer

One outing to Ascot Races organised by A.J.S. in 1925 or 1926 was filmed by Sydney Bird – a valuable record of the personalities attending and of the attire then considered fashionable. When I saw the party off I thought Jennie looked just wonderful but – Oh, dear! – however did anyone suffer these extraordinary designs for so long? I projected the film for occasional charity shows in spite of attempted bribery by Jennie to keep it from being exhibited.

That period must have been the only one that attempted to conceal the shapeliness of the female figure completely. A droll and unimaginative flat-plank effect was created by putting the waistline somewhere below the hips and the result, helped by the wearing of a camisole, appeared to be modish, with some variations, until about 1929. The suppression of femininity was lightened by a modicum of excitement when the hemline was raised from three-quarter to knee length, and so, with a careless or brash manipulation of the legs when sitting down, the sinful but exhilarating glimpse of an elegant and colourful garter, or even the suspenders, may have been observed! Not before time came the breakthrough to a new era – corsets and combs were discarded, brassieres appeared, the bust was in favour again and womanly gracefulness reappeared.

Thank goodness the male has never suffered the extremes of fashion or whims of 'way-out' designers. Men's attire since the last decade has been almost devoid of change, except perhaps for the elation of a change from the double-breasted to single-breasted jacket or the devilishness of an inch off the width of the trousers. One extreme change of this period was the introduction of the ridiculous and ungainly 'Oxford Bags' – so wide were some that given a wind and an umbrella one was almost certainly out of control. The 'plus fours', although primarily designed for golf, were commonly worn informally. They were, indeed, extremely comfortable and were invariably worn with a colourful pullover.

One item of male clothing which seemed senseless were 'spats', the buttoning operation which often called for the use of a button-hook. Then there were the stiff white collars which, during dressing, were capable of sending any placid-minded person into blind fury.

An attempt was made to popularise brighter footwear with white and brown brogue shoes, but a man had to be careful not to appear too rakishly dressed otherwise he could easily be stamped as 'one of those'.

Tails and white tie were normally worn at all ladies' functions, and dinner jackets the invariable dress when attending the theatre – now one has more chance of seeing a streaker than such a fastidious dress. Almost everyone possessed a trousers press to sharpen up the razor-like creases.

Edward, or Teddy as he was affectionately known, the very respected and idolised Prince of Wales, appeared in gayer shirts and shocked many by wearing them outside his trousers – well, I never did! Whatever will they be up to next? The new look soon caught on. The prince was, without doubt, a great ambassador for Britain.

The girls were beginning to be freed from their shackled lives, and a general relaxation of the orthodox way of life was in progress. Hairstyles were changing – out went the bun and plaits and in came the bob, shingle, Eton crop and the Marcel wave. A permanent wave was to be had but I believe the operation was quite an ordeal.

Although the sentimental ballads have never really faded, the popular old music hall songs have lived through without ever losing their popularity. In the Twenties there was a vast change in popular music. The tempo changed, beat music was introduced and with it came the rhythm, blues, jazz and syncopation. The Black Bottom was the first stamping type of dance. I remember this was followed by the rhythmic and eccentric Charleston and, of course, the foxtrot, one-step and quickstep were popularised. Some of the first bands in the world dispensed the new tempos – Jack Hylton, Billy Cotton, Debroy Sommers, Jack Payne, Roy Fox, Harry Roy, Ambrose and Oscar Rabin, also the Savoy Orpheans. Len Franks, the licensee of The Duke of Abercorn (at the rear of The George), was a member of the latter band for many years playing the saxophone and clarinet.

To anything of high quality or pretension to superiority the word commonly applied in a jocular sense was 'posh', the derivation of which seems to refer to the custom of the more affluent passengers travelling by liner to India or the East who would book their cabins Port Out, Starboard

Home... This is said to have had its origin in travelling conditions through the Red Sea, when the cabin would have the benefit of the sun during the morning and the coolness of the evening on the outward journey, and *vice versa* in the opposite direction.

In 1926 brother George resigned from Standard Telephones, where he had been employed as a toolmaker at a basic wage of 18s 0d (90p) including bonus, but with piecework he would draw something comfortably over £3 per week. On leaving he was slapped straight into the fish business. A.J.S. had purchased a redundant pub at Stratford and changed it into a wet and dry fish shop with a restaurant above. Considering George had not the remotest idea of the trade he made a remarkably good job of the operation. Unfortunately the general strike brought the country to a complete standstill on 4th May of that year and although it lasted nine days (the miners stayed out until November) the exercise was to say the least disrupting, and this greatly contributed to the early closure of the business.

I well remember visiting George at the shop, having ridden his Matchless motorcycle from Enfield. On arrival he gave me a furtive and smug look and announced, 'I want the bike for market tomorrow – how will you get home?' knowing full well the only way was for me to walk with the strike in full swing!

Just to jolly-up my depression a little he said gleefully, 'Throw up a couple of herrings whilst you are there' – slimy things! Oh, and didn't George 'winkle and shell' when he came home!

The eleven miles home took me about four hours, including a stop at a coffee stall at the top of Kings Head Hill. Unfortunately, I jumped a lorry near The Green Man, Leytonstone, and instead of being taken to Woodford I found myself speeding along Whipps Cross. I had travelled over a mile before it slowed sufficiently for me to jump off.

Considering the magnitude of the '26 strike, the operation was conducted in an atmosphere of responsibility by all factions. Bearing in mind the thousands of volunteers (by the third day London had mustered about twelve thousand five hundred) who answered the call to man the essential services, drive the buses and trains, etc, there was comparatively little violence.

Naturally some ugly scenes occurred, such as attempts to stop motor cars conveying people to work and attacks on buses manned by the volunteers, but overall there was not the hot-headed and violent extremism that would erupt today and, my goodness, there is little comparison in their demands and needs then!

The first half of the Twenties witnessed a new priority with the prices of the motor car beginning to be within the reach of a wider section of the public. The outstanding difference in motoring then was the pleasure and excitement of the unknown; today it is the frustration and displeasure of the known! Can one's imagination really visualise our roads with only finger-post signs and no other distracting impediments. To know where one is going on strange territory today a passenger lookout is imperative if one is to ever think of reaching a destination on time. Imagine – not a marking on any road, not a crossing, not a beacon, no traffic signals, no white lines, no yellow lines, no lanes, etc., etc. But then the driver had to think and drive with the utmost discretion, and running over a point duty policeman was a good deal more serious than knocking an obelisk down. The motorist then was well-compensated for his unsophisticated machine by having the freedom of the road, absolutely no complications in finding anywhere in Britain and no parking problems. One could pull in almost anywhere for a picnic. There were no one-way streets – today if one should slip-up, the consequence almost heralds the end of the world. Hordes of confident motorists (who know where they are going) take on this attack of their right of way with blasts on horns, flashing lights, cannibalistic screams and glares registering anything from plain disgust to murder. Always, however, despite all this there is usually some kindly spirit who reacts to this desperate plight and helps to extricate one from a whirl of now-idle vehicles! These same pent-up, nerve-racked drivers when away from the crazy busy thoroughfare though, can be embarrassingly and insistently courteous in giving way when driving in narrow lanes with their passing laybys. Oh, well! 'If born in China you talk Chinese.'

In 1925 A.J.S. bought a great old seven-seater touring car called a Paige, with a six cylinder engine which, I believe, was 40-odd horse power. (In 1921 another model held the speed record of 102 mph.) It resembled a small charabanc and to pull the hood over in stormy weather by oneself was a man-size job. The tax was then £1 per horse power and with the car's gluttonous thirst for petrol it was understandable when A.J.S. disposed of it and purchased a new Wolseley tourer of 11-odd horse power for £225.

Saloons and limousines could be obtained and were quite common in the early Twenties, in fact they were produced as early as 1906 but the cost was prohibitive for the average person. We had many happy trips in the new Wolseley, especially on Sunday afternoons to The Crown Inn, at Elsenham, in Essex. The licensee was George Haylock whose son, George, was living with us as one of the family at The George Inn. A personal friend of brother George since 1919, he was one person sadly missed at the fiftieth anniversary on 24th June, 1974, he having passed away in the latter part of the previous year.

On one occasion I accompanied George to Elsenham on his Matchless motorcycle, and a hectic day ensued. George Haylock and his family were all there and an early start was made in the bar by an attack on some scrumpy, or rough cider, and as the two Georges seemed not to have a palate for it, I consumed their share as well. After the morning session we all went to Sir Walter Gilbey's estate to look around the stables and to see the race horses. I remember little, my head was spinning and, in fact, if someone had asked which horse I would have put my money on I would have bet on the stables by the speed they appeared to be moving! I was still feeling distinctly peculiar on the way home and somewhere along the road in Epping Forest I requested George to stop to allow me to ease my discomfort in the woods. I walked to a cluster of trees by a large filthy and stagnant pool thinking, 'I can't hurt that'. Whether the pool thought differently or not I shall never know, but I was executing the last act of this undignified proceeding when I fell in. My foot caught in an above ground root, I pitched face down with arms outstretched and my hands entered the slimy watery mud. Down and down I sank to my elbows, slower and slower until I realised the serious plight I was in. I shouted for George and, being unable to turn my head to see if he was coming, became a bit frantic. However, he arrived in time to pull me out when my face was within three inches of that foul slime. The new light-coloured tweed overcoat I was wearing resembled a sack which had been dragged out of a tar-boiler – and the stench made farm silage smell like roses.

When the lounge bar of The George was closed for alterations, as has been mentioned previously, a temporary bar was erected in the hall on the first floor. It presented a novel and popular change and, with a pianist and violinist engaged, it was business as usual. Occasionally artistes were engaged and I remember A.J.S. having some of the old timers whom he knew, to entertain. They included Tom Costello, who popularised the songs 'Comrades', 'At Trinity Church, I Met My Doom' and 'In the Nineties'. I remember being sent out to give Tom Costello something he had left behind after he had just boarded a tram. They were hard times for a good percentage of the great ones in all spheres.

A.J.S. loved the theatre and the music halls of which his knowledge and memory were amazing. A book was presented to him in 1953 by a great friend, Vallance Lodge, who was known to so many of the well-known names in the theatrical world, who inscribed in the book: 'Alfred – the master historian of the 'Halls' from a humble also-ran, Vallance.'

Sometime during this period A.J.S. had a very fine temporary bar constructed for use at functions. It incorporated all the fitments and amenities of a permanent bar and replaced the old trestle tables which had been masked by white cloths. There was a peculiar ruling under the licensing laws that there must be no appearance of permanency or professional image of a temporary bar. Soon after the new bar was operating members of the licensing section, headed by Sir Henry Bowles, paid a routine visit. Just one look was sufficient for them to size up this new piece of useful furniture, and we waited to know its fate. A little muttering together resulted in a decision that the bar was too much like a bar and that the height would encourage people to lean or loll on the counter! Back came the benches, which must not exceed table height and which had clean cloths for every function.

In 1926 brother Alf was married to Edna Tyrie, the daughter of Tom and Flossie Tyrie, who were then licensees of The Sir Robert Peel, at Woolwich. They were also hosts at a number of other pubs, including The Telegraph, at Stratford, The Railway Inn, at Enfield, and The Railway Arms, at St Albans.

Following the wedding at St Andrew's Church, at Enfield, reception at The George and their honeymoon at Westbrook, Cliftonville, they became hosts of The Lord Brooke, Shernhall Street, Walthamstow. Alf was then only twenty-one years of age.

Several times I went to The Lord Brooke and relieved Alf and Edna from their duties for a few hours, and it was on one of these duties that I had my first experience of fiddling. The barmaid was dropping two shilling pieces into the pewter washing up well, but I pulled the plug out first!

On one occasion when I had promised to relieve Alf it was so foggy that Jennie said I would be crazy to make the journey by road. I was of the same opinion a little later. The two-stroke motorcycle I then possessed refused to start, not a sign of life – up and down the road I pushed it, nearing exhaustion. I made one final attempt, opening the throttle and ignition inspired by a bit of temper. I had arrived at a maximum running speed when I let in the clutch but, instead of the normal signs of starting that encourages one to keep going, the machine leapt forward like a rocket and out of my hands. I just managed to grab the rear carrier bar and momentarily I was dragged horizontally along the ground. Needless to say I was a little shaken after picking myself up from the gutter but the stupid climax was that I had lost the motorcycle. The one and only person who had appeared displayed a curious, questioning and suspicious attitude when asked if he had seen a motorcycle laying about somewhere. I eventually found the thing in another road, fortunately not damaged sufficiently to stop me groping my way to Walthamstow.

Brother George replaced Alf as cellar man and right hand for A.J.S. It was not exactly a paradisical way of earning a living but, as one used to long hours and very little free time for relaxation, eighty hours per week seemed not unduly amiss. George always made the best of everything, was almost abrupt in his decisions, was determined, and, moreover, with an infectious sense of humour without a little of which in those days life would have been much the poorer.

I remember one evening when the family was sitting out on the verandah after closing time and A.J.S., giving George a little advice, ended by saying 'You're a fool.' Undaunted and quite cheerfully George retorted:

'He said to me, "You're a fool."
'I said, "Who?"
'He said, "You."
'I said, "Me?"
'He said, "Yes."
'I said, "No."
'He said, "Oh!"'

How stupid, but quoted snappily it fitted the moment and tickled A.J.S. so much everyone finished up laughing at each other's amusement.

A.J.S. also had his favourite little sayings and phrases – two of which were always being offered to the boys: 'You can't put an old head on young shoulders' and 'The proof of the pudding is in the eating'. His 'hokey pokey', 'golly wobbles' and 'abso-bally-lutely' were regularly quoted in their suitable context.

In the young upper middle class one would use words such as 'Spiffing!' and 'Ripping!' and one's parents were referred to as Mater and Pater.

Enfield's Bycuflah Athenaeum, which was destroyed by fire in 1931, stood where now stands the Old Oak Garage, Windmill Hill. Later to be known as the Assembly Rooms the premises offered the town's only hall suitable for concerts, musical productions, etc. A.J.S. promoted a charity dance band contest there with all profits from the bar being donated to the local hospital. What a sweat A.J.S. had worked up that night; Cecil Charrington, the chairman (1923–1949) of Charrington & Co, a kindly and affable person, was the guest of the evening – an extremely important night for Father which warranted a brand new outfit of white bow tie and tails appropriate to this dignified occasion, but George quickly put a stop to all this propriety. Being in charge of the victualling he had forgotten the port, not once, not twice, but – well, Father for the third time (having now dressed for the occasion) asked, 'You've taken the port, George?'

Before George could answer, Father said excitedly, 'Give the bottles to me, I'll — do it myself' (Bottles were then filled from casks.) He dashed across the main beer cellar, bottles in hand, tripped over a beer pipe and fell full length in an open drain! (George had taken the grating off for cleaning.) His suit was ruined, immersed in all the bar waste water and he was just ready to explode. George walked over to him, took one look down and burst into laughter. (How he ever got out of that cellar alive always baffled me.)

One outcome of the dance band competition was that Billy Sears, the leader of La Boheme Dance Band, led his men into second place and he has been engaged from then on to officiate on various occasions at The George and elsewhere, including the fifty years celebration on 24th June, 1974.

Until the evening of the dance band contest A.J.S. had not spoken to me for weeks because I had purchased a car for £27 10s 0d – a second-hand Swift – and he made it very clear that I was in no position to buy even a pair of roller skates, let alone a car. However, that evening the car was useful and when the hectic and successful evening was eventually over everyone finished in a merry mood over a drink, with Father all smiles.

However, the car was once again to attract the displeasure of A.J.S. when I thankfully sold it to the two sons of one of his esteemed and regular customers. It appears that on their second or third outing one of the wheels became detached, another was just hanging on and I believe the other two were cracked.

One of my early mechanical purchases was a Scott Squirrel motorcycle from Reg Pointer. His family were the proprietors of the town's main newsagents situated next door but one to The George and, incidentally, the premises in which John Meyers once published the *Enfield Gazette & Observer*.

Why I so much as thought of paying Reg £26 10s 0d for this machine, knowing the rigours it had undergone, I shall never know. The whole town was disturbed in the early hours when Reg started his round of deliveries, and the way he rode would have done justice to a Brooklands racer cornering, or a 'wall of death' rider gone berserk. The noise would have competed favourably with a flight of Concordes!

Reg became one of the early, well-known dirt track riders winning the first ever race on British soil at High Beech, Epping, on 19th February, 1928, and he later captained the Harringay team. He also won the MacMillan Cup at the Enfield Motor Cycling Club meeting in 1926, on my 494 cc Scott Squirrel, No. EP 2365. Jessie and Bill Pointer continue to run the business but now from London Road.

Early in 1927 I was eventually allowed £22 10s 0d in part exchange for a new Dunelt for which I paid £43, leaving the remainder on hire purchase at £2 6s 8d per month. This had the luxury of dynamo lighting.

# Chapter XXIII

The Tudor Room at the Palace and the new Constitutional Club – Elizabeth I visits the Chase – the country then and now – George marries Phyllis Chandler – I eventually enter the business – the cellar then and my early experience of the trade – the Performing Rights Society – The Thirteen Club – Whitewebbs Golf Club – Whitewebbs and the Gunpowder Plot – 1930 – FA Cup Final

By 1928 the development of Enfield was progressing rapidly. One of the major alterations was the demolition of the old Elizabethan Palace which has been referred to earlier. This was followed by the felling of the Uvedale Cedar tree. and later the offices of James Neilson, together with three other properties – Charlie Lamb (butchers), Youngs (photographers) and Stapleton's (dairy) were pulled down.

Prior to this uncivil undertaking I had been detailed to take the measurements of the large panelled room, which contained a very fine carved stone chimney piece, and the original thick ornate plaster ceiling in geometrical design, displaying alternating impressions of the crown, rose and fleur-de-lys. When the exact measurements of the perfect and imperfect parts of the room were ascertained, Ben Liffen designed a building to contain as much of the interior as was worthy of inclusion. This building, known as the Tudor Room, was designed as an extension to Major Leggatt's house, Little Park, in Gentleman's Row. Ben had one of each of the ceiling motifs framed, which he later very kindly presented to me, and these were on show in the Elizabeth Bar at The George, but are now on loan to the Borough of Enfield and displayed at Forty Hall. Little Park, Gentleman's Row, now owned by Godfrey Groves, JP, who has fortunately nurtured the town's ancient past by adding his important collection of records and books, and many other items of interest, which enhance this delightful room – the only piece left of Elizabethan Enfield, apart from the Tudor Building of the grammar school.

Ben also designed the new town Constitutional Club premises in Old Park Avenue, having previously had the palace as their home since 1906. Unfortunately, the original design was too costly, resulting in paring down the existing design, which invariably is uncomplimentary to the original as happened in this instance. What a job tracing those four sets of plans.

The official opening of the Constitutional Club and Bowling Green, known as the town Conservative Club since the late Forties, was on Saturday, 30th June, 1928, with Col. Sir Henry Bowles and Maj. P. Leggatt officiating; the former had been the club's president since 1890 when their headquarters were originally opened with premises in London Road. He and Major Leggatt also contributed practically and financially towards this new project. The officers then were: chairman, Frank Robbins; vice-chairman, Bob Laing; treasurer, Jim Neilson and secretary, Dick Spratley.

It is not known whether Princess Elizabeth visited her manor house or palace on Enfield Green when in April 1557 she journeyed to Enfield Chase to hunt the hart (male red deer). Leaving Hatfield Hall (now Hatfield House) the retinue consisted of twelve ladies in white satin riding the light ambling saddle horses known as palfries, accompanied by twenty yeoman on horseback and dressed in green. Arriving at The Chase the royal party were met by fifty archers wearing scarlet boots, yellow caps and armed with gilded bows, each of whom presented Her Grace with a silver-headed arrow winged with peacock's feathers.

Another interesting and unique house named Claysmore, which stood on the lower north side of Clay Hill was demolished, much to my sorrow, in 1937. The site was later purchased by Mr and Mrs Stevens who erected a modern house on the location in 1954.

Claysmore was built by Mrs Hume after purchasing the land between The Rose & Crown and The Fallow Buck, ten acres of which was conveyed by Mary Turpin in 1765. There is little doubt that the latter was connected with the notorious Dick Turpin, whose grandfather is said to have kept The Rose & Crown. The house was purchased by James W. Bosanquet in 1847 and continued to be in the family until the mid-Twenties. His grandson, B.J.T. Bosanquet (1877–1936), invented the googly by experimenting with a tennis ball on a billiard table which eventually revolutionised spin bowling. B.J.T.B. played for Oxford University, Middlesex and England in the great period of C.B. Fry and Jack Hobbs. Reginald Bosanquet, a well-known controversial newsreader of ITN is the son of Bernard. When the family vacated Claysmore the property was let for, I believe, £125 per annum to Lady Tree (daughter of Sir Herbert Beerbohm Tree) a well-known and popular figure in theatrical circles. (Neilsons were responsible for collecting the rent.)

When the house became vacant I viewed it with the intention of creating a first class residential and dining club there. The premises were ideally suitable with unusual amenities including an exciting dining or function hall some fifty feet long with a great open stone fireplace and several large distinctive old stained glass windows, one of which covered one end of the room and contained some remarkable specimens of the thirteenth century. I tried extremely hard to find someone to finance the project but without success.

Whatever A.J.S. was doing staying at the Charing Cross Hotel on 26th June, 1928, on his own, I shall never know. He must have had an extraordinarily good excuse for Jennie to sanction the night away, but it has left proof that a night's stay with breakfast was 9s 6d (47½p) – the cost today (1974) is £15.95 including gratuities and VAT.

The country was comparatively poor pre-war, but there appeared a far more collective enterprising projection than now, and no wonder! Today the defence of a business, home or job is almost made aggressive by the precariousness of life, and in the main the extreme radical changes are far too frequent, no doubt due to crazy world changes, high bank rate, taxation and rates. No wonder the powers that be bear conflicting ideas for the cures, and it is very understandable that a normal minded person pulsates with frustration.

In contrast I well remember the Enfield Shopping Festival in 1929 between 20th April and 11th May, promoted by the Chamber of Commerce. The spirit of the whole promotion was so amicable and light-hearted. The shops entering had a blue star displayed in the windows, and through the issue of coupons, which were exchanged for voting papers, various prizes could be won, the first prize being £100. Children's competitions were also included. The three-penny souvenir handbook also contained about three thousand words of Enfield history with many photographs; some one hundred or so; shops and firms advertising.

On 4th June, 1929, brother George married Phyllis Chandler, the youngest daughter of Ben Chandler of The Holly Bush, Enfield. What a charming and pretty girl she was, always composedly dignified with all the qualities essential as a partner in the licensed trade. Following their honeymoon at Westgate they commenced their new life the hard way by managing for A.J.S. at The Eagle, Stratford, a fairly tough assignment at the age of twenty-one. I was approached by A.J.S. to see if I would like to join the business and take over the 'cellarman come all else' job George had vacated, but it had little appeal, because basically I was a fresh air and freedom crank. Those hot evenings spent relieving in the bars on Saturdays, heads down, swimming in beer, toddlers and prams outside, noise with the general kerfuffle sometimes nauseated me – no, it was not for me! Somehow though, I felt somewhere along the line I would finish up in the business, but not just yet! Father had a saying with which I never fully agreed, but more often than not it was right. 'There's a price on everybody's head,' and so when I was offered the same wage as George had been receiving the job seemed to be viewed in a lighter aspect, and I accepted the position at an exciting wage of £3 10s 0d (£3.50) per week.

My sister, Peggy, was working in the business then, having recently left Godwin Girls' College at Cliftonville. This was comforting, as the change for me was a little disturbing, having reluctantly left James Neilson and, of course, my wife-to-be; rather different after working with her and also being free at least three evenings a week. Now I had only one evening a week off duty. A depressing change, but one quickly acclimatises and adjusts to a new life.

The first move I made was to try and be rid of troublesome persons, and the start was made with an extremely quarrelsome individual whose family was known to almost every publican in Enfield, and, therefore, shall be nameless. He was a tall, lithe, wiry character who could easily have fallen out of the story of *Treasure Island*. He displayed a shade over one eye, that appeared the focal point of a face with bloodless, slightly scarred skin that seemed to be stretched unevenly on a frame which pulled the mouth higher one side than the other. Well, I called him to one side before he started drinking, and explained my intentions. We entered into a pact that the only time he would use violence was if I was in trouble! He had the offer of behaving and staying or leaving then; he chose the former, and from then on we were good friends, and I cannot remember any incident that followed that was uncivil.

In those days the hub or focal point of a licensed house was the cellar. In many ways they were more easily organised in so much as the cellarman was working with only four or five draught beers and possibly eight to ten bottle beers, but there was far more work attached to its operation. For instance, all the dark beers were fined down in the cellar; a simple operation requiring more feeling and care than skill. One could sense the amount of rousing before and after the finings were added by condition or look of the head on the surface; the finings used being Isinglass, which is the air bladder of a fish, invariably sturgeon, that is dissolved in an acid solution. The liquid that coagulates resembles a very thick colourless oil and when applied will clarify the beer in a matter of hours by throwing out all the suspended yeast and other particles. There was a sense of achievement when after clearing the tap and drawing the first glass of crystal clear beer it was tasted – ah! none better.

Cooled cellars were unheard of then and when one looks back, it appears almost miraculous that the same cellars only touched sixty-five degrees during the hottest weather. The temperature was controlled by covering all the barrels with sacks, also the opening to the delivery flaps, and soaking them in water at least four times daily.

A partition was built across the lounge cellar whilst Alf was cellarman, making another cellar for coal. Three or more years later I found a full barrel of bitter beer under the coal in the lounge cellar. I can only assume the cask was there when the cellar was partitioned off, and a load of coal was delivered whilst Alf was off duty. How it went unnoticed we shall never know, but over a period of three or four years, considering the amount of coal used at that time with the minimum of eight large fires regularly burning, one would have thought the stocks must have diminished sufficiently to have exposed it? The beer was not bad when I sampled it – somewhat vinegary! I bet A.J.S. had Alf on the carpet one month for bad stocks!

An early experience of being tuned up to the customers' level of thinking was when a miserable-looking, shag-smoking regular sitting in his arm-chair at the end of the counter in the public bar called me over and ordered a pint of ale. Having, as I thought, put a perfect convex head on the beer, looking enticing enough for an advertisement, I took his money and returned with his change from his sixpence. When leaving he called me back – 'Hi, Boy, can yer get a double gin in there?' 'Think so,' said I, and promptly did as I was told, and awaited payment. He looked up at me with a smug grin and said, 'Isn't it the law that you must serve a pint?' I answered, 'Of course.' 'Well, how the bloody hell did you get that double in there?' he retorted. I paid for the large gin – one shilling. The incident never happened again!

The following was served to the Enfield Masonic Lodge on 14th October, 1929, at 5s 6d (27½p) – hors d'oeuvres, tomato soup, fried fillets of sole, anchovy sauce, roast rib of beef or roast leg of lamb, peach melba, cheese, coffee.

An extraordinary contraption A.J.S. purchased in 1928 was a Panatrope, a double turntable record player with speaker amplification to the bars. An enormous piece of equipment requiring large electric motors which were housed in the cellar. The apparatus was designed for use in cinemas. There was one particular record (could have been more), that struck a note or notes that frequently took about a quarter of an inch from the top of certain glasses as if accurately cut with a diamond; they were mainly glasses standing on the pewter under the counter. Fortunately there were no accidents, but there were occasions when the detached ring was found on its own on the pewter giving a clue to the remainder being in use!

This system of relayed music in the bars was quite a new innovation, but it was not long before somebody pounced on the idea of not being satisfied with the royalties paid, and invented a new system of extracting money from the persons playing the records in public which was named the Performing Rights Society. One may imagine my annoyance at being told by (as I thought) a customer, the numbers of certain records that had been played and that we would have to pay a fee for doing so; what impudence. To have the impertinence to tell me what records we were allowed or not allowed to play! It must be remembered at this period the business man was not plagued with the modern inflationary methods of employing so many administrators and snoopers to see everyone conforms to the hundreds of rules and regulations that beset the hunted retailer or manufacturer. So neither we, nor any other licensees, took any notice, especially as our trade paper gave the impression that everyone should ignore the notices, until a licensee was taken to court and lost the day, suffering a £100 fine. This completely changed the situation, especially as our final notice expired next morning! Never before had I seen Father so anxious to drive to London – with the cheque of course!

A.J.S. and twelve friends formed a little dining club – the main object seems to have been to defy superstition by naming it the Thirteen Club. The menu dated 5th December, 1929, is preceded with the following verse:

## *The Rime of the Club Jester*

> The bold Thirteeners dine tonight
> In a brotherhood that's glorious.
> Vain superstitions we'll put to flight
> Pell-mell by rites uproarious.
> 'Gainst ladder, salt and looking-glass
> We fight, their powers scorning,
> So here's to the sailor that love a lass –
> And – we won't go home till morning.
>
> Dickon

The club lived but a short while; fate decreed a cheerless sequence of hapless events. I remember a number of the unfortunate occurrences, but I am certain every member, or one of his family, suffered one way or another, with A.J.S. being the last to be involved in 1939 (of which reference will be made later).

My old friend Wally Hunt and his father, Micky Hunt, were regular customers and friends of A.J.S. Wally won the lightweight amateur boxing championship in 1927 and again in 1929. I accompanied Father on both occasions. Wally gave me a fascinating book called *Fancy-Ana, A History of Pugilism from 1719 to 1824* – a record of every major contest, compiled one hundred and fifty years ago.

The impression is often given today that pub catering is something new, but from 1925 I remember the appetising snacks that were prepared for the bar, including prawns (hand peeled) on toast, anchovies, sardines, every type of sandwich which could include fresh lobster, crab or home-made brawn, and there was always a counter hot cupboard with sizzling sausages or welsh rarebit on sale.

Bill Pratt, later known as Boris Karloff who portrayed the Frankenstein character in the horror series, would call at The George when on a visit to his home town from America. Some years before he was a regular playing member of the Enfield Cricket Club.

Wherever one stands in Enfield there seems to be a fragment of history attached to the spot or thereabouts. I wonder how many out of the thousands of golfers and visitors to Whitewebbs Park and Golf Club realise the fascinating, but little known, history of the estate.

The original White Webbs House which was sited on the north side of White Webbs Lane was built within the estate of the Manor of Worcesters and in 1570 or thereabouts was granted by Queen Elizabeth I to her physician, Robert Huicke, who had also attended King Henry VIII and Catherine Parr. From evidence produced following the Gunpowder Plot the house was said to have played an important part by the perpetrators using the premises with its numerous secret passages and priest holes to meet and survey the progress of their conspiracy.

Catesby, the leader, was impassioned by the suppression of the English Catholics and requested their complete liberation, but without success. Thomas Winter was the first to be taken into his confidence after which John Johnsonne (alias Guido Fawkes) soldier of fortune, was introduced by Winter to play his part in the scheme. They were later joined by many others, but the original eight conspirators took the oath in a lonely house set in fields near St Clements Inn, London.

Following the first intimation of the method of warning their friends and relations who would be attending parliament at the time appointed for their revengeful deed, Catesby, Winter and Fawkes met at White Webbs House. They were later joined unexpectedly by Tresham who was related to Catesby and although he was a mean dispirited man and not completely trustworthy, he was furnishing the enterprise with the immense sum of £2,000. In all probability his later action saved England from the ghastly plot. He passionately pleaded the discretional warning of his brother-in-law, Lord Mounteagle, but was refused with great determination, and so he desired the plot to be deferred on the grounds of being unable to produce the money at that time.

There is little doubt that Tresham was the perpetrator of the anonymous letter received by Mounteagle obviously warning him of the forthcoming horrific act. The letter was immediately conveyed to Whitehall and shown to Cecil and other ministers; the king was notified on his return from Royston where he had been hunting.

Tresham was absent for several days, but eventually faced Winter and Catesby who had already pronounced his betrayal of them and were prepared to murder him, but his denial was offered with such conviction he was spared.

Every evening until 5th November Guy Fawkes, checked the cellar that had been secretly entered from adjacent premises by seven of the conspirators breaching a 9 ft stone wall (all of whom were 'gentlemen of name and blood'). On 4th November, Suffolk the Lord Chamberlain with Lord Mounteagle visited the House of Lords, and after a period they visited the vaults and cellars on the pretence certain items belonging to the king had been reported missing.

Opening the door of the prepared vault they encountered Guy Fawkes standing in a dark corner and when asked who he was he stated he was a servant to Mr Percy and was looking after his master's coals. 'Your master has laid in a good stock of fuel,' said Suffolk, after which he and Mounteagle casually left.

As there had been no warning, Fawkes returned to the cellar after relating the incident to Percy, still thinking their plot had not been uncovered and at midnight sallied forth to check; as he stepped out of the cellar his arms were pinioned in the presence of a company of armed men under the command of Sir Thomas Knevet. The party went into the cellar and removed the faggots revealing the horrendous operation – thirty-six barrels of gunpowder, and on Guy Fawkes was found the necessary means of firing.

He defied king and council, refusing to give the names of his accomplices. Submitting to the 'gentler tortures' and by reason of his signature on the deposition on 8th November compared to his signature on the 10th it suggests he underwent appalling types of torture. He was executed on 31st January, 1606. Garnet, an accessory to the plot, confessed that he had been with the conspirators at White Webbs House in Enfield Chase. He was executed after a trial at the Guildhall. When the house was searched Popish books and relics were found but no papers or munitions.

Several of the conspirators fled north and died fighting to the bitter end when the house they were sheltered in on the borders of Staffordshire was surrounded and attacked by men under the command of the County Sheriff, Sir Richard Walsh. The others involved in this immense and intriguing undertaking of blowing high the king, Lords and Commons at one blast were hunted down and ruthlessly dealt with as extreme brutality of torture and disembowelling were permitted at that period – their fearful penalty was paid in full for the unaccomplished plan of conspiratorial treason.

An example of how repression of a bigoted type may make fiends of normal persons when driven to such wild extremes.

Old White Webbs House was pulled down in 1790; the existing building was erected in 1791 by Abraham Wilkinson and is now a delightful residential home for senior citizens where loneliness may be their only enemy. The Sportsmans 68 Dinner Club (founded at The Cambridge in 1968) and the Enfield Standbrook Bowls Tournament continue to supply Christmas fare to the old folk and generally help wherever possible, and similarly to four other homes for old folk.

The very popular public golf course was opened in 1932 and may hold a record by the fact the club's very amiable professional, Reg Wilson, was there for the opening and stayed until his retirement in 1972.

Several menus have been quoted, but I feel the following at 6s 6d (32½p) per head would require some beating for costing even in 1930:

Hors d'oeuvres  
Soup – Tomato Puree

Fillet Sole – Anchovy Sauce  
Fillet Steak Garni  
Chicken and Ham Salad

Pear Melba  
Cheese, Biscuits, Butter  
Coffee

April 26th that year I attended Wembley Stadium with A.J.S. to see the FA Cup final, and witnessed Arsenal win the cup by beating Huddersfield Town 2–0; James and Lambert scoring. The Arsenal team was: Preedy, Parker, Hapgood, Baker, Seddon, John, Hulme, Bastin, Jack, Lambert and James. Herbert Chapman, one of the most renowned names in football, was then managing Arsenal. The grandstand tickets were 10s 6d (52½p). 1930 saw floodlight football forbidden by the FA and that year witnessed the first World Cup presentation when Uruguay won the trophy in Montevideo.

# Chapter XXIV

A.J.S. has an arm amputated – We smash the Buick up whilst uninsured – The 1931 depression – improvements and drawbacks to cars – The normal LVA menu 1931 – ABA Championships and professional boxing – Primo Carnera and Larry Gaines

I am uncertain when the Thirteen Club terminated, but it was either before 1930 or that year, and it has always been vaguely linked with the severe accident A.J.S. suffered when taking Ben Chandler to see his wife and bring her home after a period of convalescing at Clacton. The accident happened at White Lodge Corner, Little Clacton, early Saturday morning, when the road surface was greasy following severe storms the previous night. The Buick skidded on the bend, hit the grass verge on the other side of the road and turned over. Ben was able to get out, luckily suffering from nothing more than a strained back, and seeing A.J.S. could not move he immediately started for help, but by now some nearby residents were at the scene, one of whom immediately applied a tourniquet and stopped the bleeding; but for this A.J.S. must have died, as it was two hours or more before the ambulance arrived at the hospital. His arm was so badly lacerated and crushed the surgeon made an immediate amputation. I was scrubbing in the cellar when the news came through on the telephone, and what I thought was exaggerated laughter was poor

Jennie crying hysterically. Mother went off to Clacton leaving Peggy and myself to run The George.

A.J.S. made such an amazing recovery the doctor let him stay at the Beaumont Hall Hotel provided Jennie looked after him. In fact, by all accounts, A.J.S. was back to his old form of seeing the funny side of all that happened. One such instance was the first time Jennie shaved him, and plastered his face without getting any lather. The more hot water used the more plaster-like the expected lather became, until A.J.S. said to Jennie, 'Show me the soap you are using.' Jennie passed it up, and almost before it was at a readable distance, he retorted, 'Why, you silly cat, you're plastering me with Meltone shoe cream!' Everybody was so kind to A.J.S. in the hospital that he reciprocated by making a donation, after which he was made a Life Governor.

I only remember one touch of sadness following the accident, and that was, on my first visit to hospital, before he said, 'No more golf, Stan.' It was the tone and suppressed way he said it, and when I saw his eyes well up, I just couldn't answer. We played golf at the Enfield Club nearly every Thursday morning.

Well it was only a matter of six weeks or so before A.J.S. was driving and enjoying the pleasures of golf. He quickly had his driving test, in which the instructor was so amazed at the way the large car was manoeuvred out of the garage he passed him as a worthy driver before he arrived at the end of the passage at Sydney Road! The instructor could not understand how we managed to put the car in let alone drive it out.

About this time another incident occurred that understandably brought forth little joy from A.J.S. Brother George, Ronnie Neilson and myself had made arrangements to meet at The George and from there we intended visiting some old haunts including The Royal Hotel – Father's old house in the Leytonstone Road; Ron was to drive us in his open two-seater Morris but the rain having started necessitated somebody getting very wet sitting in the 'dicky' seat. George had a stupidly brilliant idea and said, 'Ask Father if we may take the Buick,' followed by 'and who's driving?' I said, 'Not me the car's not insured, you get it, you drive.' A.J.S. naturally said, 'Yes, and let Stan drive' – I assume because I was used to it. So off we went to The Royal where I only had two shandies after which we went on our way to see Alf and Edna at The Lord Brooke, Walthamstow. As previously mentioned there were no signs on secondary roads that warned who had the right of way at crossroads and in this particular case both I and the driver of a lorry loaded with acid jars thought we both had, resulting in my hitting him admidships and being dragged broadside on for several yards – there followed a fine old rumpus with who was and who was not responsible. Fortunately, other than a few bruises, no one was hurt, but oh dear! the car wasn't looking at all well. I seem to remember the bonnet being on the roof, the radiator was all tangled with the engine and somehow the front wheels had become the wrong way round. However, we went to Tom Tyrie's pub The Telegraph and telephoned Father, who didn't appear at all happy. On arriving back at The George I shall never ever forget the picture of Father sitting in the armchair by the side of the fire in the office, hand on the wooden arm, his body swaying from side to side and literally puffing and blowing in rhythm with his body – it was the insurance position that encouraged his rage. However, when he had exhausted his supply of adjectives that appeared relative to the questions I took my leave and completed my one day off duty.

On my arrival back A.J.S. was in a reasonably cheerful mood and I improved it by saying I may have exaggerated the damage, due to the shock I was suffering. 'Well, it's no good crying over spilt milk, let's all have a drink,' said he, and so to bed all reasonably content. Next morning the sun was shining, just one of those mornings to dissolve depressions. A.J.S. looked in good cheer and again this was improved further when I considered the damage to be less than I had intimated and he would possibly find most of what I had described superfluous, and so off he went in a happy mood to see the car. Some three hours later I was requested to go to the office; there was A.J.S. his looks offering something between mockery and murder. 'What condition did you tell me that b— car was in, the b— thing looks like a b— concertina!'

Another depression came in 1931, wages in many cases were cut back and there was little room for manoeuvre in this field, the wages being so low with the bread line estimate being £1 14s 0d (£1.70) per week. The unemployed numbered some two million soaring to more than 2,750,000 by 1933 (Enfield in 1931 was 3,600), but again London and suburbs, although affected, were suffering more from anxiety than serious disruption, unlike most northern areas where people were finding the times much tougher. Perhaps my thinking was wrong at the time but I well remember how annoyed I and the family were at not having a reply to several advertisements inserted in northern papers, after having tried without success in the London papers. The advertisement was for a married couple to live and sleep in, absolutely no outgoings with a joint wage of £6 per week. (This may be thought a ridiculously low amount, but three years later our joint wage was only £6 weekly when we managed The George.)

On 17th January, 1931, I purchased a 1926 two seater Clyno and what a fine little car that was; considering the condition generally, body, engine, hood, tyres and even the mica side screens were clear and unscratched, and so for £12 10s 0d (£12.50) I thought it a bargain. Audrey and I had a good deal of trouble-free motoring, including touring Devon without a hitch. The windscreen wiper had to be pushed back and forth by hand, but invariably I would open the top half of the windscreen for better vision when it was raining.

The automatic turning signals, trafficators (known as flickers), came into being about this time, and for those who have not suffered the discomfort of driving in heavy rain, especially at night, imagine driving with no automatic wiper, flimsy yellow sidescreens with a small flap in the corner where the driver's arm had to be threaded through for turning signals and, without a passenger, one was often compelled to take a chance. It is amazing why some method of signalling was not discovered before!

Triplex windscreens were beginning to be fitted and the synchromesh gear box was introduced. The whole act of driving then was in the use of the gears and a large degree of satisfaction was attained in knowing your engine revs when performing the essential double declutch when changing gear. The balloon tyre which was now becoming quite universal added a fair degree of comfort to motoring. Another natural operation then which would be a real chore today was draining and filling the radiator in cold weather every time the car was taken out, and, of course, cranking it to start the engine.

Although I do not remember owning two cars at the same time, it appears I purchased an Amilcar by the receipt dated 27th January, 1931 – only ten days after buying the Clyno. This was a racy little sports car, a real eye-catcher but little joy did I have driving it; the one time I had it running nicely brother George happened to be at The George so I invited him for a run. His face showed little signs of happiness when struggling to wriggle into the hole with its seat on the floor and when I revved up and turned into the town it roared up to an exciting thirty miles an hour and the engine cut out; all eyes were on this triple colour contraption with George looking and wishing he had never accepted my offer. 'What now?' said he. 'Push it to the garage,' said I. 'She's probably out of petrol.' Upon arriving at Graham's Garage I requested petrol, but before the amount ordered was dispensed the tank overflowed, so the fault was not fuel but it still would not start. Eventually the mechanic found the petrol supply turned off; George had put his foot on it, probably when pressing the floorboards with fear!

In December 1931 the family and friends attended the annual function of the Fulham and South Kensington Licensed Victuallers Association in support of Mr W.S. Walker, president of the society who was then the general manager of Charrington & Co, and a man with an extremely charming personality. I quote the following menu as a typical example of a normal meal then served at a ladies' festival.

Oysters
or
Side dishes

Consommé of Turtle
Cream of Tomato
Boiled Turbot and Lobster Sauce

Calf Sweetbreads
Roast Chicken and York Ham
French Salad
Chips

Ice Pudding
Wafers
Dessert
Coffee

One day of the year we all very much looked forward to was the Amateur Boxing Championships which were held at London's Albert Hall. A.J.S. would have the lower tier box that held ten and I would have two on the upper tier which held five in each. The boxing would commence at about 11 a.m. and continue until 11 p.m. with the competitors boxing probably on four occasions to win the final. In two's we would visit Father's box at intervals, the main object being to suffer their hospitality which included St Neots pork pies and champagne!

When I look at the 1931 programme and see the names in print, so many memories fill my mind, the little fly weight – T. Pardoe – who won the championship for five consecutive years from 1929. Harry Mizzler (later to be my guest at charity functions) who won the bantamweight title in 1933 and went on as a professional to win the British lightweight title in 1934. Benny Caplan who won the featherweight championship in 1931 boxed as an amateur at Enfield, later, as a professional he was beaten by Jim (Spider) Kelly for the British featherweight championship in 1938. J. Waples won the lightweight title in 1930. Dave McCleave won the lightweight title in 1931 and the welterweight title in 1932 and 1934. Ernie Kemp from Enfield was unlucky not to win the lightweight title after getting to the finals three times and unfortunately failing his medical, I believe on two occasions, once when I was with him. What exciting all action bouts he had with Freddie Frost at Enfield; Frost went on to win the lightweight title in 1935, J. Barry won the welterweight title in 1931. Harry Bone, who was well-known to everyone in Enfield, won the welterweight title in 1928 and later was a tower of strength to the Enfield Amateur Boxing Club, but lost his services when he became the licensee of The One Star at Hoddesdon. Freddie Mallin won the middleweight title in 1928 and held if for five years equalling his brother Harry's record from 1919 to 1923. (Excluding his Olympic win in 1924.) The greatest bout on the 1931 programme was between J.W. Goyder and Jack Peterson, the latter winning and becoming the light heavyweight champion and the following year, after turning professional, he beat Harry Crossley for the British light heavyweight championship and the same year he KO'd Reggie Meen in two rounds for the heavyweight title and, having lost and won the title with Len Harvey, he finally lost it again to Ben Foord in 1936. M. Flanaghan became the amateur heavyweight champion in 1931 by beating C. O'Grady, the latter winning the title in 1933.

On several occasions we had the pleasure of having in our company H. Brewer the ABA lightweight champion in 1899 and heavyweight champion in 1907.

Don McCorkindale won the light heavyweight title in 1926 and later joined the professional ranks; he fought most of the leading boxers of that period including a twelve round draw with Walter Neusel (in their first contest he won on a foul). He also fought Carnera losing on points over twelve rounds. He entered the licensed trade and his early insight into the business was obtained at The George.

Fred Webster had the unique experience of winning three ABA titles consecutively; bantam, feather and lightweight in 1926, '27 and '28. He turned professional and won the British lightweight championship in 1929. His younger brother Charlie and his wife Rose are now hosts at The Tollington Arms. Holloway also established himself as a leading boxer. He won the important American Golden Gloves Amateur tournament in 1936 and in 1938 he won the ABA welterweight title. Joining the professional ranks he fought many well-known boxers of that period. Charlie and Alf Paolozzi, with the assistance of Jack Powell as honorary secretary, instigated the London Ex-Boxers Association, the headquarters being at The Tollington. Alf is the present chairman.

One memory of A.J.S. and the Albert Hall was when a customer friend borrowed £50 from him. After two years of waiting, the debt had been written off, but the friend called and gave it back to A.J.S. just as we were leaving for the Albert Hall. Bert Greenall the bookmaker and a great friend was in the office at the time and so too was Jennie (who loved a little gamble with a maximum stake of about two shillings). A.J.S. said to Bert, 'Well, it's money written off put it on (so and so),' but Jennie smartly put her foot down saying, 'No, you are not going to gamble like that,' and so the money was locked in the safe. The whole thing was forgotten until the result of the race was announced on the microphone and the horse A.J.S. wanted to put the £50 on had won at 15 to 1! A.J.S. phoned Jennie immediately to dispense a little of his wrath, after which he transferred to the bar and little was seen of him until our departure!

The boxing contest that seems foremost in my memory of pre-war battles was when Larry Gains (also my guest at later charity functions) then Empire heavyweight champion, fought Primo Canera at the White City on 30th May, 1932. I attended with A.J.S. and Alf Overall, the latter being a personal friend of Larry's. Normally I disliked open air boxing but this night offered every ingredient to favour it; the weather was perfect as were our seats – centre front row. Larry came over to speak to Alf before the bout commenced saying something about seeing us all in the dressing room afterwards. The contest was never a classic but for excitement could offer no more. This mountain of a man weighing almost nineteen stone with a height of approximately 6 ft 6 ins and carrying no surplus weight looked so huge and menacing against his opponent Larry who weighed 14st 4lbs and a height of 6 ft 1½ins.

No matter what has been said about Carnera he could move quickly considering his size, he had courage but lacked the real power in a short punch. That long powerful right uppercut that won him the world championship when he KO'd Jack Sharkey in six rounds had been attempted but Larry seemed to be aware of the tactic almost before the intended blow had started, only once did it nearly connect, if it had, who knows? It appeared the most devastating punch that I have ever witnessed, Larry gainfully used his unlimited ring guile and outwitted Carnera on points over ten rounds. When Carnera came to London in 1929 his exaggerated height, weight and measurements, wherever these rumours started from, were lapped up by everybody. No boxer has ever been exploited more than Primo Carnera the 'Gentle Giant'. Larry Gains was empire champion from 1931 when he KO'd Phil Scott in two rounds and lost it to Len Harvey in 1934.

Apart from Carnera Larry beat Schmelling and drew with Mike McTique; all were world champions.

# Chapter XXV

The piano plays in the night – A.J.S. and greyhounds – the parrot – 'Charlie Boy' – flying 1927 – Peggy married to Reg Handisyde – Herts and Essex Flying Club – northern suburban LVA function and menu – cheese and the pub

A.J.S. certainly kept abreast of the times with regard to music. I remember another of the methods used to dispense music was a 'penny in the slot' electric piano that cost several hundred pounds to buy. The switch for the electricity supply was under the counter, and due to dampness this would short out and electrify the pewter which was continuous around the whole bar, the shock at times being quite severe. One night I awoke to the sound of a piano playing. At first I thought it was a dream, but soon realised it was really happening! The next morning at breakfast I told A.J.S. of my experience, but he was not moved in any way – just retorted, 'You want to take more water with it, son.' A few days later I was walking along the drive-in during the afternoon when the piano started playing again, and dear old Maggie, the wonderful old-timer who helped the family at all levels, was on the first landing. I called to her, 'Maggie, listen, the piano is playing again.' I obtained the keys and with Maggie rushed in immediately noticing a wisp of smoke coming from the back, but before I could turn the live switch off, to my horror Maggie had thrown a bucket of water over it! What a sight – flashes, crackles, billowing smoke – we had everything except the right day, 5th November. A.J.S. after looking at the piano never doubted it had been playing without the help of a human!

The popular saying, 'He's gone to the dogs' applied to a tremendous number of people in the early days of Greyhound racing, in fact eight million persons paid for admission to six tracks in London alone during 1929. The first Greyhound races were staged in Manchester in 1926, and the first track to open in London was the White City in 1927 in which year the Greyhound Derby was instigated, the winner being Entry Badge owned by E. Baxter and trained by J. Harmon. I accompanied A.J.S. and my mother to one of the early meetings held at the White City, but this outing has left me with only two memories. The first was arriving in the new two seater open Morris Oxford which A.J.S. had just acquired, and following a rather sudden application of the brakes, a taxi driver, leaning out of his cab shouting, 'Why don't you take that bloody thing over the park?' That was one thing about sitting in the 'dicky' seat, one knew generally all that was going on! The other memory was an observation regarding the general atmosphere in the stadium and of those attending which made it easy to prompt a thought, like 'Ascot at the dogs'.

A.J.S. owned several popular greyhounds, two of which I remember well; named Nobby McNab and Wyndways. A good dog would always pay for his keep at the kennels with the win and place prize money it won. The cost of keeping a greyhound at Harringay at this period was £1 10s 0d (£1.50) per week and the normal prize money would be £20 for a win, also £1 for appearance money.

A.J.S. had a great deal of enjoyment from the sport, apart from the racing there developed a social side which through A.J.S. and his most likeable colleague and partner, Bert

Greenall, also the trainer Jack Harvey and Mac McCorkindale, Jack Kennedy and Sid Jennings encouraged people who had little or no knowledge of the sport to take an interest. Jack Harvey won at least two greyhound derbys. Of course, there were many who had the infallible betting systems, but none to my knowledge stood the test of time.

Another great family friendship which was created from the sport in question was with the Lake family, the highly respected North London Commission Agents. I remember A.J.S. leaving the Harringay dog track early one evening and collecting his Buick, and finding that when he arrived home, he had taken the wrong one – Harry Lake's.

Following the death of Harry in 1940 his two sons, Harry and Leslie (just two of a very large and jolly family), carried on with the business.

The following are reprinted from the *Enfield Gazette and Observer* in January 1931:

## *The Countryman's Story*
## *or*
## *The Value of a Telescopic Neck*

Yes, Sir, there's a good dog, dear old
    Wyndways,
whose story you've asked me to tell;
How he ran for world fame and fortune,
    and for Alfred and Albert as well.
How he saved their baronial halls, Sir, from
    the blood-sucking income tax crew,
And brought smiles to us all at The George, Sir
…a pint? I don't mind if I do.

Wyndways, Sir, was never a fav'rite; in fact he
    was reckoned small beer
By the starting price merchants, who laid him
    at sixes and eights without fear.
But that dog knew the hopes that he carried,
    and he
whispered to Alfred and Bert;
'An outsider? Rot! This is a cake-walk. Shove
    the dough on and then shove your shirt!'

There were moments of terrible tension ere
    nine by the course clock was struck;
Would Wyndways retrieve all our fortunes – or
    leave us again in the muck?
And I thought of the money he carried and
    prayed to the fates he's come through;
And my throat was that dry... Drink a pint, Sir?
Yes thankee, don't mind if I do.

Now they're off, with each dog at full stretch,
    Sir; they're moving all bunched in a crowd;
Like a pack racing Hades for leather, or as if
    with lightning endowed.
Nearing home, Sir, old Wyndways looked
    beaten, and my heart went as heavy as lead;
*Then the gallant old dog stretched his neck, sir,*
    *and won a good race by a head.*

                                    'Wanderer'

## An Enfield Dog Lover's Story

Did you say a good dog's a real pal, Sir – well that's
    as may be, Sir, say I;
Some dogs, like some humans, are vicious and like
    to see things go awry.
Have I told you the story of Wyndways? – a racer of
    pedigree he –
Who carried the money of Alfred and Albert and
    Harry and me.

'Twas at Harringay course, Sir, we loosed him to win
    us of money a pot;
All the mid-day newspapers had tipped him, and so
    had 'The Man on the Spot';
It was 5 to 2 on Wyndways, Sir, a rather short price,
    you'll agree,
But – 'Our dog can't be beaten,' said Alfred and
    Albert and Harry and me.

They got off to a flying start, Sir, with Wyndways
    a-racing in front,
And I thought of the quids that I'd gather from out
    of this dog-racing stunt;
So I shouted 'Good dog!' to old Wyndways, and
    then on his haunches sat he
A-grinning a good'un at Alfred and Albert and Harry
    and me.

Is he still running, sir? Well, I wonder? More like
   he is still sitting there
Just biding his time, with his ears cocked, awaiting
   the next bally hare;
But Alfred and Albert and Harry, who fell to that
   5 to 2 call,
Are now singing songs in the street, Sir, with Uncle
   Tom Cobley and all.

'Wanderer' (Charlie Maunder)

Only six months after entering the business I arranged my first function, and from then on for the next forty years (war years excluded) I made a bed that I had to lie on – sometimes feather, many times lumpy! This inaugural dinner was held on 28th January, 1930. the guests were all from the saloon bar, and not the lounge, and just to establish my bar on a par to the lounge the menus were headed 'A few gentlemen of The George'. They were a great crowd of customers and from all walks of life, with perhaps the building trade offering the largest representation. Although the times were projecting anything but luxury, and considering the suffering in the building industry when severe weather brought about a complete shut down (often for as long as four to six weeks), there was nowhere near the discontent of today; they had not had any experience of it being otherwise! The building trade was the barometer to the licensed trade – when the building growth progressed, Britain flourished.

That one day off duty was really something to look forward to, especially after being on duty for approximately seventy-five hours for the other six days; alas the day was rarely used for relaxing, because apart from the afternoons from 2 p.m. until 5 p.m. there was no other time for sport. I have commenced with a game of bowls around 9 a.m. at the Bush Hill Park Sports and Social Club, then adjourned to the tennis courts, and finished there with a few games of table tennis; after lunch to Theobalds Park to play golf, followed by a spell in the attached swimming baths, and afterwards to complete the day we used up any surplus energy in the gymnasium.

My memory is jogged by the most enjoyable games of tennis. I would have some afternoons with Henry Crick on a private court tucked away in tranquil seclusion, spoiled only by Henry dashing off in the middle of a crucial game to wring the necks of some geese he had forgotten to prepare for a customer!

About 1926 a parrot joined the family, an African grey which was brought home by George Daniels from one of his tours in the merchant navy; there will never be another Charley Boy! for that was his name; he would talk, sing, whistle and dance... his favourite little piece was 'Up and down the City Road, in and out The Eagle, that's the way the money goes, pop goes the weasel', and to project his act, he would perform a little dance – three steps to the right, his head cocked to the left, and reverse; having completed the verse he would lower his body, flap his wings, push his head forward, and with a low meaningful grating voice he would say, 'Gert you old bugger', repeating the latter word quickly four or five times.

A local vicar would call in the saloon bar midday once or twice a week, and have just one gin and Italian; one of these mornings Charley Boy was strutting up and down on the bottle basket; having served the drink and taken the money I stayed with him, starting a conversation because I could see Charley was starting his dance and preparing for the worst – when he did, it was! I had never heard him in better or worse form – 'What's the time', 'What's the time, ain't yer got no 'omes? Gert you ole b—, b—, b—, b—,' he was saying – it was the venomous way he was looking at the vicar; 'twas all taken in good part.

Poor Charley went into solitary confinement for a week or more down in the cellar. This was due to a barman who would say one certain word to him every time he went through the office that could not be tolerated in the bar, or in front of the ladies; a word easier for a parrot to pronounce than the one quoted earlier. The extraordinary outcome was that he seemed to enjoy the anti-social word so much he hardly touched his old routine.

Charley was no fool; I remember Captain Phillips of the Cornwall Aviation Co. when he stayed with us whilst he promoted air flights, etc. in Enfield, would tease Charley by blowing smoke in his cage; this was reciprocated by Charley snapping at him and raising his feathers until they were almost standing on end. One day Charley was on top of his cage, and when the captain came near, instead of him being spiteful he lifted and extended his foot, as he would when wishing attention, or to be picked up, and so the hand was offered. Charley gripped the finger, and in a slow and friendly manner made his way up his arm and on to the shoulder; having arrived at the desired spot, he took one vicious nip at his ear, biting right through the lobe. He hopped on to the cage and clambered inside, swearing, cursing and cockily saying, 'Haaall-o Chaaalie.' Captain Phillips said to me, 'If it wasn't for your father thinking so much of that b— parrot, I'd have rung its b— neck!'

I had my first taste of stunt flying with Captain Phillips in, I believe, 1927. The exhibition was arranged for the end of the day's flying – poor plane, it had been taking off and landing since about 9 a.m. that morning, and to make matters worse the buffer spring on the under-carriage had given up on the last flight, leaving the flimsy plane lolling on one side. However, the mechanic bodged it up and away we went. I think every stunt known to flying was performed, which included the spiral dive, the falling leaf, flying upside down at almost nil altitude, also the other occupant sitting behind, handed his scarf to me and precariously scrambled over with one foot either side of me on to the fuselage and up on to the wing. I must admit to a little feeling of unsteadiness on arriving back to earth.

Charley Boy should have been named Connie Girl, because an entry in my diary dated 1st February, 1940 says, 'The parrot, Charley Boy, whom we thought was a cock has laid an egg after all these years!' The poor thing had an untimely end at the Cuffley Hotel whilst Peggy was managing the business for Father during the war. Charley was strutting about on the counter when somebody caught the heavy counter flap, knocking it down and crushing his head. A.J.S. never did know, he was told she had laid another egg and died with her efforts.

A gammon ham has always been on show behind the bar, and on this occasion, skinned and breadcrumbed, a fresh one was proudly displaying itself on a stand. A customer who was drinking at the counter called the barmaid, who had just arrived from the country and a newcomer to the business, and said, 'Half a Boars Head (tobacco) please, miss.' She nervously stammered back, 'Wh-what did you say?' He repeated his request, 'Half a Boars Head, miss.' She looked around furtively at the gammon and remarked, 'I'm sorry, but we only have ham.'

The Piccadilly underground was extended to Enfield West in 1932; the station was named Oakwood. The following year the line was extended again to the terminus at Cockfosters.

The Rover cars made between 1925 and 1927 sold for £215 were 9/20 hp and were small comfortable four seater tourers. I purchased one in 1932 for £4 10s 6d (£4.52½) and had little or no trouble with it, except in a traffic jam, when one was likely to be asphyxiated with fumes coming through the floor boards.

About this period The George became the town's main bus stop and terminus; one could almost have jumped from the verandah on to the old open deck buses. The open top was appreciated in fine weather, but when teeming with rain and lashed by wind, huddling behind a sheet of oilskin which was permanently attached at the top to the seat in front and the bottom was pulled over both passengers and fixed at the rear, could have really only been appreciated by a courting couple? The first covered top was introduced in 1925 but met considerable opposition on the grounds of safety. The open bus was running well into the Thirties. 1925 also witnessed the first bus fitted with pneumatic tyres, but these were energetically opposed for safety reasons. The last bus fitted with solid tyres was on route 108 and taken out of service as late as 14th April, 1937!

Although work permitted only one day a week when I could play golf, the enthusiasm was always with me sufficiently so that I owned two extra sets of clubs, which I would loan to anybody should they be interested in playing. Perhaps this appears extravagant, but we must take into consideration that the sets were made up of clubs I had purchased second-hand for between one shilling and four shillings per club, with balls by the dozen from a penny up to threepence each!

Speaking of golf I remember on several occasions a message coming through asking me to tell the golf caddies to report to Trent Park, Sir Phillip Sassoon's residence as quickly as possible because the Prince of Wales was on his way and would be playing golf there.

My sister Peggy married Reg Handisyde in 1933. Reg was an extremely likeable personality who much preferred the lighter side of life, and so it was always a tonic to be in his company. I must admit a slight feeling of loneliness understandably crept into my life; Alf, George, George Haylock and now Peggy had all left within the space of seven years. Alf was now works manager for Gaymers Cider at Attleborough; George and Phyllis were managing The Holly Bush in Enfield for Ben Chandler, and George Haylock had moved to Surbiton.

I now found myself more involved in organising, and in some selfish way thought that if I liked a given sport or a pastime, then everybody should like it! If anyone disagreed with my enthusiasm I would move heaven and earth to prove them wrong. An instance was when the subject was flying, and being a member of the Herts and Essex Flying Club at Broxbourne, which was run by Roger and Buster Frogley, I invited a party to sample flying, two of whom were in favour and one against, and another named Bill Last was so anti flying he worked himself into a rage thinking about it! I phoned the instructor and stated that a party would be there at 3.15 p.m., allowing time to close and carry out the normal chores. When we arrived the plane was standing by, with engine running all ready for the off, and who was in first? Bill Last of course! He must have had a word with the pilot, thinking, 'I'll show 'em!' They certainly were performing some antics. I can see him now, his very florid face crowned with thick white hair, looking like a snow-capped sun, and wearing a winner's smile!

Another function I must mention was the Jubilee Dinner Dance and Cabaret arranged by the Northern Suburban LVA in the Grand Hall, Connaught Rooms. The President that year was Brigadier-General A. Courage, and the Chairman was William Davis of The Woodberry Hotel Tottenham. The toast list offered some very interesting speakers with no less than four members of parliament replying to the toast of 'Imperial Parliament' proposed by Captain A.J. Dyer. They were L. Col. R.V.K. Applin, Edward Doran, J. Rutherford and F. Noel Palmer. Luke Brady proposed the President. A.J.S. being on the committee mustered a sizeable party for the evening, as did the twenty-five other well-known licensee committee members. The following menu that was served would require tranquillisers today before the costing was announced.

>
> Oysters
> or
> Hors d'oeuvre
>
> Real Clear Turtle
> Tomato Cream
>
> Fillets of Dover Soles
> Champagne Sauce
>
> Quail Pie Connaught
>
> Curacao Sorbet

Saddle of Southdown
Duchesse Potatoes

Pheasant in Casserole
Ninon Salad

Cherries in Liqueur
Vanilla Cream Ice
Petits Fours

Coffee

Not only were all of the courses consumed by almost everybody, but a welcome buffet of assorted patisseries and fruit tartlets, ice cream, fruit and claret cup, also tea and coffee, and lastly to be certain no guest went home hungry a wonderful selection of sandwiches was served after midnight! In more ways than one a 'full' evening, especially with the inclusion of a first-class cabaret.

Why does cheese in a pub appear to be that much more agreeable and palatable than elsewhere? I am positive the reason can only be environment, plus the fact that it is so often eaten as a snack between meals when the appetite requires appeasing. How unfortunate that so many only have cheese following a meal when the taste buds are working overtime and the appetite is waning. A good cheese should be treated with more reverence. I cannot think of a tastier or more sustaining snack than my friends and I would have when playing golf at Whitewebbs; we would tinkle the cow bell at the old King and Tinker to warn the landlord of our entry from the rear. We would have a room with a large round table and were served with bread that appeared so much better than we had at home; the cheese had a bite in it which seemed just a little superior to any other, and the pickled onions were almost walnut coloured, mild and soft, but crisp enough not to erase the inevitable juicy crunch. This rustic lunch would be accompanied by a smooth mellow Guinness (then bottled in Ireland). What better fare when joined with the right environment and company.

# Chapter XXVI

The Cambridge, Palmers Green – our wedding – Audrey in a strange business – the Cuffley Hotel – site and plans – staff – Cook Cushney and Alice – general election 1935 – Bartle Bull MP – application for license, Cuffley Hotel – pubs – violence then and now – staff and relative thoughts – signs of war – presentation at the Rialto Cinema

The license of the off license at number one Huxley Parade on the Cambridge Road, Edmonton was granted on 4th February, 1931, in the name of George Henry Standbrook, who temporarily managed the business. This was the forerunner to the application for the full license of The Cambridge Hotel. After intensive canvassing A.J.S. was successful in acquiring the provisional license for Charringtons on 8th February, 1933, The license was confirmed by the licensing bench on 28th April. At that period and indeed until the Finance Act of 1959 all new licenses were subject to what was known as monopoly value; in money terms this meant briefly the difference in the value of the premises licensed and unlicensed. This to a great extent safeguarded the landlords against another license being granted within a given area. The MV in this case was £5,000 payable over a period of five years, a large sum of money to be added to the total cost of land and building, which was in the region of £30,000. The difference between that era and the present age is that then, with the bank rate at something like five per cent, it was gainful to make money work, but today, with the interest rate at anything up to fourteen per cent, many have found it more advantageous to dispose of their businesses, together with all the pressures and frustrations involved, and so reverse the situation! Considering the enormous amount of money at stake Charringtons were very fair with A.J.S. in granting a five-year term at a nominal rent which rose to £250 per annum only in the last year. The licensee also had a substantial outlay when equipping, furnishing and stocking such large premises, but again if the cash was not available the brewers would almost invariably co-operate by making a loan.

The Cambridge was an instant success and within a short period the bars were enlarged. The banqueting hall was yet to be built, but the site which it later occupied was wisely used for well-planned gardens which extended to the banks of Salmons Brook (this section known as The Weir), the scene presented being quite rural. Unfortunately the licensing bench had granted the license, subject to the weir being covered and, after culverting, the area subsequently became the rear car park. Although it was felt at the time that a retrogressive step had been taken, time would have proved otherwise with the increase in vandalism in later years, A factor to which may be added the wayward growth of population, that has brought degeneration to the country's inland waters.

The Cambridge was opened by A.J.S. and Jennie in June 1934 after a busy but compensating period of furnishing while at the same time establishing and interviewing the various staff required. The only possible help I could offer was to make a complete schedule of all equipment required for bars, cellars and of the entire opening stock. After the opening there followed quickly an extremely happy atmosphere which was created by the sheer personality of A.J.S. and Jennie. I later met so many old characters who alas, together with the hosts, have since run out of time – so many of those boisterous and fun-loving types who were the first to open their hearts and purses generously when the occasion arose. There were a few old stalwarts who patronised The Cambridge on the opening day, and who were still doing so until our farewell gathering on 4th April, 1974.

Brother Alf and his wife Edna took control of The Cambridge sometime in 1936, allowing A.J.S. and Jennie to move into 'private' though both still remained active in the business. Jennie's father, Fred Pluck, thought them out of their minds for paying £1,200 for Oakwood, Slades Hill, Enfield. Admittedly the interior was slightly dilapidated, but he declared the building would be a heap of rubbish in a few years. Fred Pluck later had many happy moments there, and when sipping his glass of bubbly he certainly never seemed apprehensive of the crash of debris!

I must undoubtedly have been so bewildered during the few days preceding, and the days following the Cambridge opening that my memory is clouded, and I cannot remember how I ran The George on my own, especially in view of the fact that my wedding day was to dawn on 21st June. One vague memory of my wedding eve was of swashbuckling Joe Nichols, the Spurs keeper joining me for a drink.

The wedding service was arranged for 11 a.m. at St Andrew's Church, almost opposite The George, though Audrey was late, owing to a misunderstanding, and the reverend, officiating, regularly reminded me it was the longest day of the year, everything went placidly. At the reception which was held at Freeman's restaurant, I made a request for our early departure owing to uncertainty as to whether or not my Morris car, which had been re-bored, would achieve the trip to Bournemouth. I stupidly declined Ben Liffen's offer of the loan of his car, and took the risk of an eventful journey. After our farewells we made a happy enough departure, but after only a few miles the car resembled a steam engine, sadly overheated and with the pistons seized up in their sleeves. To have to wait until an engine cooled sufficiently to restart on one's wedding night was anything but pleasing and the thought that we had more than one hundred miles to cover was yet more exasperating. However, driving with great care we managed to stop only four times for a cool-off – thankfully arriving at the hotel about 9 p.m.

We spent our honeymoon at the Abbey Mount Hotel in Priory Road, the proprietor of which was Leonard Shevill, who was previously a musician, playing for the Savoy Orpheans. I quote his confirmation for the booking: one double room on first floor, facing sea, for the period 21st June to 29th June at terms 3½ guineas each per week inclusive!

This illustrates the tremendous gap between hotel prices today (1974) and those of 1934, but perhaps the most marked difference was to be seen in the service, the care and the tremendous effort to please which was then lavished on guests.

Fred Emney was playing at the Pavilion, and occupied the table next to ours at the hotel. I have never since seen anyone play two such opposite roles – on the stage he would have made a drowning man laugh, but in the hotel he would have reduced a Pools winner to tears. And so, after only eight days, we were back to manage The George for A.J.S. I never felt at all sorry for Audrey who was being introduced to the business of pubs after having known only a sheltered, satisfying and pleasant life with a hard-working but delightful and discreetly disciplined family, among whom all the basically nice things in life were practised. I think the impact of the change may have been softened by the artful and astute understanding laid down that Audrey's department would not entail serving in the bar. She would only have to deal with all the office work together with wages, linen and laundry, as well as the cash, and to assume responsibility for the books and the compiling of a weekly balance sheet. As a fully trained and experienced secretary these duties were not very awesome but the unsocial hours and almost non-existent home life must have been strange to her. If that were so, I have never heard her complain.

How environment may so easily change, for better for worse, a person's attitude of mind. Audrey had no experience of the workings of a bar nor of the fascinating friendliness and companionship that exists among the great majority of customers. The first introduction happened on our first morning on duty, when dear old Jack Lisney, of Turner & Lisney, came in and insisted on buying champagne for Audrey and me, a gesture accompanied by Jack's good wishes. The next time was a little less successful. Whilst I was in the office just after opening time the next morning, a customer approached the counter, meeting Audrey face to face at the bend and with his hat pulled down over his eyes, coat collar turned up, and with a hideous distorted look on his face rudely blasts out in a harsh and grim voice, '*Guinness*' – not even a 'please'.

Audrey came rushing into the office on the verge of tears saying, 'There's such a rude man out there!' I went to the bar and who else could it be but the one and only Dicky Bird! However, it was not long before Audrey was inveigled into the bar by numerous persons to whom she had been secretary, together with their clients, many of whom were also well-known to her. So the inevitable happened – another added chore, bar service! Our contract was soon broken – extra duties, but no extra wages. Hardly surprising, with our joint wages at £6 per week! The money appears so ridiculously small now but it was substantial enough for us both to appreciate and, as has been mentioned previously, with accommodation and our victualling taken care of we were really in a happy position.

I had the public telephone in the inner entrance hall installed, mainly to relieve me of continually answering the office phone and taking messages to Jack Tranter and Dicky Bird regarding their continuous buying, selling and general information on stocks and shares. They were a comical couple, seriously funny, in fact parts of their repertoire would not have been amiss as inclusion in the script for Morecombe & Wise. The theme of their conversation was the Stock Exchange and who was the poorest or the richest, who hadn't bought a drink – why a scotch when I pay; who was going to die first and what arrangements had been made for all the money they had stacked away. Jack Tranter bought the little tobacconists shop opposite The George and when Dicky Bird heard of the deal at £5,000 he suggested phoning a psychiatrist or Napsbury to have him taken away!

A welcome break would occasionally come by way of a telephone call from The Cambridge – 'Pressure system out of action – can you come?' I remember this happening once at the peak trading time on a Saturday. When I arrived the staff were attempting to keep pace with the thirst of hundreds of customers by filling jugs or any other suitable receptacle from the cellar, beer being slopped over everything and everybody! Knowing so little about this new installation I was thankful when the system did start working again. Apart from a new system of valves and supply lines the original compressors are still working efficiently to this day.

An expression seldom used today when one is about to descend the cellar stairs is the verbal warning cry 'be-lo-w' (below) as a warning of approach to the cellarman or to whoever might be in the cellar. At least it gave a person a sporting chance to conceal an artfully acquired drink!

I will always appreciate being invited to the police station by Sub. Div. Inspector Harris immediately after taking over, just for a chat. The main theme was that should I require advice, or be in trouble in any way, never was I to be afraid of contacting the station. A trivial seeming point, but it reflects on the difference between the past and the present. I regret now the fading away of the meaning of trust, sincerity, loyalty, courtesy and the distinct reduction in faith towards life itself.

A site for new licensed premises offered by James Neilson to A.J.S. in 1934 was immediately passed on to Charringtons for the board's consideration, and resulted in the purchase of the site at Cuffley. This was followed by the routine procedures for application for the license. A.J.S. had purchased all the available land on the north side of Station Road at £8 or £10 per foot. I became involved in the project when I received the following letter from James Neilson:

*James Neilson*
*37 London Road*
*Enfield*
*Middlesex*
*26th November, 1934*

*Dear Mr Stanley,*

*I enclose a small plan of land at Cuffley, from which you will see that it has a frontage of 100 ft by a depth of about 150 ft.*

*There is a 9" sewer crossing the land as shown, and therefore the building would require to be to the West of this sewer. The line of the sewer would make an entrance to the yard of the Hotel.*

*Get a move on with your internal plans, as I have promised Mr Walker that I will be up there at the earliest possible moment.*

*Yours faithfully,*
*J. Neilson*

At this point in time both Audrey and I were really under pressure, especially with Christmas looming ahead, but somehow, with the odd afternoon and an hour out of the bar occasionally, I managed to finalise the ground floor plans by working after closing from 11 p.m. until about 2 a.m. to complete the task. When the plans were submitted to the brewery for approval they were rejected owing to the cost. So far as my memory serves me the difference was approximately £1,200 more than the calculated expenditure of £6,500. Once again, probably through haste, the building was not re-designed. The existing plans suffered certain curtailments until the cost was roughly trimmed to the estimate. The main theme of my plan was executed to with an alteration nearly thirty-five years later.

The green belt land was purchased in 1934 by the Enfield council and the 2,500 acres involved cost nearly half a million pounds, but the cost to Enfield was only £40,000; little perhaps compared with today, but still an enormous amount of money forty years ago!

Though Cook Cushney, who was with the family for years, was completely deaf, little difficulty was found in communicating with her, but one natural reaction was that when anyone else was talking to somebody without her being in the conversation, she was under the impression that the conversation was detrimentally concerning her. I remember some years ago little Alice, the housemaid, was writing a letter or she could have been writing tomorrow's winners out (she loved a little gamble). The ink bottle was somehow knocked over on cook's newly scrubbed kitchen table. This was the only evidence I had when alerted by someone shouting 'Murder' and on arrival I found cook, enormous looking, with a great carving knife in her hand, chasing round the table tiny little Alice who had her stockings half down and her little lace cap flopped over one eye. One never finds the absolute truth regarding these little differences. Alice may have knocked the ink over purposely to annoy cook, or she may have made some exclamation that was misinterpreted such as, 'Oh, blast it,' cook reading it as, 'You b—'

One summer afternoon between closing and opening times I was sitting on the front verandah when there was a colossal bang that shook the whole building. I dashed towards the kitchen and en route I found cook laying in the passage outside the staff bathroom saying, 'The geyser, the geyser.' The pilot light must have gone out when she swung the burners in and, being deaf, she had not heard the hissing of the unlighted gas, and later, finding no hot water, she had attempted to relight the pilot, when it blew up. How lucky she was not to be severely hurt. The large old Ewarts geyser was in bits and the window blown out. Those old geysers unless carefully used, were a constant danger especially to children.

During the 1935 general election I had the pleasure of looking after Bartle Bull, later the Conservative MP for Enfield. What an unusual and interesting Canadian family, full of charm in their courteous, humble and decidedly down-to-earth manners. Michael, one of the brothers, was a barrister, and Billy, the other brother, was a member of the Stock Exchange. I must admit that if there were any demonic features in the family, he was the one with them. The father could have been a blustering, powerful rugged character playing the lead in a way-out Canadian logging camp; heavily bearded, with a great overcoat heavily trimmed with fur – it was all I could do to hold it out in front of me when getting him into it.

I remember on one occasion Sir George Henessey's daughter, after being out electioneering, tasting bitter for the first time, and after a short while, leaving the bar and re-appearing excitedly happy, saying to me, 'Who is that priceless person upstairs?' I replied, 'That's Maggie – what's happened?' 'Well I asked her for the ladies' toilet and she said the key had been lost, and with that she took hold of my arm and led me to the Gents and said, "There you are, dear, slip in there, I'll keep diggy," which I did while she stood guard!'

We also had William Mellor, the Labour candidate using The George for his headquarters, and quite often both parties were in the lounge at the same time, but all the way through the campaign the bars were busy with a boisterous, light-hearted atmosphere.

Once when Bartle found he could not keep his appointment with Lord Selsdon at The George, until later. He therefore requested me to meet and look after him until his arrival. I found this most interesting and enlightening with his chat regarding Lord Seldons's experiences when he was postmaster general between the years 1924 and 1929. Also his recent appointment as the chairman of the Television Advisory Committee from 1934.

Poor Bartle wanted so desperately to do everything right. He always thought deeply and was so sensitive and touchy about Britain that should anyone express opposition to the ideals of King and Country and heckle him at meetings he would off with his jacket!

A noticeable reflection regarding people, was the flippant sense of humorous quotes that tended to create a liveliness of atmosphere in the bars that is often missing today. An example of unpremeditated wit comes to my mind. A customer was asking a friend (who was some way along the counter from him) to join him in a drink, but there was no response and so he called very loudly a second time, 'Jack, what are you drinking?' He replied, 'Oo-er, mine's a light.' The immediate satirical retort was, 'Well put a bucket of water on it!'

How I would love to see the horses back in the town and again welcome our old friends from the Empston Riding School (later the Hollyhill School when they joined Wilf Fountain of Holly Hill Farm). The party including Doris Darter, Jo West, Bid Giles, Daphne (who was later to marry Wilf Fountain), and Gill Robinson were a tonic to serve and converse with – bright and fun-loving.

The Cuffley residents were unsuccessful in their opposition to the proposed new Cuffley Hotel at Hatfield Petty Sessions on Monday, 4th February, 1935. The license was opposed very strongly and the report of the court application in *The Potters Bar Gazette* which detailed residents' views and voting, together with the opposition of The Plough, which was then only a beer and wine license, makes it appear surprising that it was granted. When A.J.S. was questioned he most certainly appeared to have the answers. One telling response was made to Mr Clayton:

| | |
|---|---|
| MR CLAYTON: | Do you know there are sixteen firms delivering almost daily to people who require supplies? |
| A.J.S.: | No. |
| MR CLAYTON: | Does that surprise you? |
| A.J.S.: | It makes me think a public house is needed more badly than ever. |

There were then three hundred and forty-two season ticket holders and the number of passengers using Cuffley station during 1934 was one hundred and ninety-two thousand. St John Hurchinson, who made the application on behalf of A.J.S., quoted these figures, and to substantiate the growth of the district he stated that in 1929 the number using the station was only ninety-two thousand.

Although the average licensee of this period never suffered the offensive vandalism, violence, bombings and the disturbing drug hazards, nor the confusing under-age drinking of the last decade or so, he still had to be wary and continually vigilant for trouble-makers. Most of the licensees knew the brawling and quarrelsome individuals as families in the surrounding district, but the worst disruptions were caused by persons attending local fairs such as Barnet Fair. One or two evenings a year were a certainty for a rumpus and one in particular was when Enfield football team played Barnet at home. One such evening a stupid person insisted on being given a clay pipe with his half-ounce of 'bacca'. Despite all the diplomatic explanations, that those days had passed by, he was still adamant and started thumping his fist on the counter and shouting, 'It's the law of England that you supply a clay pipe with my tobacco.' That was enough of that nonsense so, following his attempt to throw a pint mug at me, he was put out forcibly but unknowingly with a pint mug. This came sailing through the large plate glass window, but fortunately I had seen his hazy form through the frosted glass moving around like a discus thrower, and realised his intention.

I shouted, 'Get down,' and we were able to duck below the window out of harm's way.

We dealt with more silly and stupid souls then than we do today. Some offenders were sleeping rough, of whom a high proportion were meth drinkers. There is nothing worse than dealing with a sub-normal character who has been reduced to a demented state of mind by drink of one sort or another.

When I think of all the luxuries and freedoms of the present world and the harshness of the between war years I often wonder has there ever been a period of uniformity when our priorities are right and equitable. The answer is, shamefully no.

I recall a poor old retired railwayman who had for years helped at The George as an odd job man, liked and respected by all. He had a fine-looking, well-built son who had a dreadful mental affliction which necessitated periodical residence in an asylum, and with this added burden he was only able to live with the additional money he received from his part-time job. One evening I had occasion to go to the annexe, and while there I noticed the top of a bottle poking out of some firewood in a bag – Frank's bag! In it were three barley wine and three guinness bottles. The firewood he was always allowed to collect and take home. He apologised after offering several excuses, and all was forgiven. About two weeks later he was caught again – this time it was cigarettes. He would come behind the bar to empty the bottle baskets; pretending to use his handkerchief he would lay it down on the cigarettes and one packet of twenty would be attached when he retrieved it. I followed him into the cellar and when face to face I asked for the cigarettes, which he gave to me only when he had exhausted the usual excuses; and so I sacked him, with extreme regret. It was touching to see a man so upset but I could not retract. The following morning Frank had already started work when I met him and said, 'What are you doing here?' He replied, 'I couldn't tell the wife, it will upset her so.' Tears were streaming down his face! What the hell could I do – two old persons' lives shattered over a few bottles of beer and a packet of cigarettes, which he couldn't afford to buy! There was no alternative but to say, 'Forget the whole thing,' and walk away. Inevitable but shameful that we have to wait for tomorrow to truly see yesterday.

In October 1935 A.J.S. was requested to present a cheque on the stage of the Rialto Cinema to Mr A.R.W. Wiseman, managing director of *The Enfield Gazette and Observer,* in aid of the Enfield Central Band. But, A.J.S., unfortunately, had another engagement. A.J.S. like the rest of the Standbrooks, would have come last in any competition if the prize was the honour of making a speech! If A.J.S. had been asked to perform a little tap dance and may be tell some funny stories, he may well have cancelled the other engagement. However, I myself accepted the challenge as a duty, but with little enthusiasm. I had little idea how quieter than quiet a packed cinema could be immediately after a brass band ceased playing. The embarrassment was so great that every word I was going to say just vanished. I must have mumbled something or other because I received a letter of thanks from the band secretary almost overwhelming in its kindness.

# Chapter XXVII

1936 expansion but ominous future – death of King George V – functions – costs of amenities – Enfield Georgian Golfing Society 1936 – Enfield Standbrook Bowls Tournament

To me the year of 1936 was the liveliest period since the first world war; there appeared to be no more money circulating, but a definite atmosphere of expansion prevailed, part of which could well have been attributed to preparations in view of Hitler's warlike antics. There must have been many worried and frustrated people when Germany created a peace-time army of half a million in 1935 and compulsory service was also introduced. Great protestations were made by the League of Nations but there was not the remotest sign of action. The Versailles Treaty was virtually torn up, and Britain gave Germany the right to provide herself with submarines, and to build a navy of a stipulated size. Britain and France were, shamefully, in no position to resist and so in 1936 German troops marched into the Rhineland, the Versailles Treaty and Locarno Pact broken. To cloud and complicate the outlook still further Hitler created the Rome-Berlin Axis by signing an agreement with Mussolini to defend Europe against communism. By and large our good old British complacency came to the fore and continued more or less until the sirens screamed on the Sunday morning of 3rd September, 1939.

The year was an extremely busy and commanding period for The George and for the Standbrook family. Such records as I have in my possession may only be touched upon owing to the lack of time and space.

The Jubilee of King George V in 1935, marking his succession to the throne culminated in a Thanksgiving service at St Paul's Cathedral on 6th May, but little did the Royal family and those attending celebrations throughout the Commonwealth think that eight months afterwards, on 20th January, 1936, the nations would be mourning the King's death.

His reign with Queen Mary was perhaps the most tumultuous twenty-five years suffered by any British monarch – the Ulster crisis – the merciless and bloody First World War – the general unrest culminating in two general strikes. Notwithstanding all this he was the right man in the right place at the right time, especially being a great naval personality and, above all, the king who had the right tolerance, discipline, humility and the challenging strain relative to the British Empire being at its territorial summit.

There was a distinct upsurge of functions and general bookings during 1936 and looking at many of the menus and prices, also letters of thanks, nostalgia floods the mind. Was it all worthwhile? So few years can wipe out the association of so many friends and characters, and it makes one wonder. We had bookings for four property sales in just over three weeks by James Neilson, Goodchilds, Broad and Batey, Baynton and later Bowyer and Bowyer. The hall charge was one guinea.

A few of the dinners I have information about were – Enfield Football Club, Edmonton Invicta Athletic Club,

Thirty-Three Club, St Michael's Sports Club, Enfield Conservative Association, Enfield Motor Cycle Club (with Graham Walker and Professor Lowe), Lea Valley Motor Cycle Club, Enfield Chase Tennis Club, North Enfield Cricket Club, The Prudential and the Pearl Assurance Co., Plant Bros., Enfield Old Centrals (with dear old Jack Oliver in the chair who passed away in the Sixties aged one hundred), British Sangamo-Weston, Enfield Central Band, and Elms Athletic Club. This was Elms AC's first dinner and dance with an attendance of forty-one. The menu cost 3s 8d (under 18½p) the bill being 17 10s 4d. The wines cost more than the food: ten bottles of Spanish wine at 3s 6d (17½p), two bottles of Golden Guinea at 12s 6d (62½p) – total £10 10s 4d.

When The George was rebuilt a very poor attempt was made to provide Masonic facilities. In fact, bearing in mind the numerous types of other functions involved, the only way to operate efficiently then was by the use of careful planning and the zeal of a removal enthusiast! Numbers were not large – the Manor of Worcesters Lodge would be the only one to exceed sixty. The Lodge meeting was held in one half of the hall and the other half would be laid for dining, which was, if possible, to be completed before the meeting commenced at about 3.30 p.m. or 4 p.m. This was because the noise easily penetrated the monstrous wooden partition which had to be covered with enormously heavy curtains hung on great sliding rings to help muffle the sound. The heavy furniture and the chests used to store the small equipment all had to be stowed in the ladies' toilets, and so after all the equipment had been put in the meeting room and curtains set up, everything was moved again when the meeting terminated to allow the dining tables to be extended into the other section. All hands were mustered for clearing, laying tables and to open the bar for service.

Another handicap was that no staff were allowed to use the passage through the hall whilst the meeting was in progress. There were no departmentally responsible staff then, but all regular staff joined in the melee without any fuss. I would not like to go back to these particular operations – it meant a non-stop day from 7.30 a.m. until 11.30 p.m., and I was lucky if I managed to have as much as an arrowroot biscuit and cheese for my evening meal!

When one receives letters like the following it certainly helps to promote a willing spirit for the next event!

*18 Little Park Gardens*
*Enfield*
*Middlesex*
*13th September, 1934*

*Dear Mr Standbrook,*

*As Worshipful Master of the Earl Strafford Lodge, I should like to express to you, and to your wife, the sincere thanks of the members of the Lodge and myself for the arrangements you made on our behalf last evening. Everyone was satisfied, and I hope this is the fore-runner of many happy evenings at the George Hotel.*

*Again thanking you,*
*Yours sincerely,*
*F. (Frank) Robbins.*

*Burton House*
*Mill Hill, NW7*
*20th February, 1935*

*Dear Mr Standbrook,*

*Herewith cheque for £13 5s 6d and the account in respect of the last Lodge meeting and I shall be glad of your acknowledgement in due course.*

*I should like to express our appreciation of the prompt and courteous attention of your staff, also of the far greater comfort of the members owing to the arrangement of the tables which greatly facilitated the movements of your staff during dinner.*

*Yours faithfully,*
*W.E. Hammerton, Major RE (Ret.)*
*Treasurer of the Earl Stafford Lodge No. 3500*

I designed an entirely new game of darts which I patented on 7th April, 1936, but after having one or two prototypes made, and privately playing the game to consider the rules, I shelved the whole idea when approached for a board to be displayed in a well-known London firm. The game was 'golf' played over nine holes, and it was possible to play and score stroke for stroke, as golf is played – everything except the weather element! One very important and advantageous point regarding the game was the ability to play it under handicap conditions.

This was also the year in which the golf craze was seriously developed at The George – the game had become so popular since the opening of the municipal course at White Webbs. I organised a competition among the customers under the title of the Enfield Georgian Golfing Society, which continued in being with Dick Clark as secretary and Percy Homewood as treasurer. There were sixty-four entries for the first round to be played off by 30th May. As so many of the competitors are still residing in Enfield and district, I feel it obligatory to enumerate the contestants. I only wish there was room to relate some of the incidents that happened in the competition.

*Enfield Georgian Golfing Society*

Alf Standbrook v Frank Newton
Sid Crowl v Bert Greenall
Charles Marshall v Charlie Berry
Michael Bull v Jack Brown
Trevor Brown v Billy Bull
Bid Giles v Gill Robinson
Lewis Dixon v Percy Homewood
Dick Clark v Josh Brown
Dennis Crame v Tubby Morrell
Les Morris v John Bowman
Jack Squires v J. Clark
Karl Darter v Gordon Keene
Fred Pointer v R. Exton
Ernie Carter v M. Sentance
Mr Bartle Bull MP v Councillor William H. Bishop
Charlie Chapman v Bill Ricketts
Tom Sweetman v Frank Stanmore
Stewart Brown v Len Oxley
Edgar Dipple v Freddie Sheldrake
Les Pratt v A. Calvert
John Sutton v Nobby Sweetman
L. Rota v H. Farrant
Fred Hodgkinson v G. Cutters
Alan Kime v R. Pulker
Councillor William B. Anderson v Bill Neilson

Harry Walton v H. Haycock
Councillor Ron Neilson v Harold Townsend
Arthur Skinner v Tom Bull
Bob Payne v Bill Marchant
Bill Wright v Cyril Attwood
G. Smith v Ted Eustance
Bob Vernum v F. Rolls
Stan Standbrook v Alf Sales

The following year a concert and presentation was arranged with Dick Clark (the oldest customer at The George now) occupying the chair. A.J.S. had donated a silver cup which he duly presented to J.S. (Nobby) Sweetman, the winner of the tournament, and I presented a tankard to H.G. (Tubby) Morrell, the runner-up.

Golf now seemed to be the prevailing interest and I was a little perturbed at the over-riding influence it was exerting, especially in regard to its effect upon other clientele, and so I gossiped with the bowlers, who were strongly represented in the lounge bar. Finally I offered the idea of an Enfield Bowls tournament to Charlie Maunder, a great friend of A.J.S. and editor of *The Enfield Gazette and Observer*. He was very keen, but pointed out that a similar promotion had been attempted some years before, but without success. We agreed to a notice being inserted in the local paper requesting that two delegates from each Enfield Club be invited to a meeting.

The response to the notice and to the enthusiastic personal contact with bowlers generally, led to the first meeting. I had previously approached A.J.S. regarding a trophy, to which he acceded and said he would be delighted to assist and help in any way whatsoever. The inaugural meeting of the Standbrook Bowls Tournament followed a preliminary gathering, and was held on Friday, 22nd May, 1936. The Clubs represented were:

> Enfield Constitutional Club (later the Conservative Club)
> Bush Hill Park
> Enfield
> Durants Park
> North Enfield Conservative

The tournament commenced with a single-rink competition, with an entrance fee of ten shillings per rink which, together with other monies raised, would be donated to the Enfield War Memorial Hospital. Officers elected to run the tournament were: chairman – Charles Maunder, secretary – E. M. Andrews, president – A.J.S., with myself as vice-president. The committee consisted of one delegate to be nominated by each competing club. I must record that the *Gazette and Observer* played an extremely important part in promoting this charity tournament.

The Bush Hill Park Bowls, Tennis and Social Club staged the first final on Friday evening 7th August and carried it through with an enthusiasm that would have done justice to a national final! The club's general secretary, Percy Dashwood, and Billy Bales, the bowls secretary, did everything in their power to ensure a successful evening. Enfield bowlers strongly supported this first final with onlookers numbering anything up to two hundred. The winning rink representing the Constitutional Club were: S.G. Edwards, W.A.J. Williams, H. Hird and A.G. Hinkins (skip). The losing rink from Enfield Bowls Club were: F. Martin, P. Skelding, T. Brain and W. Homer (skip).

The first year culminated in a dinner and presentation, at which a cheque for £32 10s 0d was presented to Hugh Collingridge, who received it on behalf of the Enfield War Memorial Hospital. A.J.S. presented the cup to Bert Hird and I presented a tankard to each winning rink. Charlie Maunder, in proposing a toast to the donors, said of A.J.S., 'Most of us have got beyond the state of mere acquaintanceship with Alfred Standbrook, we call him our friend and we are proud of that friendship.' Of me he said, 'Stanley Standbrook, our vice-president, has also taken a great interest in the tournament – an interest that will increase when he becomes a bowler proper.' Well, it's nearly forty years on and the quote has failed to fulfil itself. I take a greater interest, but I am anything but a bowler proper! However, thirty-two years later I was extremely proud when my rink won the competition, although I must humbly admit this achievement could never have materialised had it not been with the support of my three meritorious colleagues, Tom Turner, Sid Lamb and George Lawrance who supervised and encouraged my game. My bowling shoes are the newest looking pair I possess and they were purchased about thirty-five years ago! The dinner account, incidentally, reads – 52 Dinners @ 4s 6d (22½p).

The tournament developed with the addition of trophies kindly presented by Arthur Harston (triples), Alderman W.D. Cornish (pairs) and Arthur Martin (singles). The tournament is now helped with a sponsorship by the Ancient Order of Foresters, the amazing sequel relating to this kind gesture is that the photograph displayed taken over one hundred years ago portrays the Foresters outside the Old George Inn, the banner displaying 'Court Old Oak No:1620'. A copy has recently been handed to this court's secretary Mrs Launchbury of Enfield. I also possess three menus of this court, one of which is displayed dated 27th November, 1930.

Enfield Town-early sixteenth century.

The Stonehouse Hotel, Hatfield, Herts.
Offered to Standbrooks by James Neilson-refused due to war situation. Purchased by Charrington's: Standbrooks became tenants at £1,000 pa rent. Demolished to facilitate road improvements. Watercolour by J. Montgomery 1945/46.

The Norfolk Hotel, Arundel, Sussex.
Leased by Standbrooks-sold 1948.
Watercolour by J. Montgomery 1945/46.

The George Inn, Enfield, Middlesex. Standbrooks 1924-1978.
Watercolour by J. Montgomery 1945/46.

The Cambridge, Palmers Green, North London.
License obtained by Standbrooks. Demolished early 1990's.
Watercolour by J. Montgomery 1945/46.

Cuffley Hotel, Cuffley, Herts.
Site obtained by James Neilson-license obtained by Standbrooks
on behalf of Charrington's. Watercolour by J. Montgomery 1945/46.

The Gryphon, Grange Park, Enfield.
Full license obtained by Standbrooks.

The Bulldog, Bullsmoor Lane, Enfield. Full license obtained by Standbrooks on behalf of Charrington's.

The Railway Tavern, Buckhurst Hill, Essex.
Where the author was born in 1909.

The Castle, Woodford, Essex.
Owned by Fred Pluck, the author's grandfather; his daughter,
Jennie, eloped from here to the Isle of White with AJS in 1903/4.

*Left to right:* The Potman, Mine Host and Jennie, Enfield Horse Show, Theobald's Park in 1953. The coach four-in-hand visited The George.

A precious photograph of Audrey and Brian, kept with the author during his war years with the RA in World War Two.

The Cambridge roundabout before demolition. The Cambridge
and car park centre, right, were demolished along with the roundabout.
The latter was enlarged, and an underpass constructed from right
(Palmers Green) to left (Woodford). It was reopened in spring 1990.

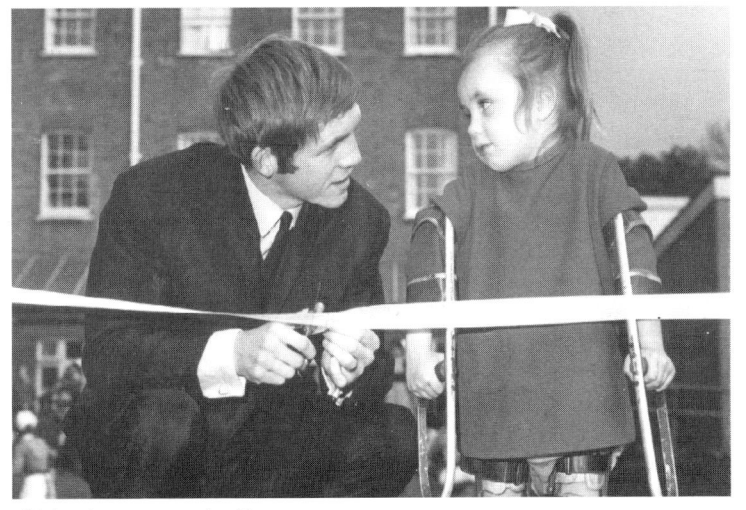

This picture says it all.
The presentation of the summerhouse to the Halliwick children-
Alan Rudkin is shown cutting the tape, a few days after his attempt
to take the world championship from Lionel Rose in Australia.

1939: When The George played Arundel at cricket we flew on a Scylla class airliner which could carry thirty-four passengers and five crew-all for £35.

The first 'ESCBT' presentation at The George, 1936.
*Left to right:* Charlie Maunder (editor of the *Enfield Gazette* and chairman of the committee, E. Andrews (AJS president), SWS, Bartle Bull (MP for Enfield).

# Chapter XXVIII

Brian is born but work continues – Frascati Restaurant – A.J.S.'s fiftieth birthday – George introduces table tennis at Holly Bush – George and Phyllis open Cuffley Hotel – Edward VIII abdicates – ABA titles 1936 and professional boxing

An appropriate quotation: 'One will never know how unintelligent one is until the years remind one how unintelligent one has been.'

This applied to me when I started catering for bars off the premises – as if we had not enough to do! This entailed collecting the van from The Cambridge and returning it; working all the afternoon and setting up a temporary bar and stocking it and completing stock sheets. After everything appeared to be under control, I would return, after closing the George, and see the occasional license through until midnight, after which we would leave everything ready for collection early next morning, only taking back as much full stock as possible.

Whether I purposely became involved in so much work that year to keep my mind off the fact that Audrey was having a baby I cannot remember, but I thought sufficiently of the business to ensure that the baby was born at The George, so that Audrey could carry on with the weekly books, etc. No Standbrook would actually plan this, the procedure was a natural inborn trait! Audrey never gave up any of her chores, except serving in the bar, until shortly before Brian was born – even completing her routine job of cashing up, and retiring at nearly midnight the night before baby was born.

Somewhere about 2 a.m. Audrey woke me, and made some silly remark that amused me. It brought forth a sillier reply from me, and so we were both sitting on our beds laughing our heads off, so much so, in fact, that I found it difficult to be serious enough to phone the doctor. The culmination came happily next morning, Sunday, 28th June, with Dr Toop officiating. Only a short time elapsed before the laughing was curtailed – poor Audrey!

At the Masonic meetings during the afternoon, when a triple hush had blanketed The George, screams would rip through the stark silence that had me streaking up the stairs three at a time to order Audrey to do whatever she must to stop him. The aggravating condition was the Tyler of the Lodge telling me the baby was screaming when I was frantically en route!

A.J.S. celebrated his fiftieth birthday on 28th April at the Frascati Restaurant in Oxford Street; I cannot remember enjoying an evening more – a delightful meal, an extremely enjoyable gathering, and such pleasant surroundings. Bert Greenall was the only guest outside the family – wonderful company, A.J.S. had only to make the most naïve remark to get him chuckling away. Jennie's father, Fred Pluck, was also with us, although then seventy-three, he behaved as youthfully as the youngest in the party. It was my firm intention to repeat that evening for my own fiftieth, but alas, this very well-known London restaurant underwent a change of function in another development.

Brother George with his wife Phyllis, had been managing The Holly Bush for Ben Chandler for the past few years, and very successfully too. George may have been the first licensee to popularise table tennis in a pub.

Exhibitions were regularly promoted, with several of the players who represented England's team taking part, including Jimmy Dass, Eric Findon, Bill Stennett, Jack Carrington, Eric Shalson, Alec Brook, Tommy Sears.

The large hall and bar, would be crowded on these occasions as they would also be on match nights. At twenty-nine George was then ageing a little for the game! But, despite this and his hectic life, he played but lost in the finals of the Middlesex championships at the Regal Cinema, Edmonton. All this terminated when George and Phyllis decided to open the new Cuffley Hotel on behalf of A.J.S. in May 1936. They had a lively following and quickly had the place buzzing; a super snack bar was soon in operation and proved very popular and the local clientele was glowing with characters. Jack Hawkins was a regular visitor then and continued his visits after Audrey and I took over in 1946.

George later took up horse riding which was then a popular pastime in Cuffley, but it was not long before he had a fall and broke his wrist. This certainly did not amuse A.J.S. and according to information I had gleaned his confrontation with George would have been on such lines as, 'How the devil can you find time to go gallivanting around on a horse when you're supposed to be running a pub?' and, 'Look at you, out of action, useless, with a busted arm!' I believe that the views expressed to George were actually offered in a much stronger vein.

On one occasion I visited The Cuffley Hotel with A.J.S. when George, well mounted on his steed, was about to move off with his party. A.J.S. stopped the car and very casually got out; passing George he slowly raised his bowler, and performing an aristocratic bow, with a subservient and solemn look on his face remarked, 'Mornin', sir,' and walked to the bar. Superb acting!

I wonder if the two thatched cottages opposite The Cuffley Hotel would have been saved for posterity if they had not been gutted by fire a year or so after the hotel was opened. Charlie Lamb, the Enfield butcher, opened a business in one of them. His wife had her father, who was one hundred and one years old, staying with them when the fire quickly swept through the old timber. Everybody had evacuated except the old man, and he was up in his bedroom. It was George who went up for him – not easy when a man over one hundred insists on putting his long johns and trousers on whilst choking with smoke and with the crackling timbers spitting sparks (a younger person could have been dragged out). However eventually George managed to get the old boy, quite unperturbed, downstairs! Minutes after, the house was a raging inferno and the heat so intense that some of the windows of The Cuffley Hotel cracked!

Misfortune struck the monarchy in 1936, when Britain was ruled by three kings in one year: George V, Edward VIII and George VI. This was due, of course, to the Prince of Wales being the next in line for the throne on the death of King George V, and to his subsequent abdication on 10th December, 1936. The broadcast by Stanley Baldwin was touching, and the majority of people were numbed by the melancholy statement. Baldwin had previously stated that the Cabinet would not agree to a morganatic marriage (briefly, an inferior marriage) with Mrs Ernest Aldrich Simpson. Prince Edward's speech explaining his abdication was a very deliberate statement and one extremely sad for the millions listening with heavy hearts. One passage of the speech tells it all:

At long last I am able to say a few words of my own. I have never wanted to withhold anything, but until now it has not been constitutionally possible for me to speak.

A few hours ago I discharged my last duty as King and Emperor, and now that I have been succeeded by my brother, the Duke of York, my first words must be to declare my allegiance to him.

This I do with all my heart. You all know the reasons which have impelled me to renounce the Throne, but I want you to understand that in making up my mind I did not forget the Country or the Empire which as Prince of Wales and lately as King, I have for twenty-five years tried to serve.

But you must believe me when I tell you that I have found it impossible to carry the burden of responsibility and discharge my duties as King as I would wish to do without the help and support of the woman I love. And I want you to know that the decision I have made has been mine and mine alone. This was a thing I had to judge entirely for myself. The other person most nearly concerned has tried up to the last to persuade me to take a different course.

I have made this, the most serious decision of my life, only upon a single thought – of what would in the end be best for all. This decision has been made less difficult for me by the sheer knowledge that my brother, with his long training in public affairs of this country and with his fine qualities, will be able to take my place forthwith without interruption or injury to the life and progress of the Empire. And he has one matchless blessing enjoyed by so many of you and not bestowed on me, a happy home with his wife and children.

During these hard days I have been comforted by her Majesty, my mother, and by my family. The Ministers of the Crown and in particular Mr Baldwin, the Prime Minister, have always treated me with full consideration. There has never been any constitutional difference between me and them and between me and parliament.

Bred in the constitutional traditions by my father, I should never have allowed any such issue to arise. Ever since I was Prince of Wales, and later on when I occupied the Throne, I have been treated with the greatest kindness by all classes of people, wherever I have lived or journeyed throughout the Empire. For that I am very grateful.

I now quit altogether public affairs and I lay down my burden. It may be some time before I return to my native land, but I shall always follow the fortunes of the British race and Empire with profound interest, and if at any time in the future I can be found of service to His Majesty in a private station I shall not fail.

And now we all have a new King. I wish him and you, his people, happiness and prosperity with all my heart. God bless you all, [*raising his voice almost to a shout*] *God save the King.*

It was the most controversial happening of this century. One thing is certain, should there have been a referendum, the king would never have abdicated. I must admit that I was one who was against the marriage with Edward staying on as king. I think most people were pleased that the happy relationship continued until the Duke of Windsor passed away in 1972.

Little did I think when I watched, with so much enthusiasm, Wally Pack win the ABA welterweight title in 1936 that he would become not only a licensed victualler, but one of the most energetic and enterprising officers on behalf of the trade. He was governor of the Licensed Victuallers Schools for the year 1964–65. He very sadly passed away on 28th July, 1974, whilst he was the licensee of The Cricketers, Southwick, Sussex. His wife Joan, who was a tower of strength in her support of him in his many duties, continues to hold the license at The Cricketers. His brother Harry, with his wife Maureen, are hosts of The John Baird, Fortis Green Road, and have only recently relinquished the license, after eight years at The Noble Art in Hampstead.

Previously known as The Load of Hay this pub has now reverted to that name after new management had been installed by the brewers. The British Boxing Board of Control gymnasium is at present still operating on the premises. Harry boxed as an amateur. He became the police champion, and later won the ABA divisional championship, but lost to Charlie Webster in the semi-finals of the ABA championships in 1938.

Jack Peterson beat Len Harvey for the British heavyweight championship at Wembley – the first heavyweight title fight to be staged there. Both boxers would have been helped by being another stone heavier for the heavyweight class and I am certain Peterson would never have lost to Walter Neuse given the extra few pounds. Three times I saw them box and each time Peterson lost but gave the public a great deal of excitement. Considering his weight Len Harvey could hit with much greater power than a lot of people thought. To me he was the greatest artist of boxing ever, many thought sometimes dull to watch, but this was due to the way he nullified the antics of the most aggressive opponents – a sportsman and a gentleman.

I and my party of twelve were pleased to see the first boxing promotion to be held on 18th November, 1936, at the new Harringay Arena, which had been officially opened a few weeks before. The show was promoted by Sydney Hulls. The main bout was between Ben Foord (who had recently taken the British and empire titles from Peterson) and Walter Neusel, the latter winning on points over fifteen rounds. Foord was comfortably in front on points when he faded away during the last few rounds. Boxing on the same programme were two of my favourites, Dave Crowley and Harry Mizier, in the former's first major contest as a lightweight. Dave won on points over eight rounds. I was delighted to have the pleasure of having them both as my guests at a charity function recently.

# Chapter XXIX

Catering prices 1937 – con tricksters – catering at Theobalds for three day sale – Temple Bar – flying – Herts and Essex Aero Club and to Ostend by Imperial Airways – coronation King George VI and Queen Elizabeth – amateur and professional boxing – the ceremony of the keys – Tower of London – Christmas

Until 1939 The George always catered for Sunday luncheon. The demand was small but although we were well aware of the fact that it would never be a viable proposition, it was quite natural to offer food on a Sunday as a duty or a genuine service to the public. This, quite honestly, was not a bighearted or self-sacrificing act; it was simply an example of goodwill which the majority of pubs then offered in one way or another. Today, circumstances make it almost impossible to suffer the departmental financial losses.

Another comparison that really amazes me is the effrontery using paper serviettes at normal functions and in general catering (by Standbrook's included) when right up until 1940 we used linen serviettes for all meals' including a half-crown (12½p) three-course steak and kidney pudding dinner for a smoking concert.

The following account and the subsequent letter from Enfield Cricket Club is an example of the amount of money involved in catering for nearly one hundred persons (linen serviettes used) and also the pressure The George has always been under for room and general amenities.

*Enfield Cricket Club – 12th February, 1937*

|                                       | £   | s    | d |
|---------------------------------------|-----|------|---|
| To 98 Dinners @ 4s 6d                 | 22  | 1    | 0 |
| Coffee                                | 1   | 0    | 0 |
| Flowers                               |     | 10   | 0 |
| Artistes' refreshments and sandwiches |     | 4    | 6 |
|                                       | £23 | 15s  | 6d |

No percentage was added for gratuities, a plate was sent around the tables instead.

<br>

ENFIELD CRICKET CLUB
Founded 1856
*President:* S.H. Hill, Esq.

*Hon. Sec. (Tennis Section):*
Mrs E.S. Harris
'Arley', Abbey Road
Bush Hill Park

*Hon. Gen. Secretary:*
Mr A.W. Buckenham
17 Downs Road
Enfield

*Hon. Treasurer:*
Mr F.S. Michell
40 Abbey Road
Enfield

*Hon. Match Secretary:*
Mr J.R. George
Glenesk
Hoodcote Gardens N21

*28 The Meadway*
*Bush Hill Park*
*Middlesex*
*1st March, 1937*

*Dear Mr Standbrook*

*I wish to thank you on behalf of the Committee of the Club for the way you carried out the arrangements for our Dinner on the 12th ulto. I have received many congratulations on the success of the function and we appreciate how much we owe to you and your efficient staff for the way you catered for us.*

*What a pity your accommodation is so limited; as you know I had to close the list some time before the due date, and next year, from what I hear, it will be more popular than ever. I think I can safely say that 130 will want to be present; I don't like to think that the oldest Club in Enfield may have to have its Annual Dinner out of the district through lack of space. Can nothing be done in the matter?*

*Again thanking you and Mrs Standbrook for the thought and care you both gave to the function and which very much lightened my work.*

*Yours sincerely,*
*S.A. Patman,*
*Dinner Secretary*

There is one interesting answer I have yet to find. However did we cope when producing much larger and more complicated menus under such inferior conditions and circumstances, completely without any of the modern equipment, with little or no prepared food to use, and while for service at functions there was only one less than six foot cast iron hotplate to store and serve from! Our normal 'Ladies' Night' menu would consist of six courses plus cheese and coffee; four of the courses were served hot consecutively! Furthermore, from 1924 to 1940 we employed the same number of kitchen staff as we did after the war, with everything being accomplished by hand without any of the 'it-does-it-for-you' equipment so described for the gullible. All meats were carved and served straight from the oven; all soups were home-made (until about 1956), the old-fashioned stock pot was simmering day and night. Apart from all this extra work all food sold in the bars was prepared in the same kitchen, and the same staff was responsible for the cleanliness of the staff room, still room, passages and service area – and *no* unhygienic mops were allowed! The outstanding difference, even up to almost 1960, was the comparative lightheartedness that prevailed, and it was not uncommon to issue a request for a little hush when whistling or laughing distracted those working in the office and attempting to concentrate!

There were numerous con men floating from town to town during the pre-war years, extracting money from easy-going people by relating very plausible tales of their background, and their social or business connections with the 'right' people. Generous in conversation and paying their corner at the bar they would maintain this attitude for a short or long period, depending on the magnitude of the operation and the extent to which the trickster thought he had softened his prey. He would then introduce to his new-found friends some plausible or enticing proposition which could be anything from a share in a race horse to a plan for the purchase of the crown jewels! Petty and unimportant now, but a frequent talking point in a pub, when tales are related of those who have or have not suffered some indignity in being conned.

One simple and impudent trick worked by the minnow swindlers was for a person to purchase a bottle of whisky at the counter, pay for it and place the bottle in his carrier bag, at which moment his colleague opened the entrance door and called out, 'Forget the bottle of scotch, Charlie's already bought one!' and so the bottle was put back on the counter. The person who served it having heard the remark would hand back the cash without compunction, but alas! when the bottle was required later for use from the cabinet it was found to have been switched and to be filled with coloured water! Now what comparison may we make with today? Television? It is a boon to so many people if used correctly, but rarely does conversation follow viewing. The facts are final: 'You have been told!' Even if one does wish to make a remark, before the head is turned and the mouth is shaped to form the first word, the box is in full blast again. Back the head swivels and the eyes are glued once again on something one wouldn't switch on to see from choice, but, oh well, the wife seems contented with it, and so it goes on. The remark which was about to be made is forgotten anyway! We have moved on from the days when the simple confidence trick was conversationally of sufficient importance to be sympathetic or amusing; to a con trick phase now so gigantic that the situation has been reversed, and so we now have an outstanding point of conversation when we have *not* been conned.

We were requested by James Neilson to provide the general victualling for the three day sale at Theobalds Park on Monday, 24th May, 1937. Following the death of Sir Hedworth Meux the mansion was little used; it was eventually leased to Kate Meyrick, the notorious nightclub hostess, who had generated a shady reputation at her London club. Theobalds was raided for late drinking on several occasions, and police later found evidence of more serious practices, in fact involving one of their own members. For her nefarious deeds she was committed to Holloway prison for two years.

The forty bedroomed mansion was at that time being developed as a fully licensed hotel under the auspices of Alderman Sir George Collins, JP, but the enterprise was unsuccessful resulting in the auction. There were 1,249 lots, many of which were left over from the 1911 sale, with which the contents generally would not, in 1937, bear comparison. The mansion was sold to the Middlesex county council, and after being put to several uses it has now settled down as an adult residential college under the responsibility of the Borough of Enfield, who have attempted to restore Theobalds to some of its past glory. The present principal, Peter Padwick, is making great efforts to acquire furnishings or any small articles that would add to the elegance of this lovely old house. I am in the process of having a copy made of the painting of Lady Meux with her horse Volodyvski for the college. (As previously stated, the original painting has since been loaned.) Sir George became bankrupt and I never understood why he bid for and bought so much of his own inventory at the sale. I remember having quite a tussle with Lady Collins, who, for reasons known only to herself, became very discordant when it came to agreeing the refreshment site.

Although we bid for several items, very few came our way; in fact many would have been knocked down for much less but for the bidding of Sir George. Apart from pieces of silver-plated catering equipment only two items bought were of consequence; one an upholstered low-backed armchair which was in the first sale in 1911, and an original fixed oak seat from Temple Bar.

Len Harvey, who won the British heavyweight championship the following year, attended the sale with Florence his very vivacious wife. I found them so delightful to chat with. I was not to meet them again until some thirty-odd years later when Audrey, Brian and I, together with Brian and Maureen Verlaque – who were later to manage The George at Enfield – called in The Star and Garter at Islington (when Len was the licensee) when coming home from a catering exhibition promoted by Charringtons. I wrote to Sir George during the latter part of 1936 asking if the sports complex would be available for rent. My intention was to create a first-class sports club which would offer catering and bar facilities. The following was his reply:

*Theobalds Park Hotel*
*Waltham Cross*
*Herts.*
*4th January, 1937*

*Dear sir,*

*A few weeks ago you wrote asking if the squash courts here could be rented.*

*I am now in a position to sell them with the swimming pool and tennis courts, as a freehold lot.*

*If you are interested we could meet on the site.*

*There appears a strong demand for them, and perhaps a club could be formed to acquire.*

*The money could easily be borrowed from the bank, the interest being debited as rent to the Club.*

> *The premises are fully licensed, but it might be better to take out a 5s 0d club license, and pay the annual Excise levy on purchases.*
>
> *Yours faithfully,*
> *D. George Collins*

This produced something of a surprise, and I was informed by James Neilson quite emphatically that he was in no position to offer any portion of the estate for sale freehold, and so the matter was dropped.

Temple Bar, the old gateway to London is now one of the most forgotten and dilapidated pieces of historical stonework anywhere in and around the capital (my apologies to those who have tried so hard for its restoration). This very famous gateway was built by Wren in 1670 and officially opened in 1672 (at a cost of £1,397 10s 0d); it replaced an older wooden structure which had escaped the Great Fire, but it became a hindrance to the ever-growing amount of traffic. It is probable that at this a barrier had existed from the twelfth century point dividing Fleet Street from the Strand and the City from Westminster. When the building was dismantled in 1878 every stone was numbered and placed in an open space in Farringdon Street, and there these thousands of pieces of masonry incorporating some wonderful craftsmanship and weighing about 400 tons lay for ten years until Sir Henry Bruce Meux, Bart purchased the numbered pieces for £3,000, and had them transported by sturdy horse-drawn brewers dray and re-erected at one of the entrances of his estate at Theobalds Park.

The last of the grim displays of human heads and quarters on Temple Bar was in 1746 following the Jacobite rebellion when Townely and Fletcher had their severed heads exhibited. The head of another Jacobite, Christopher Layer, remained on show impaled on a pole for thirty years, having been placed there in 1723. Several of the well-known diarists mention these gruesome exhibits, and some persons used the macabre scenes for their own benefit! Sir Horace Walpole refers to mercenary people 'making a trade of letting spy glasses out at halfpenny a look'.

In the small room in the archway over the gate of Temple Bar was displayed a large leather-bound book that contained the signatures of a host of famous names, including royalty, who had been guests at the mansion from the late nineteenth century until Bill Neilson and I signed it between the years 1926 and 1928. if memory serves me correctly these signatures were on the same page as that of the Prince of Wales. I was under the impression this book would be offered for auction, but on reflection it must obviously have been a fixture and therefore part of the Meux estate. I did say to Jim Neilson that if the book was entered in the auction I would go up to £50, but to my knowledge this priceless reminder of another era was never spoken of again – I would dearly love to know where the book is now. The little room that contained the book was rented at £50 per annum by Messrs Childs, the bankers, in 1670, and used for keeping their valuable old documents and account books. In 1770 it became the first office of the Legal and General Assurance Society. Jim Neilson was taken ill at the sale and his son Bill made his debut at this public auction – a rather frightening experience!

Temple Bar derived its name from the property adjoining which was owned by the Templars, an order of Knights founded in 1119, the most powerful of military and religious orders founded in the Middle Ages, and born of the Crusades. The original vow of nine French Knights was to maintain free passage for pilgrims to the Holy Land.

Life was so varied during these pre-war years. There was always something different to create or promote. Apart from golf and darts competitions, for which tankards commemorating the Coronation of George VI were presented, two were also presented for bowls and darts at the Constitutional Club. A.J.S. also presented Coronation tankards to all winners of the Enfield Standbrook bowls tournament. Tournaments were arranged for bagatelle, crib, skittles and dominoes. A trophy was presented at the Herts and Essex Aero Club for a balloon-bursting competition held at the Broxbourne air display, which turned out to be a tremendous success. This club was commenced in 1930; instigated by Buster and Roger Frogley, who were among the earliest dirt-track riders. W. Bannister became the flying instructor and F. Barlow the secretary – In 1931 the club was officially opened by Amy Johnson. The cost of obtaining a pilot's A license then was as follows:

|  | £ | s | d |
|---|---|---|---|
| Monthly Member's subscription to Club | 1 | 1 | 0 |
| Eight hours' instruction at £2 per hour | 16 | 0 | 0 |
| Three hours' 'solo' at £1 10s 0d per hour | 4 | 10 | 0 |
| Royal Aero Club and Air Ministry fees for Certificate and License | 1 | 6 | 0 |
| Medical examination (approx.) |  | 10 | 6 |
| Photographs for the Certificate and License |  | 3 | 6 |

Flying clothing (helmet,
telephones and goggles, which
may be obtained in the Clubhouse)     <u>1   5   0</u>
                                                           £24 16   0

Whilst on the subject of flying, I must record our air trip to Ostend, which was organised by A.J.S. through a friend who had connections with Imperial Airways. The object was to visit the Grand Prix Races on 29th August, 1937. The plane chartered was of the famous Scylla class, called Hercules or Heracles. My party from The George included Karl Darter, Gill Robinson, Jack Squires, Herby Ellison and Maurice Derrick. On arriving we decided not to attend the races, but to go sight-seeing. Hiring a car we sought information from the driver, deciding to visit Zeebrugge and the Mole after his initial approach of, 'Where to? Visit the ladies?', Both parties appeared adamant regarding their intentions, so much so that the driver went inland off the coast road to a town. Here he made his final bid, pulling up opposite the female Love Shop and saying; 'There, it is your last chance!' Only one of the party made an effort to depart – jokingly? – and so we went on to our original suggested destination, which we indeed all found very interesting

May 24th, 1937, was a day never to be forgotten: the Coronation of King George VI and Queen Elizabeth following the abdication of Edward VIII. Public houses were open all day – that in itself was reasonable enough – but the trade developed early and continued without a lull until customers and staff were out on their feet. I was very thankful when the doors were finally closed, and grateful to get away from an extremely hazardous situation without suffering any serious incidents. Christmas Eve, in comparison, would have resembled a temperance outing!

The following sixteen years were indeed confusing for their majesties, but the storms were all weathered with a dignity and strength of purpose, sometimes against great odds, that set a fine example to us all. No king could have had a more perfect partner, and to this day she continues to carry out her duties as Queen Mother in a manner undeniably faultless – one of the world's most gracious and kindly ladies.

The Enfield Athletic Club (boxing section) promoted a tournament in January, 1937, at the Drill Hall, on which occasion I organised a party of sixty to attend. I received an extremely appreciative letter from Norman Easlea on behalf of the committee. When one considers the enormous amount of work and thought needed to produce an entertaining show with one hundred per cent voluntary labour, including all of the ABA officials – perhaps the procedure should occasionally be reversed, with a complimentary letter sent to the organising club for the entertainment provided. One remarkable fact relating to the evening in question was the value of the prizes presented. The open novices winner's prize was valued at five guineas (between £35 and £50 today). The maximum permitted cost of a prize today (1974) for a similar event is £7.50. The only officers officiating that evening whom I knew personally who are still around, are Lindley Armitage, Councillor Wally Nunn, John Miller, Stan Blumner and Mary Amies.

This year we saw Walter Neusel beat Jack Peterson at Harringay in February, and again in June at Wembley. At Harringay we also saw Dave Crowley beat Peter Sarron (the latter holding the world's featherweight title). Boxing on the various programmes were Buddy Baer, Jim Wilde, Harry Mizier, Dave Finn, Kid Berg and Alby Day. I was present at what was probably one of the most comical contests ever seen among heavy weights, that between Jack Doyle and King Levinsky. If I had been a sea scout I may have been able to identify the knots they managed to tie between them – the referee seemed to know it because he managed to untie them, in a confused sort of way. There was a surprise for our party at Harringay Arena when Tommy Farr knocked out Walter Neusel in the third round, although at the same stadium Walter had recently outpointed Max Baer. The ringside seats then averaged three guineas, invariably rising to five for championship contests. We normally had seats priced at twenty-four shillings.

The great Joe Louis became the heavyweight champion of the world this year by beating James J. Braddock in eight rounds, and what a tremendous effort was made by Tommy Farr when he took Louis to fifteen rounds in a hard, gruelling contest that was extremely evenly matched. Joe Louis reigned as world champion until 1949, and in that twelve year; he put his crown at stake on no fewer than twenty-five occasions and only three opponents went the distance with him. Two of them were stopped inside the distance at their second meeting, and so Tommy was the only man who can say he went the distance with him without being beaten the second time. I had the pleasure of being with him at a later function.

I was introduced to G.J. Ford, one of the Yeoman Warders at the Tower of London, and organised the first party to see the Ceremony of the Keys at the changing of the guard within the Tower. These outings continued until the outbreak of war. I will never cease to be fascinated by this ancient custom. There is one little, but important, difference in the ritual – before 1940 we adjourned to one of the numerous towers after the ceremony for some liquid refreshment, and this period between about 10.30 p.m. and midnight was long enough just to sense the pressure of the centuries of old emotions and passions held captive among the very blocks of these time-worn stones and, in fact, the very bottles from which we drank actually came from small niches in the walls. Now, following the ceremony, the party adjourns to an attached modern club room where it is impossible to generate the fantasy inspired by the natural environment. Yeoman Ford was enthralling with his tales of the Tower and in the interesting articles he had made or collected. One of his special tales and exhibits related to World War One prisoners who had been found guilty of treason and were shot in the Tower whilst he was stationed there. He would relate in detail every prisoner's reactions when led out to die, and actually had the chair on which the prisoners were seated and bound before the firing squad about turned and received the nerve-racking order, 'Fire!'.

One of the most despised persons at this period, who had enjoyed the country's favours and then schemed for its downfall, was Sir Roger Casement; although imprisoned in the Tower he met his end as a traitor on the end of a rope at Pentonville prison.

The Yeomen are commonly known as Beefeaters, but this rather derogatory expression is very much frowned upon within the Tower! The cost per person for the evening's outing was 3s 6d (17½p).

At this period there seemed to be little difficulty in obtaining tickets to see the Spurs play. I seldom attended, because of the business, but records exist of large parties which I organised for special games. The stand seats were then 5s 0d (25p) which makes them cheap at £1.50 in 1974. Willie Hall, a Spurs inside forward, was one of the regular visitors to The George – an extremely likeable and modest person. The introduction of numbers to be displayed by football players on their shirts was introduced during this period, in fact during 1939.

Christmas has always been, and always will be, a crazy period in a pub, and in 1937 it was no exception. A catering house can become an absolute nightmare if the requisite staff is not available, especially when commitments include catering for functions, luncheons served at three focal points and with license extensions. This particular Christmas Eve, with an extension of license until midnight, terminated with the grand total of £200 in takings. The amount appears ridiculous today, but to take this money it required a staff of fifteen to handle the bars and catering during the morning period; and fifteen again in the evening, but for the bars, snacks and waiting only.

We would complete the stocking up and cleaning of bars after morning session at about 4.30 p.m. After a wash and brush up and a cup of tea the live-in staff were on duty again to prepare for opening and for the onslaught at five thirty. All staff worked through their Christmas week without any time off duty. This included Christmas evening, and on that night, after closing and cleaning up, everyone was invited to a party. (The operation is still very much the same today.) I was completely against opening in the evening on Christmas Day but A.J.S. insisted, and it was not until 1939 I won my point and closed – if ever anyone deserved a break at Christmas it was the employees in the pub business. The same problem existed then regarding teenagers, but it was, fortunately, only once a year, and the majority of people would be feeling sorry for them rather than annoyed. They were perfectly harmless, but simply not used to alcohol – about four lemon and ports and 'whoops-a-daisy!'

# Chapter XXX

The George cricket team 1938 – A.J.S. Chairman NSLVA – The 6s 6d (32½p) menu and toast list – the last tram car leaves The George – command performance 1938 – preparation for war and the Spanish Civil War – cars, gold and prices in comparison – 1939

The events of 1938 were very similar to those of the previous year, except that requests for functions were still growing and outside bar catering was increasingly in demand, but to these many commitments I added a George cricket team. The blame rests initially with Harry Street, Det. Supt. in charge of Y Division who, when talking sport one day, suggested I raise a cricket team to play the Division Athletic Club. I declined on the ground of being far too deeply committed in so many other spheres, but his strategy quickly broke down my defence. 'You won't have to worry, just get the team, we'll do everything else…' It sounded so easy but things seldom work out that way.

However, the first of many matches to be played at the Winchmore Hill CC was arranged for 19th May. I was thankful for Harry Street's introduction, because for team spirit and after-the-game warmth and friendliness, few sports equal cricket. I had good reason for not playing in this game because I didn't wish to weaken the side, knowing they had Herbie Taylor playing for the opposition, and he had recently taken something like five wickets for twenty-odd runs when playing against the West Indies! Still, I had confidence in the strength of my team with

Harry Walton, as captain, supported by Doug Wheeler, Rex Bullock, Harold Dupont, Geoff Gaunt, John Maxwell, Ken Haynes, Doug Hutton, Bert Fitch and E.N. Field. I have no record of the eleventh man, not having a score book for this game. Herbie ploughed straight through them all – all out for thirty-four – and so afterwards to the bar at the Winchmore Hill clubhouse for the inevitable inquest, and to arrange a return.

The return match was played on the same ground exactly four weeks later but The George side was looking quite sick with the loss of five of the team's best players, and so the side was represented by the following substitutions: Bill Garlick, from Upper Clapton, who later played for Enfield; Doctor Forde, from University College Hospital, a charming person from, I believe, the West Indies; Tony Turnbull, also from Upper Clapton and later Enfield; George Chalkley, a fast bowler who was not on top form until his shirt was moist enough to wring out! And, of course myself, which virtually left the team with only ten men.

The game was extremely tense, so much so that I couldn't watch the early balls from Herbie Taylor, but the batsmen soon gained confidence and The George team, aided by a little luck, passed the police score with three wickets to fall. This gave me a chance to take two overs from Herbie – the five I believe I scored consisted of a four from a ball which hit the edge of my bat before my reflexes allowed me to move it, and another cannon-ball I stopped with a shudder that shook my whole body. It was only when the batsman at the other wicket called upon me to run that I realised the ball had bounced off my bat and was equidistant between us in the middle of the wicket. Herbie, knowing I would never make a stroke and hit the ball forward, had half the fieldsmen in the slips waiting for an edge. Dr Forde was quite a cricketer and played an excellent game I wonder where he is now, and what fate has decreed for him? Apart from Harry Street, Herbie Taylor, Sydney (Sandy) Powell, and Ray Pulker, I have no record of the other players representing Y Division.

The majority of these games were played to raise money for charity, and one such event which aroused great interest was with the Enfield fire brigade, when Supt. A.H. Johnstone, a keep-fit fanatic, skippered his side to victory. The return was played during the following month and resulted in a win for The George. The end product for this game – just over £13 – which was donated to the War Memorial Hospital, seems pitifully small when compared with today's bewildering money values, but the sum must have represented an inflationary amount of about £150 today (1974).

All the games were played at the Winchmore Hill Cricket Club and, considering the amazing facilities offered, the charges were very moderate. The total account for the police game was £3 1s 10d – this was for thirty-four teas, the ground and facilities, and gratuities to staff and groundsman. A great day for so little!

We had some great sporting games with The Cambridge in which A.J.S. played, with brother Alf as captain. I had a model dustbin made in which were placed the burnt remains of a very old bat, and so the 'Ashes' were the annual trophy.

A.J.S. was chairman of the Northern Suburban Licensed Victuallers Association in 1938, and a reflection of his decided popularity was demonstrated by the number attending the annual function in the Grand Hall of the Connaught Rooms (where the annexe was also used), about five hundred and fifty diners attending. The George made up a party of nearly fifty, whilst The Cambridge mustered a similarly large supporting group.

Confirmation of the fact that the cost of living was not rising is afforded by the following menu which we served to the town ward of the Enfield Conservative and Constitutional Association, The account reads as follows: seventy-four dinners @ 6s 6d (32½p) £24 1s 0d and is dated 4th March, 1938.

Hors d'oeuvres

Cream of Tomato Soup

Fried Fillet of Plaice and Anchovy Sauce

Lamb Cutlets and Peas
Pommes de Duchess

Roast Chicken and Ham
Game Chips and Salad

Biscuits, Cheese and Butter

Coffee

The names on the toast list were: Douglas Wait, Bill Bowyer, Mrs Hornsey, Bartle Bull, MP, Mrs R.G. Porter, Mrs Holman and Councillor W.H. Bishop. Chairman was Bob Laing. The normal charges rendered for drinks at the table then were as follows: champagne 12s 6d (62½p); Beaune 4s 6d (22½p); whisky, per bottle including a syphon of soda 14s 0d (70p).

The George had a party of forty-odd at the CID Y Division Athletic Club function at Alexandra Palace in November. The toast list was supported by Dist. Supt. George Yandell, Div. Insp. Charlie Coates, Det. Insp. Tag Bishop, Deputy Asst. Commissioner Major de Chair and Bartle Bull, MP.

On 8th May, 1938, the last tram from Enfield left the terminus outside The George. This represented a relatively short life for this mode of public transport for it was only thirty years after the old town had been knocked about to let the first trams in. There were hundreds of sightseers and souvenir hunters in the town, and the vehicle was stripped of everything that was detachable. We were relieved the next morning to have dispensed with that customary dropping of the tram step which created enough noise, together with the general hullabaloo, to have awakened a mummy. The driver lowered the step for the use of passengers before removing the driving control handle and going to the opposite platform for the return journey.

A.J.S. and Jennie attended the Command Performance on 9th November, 1938, at the Coliseum. The show was performed before King George VI, Queen Elizabeth and the Duchess of Kent. The cast included the Tiller Girls, the Two Leslies, Murray and Mooney, Evelyn Laye, Renee Houston and Donald Stewart, Jack Payne with his band and the Dagenham Girls Pipers, Les Allen, Elsie and Doris Waters, Vic and Joe Crastonian, Richard Hearne, the Stuart Morgan Dancers, Ken Davidson and Hugh Forgie, the Three Aberdonians, Will Hatton and Ethel Manners, and, for the grand finale, excerpts from the Victoria Palace production of *Me and My Girl*. The evening ended with the new world-conquering tune by Noel Gay 'The Lambeth Walk', and lustily joining Lupino Lane in the song and walk were many of the old music hall favourites including Irene and Violet Vanbrugh, Mabel Love, Seymour Hicks, Ellen Retford, Harry Tate, Vesta Victoria, Jack Barty, Arthur Reece and Harry Champion, the full company of three hundred and seventy joining in with the 'Oi!' Gary Cooper attended with his wife, also Douglas Fairbanks, junior. The financial result was £4,750 for the Brinsworth Home.

The ushering in of the year 1939 was almost jubilant in its complacency, although the previous year had seen Britain on the brink of war with Germany, an event only deferred by an appeasement deal with Hitler and the Munich agreement which involved the handing over of the Sudetenland to Germany. Some preparations had been made, such as the call-up of reservists, positioning of guns and preparation of ambulances. Trenches were dug, but one gloomy aspect which I believe the population felt most emotion about was the issuing of gas masks, with which came the chilling thought of bacteriological warfare.

The country and the world was aghast when, later in 1939, Russia signed a non-aggression pact with Germany after Britain and France had guaranteed the territory of Poland and were negotiating a military alliance with Russia!

Early in 1939 the Spanish Civil War ended with Franco emerging the victor after three years of extremely controversial, brutal and merciless killing in an atmosphere of extreme hatred. A number of idealists who enlisted to fight were customers at The George, several of whom never returned. Rightly or wrongly I thought at the time how stupid and wrong the whole exercise was, interfering in another country's affairs when poor old Britain required a mite more forthrightness and gusty promoting to get it off its knees.

I purchased a Chrysler saloon, in immaculate condition, for £16, but on arriving home and making a further examination I noticed one of the tyres was just showing the canvas, and had the audacity to take it back and request a replacement, which was provided without question! The greatest drawback with second-hand cars then was that they were inclined to rattle or squeak, owing to wear on the many coach built parts where wood and screws were used. The spring clips that held the folding bonnet in place either side of the engine could also be irritating. I later acquired a sports coupe SS.1, which could have been named The Rattler, but for £17 10s 0d, with almost new tyres, who could grumble?

A Ford eight saloon was then £115 and capable of 60 mph. The Daimler saloon or sports 2.5 litre six cylinder was priced at £485. Petrol had risen to 1s 6d (7½p) per gallon, but generally all commodity prices had remained static over the preceding fifteen years.

Gold was £7 5s 0d per oz, and sovereigns were priced at £1 14s 6d (£1.72½). There appeared to be no apparent increase in wages. For example, The GPO was advertising for engineers at £3 13s 0d (£3.65) per week, and for a male clerk who was expected to have matriculated, to be efficient in shorthand and typing, and to be able to pass a health and fitness test – all this for £145 per annum, rising to £175 maximum, at an annual increase of £15 per annum! The LCC was advertising for cooks at £2 12s 0d to £2 16s 0d per week, with meals to be charged for but uniforms supplied. Probationary nurses were paid £2 per week, including lodging and meals. The minimum working week was forty-eight hours. The standard rate of income tax was 5s 6d (27½p).

If only the same people could be brought back today uncontaminated by the post-war lethargic, something-for-nothing attitude but given the present day money and conditions – Britain would be rebuilt and thriving within one year. Of course, there will always be a percentage of people who are not particularly attracted to work. I interviewed a number of barmen who presented their green cards for signature, declining the job before an interview. Or they would say to you, 'What, me work for ten bob a week, guv?' That was about the difference between working and attending the labour exchange in some cases!

The differences prevailing in customs then and today are in many instances incomprehensible – quality and service do not bear comparison. Then the twice weekly delivery of draught beer by all breweries was an absolute essential, and today the licensee is fortunate if he gets the single delivery at the correct time. All this is due to today's destructive forces for which nobody ever really appears to be responsible.

# Chapter XXXI

Harringay Arena – Boon v Danahar – cricket – George XI v Enfield – cricket – Arundel by air – Arundel as a youngster – George and Phyllis over The White Horse Potters Bar – A.J.S. offered the Stonehouse Hotel, Hatfield

I was pleased not to have missed the great Harringay promotion by Sydney Hulls when Eric Boon put his British lightweight title at stake against Arthur Danahar (both my guests at a later charity function). This was a classic contest between a born hard-hitting, tough and aggressive fighter, and a classic stylish boxer who, in the early rounds, through sheer ringcraft gained a point's lead. As the contest progressed Eric connected more and more with his lethal left hooks, until the referee stopped the contest in the fourteenth round, but not before Arthur had inflicted on his opponent punishment enough not to have made it by any standards a one-sided dispute. Memories flooded back when the were both my guests at a charity function thirty-odd years later. In just over ten months Eric had been involved in fourteen contests, winning nine by knock-out, three within the distance and two on points. Arthur, in approximately the same period, also had fourteen contests, winning eight inside the distance, one KO and five on points.

When we saw Bruce Woodcock, then only eighteen years of age, win the light-heavyweight ABA championship by beating A. Ford, little did we think he would become

British and empire heavyweight champion in 1945, three years after turning professional in 1942, and after nineteen contests.

The cricket team representing The George was full of enthusiasm and played many new teams, including the Chamber of Commerce who through the secretary Stan Walker, was kind and helpful in all our charity games. I have some snippets of coloured film of this game played at the Edmonton CC ground in which brother Alf is portrayed, and Harold Dupont is shown completing his century for The George. We also played Charringtons Brewery, Marshall Taplow, Aldsmede, and Enfield. The latter proved to be a hair-raising game, in fact so exciting that A.J.S. who had the keys of The George, had to stay to see the game concluded, with the result that The George was opened at 7.15 p.m. instead of the usual Sunday opening, which was 7 p.m. In this match fortune smiled on me when I made an apparently sensational catch. In fact I was looking at everybody else, at the boundary where the ball should have been, until one hand felt a little heavier than the other when I arose from an acrobatic dive and found my right hand contained the ball! Rex Bullock was just settling down to his batting with fifteen on the board when he blasted another intended four, but so perfect was Sid Chapman's bowling during this game that I crept closer to the wicket and my reflexes must have instructed me to dive before Rex had made his stroke! The score then was sixty-four for five wickets, with only fifty-five runs required to pass The George's total with Merle Gaunt and Doug Wheeler well set and taking the score to one hundred and eight with four wickets to fall and eleven runs wanted to win. Sid Chapman took the last three wickets for two runs, and the other wicket was taken by Dr Forde by means of a catch by Stuart Roach. Sid took eight wickets for forty-two runs in fourteen overs, five of which were maidens. I must quote another unusual feat from me – I scored eight runs!

### A WIN FOR S. STANDBROOK'S TEAM

Sunday matches on the Enfield ground this season seem destined to provide thrilling finishes and the matches versus Mr Standbrook's XI again caused palpitations before the visitors won by six runs. The slow bowling of Rex Bullock took 6 for 52, only Dr Forde batting well. W. Buckenham made a valuable 28, but the fielders were very kind; in fact Enfield took things too casually and without deprecating in any way the merit of the visitors' unexpected win, several easy catches were badly missed, and the wicket-keeping was poor. Nevertheless, with only 118 to get Enfield, with a good batting side, looked easy winners, and with 60 with only four out, it seemed quite comfortable. The turning point came when Standbrook took a brilliant catch from a very hard hit from Bullock – and one of those catches that fieldsmen dream about. After Gaunt had gone for 20 Wheeler (20 not out) could get no one to stay with him against the devastating bowling of Sid Chapman who, not quite so fast as hitherto, bowled unchanged to take 8 for 40 – a very fine performance. A word of praise must be given to the visitors on their fielding, the whole side were on their toes from start to finish, Congratulations to the victors of a very sporting game.

*Enfield Gazette* Report

The teams were as follows:

Enfield: Jock Whyte; Sid Garbett; Harry Walton; Gordon Chadwick; Rex Bullock; Merle Gaunt; Doug Wheeler; G. (Topsy) Turvey; Trevor Evans; Bob Crowl; Gordon Chidwick.

Stanbrook XI: Stuart Roach; George Wrigglesworth; Bill Garlick, Dr Forde; Ken Haynes; Wally Buckenham; Gordon Holden; Bernard Christmas; Stan Walker; Sid Chapman; Stan Standbrook.

The outstanding day of the year was Saturday, 21st May, when The George went by a chartered air liner to play Arundel town at cricket. The novel outing appeared to have stirred people's imagination, even the London newspapers had posters about 'Enfield's Flying Cricket Team'. The outing obviously created a great deal of work and organising, but everybody was prepared to help where possible, with my old friend Bernard Christmas acting as my right hand. The match date was confirmed early in February, and at this stage it was not intended to travel by air, but as an afterthought I fancied it might be worth enquiring from Imperial Airways about the possibility and cost. To my surprise the quotation was extremely realistic, and so the air liner was booked. When I see the twenty or so letters from the company, and consider the care, attention and the effort to please contained in them, I marvel that all this wonderful service involving a thirty-four seater aircraft all day, with five in crew, was secured for a total cost of only £35! Our dear old friend Horace Clark, the proprietor of Alexandra Coaches, was booked to take the party to Croydon and return for £5 5s 0d, Horace to be the guest of the party as a passenger on the plane. Another coach was booked from London Coastal Services to meet the plane at Ford Aerodrome (now an open prison), a mile or so from Arundel, and take the party to The Victoria Hotel at Bognor Regis for lunch and back to the cricket ground afterwards for which the charge was £5 5s 0d. The proprietor of The Victoria, F. Hallerman, was well-known to Sydney Patman of the Enfield Cricket Club, and it was he who introduced me, making the arrangements so much easier. The lunch was cold with a choice of meats and salad, etc, as well as a hot or cold sweet and biscuits and cheese, for which the charge was 2s 6d (12½p). The two largest hotels in Arundel, The Norfolk and The Bridge, were both approached, but were unable to cater for large parties. Tea was served at the ground and supper was arranged at The Eagle Inn, in Tarrants Street, Arundel, the hosts being my relations Roger and Tot Martin. Every passenger was insured for £1,000. A hired car was also arranged to take the air crew from The Eagle to the airfield.

The chartered plane was one of the Scylla class, named Horatius, constructed by Handley Page Ltd of Cricklewood. This air liner was one of a luxury fleet of that period, and possibly the safest class of air liners ever built. In service all over the world, they flew millions of miles without one fatal accident. The plane represented the acme of comfort, with little noise from its four great prop engines, but of course it was comparatively slow, with a top cruising speed of about 110 mph and maximum speed of 130 mph. Being a large winged bi-plane the lift was so great that one could imagine it being able to land anywhere. The span of the top wing was 130 ft, and the overall length 86 ft 6 inches, with a height of 27 ft 3 inches and an approximate all-up weight of 13 tons. The fore and aft cabins were connected by a passage, on either side of which were the kitchens, toilets and bar dispenser.

Before we took off from the airport I was given instructions regarding two essential stipulations, the first being that under no circumstances must any liquor be taken from the plane and the second to make sure the party were all on time for take-off from Ford before dark. Several of the party had not flown before and others had never flown in an air liner, but I found great interest in observing the reactions. Knowing the short time we should be airborne the boys soon had the stewards on the move with drinks: gin, whisky and brandy 9d (3.75p); Bass and lager 6d (2½p). The one thing I wished to see from the air was Arundel with its majestic castle, the great park, and the river Arun. The pilot, Captain H. Horsey, certainly met this request by manoeuvring the plane to allow ample time to observe the stately scene.

On landing, we were met by Mr F. Hallerman, the proprietor of The Victoria, who had taken a great interest in our endeavours. Before we departed for Bognor the stewards came to me reporting that many of the party had requested the bar be taken to the ground! Very emphatically I said, 'No! Not in any circumstances.' Then everybody joined in and the pressure was on! But I stood my ground, with a final, 'No!' and so away we went. We had almost one and a half hour's drinking before lunch and the match to play after which we would be drinking again and thereafter on the plane. Enough was enough! We met the rest of the party, who had travelled by road, at The Victoria and everybody enjoyed a good lunch. After Harold Dupont had proposed a vote of thanks we departed for Arundel.

Being the skipper I began telling the team in the dressing room my reasons for not allowing the bar on the ground, when, with my shirt half over my head and facing the open fanlight I fancied, above the background of muffled voices, that I heard a glass clink, and money tinkle. I pushed the fanlight horizontal and there, to my astonishment, was the bar all set up at the rear of the pavilion, with everybody scrambling for service! Just nothing I could do about it, except to remain hopeful of propriety winning?

The game commenced at 2 p.m. with Arundel batting first, and although fielding a strong side they were all dismissed for a total of one hundred and six by tea-time Harold Dupont five for twenty-two, Sid Chapman three for thirty-four and Harold Scroggie two for thirty-five. The morale of the Enfield Soaks (the scorers' interpretation in score book) was high when going in to bat after tea, but that light-hearted confidence was short-lived. We were all out for a total of forty-five, and out of this meagre score Christmas knocked nineteen; very fortunately we were blessed with seven byes! Our team was demoralised by Ralph Blackman, who disposed of five of our wickets for six runs. Ralph later became an esteemed friend after meeting me again at The Cambridge nearly thirty years later when he was the Free Trade, area sales manager with Ind Coope. Sadly, he passed away in 1973. I was the only batsman who hadn't an excuse – one, not out! The reason for our total collapse has never been determined, but I am inclined to believe, had there been an inquest, that the fact of the aircraft bar being transported to the ground and local pub being drunk dry had a little to do with it.

After saying our farewells to a sporty team we adjourned to The Eagle Inn and enjoyed a sausage supper with a beer or two, together with the inevitable, 'What happened to the boys?' with not a mention of drink! Following a very convivial session we adjourned to Ford Aerodrome in the coach, and the crew in a hired car. Arriving at the plane in near darkness there was confusion over who had the key last followed by the usual outcome of nobody knowing or remembering who locked up! The next comical scene was lacking only Charlie Chaplin! There was the crew clambering all over the huge plane like seasoned cat burglars, hoping to find some place open, or something which would give under a little pressure. To this day I know not how the entry was made but my last recollection was of one of the stewards being pushed up somewhere by one of the crew and for all I know they may have been stuffing him up the exhaust.

I was lucky in having a chance to handle the controls of the air liner on the outward flight, and how stimulating it was to feel this enormous machine respond so smoothly to the slightest touch of the controls. On the homeward journey several of the party were permitted a spell in the co-pilot's seat, and I admit to some very peculiar performances of the aircraft. I clearly remember Captain Horsey pointing out the newly installed sodium lighting over Purley Way at Croydon. The plane glided in very soberly for a perfect effortless landing.

After leaving one pub and the plane completely dry, we all adjourned enthusiastically to the pilots' mess for yet another session! Captain Horsey expounded his views on the preparedness of Germany to raid England. He knew that most of the German planes were carrying the equipment necessary for mapping England and that all the important strategic points for bombing and elsewhere had been or were being noted should war be declared. He even quoted some planes which were already modified for quick conversion to a war role, and appeared quite upset that he met nothing but complacency when he suggested something should be done about it.

A very happy but tired party arrived back at The George somewhere after midnight. The following summarises the cost of the outing:

|  | £ | s | d |
|---|---|---|---|
| Hire of 34-seater air liner | 35 | 0 | 0 |
| Insurance @ 1s 0d per £1,000 | 1 | 14 | 0 |
| Coach – Enfield to Croydon return |  | 5 | 0 |
| Coach – Arundel to Bognor etc. | 5 | 5 | 0 |
| Taxi for air crew – Arundel to Ford |  | 8 | 0 |
| Lunch The Victoria Hotel |  |  |  |
| Thirty-four @ 2s 6d | 4 | 5 | 0 |
| Sausage supper at The Eagle |  | 15 | 0 |
| New cricket ball |  | 8 | 0 |
| Teas for team, including gratuities |  | 15 | 0 |
| Beer on coach |  | 8 | 6 |
| Gratuities – Air Crew | 3 | 10 | 0 |
| Coaches | 1 | 10 | 0 |
| Scorers |  | 2 | 0 |
| Porter – Croydon |  | 2 | 6 |
|  | £59 | 8s | 0d |

Captain Horsey was a founder pilot of Imperial Airways and at the age of forty-four he lost his life while ferrying a plane for Air Transport, crashing just off the Thames Estuary, the area in which Amy Johnson was drowned doing the same job on the previous Sunday. A pilot in the First World War, he was in his jubilee year as a pilot, and had flown nearly 1¾ million miles without a major accident, and without a single injury to any of his passengers. Not long after our party had the pleasure of flying with him, a story was told of his arrival at Cologne, when a burly German customs officer arrogantly extended his arm and cried, 'Heil Hitler!' Horsey, with a casual turn of the head, remarked, 'God Save the King!'

Between the ages of six and twelve I spent many happy periods with my relations at The Eagle, Arundel. Apart from the pub, Roger had a butcher's business in Tarrant Street, next to which was a sizeable garage also owned by the family, and run by my cousin Cyril, whose brother Stan had a grocer's shop nearby. Percy, who was my age, later held the license of The Station pub, next to the railway station. With Leslie, who managed the butchers with his father, they made up a colourful set of characters whom I knew so well individually without ever really knowing the family collectively. When I was seven or eight years of age I would help Tot Martin to prepare the teas at the Plain, as the Arundel cricket ground is known.

I am sure my memories of Arundel as a youngster are still as vivid and rich now as they were then; the stately and fascinating castle that I would sketch and sketch. From every new vantage point I would try, vainly, to express on paper the excitement of the scene that stirred my inner thoughts and imagination. The great park adjoining the castle must then have been the world's finest playground – thousands of acres of great rolling hills with patches of large and small spinneys and woods, the trees all with their under foliage at a continuous level and kept so by the nibbling deer – herds of them wandering as they willed, dignified in their safe, noiseless, and humble freedom.

We would spend the whole day in this parkland paradise, often watching the battles of the stags with their great antlers entangled in combat to decide who should reign as king of the herd. My memories seem to recall only fine weather; the park in those days was devoid of humans, and the empty silence that reigned seemed exclusive to the park – where a human cry would bounce in wavering echoes from hill to hill, where sunlight would be trapped in the breezeless valleys, and reflect its energy in shimmering waves to produce a distorted mirage effect. Every step aroused myriads of living things which all seemed to buzz and drone except the silent multitudes of brightly coloured butterflies and moths who also appeared to be demonstrating at this sudden trespassing.

The colourful peacocks were a sight to behold at the lodge entrance, certainly the finest specimens I ever remember seeing, and what a delightful background Swanbourne lake, with the wooded hills rising sharply from the lake's edge, made for these strutting, vain-glorious birds.

Today seemingly nothing has changed, but visualising the park in my memory I perceive a diminution of the almost divine solemnity of the peacefulness. The peacocks have vanished, the deer have been replaced by beef cattle which have cut up the downland valleys leading to the lake, and I suppose the weather is not the same. There is also a great increase in the number of visitors, which inevitably eliminates a little of its romance. Another alteration is the new-looking house (quite unpretentious in comparison with the castle), which the Duke of Norfolk had built in the park near to the entrance. The castle has been the home of the duke's family since the twelfth century, and although the greater portion has been rebuilt and modernised in various stages during these years the comforts and convenience of a modern home must be considerably appreciated.

Many times Percy and I have crept out of The Eagle Inn in the early hours of the morning on a moonlight night and walked to the old mill stream that issues from Swanbourne

Lake. Today the mill no longer stands, but in the Domesday book it is recorded that the annual estimated profits were 40 shillings, and in 1272 the output was so considerable that the rental amounted to ten marks, payable to the Lord, fifteen quarters of wheat and ten of barley payable to the prior of Arundel, and ten quarters of wheat and barley each to the chaplain of the castle, as well as £9 8s 0d in cash to the female lepers of the parish!

We would sit on the banks of the stream that raced from the mill pond and listen to the quiet roar of the falling water which quickly lost its turbulence and changed to the fast moving silent surge that pressured the lengthy weeds into an almost horizontal position. The many shades of green were dark in the moonlight, but in daylight the sparkling freshness of the water would tend to exaggerate and almost make luminous these gently swaying wild growths – a thousand years or more of constant flow with but little change.

Cuffley Hotel changed management in 1939. George and Phyllis requested a more lucrative deal since they now had three children to bring up. This on £5 a week, although inclusive of home and food, etc, would not exactly allow them luxuries. They acquired The White Horse, Potters Bar, for which the ingoing was about £1,100 of which George had to borrow the best part. The whole exercise proved very worthwhile, and through sheer hard work and tenacious thinking they prospered progressively during the next thirty-four years.

At some time during this period The Stonehouse Hotel, at Hatfield, was offered to A.J.S. through James Neilson, and Audrey and I were invited to have lunch with him there to assess the possibilities and to estimate its approximate worth. The business being dispensed at the time of our visit appeared inconsiderable, but the premises were generally very well maintained, and the qualified staff reflected an air of affluence. I arrived at a conclusion fairly quickly, taking into consideration the fact that the premises had not been viewed and that no information relating to the hotel department or takings had been divulged. An obvious allowance had to be made for this. When J.N. asked for my views I suggested giving him £25,000 cash on the spot – if I had to buy blind and had the money! I believe the price was £33,000. However, A.J.S. considered the proposition very thoroughly and decided, in the light of the uncertainty of war and the large mortgage to be arranged, to offer the suggestion to Charringtons. An option was obtained, but nothing had been done at the approach of its termination, and so A.J.S. intimated that if the brewers were not interested, he would make an offer himself, but Charringtons finally purchased the property, paying something in the region of £31,000 and installed A.J.S. as a tenant at £1,000 a year rental.

# Chapter XXXII

Build-up for war – menus served to Enfield Chapter Masonic Lodge from 1876 – extracts from my diary

The build-up for war was accelerated as 1939 moved on; evacuation plans were well advanced, air raid shelters constructed, conscription was introduced and the Territorial Army was doubled, but the full realisation of Britain's involvement was not fully comprehended until 1st September, when Germany invaded Poland, and on Sunday, 3rd September, the British and French ultimatum expired at 11 a.m. when Britain was again at war with Germany.

I, like thousands more, was convinced that it was Hitler's intention to blitz London from the start, but never expected to hear the monotonous moaning wail of the siren within half-an-hour of war being declared – 1,224 of these offensive but necessary noise producers were screaming in London at once. The staff were all taken to the cellars in which one old tunnel-shaped part was being converted to a shelter and a funk hole added; the brandy bottle was produced and quickly had the cook thinking again of the joint in the oven rather than of instant destruction!

Within four days six hundred and fifty thousand children had been labelled, equipped and safely transported out of Greater London in the magnificently organised great evacuation exercise and this, as in all the other great cities, was a complete success story.

The extreme efforts of many sections of Britain who appeared to grasp the war situation in its true perspective were to be admired, but my personal feeling was that complacency again veiled the country very soon after the initial shock.

I commenced keeping a diary from 2nd October, 1939, until I entered the Services late in 1940. No matter how reliable we imagine the memory to be the years blur the details and may so easily distort a story.

Most people will unknowingly tell their story in context with present day thinking and not the actual thoughts that controlled the thinking or imagination at the time of the incident. I would be a great supporter and enthusiast of diaries or manuals, old or new, but unfortunately time has not allowed me to indulge in any type of reading and so regrettably I am in that class of lazy readers who wish to absorb the maximum amount of news in a very limited time by reading only the glaring and startling headlines of the popular newspapers and absorbing so little from so much.

My first entry in the diary was as follows:

## Monday 2nd October, 1939

Officers from WX 121 C Co. for trestles and table tops. Emergency meeting NSLV at The Cambridge – had not been informed – borrowed bicycle from Horace (head man) and attended. New prices to start at 11.30 (opening time) 1d pint on beer and 1d on spirits, Went with Father to Kings Head to see Hayball.

I believe the penny addition to the pint of beer and a measure of spirits was the first rise in price since 1920 when the duty on a barrel of beer was raised to £5. In 1923 there was actually a reduction of duty payable of £1 per barrel without lowering the gravity of the brew, and so for the first time since 1660 when the first duty was imposed, the price of beer was reduced by 1d per pint. On a barrel of beer which in quantity is 36 gallons one old penny per pint (0.38 of a new penny) represented 24s 0d (£1.20) per cask.

### Tuesday 3rd October, 1939

Audrey to London to buy suitable clothing for Brian on the farm. Horace had day off to visit his wife and children. Commenced permanent black-out of windows and shutters, Nags Head changed hands. Father requested me to attend in his place.

### Friday 6th October, 1939

We are missing Brian terribly, but he seems to like very much being on the farm at Worlingworth in Suffolk. Bells fitted lounge and front bars instead of calling our 'last orders' and 'time Gentlemen, please'.

Brother George called for me at eleven o'clock – to Hunsdon where we called to see McPhearson and then on to the local. On the way home we called at The Hop Poles. Albert joined the Marines. (Barman).

### Saturday 7th October, 1939

Very busy day. Captain O'Brien promoted to Major and leaving for a posting at Southend. A concert arranged on behalf of the troops later. Elizabeth Allen and Sir Seymour Hicks to dinner.

The above entry refers to the 48th Lt. AA Battery RA, which was formed in Enfield by Major R.E.M. Wheeler (later Sir Mortimer), the HQ being established at premises in London Road (now demolished) and the officers' 'make do' mess was temporarily at The George. From this commenced my long association with Sir Mortimer Wheeler and the Battery. The first volunteer to sign on was Arnold Goodman, now Lord Goodman, one of Britain's eminent law personalities who projects his wisdom in such simple understanding.

The response from Enfield was most impressive, but sadly, as with most of the early formations, many of the early volunteers were not with us at the termination of this gigantic and second ghastly affront to a supposedly civilised world. The Battery moved to Waltham Cross on 18th October.

## Wednesday 11th October, 1939

Have now taken over the cellar work from Horace. Busy interviewing barman and waiters. Loaned the stage and glasses to 48th Battery for a concert at HQ tonight.

## Thursday 12th October, 1939

Off duty evening – to Savoy with Audrey to see *Dark Victory* – dreadfully depressing film about a person dying of cancer – cheered ourselves up by walking through the graveyard to The Old Sergeant to see Jack and Doris Fairlie – back for closing at 10.15 p.m.

## Monday 16 October, 1939

Started new waiter – Bob Bennett.

Kathleen Gillett gave in her notice because we refused to let her sleep out. Audrey and I went for a walk – the first time since the start of war. First air raid on England – near Edinburgh – now it has commenced I can see it getting worse every day. Hamburg news insists that the AC *Ark Royal* has been sunk – also the *Repulse* battered.

## Tuesday 17th October, 1939

News of air raids along the east coast – thinking of bringing Brian home. Peggy in bed with gastric flu. The shelter in cellar under passage being prepared – I think it may be needed soon. Presented a tankard to the 48th Battery for a variety turn competition.

## Thursday 26th October, 1939

Left Enfield at 7.25 a.m. – to Worlingworth, Suffolk to fetch Brian home – Len Oxley should have come along, but no sign of him went off on my own – white frost – arrived Ipswich 9.05 – Framlingham 9.40 – Worlingworth 9.55 (100 miles). Lunch at the farm after which Brian and I walked all round the land. Brian seems well at home with the life and especially horses. Left at 1.45 – back via Bury and Newmarket. Brian dreadfully sick on way – arrived home five o'clock. After seeing Brian to bed, Audrey and I went to The Cock Cockfosters for a meal. People reading the paper by moonlight.

The sickness Brian suffered was the beginning of a long worrying period, which was diagnosed as glandular tuberculosis, caused by drinking fresh cow's milk at the farm! This infection, caused by drinking the milk direct from the cows, was prevalent during the war years.

## Saturday 4th November, 1939

Managed after a lot of trouble to obtain the Stilton cheeses. Father now tells me they are plentiful. Bartle and Billy Bull came to lunch – gave 10s 0d donation for whatever fund I may start. Received a letter from Elizabeth Allen enclosing a photograph.

## Wednesday 8th November, 1939

Donations for the newly formed Soldiers' Children's Fund coming in well – George Spice gave me £5 to be put up in value as prizes.

## Friday 10th November, 1939

Received particulars of a cottage together with two smaller cottages and half acre of land at Royston – £450 freehold – tried to find someone to take me to view, but nobody seemed available. Frank Newton does not think our scheme for the kiddies fund very workable.

It seems Germany must very soon invade Holland – everything has been so quiet recently I feel something lively will happen very shortly. Called at British Legion for more poppies, also to see the chairman and secretary about our new fund.

## Saturday 11th November, 1939

Armistice Day – two minutes silence cancelled.

Father called in to say something must be done as we are nearly £1,000 overdrawn on The George account. I am now carrying a large stock and I seem to be the only one who thinks at a later date it will be needed. Audrey and I cannot work any harder – shorthanded. Total wages only £29 per week including our own (£6 joint).

Referring to the last entry. This stock was completely legitimate, the offers by wholesalers were there for anyone to buy, especially spirits, ports and all types of wine. This also applied to food, i.e. tinned hams, cheeses, etc. This stock would have proved very welcome later on.

### Tuesday 14th November, 1939

In the chair for the inaugural meeting of the proposed fund for the children of servicemen. The following friends attended: Stan Thorpe, Arthur Bridger, Bunny Crane, Ben Liffen, Edgar Dipple, Don Ellis, Percy Upton, Stan Hawkins, Stan Walker, Stan Hooker, Ted Eustance, Harry Walton, Eric Stafford, Stan Austin, Col. (Jack) Crosbie.

The meeting was asked to form a committee. Stan Thorpe was proposed as chairman and this motion was carried. The officers elected were: treasurer – Arthur Bridger, secretary – Bunny Crane and myself as vice chairman. The official name of the fund was to be 'Fund for the Children of the Fighting Forces' (FCFF). Object to provide necessities and amusements for the children. Ben Liffen – chairman of the Investigation Committee and myself of the Entertainments Committee (raise money). Already collected £17 7s 6d – handed over to treasurer. Stan and Bunny stayed after the meeting to have a chat about the new venture.

### Tuesday 21st November, 1939

Typical day for me at The George. 7.45 open office and unlock bars, etc. 8 a.m. Filled cigarette machines. 8.15 stocked cupboard. 8.40 read daily papers. 8.50 notes business and diary. 9.00 breakfast. 9.25 prepared for the Masonic dinner – stocked second spirit cupboard and filled optics. 10.00 Mr Collins phones – number increased to 53 – the whole set up for the dinner had to be changed – Horace off duty. 10.15 started on laying up trestles and table tops; in bad way in garage – hopeless job fixing them. Holdsworth called – checked delivery. 11.15 wash and brush-up. 11.30 opened up. Was mad to see Harry not yet finished yard – everyone seems behind. 12.00 commenced staff luncheons. I relieved in front bars. Charringtons Cellar Inspector called – also Lipton's representative Dewhurst's manager called to make arrangements for registration of catering. Helped Maggie to move some tables. 2.00 lunch. 2.25 turned out lounge and front bars. 2.35 collected waste beers and completed cellar. 2.45 replaced spent electric bulbs hall and kitchen. 3.00 Ted Eustance called to see me. 3.10 arranged furniture in all bars and completed black-out. 3.25 blacked out first floor. 3.50 rested until 4.30 when meeting started.

This entry relating to 21st November was by no means a hazardous day, some were very much harder from a working point of view, and so much more frustrating. The staff position was critical due to the call-up and a great number of men under thirty years of age were leaving service jobs and smartly getting into factories and so evading conscription.

Naturally all pubs were busy but there was a marked tendency for customers to patronise their local, due of course to the black-out when it was necessary for everyone to carry a torch, also the motorist was reluctant to waste petrol apart from the nerve-racking experience of driving hoods attached to the headlights allowing a very small slit to emit sufficient light with which to drive very slowly. The black-out of pubs created a great problem in maintaining an efficient ventilating system. We were having only one half day off then out of seven and even then always back by about 10.15 p.m. to close and cash up.

## Friday 1st December, 1939

Very busy preparing for Standbrook Bowls Concert and presentation. Cups & Prizes – all the donors of trophies are ill. Father, Martin, Cornish and Harston. Tickets 2s 6d. Sixty attended. Audrey presented the prizes and very elegantly too – a very successful evening all round – Cheque to hospital for £40 10s 0d. Stuart Hancock married Harold Dupont's sister.

## Saturday 9th December, 1939

To see Dr Toop during morning with swelling in arm – made appointment Enfield War Memorial Hospital at 2.30 p.m. – no lunch – walked there – gave me gas – abscess cut open – no instructions. Les Morris called for me and took me home in car. Lunch at 3.45, ate well – so hungry. Worked all evening in bar. Audrey dressed my arm at midnight – surprised at the incision – about 1" long – looks very angry.

Harry Brown (Licensee) fell down the cellar stairs at Kings Head and broke his neck – died instantly.

## Sunday 10th December, 1939

Very restless night. Busy moving Masonic furniture into Hall and checking everything for tomorrow – dinner for eighty. Packing and checking parcels all afternoon for one hundred children who will be attending the party given by our fund – some of the Committee helped: Don Ellis, Arthur Bridger, Dr Marshall, Bunny Crane, Stan Hooker, Stan Hawkins.

## Saturday 17th December, 1939

Very little sleep – asked doctor to call as I thought all along abscess would have to be opened again – arranged for his assistant and a nurse to be here at 12.00. Put me to sleep by gas – very sore for a couple of hours.

Now hot fomentations every four hours – nurse said doctor had to cut very deep on one abscess. Mrs Christmas applied the late dressing as nurse had not made arrangements to stay the night. Stuart Roach, Bunny Crane and Stan Thorpe called to see me after decorating the hall for party. Mother and Father with Alf and Bill Aitkens also called to see me.

## Saturday 23rd December, 1939

Quite foggy. Kept very busy but quite different from previous years. The town was empty after 7.00 p.m. due to black-out. Extension until midnight – no trouble except for a little singing and a spot of bother with Dan Murphy who was barred from here some eighteen months ago. The cheapest cheese now 1s 0d per lb. Very short supply – only very small quantities available. Stuart Roach left to take command of his ship which he is taking to Hull and then to Shanghai.

## Monday 1st January, 1940

I have little hope of coming year holding anything better than the last, but at least we should know shortly which way things are going regarding the war.

The 28s are being called for registration – this group should all be in by the end of the summer, then it should be my turn but I think I shall join before that although it would not be fair to Audrey as we are so busy and short of men – if it had not been for Father I would have been in the 48th battery at the beginning. Still a man short having paid Henry off.

## Tuesday 2nd January, 1940

Horace off duty – Jack Frost and Miss Phillips relieving. Have advertised for staff several times but not a single reply – phoned the Labour Exchange – thought I was trying to be funny asking for a barman. The job offered is sleep in and all found, plus three drinks per day and £2 per week.

Called a general meeting for the FCFF re the childrens' tea party arranged for 29th January – cancelled on the grounds that the money will be required more urgently for needy cases.

Bars much quieter. Stocktaking commenced at 7.50 a.m. On to Cuffley later.

## Friday 5th January, 1940

Registered for meat with Harry Walton – average weight of meat allocated to us 1 cwt. 99 lbs. Called at the printers – Hatch – regarding the next dance tickets and drew books in which we are putting up the radio. Dr Toop called to see Brian – said he may now go out for a short while. Looked at my arm and assured me the swelling is only superficial but must be poulticed. Fixed up the train that we bought for Brian at Christmas in the nursery.

To Rialto with Audrey – excellent programme *Frozen Limits* featuring the Crazy Gang and *Come on George* with George Formby. Back at 8.15. One of those uninteresting nights in bar. Father has gone shooting for two days. Hore

Belisha (war minister) resigned – succeeded by Oliver Stanley (president of Board of Trade).

## Saturday 6th January, 1940

My arm is painful – have felt all along it is not clear of the infection. Ken Haynes called in informed me Dick Horne is now farming in Cornwall. Some of our midday customers: Harris, Alf Maxwell, Jim Neilson, Les Mailer, Ben & Nellie Liffen, Charlie Berry, Stan Hooker, Jack Crosbie, Arthur Bridger, Tommy Roach, Dick Clark, Yen Skinner, Sid Lydford, Ken Haynes, Charlie Maunder, Fred Boniwell, Hambley, Len Pendross, Bob Vernum, Edgar Dipple, Fred Briggs, Bunny Austin, Stan Thorpe, Reg Maunder, John and Mrs Thirkell, Ted Eustance, Bernard Christmas, Fred and Gladys Greenwood, Karl Darter, Gill Robinson, Miss Joe West, Charles Marshall, Mr and Mrs Wally Drage, Scott, Bill Kennard, Ted West, Les Morris, Ken Hutton, Joan Jotsham, Stuart Roach, home for a short time before going to Shanghai. Barred an Irishman from lounge – would keep annoying customers by joining in their conversations. Very quiet in front bars. Freezing and foggy.

## Monday 8th January, 1940

Rationing has started for butter, sugar, ham, bacon. 4 oz butter (adults), 2 oz (children). 12 oz sugar, 4 oz bacon and ham. Terribly complicated with the staff and catering – everyone is a little lost. The new man I engaged failed to report for duty.

Nanny went to hospital to have her fingers opened – we are getting fair old customers to Dr Toop. Trade very slack.

## Wednesday 10th January, 1940

Kept to my bed – Audrey phoned for doctor – having not had much sleep for two nights I feel dreadful. Dr Toop tells me we will have to get that infernal gas machine up here again and operate. Engaged a Nurse Jones. Hot fomentations every three hours.

## Friday 12 January, 1940

Doctor insists that immediately my arm heals I must go away for a complete change – also that if another abscess forms he would recommend further advice. General meeting FCFF – held finance meeting in bedroom with Stan Hawkins, Arthur Bridger and Eric Stafford.

## Tuesday 16th January, 1940

Dr Toop brought a specialist – Dr Hamian Taylor – to see me at 2.30 p.m. Stayed about four minutes – told us what we all knew and thought and calmly walked out with £10 10s 0d cash – he must have read *The Citadel*. Doctor says the abscess keeps coming because I am run down – after this I expect them all over me. Bunny Crane, Len Pendross, Stan Hooker and Les Pratt called to see me.

Sacked the housemaid – Flossie Barnard.

## Wednesday 17th January, 1940

Doctor called – a fair chance that my arm will not have to be opened again. George and Ben Chandler called – both have severe colds. Father to see specialist to be X-rayed. The war progressing much the same – Japan is making friends with all – I expect this is on Germany's advice. They will shortly spring such a surprise. The coldest spell we have had for some years.

## Thursday 18th January, 1940

Doctor assures me that the arm will not have to be opened again – still taking M&B tablets – appear to be now taking effect. Explosion at Enfield Small Arms Factory, Waltham Abbey – five killed and about fifty injured – not heard by anyone in this house, but reports of windows out and buildings being shaken several miles away – believed to be sabotage.

## Friday 19th January, 1940

Arm very much better. Mother called with Alf and Edna.

Bad fire at Sydney Bird's factory – Cyldon works – could be sabotage – now have a number of government contracts.

Dr Toop called and signed me off, but insisted I go away. Went in Buick to see Father and Mother – both worried because I am going away – especially as Father unable to come down to The George. I explained that if customers leave because both of us are unwell they are not worth having. Visited dentist (Dimmock) to have my teeth scraped. Nanny and Brian went to Bately's to collect cine camera Steve is loaning me.

I did attempt to recuperate by having a week in Brighton and left on 25th January to stay at The Old Ship Hotel. I write in my diary, 'Brighton at present is a very depressing town' and, 'For a walk during the evening and called in the downstairs bar on arriving back – only one person there and a dingy atmosphere.'

Also, 'Visited a supposedly first class lounge bar – awful place, only one customer apart from myself – getting very bored – everywhere frozen up – quoted as the coldest spell since Waterloo.' All trains stopped, passengers staying on them all night. Another entry, 'Met a Mr Stevens (solicitor from Chatham) the only person I have met with whom I could converse.'

I felt so lonely and bored I enquired about the train service home and I note in the diary, 'Service improved to London – steam has replaced the electric trains (due to the rails icing up) – caught the 11 a.m. arriving London Bridge 1 p.m. Had a sandwich in buffet bar – what filthy holes these station bars are!'

## Tuesday 6th February, 1940

Horace away sick, also Margaret (staff maid) never turned up, I must really take it easy – have come home to a holy mess – b— awful state we are in. I am the only one left who understands the cellar and I am not able to lift anything. Four staff away – two main electric fires burnt out and no coal!

I interviewed an applicant for the bar, Trevor Bishop, to make sure of him I sent him straight into the bar to serve. Had a chat with the C in C of the Home Forces, General Sir Edmund Kirke.

The same old story – Germany short of fuel and very inferior, in fact they haven't a chance – just a matter of time! I hope there are a few who have a different perspective and can see the situation in the right light.

## Sunday 11th February, 1940

After my talk about being late on duty Bob arrives at 9.15 and expects to be served with breakfast – cook, of course, has orders not to serve them if late.

Margery, lounge barmaid off to bed unwell – looked quite normal to me. Spent a couple of hours sawing wood – no coal in stock. Dr Chisholm's nurse, Scotchie, looked after Brian for the day.

Nanny took the opportunity to go to Framlingham with Harry Walton. Apparently Brian had a wonderful day and would have liked to stay.

## Thursday 17th February, 1940

A long midday session with CID inspectors Coates, Greenhill and Ashburner. Greenhill has taken over from Inspector Arky.

FCFF general meeting – cases investigated now one hundred and thirty-six – one hundred and one having had assistance – £72 7s 6d so far spent (including Christmas tea). Bacon ration doubled – down to 1s 6d per lb and 1s 2d streaky – previously 2s 4d and 1s 10d – have been informed by Hunters it is so plentiful they are throwing it away bad!

## Saturday 17th February, 1940

Heavy fall of snow during the night. Short of coal again – spent an hour in garage sawing wood – coal now £21 1s 4d per ton.

A rumour that there might be a shortage of spirits in the near future – in my opinion this time next year we shall be short of many things. Estimated a 12½ per cent increase in the cost of living.

This country will soon have to step out of this complacent attitude – everyone seems to be making the moves except us.

HMS *Cossack* went into neutral waters and boarded *The Altmark* the German ship that has held over three hundred merchant seaman as prisoners under terrible conditions – this is a tonic – one of the few things we have done that shows the English spirit commonly known as guts.

## Monday 19th February, 1940

Violet not in – telephone call to say she would not be coming back – makes me sick, and we have lost Kathleen through her. Very shorthanded lunchtime. Horace off duty also Bob (waiter) and Margery (lounge). For a long period Audrey had the lounge on her own and I had the whole of the front bars!

## Tuesday 20th February, 1940

Manor of Worcesters Masonic Lodge – mainly local people and somehow the whole atmosphere appears lighter – very pleased with dinner – a vote of thanks was passed to Audrey who had done all the carving and serving – what a worry not having efficient staff. Jimmy Wilde the WM came in office afterwards for a drink – one of the few people who seems to think the right way about the war – recently had £500 presented to him by Winston Churchill for an invention connected with the war.

## Monday 26th February, 1940

Fixed menu with Enfield Chase Tennis Club – six shillings per head.

Hors d'oeuvres
Soup – Choice of Cream or Consommé
Fillet Sole & Tartare sauce

Chicken and Ham – Game ships –
two vegetables

Pear Melba
Cheese
Coffee

## Saturday 2nd March, 1940

Completely out of coal – the firm we have registered with, Girlings, have not a piece in their yard.

The Hannibal – same class of plane that we flew to Arundel in to play cricket is reported missing – there are eight planes in this class and each has flown over one million miles without any accident. Vera Cain (lounge) walked out after closing 2.30 – been with us fifteen months – nobody seems to know anything about it.

Ale pump broke down when very busy at 9.30 p.m. Always happens at the wrong time.

## Wednesday 6th March, 1940

Whilst waiting for Audrey I went for a walk with Connie, after to tea with her together with Brian and Nanny. Evening to Rialto saw Deanna Durbin in *Her First Love*, excellent film. Les off duty ten o'clock – had sandwich with us. Approached outside caterers – Gerrards – to cater for the Enfield Chase TC dinner/dance but wanted six shillings and nine pence per head for the same menu we are doing for six shillings.

New relief hand started – Winnie Gibson.

I wish the Labour Exchange, like every other government department, would stop wasting our time and theirs by sending girls to us who have never been inside a licensed house and with no intention of taking the job – we have told the LE so many times.

Tom Hinkens cremated.

## Tuesday 12th March, 1940

Horace off duty. Roper (chauffeur) helped me in afternoon to move all the Masonic furniture in preparation for a luncheon party tomorrow – never sat down all day – finished the furniture at five o'clock – 5.15 down preparing to open at 5.30 and putting all the furniture straight.

Brother George called in at seven o'clock.

Armistice between Finland and Russia – the latter know just what they are doing.

## Saturday 16th March, 1940

A long hard day – on from 8 a.m. until 1 a.m. next day. Enfield Chase Tennis Club dinner dance for seventy. Audrey too was very busy – did all the laying-up. Bob (waiter) sent home with German measles – in a bad way for staff but the dinner went off perfectly – I was asked in the room and congratulated. I responded. Extension until midnight.

## Monday 18th March, 1940

Masonic Dinner – Enfield Chapter – went off very well. Winnie has now contracted measles. Doctor said she could not be moved to hospital so she must stay here – difficult with the other staff – will have to arrange for them to sleep off the premises. Started a new barmaid in lounge, Anne Keating, over 6 ft tall and big all over. Sheila in to relieve. Margery took over luncheon room with Kate. Fourteen planes raided Scapa Flow – not to be used any more as a naval base! One shot down.

## Tuesday 26th March, 1940

Gave a week's notice to Anne – the very large Irish girl.

## Thursday 28th March, 1940

Les Morris stayed to lunch with Audrey and I.

To Rialto with Audrey – Arthur Askey in *Band Waggon* not very funny. Les arranged to take us for a run – called to see if he was ready and fell into a nice school. Jack and Doris Fairlie, Fred Nottage and Willie Hall, Stan Edwards and most of our fund committee – finally managed to get away after getting a round of drinks. Les took us to see the alterations he had completed at The Cross Keys, Edmonton – a very nice bar but lacking in lots of incidentals – the woodwork makes it. A Brown & Horner's house. Company houses are never the same when managed.

Told the staff off for leaving the tables out in the passage. Some silly — must fall over one as Father is leaving! I got it well and truly.

## Friday 29th March, 1940

Midday very busy in bars and luncheon room. Eric Stafford had lunch with us – said the catalogue we chose films from was about ten years old and out of date! We spent the afternoon working out a programme for the charity show.

Sydney Bird offered me his Talkie Projector for our show – also brought the race outing film in. I am annoyed at customers seeing Father about my giving notice to Anne – had to ask her to stay on!

## Wednesday 3rd April, 1940

Arranged the hall for tonight FCFF film show. Sydney Bird and his son brought their own projector and coloured films (cost £75). Took a lot off my hands. Tommy Carter had his radiogram and records delivered – he also took charge of the music for the evening. About seventy people attended and the collection was £4 7s 0d. Father, Mother, Reg and Peggy, Mr and Mrs Bird stayed until 1 a.m.

## Tuesday 9th April, 1940

Germany invades Sweden and Norway – it seems just a matter of walking in. Rumours circulating – the Navy having it tough.

Some budget details: IT up 6d (7s 0d to 7s 6d). Married allowance down from £180 to £170 – Children £60 to £50 – Surtax over £1,500 (£2,000) 1d pint on beer – 1s 9d on bottle whisky, now 16s 0d. 1d on cigarettes 5d to 6d – over 5d brands 1½d on – ½d on matches, now 1½d. Letters 21s 2d for 20 oz (1½d), Postcards 2d (1d).

## Wednesday 10th April, 1940

Germany have now complete control of Denmark, and Norway about to fall. Two German cruisers sunk – also a British destroyer and one aground. Everyone is of the opinion that Italy will not enter the war but I think she will come in just when it suits Germany.

Cancelled the cricket fixtures with Enfield and Aldsmede.

Bill Neilson's bachelor party – copy account:

|                              | £   | s   | d   |
|------------------------------|-----|-----|-----|
| Twenty-one dinners @ 3s 6d   | 3   | 13  | 6   |
| Refreshments                 |     |     |     |
| 16 qts ale @ 1s 8d           | 1   | 6   | 8   |
| 14 pts bitter @ 9d           |     | 10  | 6   |
| 8 pts ale @ 8d               |     | 5   | 4   |
| 4 pts mild and bitter @ 9d   |     | 3   | 0   |
| 2 Ports @ 9d                 |     | 1   | 6   |
| 1 Sherry @ 9d                |     |     | 9   |
|                              | £6  | 1s  | 3d  |

Dart match with North Enfield Club raised £1 0s 2d for FCFF.

## Thursday 11th April, 1940

Paid Anne off – going out all locked up and leaving kitchen door open – has been sleeping out. No wonder some customers didn't want her to leave!

The newspapers are still pumping out 'The War is all over' theme – sunk half the German Navy, etc. I certainly think we are doing well considering. but to me the war has not yet commenced.

## Friday 12th April, 1940

A hell of a day – barmaid short and two waitresses not coming in. Audrey and I never stopped all day.

Meeting for Pearl Assurance morning – sandwiches for twenty, also a private luncheon party. Evening: novel supper to raise money for the fund tickets three shillings and sixpence. Soup, boiled leg of mutton and caper sauce, mashed turnips, potatoes greens, dutch apple tart (served with a radish) and cheese including a pint of beer – not much profit but for a good cause and everybody who left the slightest scrap on any plate was fined. Churchwarden pipes and a plug of tobacco for four pence – allowed first light, after a tuppenny fine if seen lighting again – sixpence fine if broken pipe – very few whole ones left and one or two bleeding bald heads including that of Edgar Dipple – Jack Crosby's idea. Extension until 11.30p.m.

## Saturday 13th April, 1940

Shambles. What a mess to clear up – hundreds of pieces of churchwarden pipes all over the place – busy morning in bars. Alf and Reg called in lounge. A wonderful air of 'life is wonderful' – not a care in the world – I seem always to be slogging.

Audrey related a story of her father saving a kiddy of three from drowning.

## Friday 19th April, 1940

Mr and Mrs Bartle Bull and Admiral Taylor called in for dinner. Audrey out and Bob (waiter) off until eight o'clock – also Margery! Managed to get over the awkward situation – they were all very charming.

## Saturday 20th April, 1940

Stan Thorpe's birthday – also Hitler's birthday, blast him. Explosion in Powder Mills, Waltham Abbey – five killed.

## Thursday 25th April, 1940

Half pint glasses which were four shillings per dozen are now nine shillings and sixpence.

Called to see Captain Dyer at Romford – had just broken up from the Licensed Victuallers Emergency meeting – decided to raise the price of spirits from nine pence to ten pence. An extremely interesting and knowledgeable person, presented to me the Brewers Manual and another book, the *Royal Commission on Licensing*.

Evening off – went to Savoy *Gulliver's Travels*. Another dreadful picture. To Robin Hood with Les after – back to The George – bar very busy. In trouble again – Father had to be standing by when a customer fell through the wicket door in large swing gate when leaving at closing time – flat on his face – clot!

## Friday 26th April, 1940

LV emergency meeting at Cambridge – agreed to raise the price of spirits one penny per nip. Cigarettes also up – large one shilling and five pence and small eight pence halfpenny. Came home with Nelson Barber Merryhills and Bert Smith Jolly Farmers.'

All lights on first and second floor fused – reported wiring too dangerous to repair – will have to be bodged in some way – no gas on top floor. Oh to live in a modern house!

## Saturday 27th April, 1940

Very busy in lounge. Had to turn out three rough louts for singing. Refrigerator now out of action (Electrolux). Doris Darter married Bib Giles at St Stephens we were invited but impossible to attend.

## Monday 29th April, 1940

Apparently the brewers have kept the beer at pre-war price – only adding what they term War Tax – 44s 0d per barrel – we get an extra six shillings for collecting it. Several people are now using the public bar for our one shilling and threepence lunch. Joe Cleary left to go into factory – two short and I, at present, have his work to do. Surprised at being so busy considering the extra one penny pint on beer and one penny halfpenny on the stronger gravity beers – Guinness, etc. Maintenance on Lounge National Cash Register.

## Wednesday 1st May, 1940

I am still carrying on with cleaning all the pewter and stocking up – no answer to any of our adverts.

Played return match with North Enfield Conservative Club at darts. FCFF team won – benefited the fund by £1 4s 0d – Team: Stan Walker, Stan Hawkins, Eric Stafford, Bill Davis, Jack Crosby; R. Crosby, Bill Bedford, Ted West, Yorky, J. Lee and friend, scorer, Stan Hooker.

## Thursday 2nd May, 1940

Very busy morning. Down early to let in a man George recommended to clear the mice. Electrolux mechanic here to repair the fridge. Mother and Father called in and stayed until 2 p.m. Also have an interview now between 4.30 and 5.00 p.m. with a married couple – little chance of any break. With the atmosphere today (black-out, etc.) and the very unnatural way one lives it is amazing how anybody should live more than ten years in our business.

To Rialto evening – *Sons of the Sea*, coloured film – typically English, weak and slow. Les called for us at 9.15 –

went to see Frank Jelfs at The Fallow Buck. Back at 10.20 to close up – we must definitely make some better arrangements for our day off. Left Jack Frost to arrange hall for dinner tomorrow and dance on Saturday – gave him a long list of instructions.

## Friday 3rd May, 1940

Audrey taken ill and doctor called. Must stay in bed.

## Saturday 4th May, 1940

Doctor visited Audrey and she must rest.

I am in a hell of a state. FCFF dance – not feeling too well myself and so much to organise and short of staff. Bernard Christmas helping in club room. Harry Chittenden on the door for me, Mrs Eastern relieving – packed in lounge and all nice people – Jack Frost worked afternoon to finish preparing hall – Bunny gave me a hand as well.

Sweden seems to be losing faith in us now, this government seems pretty useless.

## Wednesday 8th May, 1940

Harry Chittenden started painting all the hall windows with splinter proof paint – now a regulation of the MCC.

Audrey and I to Rialto and saw *For Freedom*. Back to The George 9 p.m. Stuart Roach brought a camphor wood chest home from Japan for Audrey.

## Thursday 9th May, 1940

Sid Lydford took Audrey, Brian and I to White Webbs. We played a little golf. Tea at club – feel so much better for being out in the air. Early evening to view Two Brewers, Northaw – £600 ingoing – very keen. General meeting FCFF.

Bet Ernie Stephens 2–1 the war will not be over this time next year – ten shillings – hope he wins. Neville Chamberlain handed in his resignation, he has done his best. Winston Churchill to take over – a general change around.

## Friday 10th May, 1940

We are still in a devil of a mess for staff. Cleaned all the pewter, stocked up and arranged for tonight's function in hall. Germany invades Belgium, Holland and Luxemburg. All holidays cancelled. Audrey went to see Two Brewers with Sid, Les and Connie – all very enthusiastic – wrote to Tumbler.

## Sunday 12th May, 1940

To Northaw again with Sid – mainly to get a general idea of the Two Brewers position.

After closing we entertained in our lounge upstairs – Stuart Roach, Harry Walton, Bob Vernum and Jock White.

## Wednesday 15th May, 1940

To Cannon Brewery with Audrey – appointment with Mr Tumbler – saw a Mr Barker.

No luck – absolutely no chance – military age (call-up), terribly disappointed.

The reason we were looking for a small business was the fact that A.J.S. and Jennie had emphatically stated that Audrey would be unable to cope with The George when I eventually received my calling-up papers which were expected within six months. We had hardly sufficient money to buy a house and be left with any capital at all if the furnishings were to be completed. Our complete wealth was about £300.

## Thursday 16th May, 1940

Sid Lydford dragged me out for nine holes of golf at 3.45 – back at 5.30. Went to see White Lion at Barnet – Glen Jackerman told us it was on the market. Not suitable – just couldn't see Audrey and I there. Audrey wrote off for a job that was advertised.

Expecting a raid – barriers up at Potters Bar and guns in readiness on roofs. Everyone is talking of the danger of attacks by parachutists now – they were laughing at me seven months ago.

## Monday 20th May, 1940

Refugees now arriving and being looked after at the Oddfellows Hall: about one thousand five hundred Belgian and Dutch. A number people changed their minds and would not take them in – I hope some day they find themselves in the same position. Enfield Masonic Lodge meeting.

## Tuesday 21st May, 1940

Stocktaker.

Father called – had a chat about Audrey and I leaving. He suggested we stayed on until we found somewhere. Afternoon Audrey and I walked in park and made the most of the fresh air and a rest. Brian to Bloomfield Park for a picnic.

The German advance looking very dangerous – outlook very black – now reached Arras and Amiens, also reported to have reached Abbeville, if so they have split the two armies. M. Reynaud, the French premier, talks about miracles saving France – I hate to record or think it but it looks as if the French have been 'sold'. It seems now we shall finish up defending our island.

Florrie (cleaner) away ill, couldn't have happened at a worse time. Bought a whole Scotch salmon 9 lb @ 1s 10d per lb. (twenty good portions).

## Wednesday 22nd May, 1940

Here we are on the brink of probably the greatest disaster in our history and everyone seems so casual – nobody jumping into it.

Trade Unions demanding double time on Whit Monday or else they would strike, and butchers want treble time. I'd throw the leaders into jail. The output of this country could be doubled. Horseracing, football, in fact everything is just fine and normal and it is possible that two or three months could see us under Nazi rule!

Afternoon – took Brian to park.

Hinkins washed the front down – £2 10s 0d.

## Thursday 23rd May, 1940

Better take back some of my recent words regarding the attitude towards the war – the government is now going to do what it should have done months ago. A new defence bill is now in force which includes everybody in the country, also property. Mosley has been arrested, together with Tamsey MP and numerous others – now we should get somewhere.

German troops have occupied Boulogne – things looking very grave, but the one shining light is the RAF, which is doing well. Offered my services to the police and many other organisations but nobody seems to want any help. Played golf with Sid, White Webbs, in the afternoon. In fifteen holes I managed four bogy and one birdie – feel much better for being out in the fresh air. To Rialto with Audrey evening – saw *Tower of London*, Rathbone and Karloff. Back to close up. Engaged a Miss Hammond as relief barmaid. Fifteen French generals sacked.

## Friday 24th May, 1940

Machine guns are being mounted on all suitable buildings – if the Germans get consolidated in the Channel ports then our turn must come. I cannot think what our Army will do – half of them are cut and completely surrounded.

General meeting FCFF Sir Edmund Kirk retired as C in C of HM forces – replaced by General Ironside – good change.

## Saturday 27th May, 1940

Very busy and very shorthanded. Making arrangements to evacuate Brian again. Bombs dropped in Essex and Yorkshire. I feel quite certain that we shall not know London as it is when this is all over – am also as certain that this will apply to Berlin if they do start.

Another bet with Gifford and Bert that the war will not be over by Christmas – cannot understand people!

Age twenty-seven group called for registration.

Gave Horace (head bar-cellarman) a rise of five shillings, making his wage now £2 15s 0d plus £1 per month on stock results – also five shillings rise for Henry, now £2 5s 0d.

## Monday 27th May, 1940

We are now doubtful about sending Brian away, at least not far – if we are invaded, who will know where? Italy looks like joining in any time now. Have an idea for building simple type of tower as manned look-out posts to cover all likely landing places in country for parachutes and planes.

Catering rations cut – 2 lbs of sugar instead of 14 lbs, and 4 lbs butter instead of 12 lbs. Sent all the gas masks to have new filters fixed. Enfield Chapter – last one of the season, thank goodness.

Referring to the last sentence of the 27th May, the Enfield Chapter No. 1237 – Enfield Masonic Lodge held their meetings at The George Hotel one hundred years ago. The following menus authenticate this statement. The first is dated 1876 and costing probably between 2s 6d (12½p) and 3s 0d (15p).

### The Enfield Lodge
### Installation Banquet

at the
George Hotel, Enfield
December 11th, 1876

### The worshipful master bro. Charles Samuel Brown Presiding

### Menu

Soups
Mock Turtle, Ox Tail

Fish
Cod Fish and Oyster Sauce
Soles (Filleted) Eels

### Removes
Turkey, Haunch of Mutton, Sirloin Beef
Fillet of Veal, Boiled & Roast Chickens
Roast Goose, Ham and Tongue

### Game
Roast Leverets, Pheasants, Partridges

### Sweets
Adelaide Pudding, Plum Pudding
Lemon and Orange Jellies, Blanc Mange, Mince Pies
Tartlets, Tipsy Cake

### Dessert Wines
Port, Sherry, Champagne, Hock, Claret

## Demarcation

The following is dated 1891 – Probable cost between 3s 0d (15p) and 3s 6d (17½p).

## Enfield Chapter
### No. 1237
The George Hotel, Enfield

## Menu

### Soups
Mock Turtle, Hare

### Fish
Cod and Oyster Sauce, Boiled Eels

### Removes
Roast Turkey, Roast Fowls, Boiled Fowls
Ox Tongue, Sirloin of Beef

Sweets
Plum Pudding, Mince Pies
Maraschino Jellies
Stewed Fruits

Dessert

## Demarcation

Below is an example of many served in 1930 by Standbrooks, the cost of which was 6s 6d (32½p).

Enfield Chapter No. 1237
The George Hotel, Enfield Town
Monday – 24th March, 1930

### Menu

Hors d'oeuvres
Tomato Puree
Filleted Sole with Anchovy Sauce
Fillet Steak Garnished

Chicken and Ham, Salad

Peach Melba
Cheese & Biscuits, Butter
Coffee

Coincidentally, the last function account written out in the book before Audrey and I left The George and the last function as such during the war years was for the Enfield Chapter; the menu would have been similar to the previous one, but the following account quotes 1s 0d increase – 7s 0d (37½p).

|  | £ | s | d |
|---|---|---|---|
| 24 dinners @ 7s 6d (37@2p) | 9 | 0 | 0 |
| Wines |  |  |  |
| 3 × ½ bottles whisky @ 10s 0d (50p) | 1 | 10 | 0 |
| 4 bottles Barsac @ 6s 0d (30p) | 1 | 4 | 0 |
| 1 syphon soda @ 1s 3d (6.25p) |  | 1 | 0 |
| 5 bottles of Bass @ 9½d (3.9p) |  | 3 | ½ |
| 4 bottles grapefruit @ 6d (2½p) |  | 2 | 0 |
| 1 split ginger ale @ 6d (2½) |  |  | 6 |
| 12 baby Polly's @ 3½d (1.46p) |  | 3 | 6 |
| 6 baby tonic @ 3½d (1.46p) |  | 1 | 9 |
| 4 pints bitter @ 10d (4.17p) |  | 3 | 4 |
|  | £1 | 10s3½d | |

Wednesday 19th May, 1940

The BEF are now fighting their way out to Dunkirk where the Navy are doing a wonderful job. They must lose at least a third of their men. The Irish are not helping our cause – fancy! Ireland part of the British Isles and the German Legation sitting there!

Entertainments meeting FCFF.

Called at The Stag and Kings Head and back to close at 10.20. All signposts taken down and telephone boxes put out of action due to parachutists.

Friday 31st May, 1940

General meeting FCFF.

Looks as if the next objective of the Germans is Paris.

I cannot see anything to stop them, and it is likely Italy will join in as well.

## Monday 3rd June, 1940

Paris raided reported fifty killed and one hundred and fifty injured. We and France must have a go at Berlin. I know there is a dreadful shortage of planes – could do with another three thousand at least. Bombs dropped in Norfolk and Suffolk, no warnings given. Nearly all have been evacuated from Dunkirk – McGuire's son returned wounded. Only one hundred and twenty-five saved out of one thousand from his contingent.

## Tuesday 4th June, 1940

Apart from all else I have the pewter and bottling to do again. The last of the troops taken from Dunkirk – miraculous performance. Three hundred and fifty thousand saved. Only thirty saved out of four thousand defending Calais which made the time for the others to get away.

## Saturday 8th June, 1940

Up half the night – 12.15 there was a distinct banging just under the floor.

Nanny was also awakened by it. Police knocked us up at 2.45 for having lights showing. Went down and let them in – found passage lights on, curtains drawn back and window overlooking Ebbens Bakery open, door also open. After questioning staff it seemed clear that somebody had broken in and the banging was the window being opened – several raids whilst looking around – flying very high. Went back to police station and received a caution.

Busy day, weather very hot.

Isobel the kitchen maid gave in her notice.

Father bought a small Morris 12 car (£70). Petrol very short.

## Monday 10th June, 1940

As dark as night all day. The Weygand line generally is still holding. All troops withdrawn from Norway. Dob Ward back from the BEF.

Italy declared war on Great Britain and France – probably organised to win the first leg but they will eventually get such a bashing.

## Tuesday 11th June, 1940

Harry Walton paid his bet regarding Italy.

Dick Clark left for Llandudno.

Only a miracle can now stop the Germans going into Paris. Italian bases at Libya bombed.

Dart match FCFF and Sydney Bird's team – raised £2 3s 0d – six of our team failed to appear – my parachuting board made 15s 0d. After match cheese and biscuits and spring onions.

Started new bar waitress – Doreen Bridie.

## Wednesday 12th June, 1940

Ma and Pa off to the Derby, George and Phyl and Captain Horton called at 11.30. Extremely busy morning Bob (waiter) walked out – new waitress had luncheon room on her own – managed very well.

Newspapers report no change on the western front but reading between the lines Paris must fall in a few days.

## Thursday 13th June, 1940

For five years they have drummed into the people, 'Never again shall our soldiers be short of anything'. After only a few weeks in combat they are short of everything.

Everything seems to be far too weak that is being done for Home Defence – being carried out without inspiration in an atmosphere of 'it will never be wanted' Another six thousand troops cut off and captured. George and Phyl with some friends called in at 11.30

To Rialto with Audrey. Afterwards borrowed the Morris 12 and went to Cuffley to look at a furnished bungalow – 35s 0d per week inclusive. After to Cuffley Hotel.

## Friday 14th June, 1940

The Germans are in Paris – French retiring south of capital. Captain Jim Crame home from BEF.

## Saturday 15th June, 1940

Spanish troops occupy Tangier to safeguard territory for France! At the same time they are screaming, 'We want Gibraltar' their plan to crack the BE has been for years as clear as a crystal cut diamond. Most people, including knowledgeable ones, still think the end will come by Germany running out of petrol – if the war continues for a very long time this may be so but something must be done now.

Thinking seriously of sending Audrey and Brian to Canada.

Very busy in bars. Paid Sam off (two weeks money) found him drinking down in the cellar again. Did all the bottles and pewter myself after closing.

## Wednesday 12th June, 1940

Engaged a new waiter – Bill Ellis.

One hundred German planes raid the east coast – seems to be a try out to test defences before they try in earnest – seven planes shot down. Father to Gloucester to look for a place to evacuate the children. Strange, the cheerfulness of everyone, knowing full well that possibly in a few days we could be bombed to hell – a wonderful spirit.

## Thursday 20th June, 1940

East and south coast raided again – thirty-three down – about twenty-three civilians killed in the two raids.

Afternoon played tennis at Darters' home – Village Road. Evening to Queens Hall to see the trailer advertising our fund (FCFF) Les Morris took us to Cuffley to see the bungalow we are contemplating buying – £775 freehold, extra plot of land £150.

## Friday 21st June, 1940

Funeral of Mr Wolfenden (Charrington's Bottled Beer representative) Mr Stanford and Mr Thompson called in. Particulars of details of Armistice between Germany and France not yet known. Our wedding anniversary – six years.

## Sunday 23rd June, 1940

France has signed an armistice with Germany – there seems little hope at the moment of turning the tide with G. I think now the war will gradually spread to America, Russia, Japan, etc. I have yet to meet a person that does not think G will be starved out this winter, and the rest of Europe – I very much doubt it.

## Tuesday 25th June, 1940

Freddie Briggs passed away – a friend we shall all miss very much. AR alarm 1 a.m. All clear 4 a.m. Sid Brown came in from next door. Brian was a good little chap. Japan seems to be preparing for action.

## Thursday 27 June, 1940

Russia marches into Bessarabia – looks like a race for Rumanian oil between Russia and Germany.

To Rialto with Audrey and saw Douglas Fairbanks in *Green Hell*, after we walked to The Old Sergeant – Les Morris came for us at ten o'clock, took us back to The George to close up.

## Friday 28th June, 1940

Brian's birthday (four years old) Ronnie Bissett Howard Dixon, Shoona and Oona (Dr Chisholm's daughters) came to tea.

Les Morris took me to Plaza to obtain permission for the FCFF to advertise the fund on a film. Called at three of the contracts Les is building.

## Tuesday 2nd July, 1940

Horace (head man) off duty – Vic having his medical – Henry away sick and a waiter short. I was the only man in the house from 11.30 a.m. until 8 p.m.

Vic arrived back after his medical at 5.30 – looked as if he was going to die of exhaustion – had to send him home.

## Thursday 4th July, 1940

Mother's birthday – the family went to The Salisbury at Hertford (Tommy Lawrence) – Alf and Edna, George and Phyl, Reg and Peggy, Audrey and I – the boys paid the bill for Mother and Father – suggested the girls pay next year if all is well. Called at The White Horse, Potters Bar, going – I drove the Buick home.

## Saturday 6th July, 1940

Signed on at Labour Exchange for National Service – saw the manager Mr Gibbs which helped rather. Arrived at nine o'clock – fifty-five in front of me. Signed on for RAF.

Ordered four hundred bricks, Tipping Crown Brick works. £2 10s 0d for shelter blast wall.

## Monday 8th July, 1940

Mother and Father called. I cannot believe it – Father asked me to give him a date when Audrey and I leave The George – wants to make the necessary arrangements.

## Wednesday 10th July, 1940

Managed to see Father regarding our leaving The George – he suggested a fortnight.

## Thursday 11th July, 1940

Stuart and Les stayed to lunch – afternoon went out again viewing houses. Offered £950 for a bungalow subject to getting a mortgage – required £1,000 but will only advance seventy-five per cent – too much as I have only £300. To Rialto with Les and Connie to see return of *The Invisible*

*Man* – to Old Sergeant after to see Jack and Doris Fairlie. Les Morris met us and took us back to The George to close up.

Twenty-three enemy planes shot down over England.

## Friday 12th July, 1940

Borrowed bicycle from Horace – visited nearly all estate agents in district looking for a house – riding for two hours. Afternoon Edgar Dipple loaned us his Humber to continue house hunting. Eric Stafford moved to Wellington Road – we are keen on a house next door but the rent is 30s 0d exclusive! Thinking of making an offer of 32s 6d inclusive.

Bombs reported to have dropped near White Webbs Park.

## Monday 15th July, 1940

The Mitchies not coming here now – apparently Charlie & Gladys (Edna's sister) are taking over – Mother and Father called in – arranged to leave in two weeks – I just cannot believe it.

Jack Fairlie called up.

We had an allowance of £2 10s 0d per week but there would be no other income and so it was imperative to find somewhere to live with a rent of not more than 30s 0d per week inclusive.

## Tuesday 23rd July, 1940

Budget. Beer up one penny per pint. Tobacco up three pence per oz. Wines up two shillings and four shillings per gallon.

Les Morris took us to 6 Old Park Grove, the house we hope to rent. All we have had is information to say the owner will let. No key has been sent but time is short and we are in a very serious position! Forced a way in. Les had a painter there by four o'clock and made a start on decorations.

## Wednesday 24th July, 1940

Next Tuesday will be our last day at The George – we shall be pleased now when it is all over – terrible pressure at present, shorthanded and trying to leave everywhere clean and tidy – also trying to prepare for moving and very short time for house to be ready. We have more or less been non-stop from 7.30 a.m. until 11.30 p.m. Les has made a really good start, so also has Harry with the plumbing side.

## Thursday 25th July, 1940

Audrey and I visited the house. Afterwards called at North Met. and arranged for cooker and boiler to be installed. All hiring of equipment has now been stopped.

As promised Don Ellis, English master of the grammar school came to tea with us in his RAF uniform. To Rialto with Audrey – saw *Untamed*. Afterwards walked to Old Sergeant. Les met us and brought us back to George for closing.

## Friday 26th July, 1940

The country is waking up and certainly seems to be getting down to things. twenty-three planes brought down yesterday.

Afternoon to house with Audrey. The back of our twin beds will not fit in alcove to bedroom – have to cut a piece out.

Mother called with Gladys to look over the rooms.

Bombs dropped at North Weald. Stuart Roach stayed and had lunch with us.

## Monday 29th July, 1940

Collector from Charringtons.

Beer up one penny pint, ale now eight pence a pint, bitter ten pence, Burton 1s 0d. Wines up one penny glass.

Audrey and I are really under pressure with not a minute to spare all day.

Horace out. My schedule: 7.30 to 9 a.m. cleaned pewter with silver sand and bottled up. 9 to 9.30 a.m. breakfast. 9.30 to 10 a.m. more bottling up and cellar work. ten to eleven o'clock general ordering. 11 to 11.20 a.m. filled cigarette machines, etc. 11.30 opened up. 11.30 to 2.30 p.m. bar. 2.30 to 3.00 p.m. lunch. Three o'clock bar furniture. 5.30 open up. Bar all evening except for quick break for arrowroot biscuit and cheese.

## Wednesday 31st July, 1940

A hectic day – left The George at about one o'clock after a heavy session. Edgar Dipple drove Audrey and I to Old Park Grove, our new home. All we had for lunch was a cup of soup. In a dreadful mess. Heard's only charged £3 10s 0d for moving us.

## Wednesday 14th August, 1940

Medical 11.30. Saw seven doctors – pleased to pass Grade 1. Appears to be little chance of getting into the Air Force; stated I was free and prepare to join any services any time.

## Saturday 17th August, 1940

Siren twice today and many times during past week. Croydon has been bombed, also part of south London. Brian so far has been excellent. Father is taking over The Crooked Billet, Walthamstow, on 11th September.

## Friday 23rd August, 1940

Enemy plane woke us at 3.15 a.m., dropped three bombs before siren went off, dropped two more later.

Went to Edmonton with Bill Davis to see the damage – Alcazar destroyed.

## Sunday 25th August, 1940

At midnight a German plane was flying around – as we were dressing two bombs were dropped. Just as we were going to the shelter Ron and Babs, with Heather, knocked on the door – all to shelter when sirens started. Sixteen bombs dropped in all, also we saw a powerful flare dropped and then the sky was aglow with a fire in the same direction.

All clear about 2 a.m. – Brian and Heather were very good.

## Tuesday 29th August, 1940

Took Brian to Hugh's whilst I made several calls in the town. Ordered one hundred and sixty sandbags and two yards of sand for a blast wall. Bought a carry-cot for Brian in shelter. Les and Connie came to tea – Les helped me with the shelter. Sirens 9.30 – several bombs fell locally and two at Cockfosters, they really screamed down. Brian keeps awake through the raids but not at all disturbed and he sleeps on in the morning.

## Wednesday 28th August, 1940

Sirens 9.25 p.m. All clear 12.30. Searchlights still searching – a plane was prowling around. Ron stayed with Brian and Heather in the shelter – Babs went in the drawing room and Audrey and I laid on the bed fully dressed. Warning again; two or three batches of bombs dropped – all clear 2.30 a.m. Searchlights still on – bombs still being dropped in the distance. I hope Berlin is having a taste of this.

## Thursday 29th August, 1940

Met Mother at The George.

Dorrie Walton with David and Jean came to tea.

Warning 8.57 p.m. – several salvos of bombs. Incendiaries all around, non-stop AA fire – about three hours before we could get out for a smoke. All clear at 4.10 a.m.

## Friday 30 August, 1940

Four long warnings, one was a little frightening – about forty bombers escorted by fighters flew over Enfield having previously unloaded their bombs, seven down locally and one in Durants Road, Cat Hill and Enfield Sewage Farm. Final warning 4 a.m. Several bombs dropped.

I feel exhausted having moved two tons of sand, filled, carried and stacked sandbags from front to rear of house. Brian had no sleep last night.

## Saturday 31st August, 1940

First warning at 8.30 a.m. followed by three more. Little chance of resting. A terrific scrap after which we saw two parachutes come down in the Edmonton vicinity.

Heather Neilson's birthday; Brian, Audrey and I went to tea. Have now used up another ton of sand and still require more.

## Saturday 1st September, 1940

Three more warnings during the night making seven in all yesterday. Final all clear 4 a.m. Audrey, Brian, Babs and Heather slept in the shelter – Ron and I rested on beds in between warnings. We did not disturb them in the shelter hoping they would sleep on. We saw plenty of action, a plane caught in a searchlight never attempted to evade the position but fired incendiary bullets from nose and tail of plane directly down the beams, then the AA guns opened up and this was followed by the plane dropping four salvos of bombs.

Les Pratt called in whilst on his beat.

## Saturday 7th September, 1940

Warning 9 p.m. last night – all clear at 11.30. Brian asleep in the shelter. We all went in and had supper – another warning as we finished and all clear at 2.10 a.m.

I kept a look-out whilst everyone slept – Audrey, Brian and Nannie in the shelter, Ron, Babs and Heather in the lounge. All slept until 4.15 a.m. Audrey (who was with me after a short sleep to start with) and I then slept in the shelter until 7.15 a.m. Called at The George midday.

Warning at 5 p.m. – heavy gunfire, saw about eighteen German planes – later spitfires doing their victory rolls. One came several times over our gardens at not more than one hundred feet up.

We were having tea in the garden until the gunfire and shrapnel got so heavy we finished it in the shelter.

Terrific battle going on in London, the fires are stretching for about seven miles: East London and the docks. The light from the fire, although at least ten miles away, is so bright that the houses are throwing shadows! ninety-nine planes downed!

Carol of Romania abdicates – crown prince takes over.

## Sunday 8th September, 1940

Warning 12.36 p.m. just as we had finished a meeting of the FCFF at The George. Next warning at 8 p.m. and went right through until 6 a.m. In the garden until 3.30 – quite cold – I felt I had a chill coming on. Ron and I split a ¼ bottle of rum. The second fire of London is worse and is being continually bombed. We dived into the shelter when two bombs came screaming down but no explosions only a very loud plop as they hit the ground somewhere – maybe time bombs! Brian awake until past 3 a.m. and unfortunately kept everyone else awake. We have tried everything with him including sleeping draughts, but nothing seems to work. About the most severe raid we have had so far.

This particular period witnessed London and its people fighting against almost impossible odds; to see the second great fire of London at a distance of about ten miles (as the burning of London was seen from Winchmore Hill in 1666) made one wonder if the angry unrelenting red inferno changing its luminosity like a far distant volcano as the bombs exploded amidst the holocaust, differs much from the Great Fire of London, when the very dry timber buildings were fanned by wind that encouraged the flames to consume greedily this very same area?

Considering the many important targets in and around Enfield the town was reasonably lucky compared with inner London and suburbs but wherever one was in London it was almost a case of being sentenced to death overnight and being reprieved in the morning! When one looks at the number of casualties it was much lighter than was expected.

Out of approximately eight hundred injured only one hundred and seven deaths were recorded. The number of explosive bombs or missiles falling in Enfield including HE bombs, oil and phosphorous bombs, flying bombs, rockets and land mines, was approximately seven hundred and of course there were thousands of incendiaries dropped. Approximately thiry-three thousand five hundred houses suffered damage one way or another of which three hundred and forty-seven were completely destroyed and nearly two thousand very severely damaged.

Apart from the greatest and most heroic battle of all time which took place in the air, praise must go to all of the services that were engaged in this majestic fight for survival, not only those civilians and services who suffered the brunt of these raids but also the fireman and other auxiliary units that were drawn from the suburbs to help to stem this highly concentrated assault.

It is only possible for me to express my thoughts in a very limited field regarding my experience during this period, but I did in a minor way realistically and perhaps partly subconsciously arrange my priorities in perspective with the human element that became involved in this new frantic awakening of relaxed Britain. The early efforts of our main services were unrivalled especially the RAF who like the other services were short of equipment, but no other country could have surpassed this country's efforts in doing what it did with what we had! To complete with this immense and wonderful performance I, like countless others, was maddened by other sections of the public who had but one priority – themselves, many of whom were divorced from the war efforts complete, but reaping the rewards of the conflict!

## Tuesday 10th September, 1940

Warning at 8 p.m. last night until 6 a.m. Ron and Babs are staying at home now – worried about Heather being awake so much. The London fire is now very serious. Bombs seem to be falling all round – a new gun installed about 200 yards from us – frightening but comforting. I walked to Wardens Post and had a cup of tea. Three killed at Ponders End. Four warnings during the day. Audrey's family spent the day with us. Bill Davis and family also called. Stan Thrope and Maud called to see us. Donated one guinea and Audrey 10s 6d to Spitfire Fund.

## Wednesday 11th September, 1940

Warning again last night at eight o'clock. Went to Edgar's and had a beer. Brian asleep when I went on to the club – back at 11 p.m. in shelter. All clear 5.15 a.m. Slept fairly well. Bombs dropped after all clear. Father took over The Crooked Billet, Walthamstow – twelve o'clock change. I took Tommy Roach in his car – whilst warning going. No doubt a good house but needs a lot doing to it. A very difficult time to take over. Kept T.R.'s car – called on Eric and Ena then on to Green Dragon to tell Carter it would be impossible for Audrey and I to take over.

## Thursday 12th September, 1940

Warnings last evening eight o'clock. All clear 5.15. Brian woke at 4 a.m. A wonder he slept at all through the incessant gunfire – terrific. The barrage commenced when on my way with Edgar Thomas to The Wheatsheaf. Shells bursting all over the sky – two exploded on ground, one by the YMCA. Everyone is taking it very well, of course we have been lucky here – people are inclined to be a little optimistic, better of course than being the reverse.

Took Tommy Roach's car back – afterwards went into the town with Brian and had hair cut.

Called at The George to meet Edgar Dipple regarding a job for Audrey.

## Friday 13th September, 1940

Three warnings during the day. Caught out with Brian when barrage started – went to The Goat. 3.15 p.m. bombs were dropped near The Fallow Buck, deafening explosion. How all the windows did not come in I shall never know, probably sheltered by Clay Hill. Sirens sounded ten minutes after.

## Wednesday 18th September, 1940

Brian and I went for a walk at 8 a.m. Warning soon after. Another two followed and only 10 a.m.! Altogether six alarms up to 1.30 p.m. Picked Tommy Roach up and met Bill Kennard – went to the club.

Managed to get two gallons of petrol for Sid Crowl at Edmonton – also two for Bill Davis. Money getting very short – only £23 in the bank and £160 in defence loan, and we have yet to receive Les Morris's account which I estimate at up to £40. Nine daylight warnings altogether – last one was eight o'clock when Audrey, Bill and I were in Wheatsheaf. Molotov Basket dropped – Enfield Cricket Club pavilion burnt out. HE bombs at Bush Hill Park, Edenbridge and Wellington Roads – considerable damage.

## Saturday 21st September, 1940

All clear 5.30 a.m. Barrage not quite so fierce. Brian and I went on usual walk over the golf course – the inevitable warning whilst out. Land mine parachuted on Royal Small Arms Factory at Enfield Lock at 4 a.m. Terrific explosion. Another fell in Carterhatch Lane but failed to explode. Mr and Mrs Clarke came to tea, also Bill Davis. Later Bill and I went to the club – home before warning.

To Potters Bar with Tommy Roach and Arthur Bridger to see how George and family were after the bombing last night. One was dropped outside Robin Hood, Potters Bar – the backs blown completely out of the shops opposite and a cottage demolished in which two kiddies were killed.

## Sunday 22nd September, 1940

Warning eight o'clock last evening. At nine o'clock, whilst in the garden outside shelter, a brilliant flash seemed to be directly over our garden – thought it was a flare until I was blown down the shelter stairs; the force came from the south. Another terrific explosion later – some windows broken and the trap door to loft blown out!

Investigated in the morning. Land mines dropped by parachutes – one near the club house at Bush Hill Park golf course. All glass blown out of properties in town. Another mine opposite us on the golf course: menacing looking thing in the road, 8 ft 6 ins × 2 ft 6 ins – requested to keep doors and windows open in houses.

To tea with George and Phyl at White Horse Potters Bar – they were coming over to us bringing George Haylock but due to the unexploded land mine the roads were closed. Bombs dropped at Cuffley without warning whilst at Potters Bar – the plane was brought down at Royston. Early warning seven o'clock. Put Brian to bed in the shelter.

## Monday 23rd September, 1940

Slept right through the warnings – all clear at 7.45. Nobody has yet been to inspect the land mine.

Called for Tommy Roach and Arthur Bridger – went back to see Audrey but the road was closed so went on to Cuffley Hotel, Green Dragon Cheshunt and The Goat – tried to phone but exchange had been evacuated. I was annoyed at not being allowed through with my wife and child in the house. Apparently the only instruction Audrey had received and which sounded ridiculous to me, was not to go into the shelter as it might collapse, and to sit in the road with a coat over their heads! Crackers! The mine was successfully made safe.

## Tuesday 1st October, 1940

Warning usual time last evening, non-stop bombing and gunfire. Activity all night, bombs seem to be screaming down. Learnt later that a bomb dropped at Falmer Road, Lincoln Crescent, Ponders End Poly and direct hit on the

Two Brewers, High Street – several killed and injured. To the club with Arthur B and others.

Went with Audrey and Brian to tea with Connie – waited some time for the gunfire to cease.

## Friday 4th October, 1940

Bombs dropped at Cockfosters and Southbury Road during the day – one plane came over at about 600 feet. Every battery opened up at it, but it seemed to go steadily on its way unperturbed. The shooting generally is terrible and worse at night. Seldom do the shells burst in front of the planes, always so far behind. I suppose there must be a reason.

## Saturday 5th October, 1940

The gunfire never stopped – as soon as one plane left the area another came in. Fixed up a bunk for Brian with the spring from his cot suspended so that the earth tremors caused by bombs do not arouse him. I am very pleased also be able to stretch myself out as it must be a month now since I have been sleeping in a deck chair across the door of the shelter.

## Thursday 10th October, 1940

All clear 6.30 a.m. Four bombs fell opposite the Capitol Cinema and completely demolished three or four houses – nothing left of the centre one, just a crater! Raining hard again. Warning 8.30 a.m. all clear 9.30 p.m. Afterwards could hear the roar of many planes – sounded German, no warning. To The White Horse Potters Bar with Les and

Connie – George had gone to see Phyl. To The Salisbury for lunch – full up so went to The Cambridge – excellent lunch.

Warning 7.15 p.m. Bill and I went into the house for a beer when we heard what we thought was a train coming until it seemed to be going too fast. Suddenly realised it was a bomb – we fell flat. The whole house shook but no windows out – just how the blast goes. They are certainly having a go for London now. St Paul's Cathedral hit – altar demolished.

## Friday 11th October, 1940

All clear 7 a.m. To town with Father. Foggy. Called at Pagonnies for a reference (Gt Portland Street). Dreadful pasting around the back streets of Holloway. Called at The Cambridge, Crooked Billet and The George en route.

To see Mother and have tea at Oakwood, Slades Hill – just home in time to organise shelter, attend to black-out and have a spot to eat before the warning at 7.15.

## Monday 14th October, 1940

All clear 7 a.m. Twelve hours! Counted about twenty-five dropped but nothing very near: Queens Road, Bush Hill Park recreation ground and Isolation Hospital. The day at Cuffley Hotel – Fred and Queenie off duty. Afternoon went home for car – back to open up. Left Cuffley at nine o'clock – fog thickening, nearly gave up at Crews Hill because it was so thick. Plenty going on above. AA fire terrific – never seemed to ease once.

## Tuesday 15th October, 1940

All clear 6.30. Relieved Alf at Cambridge midday. After closing went home and prepared shelter for the night. Back to open up at 5.30. Roper drove me home after closing.

Audrey had a nasty shock when told of the bombing at Park Road near her family. Their friends Mr Small, son and daughter killed when a direct hit completely demolished their house.

## Wednesday 16th October, 1940

All clear 6 a.m. Disturbing night. We dozed off about 4 a.m. String of eleven bombs fell from the railway station just a short distance away, across to the town park – the shelter rocked and shuddered in the clay soil, also hit the water main.

## Monday 21st October, 1940

Early warning again 7 a.m. Plenty of activity when 1,000 lb bomb fell in the middle of main road at Cuffley about 60 yards from the hotel. Shops badly damaged but no casualties. I went to Cuffley in the morning. Audrey and Brian were late arriving, held up by heavy gunfire – bombs dropped on line at Winchmore Hill. Trains only running backwards and forward between Enfield Chase and Cuffley. Busy midday as only Peggy and I were serving. Brian off to sleep early – 8.30 p.m. A welcome change for Audrey and I to walk about and have some company – retired midnight.

Exploded a large bomb at six o'clock – only 200 yards away.

## Tuesday 22nd October, 1940

Very quiet night, hardly a sound after eleven o'clock. Up at 7 a.m. All had a good night's rest amongst the barrels and bottled beer in the cellar. Helped in bar midday. Rested a short while afternoon. Audrey and Brian went for a walk with Peggy.

George called in midday and asked if I would relieve at White Horse, Potters Bar on Thursday. went back with him at 5.30 p.m. to see his cellar. Came back to Cuffley by bus. Quiet in bar after 7.30 p.m.

## Thursday 24th October, 1940

Fairly quiet night, some bombs dropped locally. A lot of time bombs amongst them.

Caught the 9.40 to Cuffley to pick up my bicycle and rode to Potters Bar to relieve George. Afterwards cycled back home – the normal route closed due to the time bombs.

Poor Audrey had a nasty accident. She shut her fingers in the shelter door – about one cwt cement – split the nail in two. Ron took Audrey to doctor. Warning 7.30 p.m.

## Friday 25th October, 1940

Another fairly quiet night – Plenty of AA fire early evening. Two warnings during the morning and plenty of activity, making up for the quieter nights. The Swan, Ponders End hit and Harry Walton's shop front blown in.

## Sunday 10th November, 1940

Up at 6.45 a.m. – helped George with stocking up, empties, crates, etc. Phyl washed all the floors. Audrey did the bar furniture, polishing etc. In George's car to pick up a relief hand at Kilvinton Hall. Helped in bar midday – very busy. Les Morris called to see us. Played 'Tippet' with the experts. I actually won three games. Dougy and Billy Tibbs stayed the night, also Ken Calow and his dog. All the girls slept in the shelter and we had mattresses in the dining room. Finally retired at 1.15. If we are told the truth. Greece is battling on very well. Looks as if Italy may well soon be for it.

## Monday 11th November, 1940

Up at 7 a.m. Helped George with his work so that he could get away early. At 9.30 he left with Phyl to see the children at Burfield. I saw the brewery deliveries in, etc. Borrowed Mr Chandler's car to relieve at Cuffley Hotel. Just as well – arrived almost at Opening time.

Audrey on her own with Glades at White Horse.

I fetched Shirley from school. Weather dreadful – teeming with rain and blowing very nearly a gale. Bombs dropped at Cheyne Walk a few hundred yards from Old Park Grove, our home. Five killed and several injured. So pleased Audrey and Brian were not there. Enjoyed looking after White Horse whilst George was away.

## Wednesday 13th November, 1940

Sticky night. All clear at 7.45. To The Cambridge on cycle to relieve Alf. Afternoon went to see the aftermath of last night at Bush Hill Park – pretty awful. To Oakwood, Slades Hill, with Brian to collect his tricycle – heavy gunfire.

Bill and I took it in turns to visit the club.

## Thursday 14th November, 1940

Father phoned and asked me if I would go to Newmarket with him. Not until 10 a.m. I drove the Buick. Father won £18 7s 6d on the Tote in third race on Tobosos. The 18s 0d ring is now 20s 6d.

Weather perfect but very cold. Arrived home at five o'clock. En route we stopped at a village and Father noticed some brandy snaps which I bought for him. Whilst driving Father was in a dreadful state with his teeth and toffee – we were in tears, laughing. Met Father at The George evening.

## Friday 16th November, 1940

Coventry blitzed by hundreds of German planes – over one thousand known casualties.

With Audrey and Brian to Jeanne's birthday at The Cambridge. Alf loaned me his car to come home. Warning en route and all hell let loose as we were driving up Old Park Avenue.

## Saturday 16th November, 1940

I would say last night was by far the worst Enfield had seen since the raids started. About seven land mines came down. One was exploded in the air – terrific explosion – another fell by the New River in the Park about 400 yards away. It took our back windows out and brought the loft trap door down with an eerie clatter. Audrey got Brian under the bed. He woke up and we explained it was our guns going off. Got to sleep at about 5 a.m. Dropped at London Road, corner Park Crescent, Town Park, Willow Road, Grange Park, Slades Hill, Botany Bay. Neil Edgar and his wife were killed. Mrs Liffen and Michael had a miraculous escape at their home in London Road when the building was half demolished. Ben Liffen was at The George and it was he that got them out. Many killed in Willow Road – must be hundreds of casualties. Ben Liffen staying with Ron – went to the club with them.

# Chapter XXXIII

The Royal Artillery – Orkney's – Felixstowe – Orfordness – Bawdsey – Germany – extracts from Audrey's letters – Germany – surrender – the first atomic bomb

On 5th December, 1940, I received the 'Armed Forces Enlistment Notice' together with a four shilling postal order which apparently represented an advance on one's service pay! The following day I relieved George and Phyllis at The White Horse, Potters Bar, allowing them to fetch their children, Eileen, Susie and Jill from Burfield, where they had been evacuated. The next few days were occupied in a round of farewell visits, culminating in a family gathering for lunch at the old Kings Head, Chigwell, after a previous meeting in The Crooked Billet, Walthamstow.

So like all others who had suffered disruption and separation from their families, we found the goodbyes a profound and sorrowful exercise, particularly at this period when the future was looking anything but bright, and in many instances those left behind were in far greater danger than those entering the forces, but the one consoling feature was that Audrey and Brian were amongst a great number of wonderful friends. The operation was also lightened by the fact that after the initial six weeks training at the RA Z battery at Newark I would almost certainly be allowed home before being posted. Like hell, I went straight up to the Orkneys! I was warned never to volunteer! Only three more entries were made in my diary, the first being on January 15th, 1941:

## Wednesday 15th January, 1941

We were awakened 6 a.m. feeling a little dazed and weary and not without heavy hearts. I have learned my first lesson – conned first time! To think I volunteered for a posting anywhere subject to our party being kept together. The CO remarked, 'What a splendid idea,' and half the company gave their names in under these conditions! Were we kept together? Anything but! Our eleven was divided into four postings and only Sid Penfold and J.B. were going with me. The latter was the only person out of our party I would have left behind!

To the cookhouse for breakfast. There was a foot of snow and it was very windy – a really wild morning. An excellent breakfast was spoiled, as always, by the army's washing-up facilities – a galvanised bath, tepid water, a thick layer of grease, and bits of floating bacon rind and egg. About two hundred to three hundred would wash their tin plate, bowl and knives and forks in this!

The barrack room was where we packed our kit bags with the following: four blankets tied in a ground sheet, gas equipment, rubber boots and my personal case.

After we had completed our packing the party (nineteen in all) gathered for pay outside the BO – and were kept waiting over half-an-hour for the princely sum of seven shillings and sixpence. On looking at our party I thought, what a ragged bunch of rascals! One poor chap was half paralysed and could hardly speak – suffering from sleeping sickness.

However did he pass the doctor in the first instance? We also had two Greeks with us, both unable to speak English. A fine gun crew we would make!

After drawing our pay we adjourned to the NAAFI, where I bought them all tea and buns. After handshakes all round we went to collect our kit and await transport. Whilst waiting I had that familiar empty hopeless feeling, and my mind drifted back home to Audrey and Brian. I thought I would get home to see them before being drafted – it seemed so cruel as Audrey did not even know I was leaving the camp, let alone where I was going! I boarded the lorry with a lump in my throat.

One lorry was for our kit, but five of us found ourselves riding on the kit as there was not room in the other lorry. Major Digby the OC came out to see us off.

The party soon forgot the departing mood and on the way to Grantham station we were all in full song – there was nothing one could do but make the most of it.

What a journey that was to the Orkneys, and what a commercial it would have made for a travel agent wishing to retire instantly! Three days on corned beef sandwiches except for a rushed but welcome black sausage meal at Perth.

We arrived at Thurso, in Caithness, where we were sent to a transit camp. After being shown to our Nissen hut and issued with something like six sticks of firewood and three knobs of coal, we found a place to eat and devoured eggs and bacon like hungry lions eating a lamb cutlet! Back to the vast camp, where emptiness reigned supreme. We trudged around in the snow for over an hour trying to locate our hut; and when we succeeded, and examined what we were sleeping in I thought we would have been better off outside! The palliasses were on the concrete floor and covered with near-frozen soggy blankets. Sleeping as we were, fully dressed with our great coats slung over us, and with clammy blankets on top we managed a few hours sleep until awakened at 4.30 a.m. With our hair and eye lashes frozen we struggled to the cookhouse, to be given a breakfast of greasy sardines and toast to prepare us for the coming rough sea trip. Only one person was on his feet at the end of this wild passage across the Pentland Firth. He was, of course, a Scotsman and by the way he was singing and acting he must have had a large wee drappy of the malt and burn.

Waves were breaking over the bows of the ship and the deck was awash with floating equipment. What a relief it was when we reached the northern end of the Island of Hoy and entered Hoy Sound out of the wild and ill-tempered seas.

Arriving at Stromness we were paraded and checked out on the quay. It is unlikely that a scruffier party will ever be seen again at Stromness – white, drawn and unshaven faces offering such a wan and feeble look that if anybody had bawled 'Aa-ten-shun' we would all have fallen down! We were detailed to board different drifters (small boats that plied from place to place across Scapa Flow) each party being taken to their respective posting. What a relief it was to stand on a level deck with the fresh breeze bringing a sign of life to our drawn and pale looking faces, but as quickly as these thoughts were with us the sea banished them. Even the waves appeared to be attacking one another, and the farther we went from Hoy Sound the more vicious became the onslaught, until we were forced to go below where we were met by nauseating, sickening fumes from some kind of oil heater. My goodness we were past the sickness stage and so sat, tossed about like corks, in a semi-conscious state listening to an Orcadian giving us serious information on 'Orkneyitus' and how to deal with it!

After arriving at the quay on the Island of Flotta we made our way, with all of the kit; trudging in deep snow in a state of stupor, to the naval camp to await transport. Here we attempted to obtain something hot, but without success. Extraordinary how a degree of class difference between units could be detected in these circumstances. Maybe it was a kind of arrogant pride that prompted this distinction. Eventually the transport arrived, but only after phoning HQ. Difficulty was found in clambering on the truck, for we were stiff with the cold and had eaten only one sit-down meal in four days! After a few hundred yards one of the boys just rolled off the truck and lay, in the snow in a semi-coma. However, we all eventually arrived at Stanger Head, where the battery was sited guarding the entrance to Hoxa Sound, and where we were treated again as humans. Almost inevitably we arrived in a freeze-up, with the water rationed – one day's entire supply was a mess tin full! Strangely enough, when issued with this piece of equipment I thought it large enough for washing in!

After a few days we were taken back to Stromness for a course on coast defence searchlights, which was quite enjoyable but spoilt by the conditions and overcrowding. Our party was sleeping on the floor between the too numerous beds. The searchlights wallahs were thought little of, and I found later that in some batteries they were almost outcasts! I developed some sort of chill or flu and, although protesting, joined in a keep fit exercise after remarks had been passed insinuating that we were a lazy lot of b—s. Away we went on a mile jog-trot, with drilling and exercising on the beach, followed by a run back to camp. I remember naught after tumbling into bed, and the next thing I remember was being lifted on the mattress on to a bed which one of the boys had vacated for me. I must thank the chap in our party named Sid Penfold for all he did – if one wanted to see the MO one had to get to him regardless. When I signed off after three days the medical orderly was asked by the MO what my temperature was and he replied, 'Normal.' The b— hadn't seen me, much less taken my temperature! It must have been six weeks or more before I was completely recovered. Two other members of the party were unconscious with pneumonia and after two days were both taken to the hospital ship.

Whilst confined to bed, the barrack-room personnel suffered the indignity of an examination for those almost microscopic horrors that attack humans in a most unsophisticated way in an embarrassing part of the anatomy, but luckily and pleasingly, Sid and myself were two of ten out of a party of forty – who were clear!

The last two entries in my diary referring to our first posting following the termination of the course were the last to be made for the next sixteen years.

## Friday 14th February, 1941

Awakened at 7 a.m. – not feeling brilliant, at 8.15 a.m. walked across the golf course to collect our washing – freezing wind and bleak. Loaded our kit on lorry and left Ness Battery at 9.45. Sgt. M. Knight came and said goodbye to us and S.M. Sinclair came down to see us on the drifter. Sid, Mick and I with two others on the course went to the

Quay by lorry. Drifter left 10.30 – we were advised to put our kit below as she was shipping water – wind blew like hell let loose! Lashed with rain, the boat was tossed about like a cork and when we crossed the wake of two destroyers at full speed I really thought we would capsize. Stopped on deck as long as we could, but gave up after an hour – none of us were feeling good but fortunately we beat the sickness.

Joe Harden and friend left us at Lyness – we helped them ashore, with their kit. Amazed to see Billy Young on the drifter alongside – now first lieut. – chatted with him until we cast off.

Arrived at Flotta Island 12.30 – all of us frozen b— stiff! Nobody to meet us as usual – phoned Stanger Camp – will send transport down. Attempted to get a hot drink whilst waiting, but not successful; arrived Stanger about 1.30. Found ourselves billeted in the same room as we occupied before. Meal period over, so we collected ours from CH and took them to BR to eat – we were so hungry everything tasted good. Afternoon we drew our blankets and mattress. Moved everything around to accommodate us after which we were told our party would be going to NEB tomorrow! Had an excellent supper – stew – help yourself! Sam Buse made me a stiff whiskey boiling water and plenty of sugar.

## Saturday 15th February, 1941

Slept fairly well on the drink Sam made for me last night. Up at 7 a.m. packed up once again. An ambulance picked us up at noon. Arrived NEB about one o'clock – just in time for a meal which we found quite good, but everything is so very dirty. About ninety in the camp – the old Army filthy routine washing-up. About one gallon of stinking greasy water for everybody when you're last out the bowl would have been taken away from a pig!

One is terribly isolated here – a depressing atmosphere seems to prevail over the camp. Everywhere there is mud, mud and more mud! All the boys, some very young, have been here over twelve months and are really showing signs of degenerating. During the afternoon we were shown over the S/L emplacements by one of the sergeants. They are in a frightening position, perched on the cliffs with just a 3 ft path around a single rail. The emplacements are built of wood – both are damp and No. 2 has considerable water in over half of it! We were asked to take the night-shift – 9.30 p.m. until daybreak. Went on first shift with a SLO to see routine. The lamps are badly neglected and the procedure very slapdash! To canteen with Sid for a pint – had a hell of a job to find our way back to the hut. Went on duty 9.30 – Sid in No. 1 and myself in No. 2. A strange and lonely feeling being on duty on one's own for the first time, in charge of equipment etc. that seems so neglected. To make matters worse the wind is now screaming, threatening to lift the whole emplacement. Went through the routine drill and tests of lamp and phones. When for the first time I tested the lamp the negative carbon was badly broken. Tried twice but it knocked spitefully. Changed the carbon – hand lamp only – main light bulb u/s – managed to get it burning okay. Rang and reported then tested contactor gear and finally tested phones. The current was cut off at 11.30 and phones tested for last time at midnight. Wrote to Audrey, used a candle after 11.30. The resting unit is in the middle of earth bags, not sand, on boards about 20 inches wide. Unfortunately the bags are damp and are sprouting fungi!

Turned very cold about 3 a.m. and the boards were feeling a little hard, but managed to sleep for about five hours. Current came on again 5 a.m. I was up at 7 a.m. Had a good clean up, closed down at 8.55 a.m. Made it a little easier Sid and I being on the same shift.

The next day was a study in human nature. The behaviour of these younger personnel was, to say the least, extremely peculiar: some had been on this barren heather-coated, publess, girlless, cinemaless small island for eighteen months, and so we were witnessing our first display of Orkneyitus. We were warned by the NCOs to sit tight should the boys start anything untoward. The following day it happened. The two NCOs scarpered, whilst the youngsters gathered all the issued ammunition they could lay their hands on, opened the windows, rapidly and aimlessly firing their rifles. The din was kept up for five or more minutes, whilst Sid and myself were trying to concentrate on a game of chess. The boys were put under arrest and together with everyone in the hut were hauled before the CO, Colonel Weigel, the following day. The names Penfold and Standbrook were called, dismissing us on the grounds of being new arrivals. Who knows, in their place we may have gone one better and had a little go with the battery nine pounder guns! I believe their sentence was three months in the Glasshouse and then back to the islands! They did return looking surprisingly well, but were quickly and sensibly drafted away from the Orkneys.

We settled down to a period of anything but boredom. Sid and I cleaned the hut up, and a general change of expression in the attitude of mind appeared to prevail among everybody.

How we enjoyed those visits to the crofters' cottages, with their continuous peat fires and the quaint recessed sleeping section in the same room that we ate in.

One of these visits was made on a moonless and rainy night of nil vision and we had great difficulty in locating Sam's cottage, situated as it was well away from the road. After an extremely entertaining evening, and consumed with a goodly supply of rum under our belts we bid goodnight to Sam and his wife allowing them to tuck up in the hole in the wall. Somehow we lost the path and got completely lost in the heather. After wandering blindly for half an hour or so, I called to Sid that I had found the road – the moon peeped between the clouds just long enough to spot the glistening rainswept surface on to which I stepped, only to find no surface until I landed with a crunch six feet below. Stunned with the shock I blurted out, 'Stop, stop" to Sid, but I was too late. Down he tumbled, all six feet and 14 stone of him crashing at my side. I said, 'You silly b— didn't you hear me call?' and we both burst into uncontrollable laughter, but I soon detected that Sid's laughter was interposed with gasps of pain. Although we were not aware of the extent of the damage at the time, he had broken a leg! That was the longest two miles, I would say, that either Sid or I had ever walked: with him leaning on me between hops, progress was very slow.

There was so much to do on these islands, and we found the Orcadian people charming in every respect, and almost uncontaminated by the bustling and disturbed outside world. Boredom could never win.

One of our trips to Lyness, on the Island of Hoy, we tramped over the sometimes knee-deep heather until we were almost at the highest point in the centre of the island.

The weather was crystal clear with the sun almost sizzling the skin without seeming unduly hot. Lying all around us were the bleached bones of baby rabbits that had been eaten by the circling, screeching birds, who were now silent. The scene over the island was perhaps, up to that time, the most peaceful, panoramic view I had ever seen and so frighteningly still, silent and expressive was the calm, that it was difficult to imagine the wind would ever again be violent or the sea turbulent. Whilst reflecting upon all this the deep shattering boom of a gun from one of the tiny, grey, toy looking battleships broke the heavenly spell; the mind flashed back to reality and in that almost timeless space, I thought how utterly insignificant and stupidly selfish mankind was. Will the lesson never be learned?

One particular phenomenon that fired the imagination was the auroras, or aurora borealis. It is quite beyond me to describe adequately the magic of these gracious, wavering soft, multi-coloured folds that skipped across the darkened sky. They resembled a huge curtain being effortlessly pulled across infinite space; the swiftly changing folds accompanied by an eerie crackling and swishing as if occurring in a great, silent void. The crackling could be likened to a silken garment, charged with static electricity being taken off a human body. Actually there is a parallel there, because both are caused electrically. The aurora is created by electrical storms at an enormous height of anything up to 600 miles. The atomic particles emitted by the sun are trapped by the earth's magnetic field and follow the lines of force towards the poles, and illuminate the rarified gases; in fact the whole procedure is in principle the same as switching on a neon tube.

I wonder if the dry walled pigsty that we built near the edge of the cliff within the bounds of the camp was ever used. Every slab of stone was carried up the cliff to Dick, a pleasant and most likeable Orcadian character who was an expert at building with stones without using cement. I found it quite absorbing to take the odd spell of sorting and laying these slabs of stone under Dick's supervision. Here was a man who was like most of the Orcadians I met, self-disciplined, and it was obviously not reasonable to apply to him the same minor disciplinary touches as applied to others. Many times I observed Dick when saluting – his forage cap all cock-eyed, old pipe still in his mouth, and wearing the expression that said, when casually bringing his arm up with his hand dangling on the end, 'Watcha chum.'

## *To Orkney*

Land of the whirlpool, torrent, foam,
Where oceans meet in maddening shock;
The nestling cliff, the shelving holm,
The dark, insidious rock;
Land of the bleak, treeless moor,
The sterile mountain, seared and riven; The shapeless
    cairn, the ruined tower;
Scathed by the bolts of heaven;
The yawning gulf, the treacherous sand:
I love thee still, my native land!

David Vedder (1790–1854)

Fascinating islands with captivating people, and bewitching history. The following letter was amusing. Imagine insignificant Gunner Standbrook calling at HQ and asking if I could see the 'Brig' – not that I particularly wished to leave the Orkneys.

## The Standbrook Hospital Bowls Cup Tournament
A competition for Enfield Clubs in aid of the Enfield War Memorial Hospital
President: Mr A.J. Standbrook

*Hon. Sec. and Treasurer:*
*Mr E.M. Andrews*
*3 Crestbrook Place*
*Green Lanes, N13*
*Tel: Palmers Green 3721*
*January 26th, 1941*

*Dear Stanley,*

*We held our fifth annual general meeting today. You will be pleased to know that in spite of many adverse circumstances, owing to the war, we are able to send the hospital a cheque for £40. I enclose a copy of the financial statement which was submitted to the meeting. We had a good muster of representatives from all the associated clubs. The president presented the trophies and prizes to those who had been lucky enough to win them.*

*It was the unanimous wish of those present that I should convey their sincere thanks for the tankards which you kindly gave. You will probably remember they were won by Mr Wyld's team from Bush Hill Park.*

*I note you are up at the Orkneys. My nephew is the brigadier there. I wonder if you know him – Brigadier C.H. Peck.*

*With best wishes and good luck.*

*Yours sincerely,*
*E.M. Andrews*

Well, our time was up, and our leave had been granted to us before we reported to various units in the south of England. I shall never forget the shocking transit camp we were sent to. We were warned that to stay alive we must grab anything in sight at meal times; maybe a slight exaggeration but nevertheless the warning was worth heeding. Our first meal was tea and we were treated to an exhibition that would have done justice to Newgate prison in the time of Dickens, or a needle rugby match substituting a seven-pound tin of jam for the ball! Apart from the horseplay, the slopping out of the food was performed by three or four characters who resembled down and out buskers from an earlier era! Of course, there was the inevitable diabolical washing-up arrangement. Well, I couldn't help expressing my views in no uncertain terms, with a little explosive language thrown in. After a short time the door of our hut was thrust open, and a sergeant stamped in, and shouted, 'Who's the man stirring things up in the cookhouse?' I stepped smartly forward and said, 'Here, Sarge,' and before he could get a word in I exploded again and told him to take me straight to the CO. He obviously gathered that I was serious and the message must have got through to the right place, because at breakfast there was an NCO on duty, and all those connected with the service wore white smocks – in fact the whole scene was quite orderly, and nothing more was said to me.

That journey home after seven months away was exciting, the ship could loop the loop going back across the Pentland Firth, and as for those dry bully beef sandwiches devoured en route to the islands, I wouldn't have minded having them with chopped bullets in on that homeward journey.

Following leave I was posted to Felixstowe to join the 138 Coast Defence Battery annexed to Landguard Fort, which was the Regimental HQ and guarded Harwich Harbour. Our battery had two six-inch guns and two searchlights.

I had little to complain about at this camp, the billeting and food were good, and the personnel pleasant enough, but after a period of bull and inactivity it palled on me. I could never understand the mentality of those who almost playfully invented all the stupid, meaningless gimmicks, instead of creating something that had an end product!

I remember once I was in charge of one of the houses which billeted about ten men when orders and plans were distributed for a special CO's bulls – inspection. With every piece of equipment laid on the bed, and the bolts taken out of the rifles, the battery was virtually out of action for about two hours. This was in a period when boots were being plastered with dubbin and the routine was to present them on show between the blankets, the soles with their polished studs showing outwards. I tried to get a message to the SM, without success, and so I altered the design, telling the boys to refer any questions to me. Fortunately I was the first one to be visited – 'Wait for it,' I thought. The CO walked in with the adjutant, followed by the RSM and others from our unit. The CO remarked, 'Excellent, excellent, but tell me sergeant major, why does this layout differ from that of other billets?' Before he could attack me, I stepped smartly forward claimed full responsibility and explained my reasons. To my surprise, instead of being put on a charge, the CO turned to the others and said, 'Makes sense – make a note!' The RSM by his looks could have rammed me up the barrel of one of his guns with a shell following.

In the Orkneys it was a solo duty in the SL emplacement, with the wooden shutters closed, and a narrow board to sleep on. At this battery the steel shutters were down when on duty after the normal equipment tests, and the emplacement was manned by two men who took alternate duties: one would be sleeping in a bunk whilst the other kept watch. In warm weather it was luxury, but in freezing conditions with icy winds on a jet-black night, it was as funny as a streaker would feel at the North Pole!

On many nights Micky Mavro, my very learned Cypriot friend, and I discussed various subjects passionately, but seriously, to while away the first shift.

Micky, a remarkable person speaking several languages and with an extraordinary memory, was not always acquainted with simple army expressions, and on one occasion, when on parade, we were performing the usual dressing-up manoeuvre – arm extended, knuckles on the next man's arm, head turned, with the squad smartly shuffling backwards and forwards and getting into line. Poor Micky was doing something wrong, causing the rather raucous sergeant major to bawl at him, 'Dress up, Mavro – Mavro. *Dress upp!*' Our unperturbed Micky, completely relaxed, and with his head down, looked himself over and finally, with an effort to get his head extended over his rather corpulent tummy, he attempted to look in between his legs, at the same time running both hands up his flies to check if all was well. He will never forget the parade term for 'dress up'. He later took my place and was made up to sergeant.

Eventually I found myself in charge of searchlights which incorporated Lister diesel engines. This permitted me to do a two hour duty guarding the two six inch guns to help out. On one such occasion I had my one and only spot of action, and that concluded with me almost shooting up the camp! The orders were that the Bren gun must only be taken out of the gun emplacement on orders from the BOP, but this was an exceptional case. A lone enemy plane circled the harbour with every available gun opening up. Out to sea it flew and turning, made another run in. I dashed for the gun and stand, but in the excitement and darkness I couldn't mount the gun on the stand. Throwing the stand away I knelt, but too late. Turning sharply he repeated the operation – far too low this time to be touched by ack-ack. The cheek of it! I thought he was obviously attempting to get the guns. Kneeling and ready, with this huge ominous-looking machine flying almost directly overhead at seemingly nil altitude, I opened up, but had slightly misjudged the speed. The line being spot on, the last two or three tracer bullets appeared to hit the tail of the plane, but there the action ended, the gun having ceased to function. I went through the stoppage routine without success and decided to make an examination in the emplacement. I was holding the gun down at the safety angle, and at the end of the first step the thing appeared to change itself into a pneumatic drill – bob-bop – tracers ricocheting off the hard stony ground all over the camp. The officer on duty in the BOP must have thought it had been me on the receiving end of this little escapade, for he said, 'So you had a rough time last night, I saw the bullets flying.' I didn't have the courage to spoil his kindly thoughts by explaining to him that it was me who was shooting up the camp!

The battery had a remarkable cricket team considering the small number of personnel attached to the unit. The first game was played against Landguard Fort, the game being recorded in my score book immediately following the last pre-war game when The George played Enfield. It is now thirty-three years since I looked at this part of the score book, to provoke memories, with proof of the facts! One of the stars of our team was Vivien Broderick (Brod) who played for Northants, and who always revealed an inward sense of humour, displayed only by an amusing smile and twinkling eyes. I wonder if he remembers me clean bowling him for twenty-nine – big head, but it's in the book! What a thrill it would be to meet the following players again (rank and Christian names excluded as I am uncertain of some – Clarke, Holman, Duke, Mapleston, Harvey, Kingsman, Oxlade, Sheldrake, Dwight. In this particular game Brod took seven wickets for twenty-four runs. Incidentally 138 Battery never lost a game – by my score book!

The life in coastal defence became irksome to my disposition, I had little chance of being posted away from CD whilst holding any rank, so now I commenced looking for an outlet; meanwhile, I still continued in charge of the searchlights. Eventually I managed to get on a course for radar, but entertained doubts about my mathematics, a subject in which I never excelled, and it was then eighteen years since leaving school, but the CO very kindly helped the situation by requesting sergeant Gent to give me a little assistance.

Following the termination of the radar course I found myself posted to Orford and billeted in the old castle, which proved to be the most comfortable quarters I experienced in the service, and I appreciated the freedom which the unit enjoyed. The keep and bailey is one of the finest examples of Norman architecture and is typical of many erected during this period, when Henry II was having bother with his turbulent barons. The royal castle was built between the years 1165 and 1172, but unfortunately only the keep remains. This was completed in 1167, at a cost of £983 and the total cost of the castle was £1,407 9s 2d.

The great circular chamber reached by outside stairs was used as sleeping quarters and a room in one of the three flanking towers which had been the original garrison kitchen was our cookhouse. It had a large open fireplace and the original sink, set in the extremely thick wall, which was still efficiently dealing with the water. I would not like to hazard a guess as to the amount or weight of the castle I consumed in my stay of several months – the crumbling stone would fall from above in fine particles as dust, and one was only reminded of the fact when a sizeable piece entered the mouth and was found to be tougher than the teeth!

Above the sleeping quarters was the grand chamber which like the room below, displayed a great open fire place. This chamber was probably occupied by the captain or custodian of the castle in the bygone days, because two other rooms set in the flanking towers are offset without other means of approach. One has a fireplace and a corner waste outlet which suggests it had been the kitchen for the occupants of this section. The other room was the sleeping chamber, with a separate garderobe (toiletry) set in the thick walls. The ceiling of the great room is 25 ft high and about halfway up is a door completely without access, but the corbels at intervals around the chamber suggest that they originally supported a balcony or gallery. The corridor holding the door that would have opened on to the balcony leads to a room resembling a cell which has only a narrow opening for the window. The story of Orford castle suggests it could have been the women's domain, an early kind of medieval ladies' bower?

There is also a fascinating little chapel with the priest's room almost adjoining. This room sports its own garderobe.

The typical Norman hewn stone spiral staircase winds its way from the basement chamber to roof level and, considering the enormous wear of tramping feet over a period of 800 years, the stonework is still in good condition.

An exciting view of this cosy and unspoiled town, and its surrounding countryside was gained from the castle roof. Here were entrances to the two turrets, one of which was apparently the original bakehouse containing a great oven where, no doubt, the garrison's bread was baked. There was a smaller hearth or oven with a communicating flue. The other turret was our operations room, but the door was sealed and entry was gained from below by means of a ladder.

The original supply of water was from a deep well in the circular basement floor, which had been converted to a games room for the unit.

Obviously this old building required continuous cleaning to allow for comfortable habitation and so I suggested a new duty schedule that among other duties, allowed for the dead bats to be swept up from the spiral staircase, and to promote a little enthusiasm I volunteered to be the sanitary orderly which was at times a foul undertaking. The six or so WCs were away from the castle and consisted of a long wooden bench with holes in, each divided by a screen of sacking. I suppose the makeshift contrivance was kept as clean as possible, taking into account the inevitable percentage of those souls who even without a seat to lift, were still careless!

The function of the unit was to plot the continuous convoys off the east coast and report all information to the naval plotting room. The full complement should have been three operators, but we worked with only one on duty. This proved to be a little arduous when the next person on duty had to be awakened. First the ladder had to be negotiated then came a circular trip, two at a time down the twisting stairs to the ground floor to awaken the man on duty, praying he wouldn't slip back into slumberland again, because the man on duty doubled quickly back to the Ops room. If not relieved after some few minutes the exercise would have to be repeated. I invariably took with me a millboard which was a shield against the bats that flew continuously up and down the narrow stairway. When one flew directly at me a very quick flick downwards with the board resulted in another casualty for the sweeper in the morning. One night I killed three bats, not because I wished to but simply because of the nervous reaction to an eerie situation!

The Crown Inn (opposite the castle) which belonged to Trust Houses was extremely convenient for a bath, which cost one shilling.

Under the circumstances very few camps or stations could offer the amenities and luxuries that were enjoyed by our unit – we even had a section of the River Alde railed off for use as a swimming pool. The little inns, although busy, offered an atmosphere of welcome and homeliness not always to be found during these hazardous war years.

There were no parades, in fact I thought this was the nearest thing to complete freedom that was possible in the service, but for some it was still not enough. Such people are rarely satisfied.

One of my other postings in radar was to Bawdsey, where, on seeing our Ops room stuck on the top of a slender steel pylon, I wished I was back in searchlights! The first time on duty was frightening – fancy climbing a vertical steel ladder with blankets tucked under one arm, in all weathers, and regardless of nil visibility! I believe it was a ten hour duty split between two operators, and this meant five hours watching the tube, which was a sure quick way of reducing the efficiency of one's vision. What a laborious chore, too, when nature called upon one to make oneself comfortable.

The exercise of ascending this ladder to go on duty was child's play after climbing the 360 ft high steel radio towers at Bawdsey.

It was a simple enough job for the man whose nerves were unaffected by heights, but for those who did not know if their nerves would falter it was rather a nightmare! I personally was in a near panic when at about 80 ft, an indescribable feeling came over me, as if a mild electric shock was pushing everything from my head towards my legs – the head became slightly lighthearted and the legs nerveless and heavy. I closed my eyes, tightened my grip and made myself think I was on a small ladder that I could have jumped from – no more looking down. When I opened my eyes I kept them staring ahead, and commenced moving again.

The amazing result was that after some 200 ft I was feeling quite safe, and the higher I went the safer I felt, as one does when flying. I must admit to a sinking feeling when ascending that last very long ladder. For some extraordinary reason unknown to me this was made of wood, and it was no surprise to find it wet and slippery, in fact, in places quite slimy! What a thrill to reach the top and walk around the large narrow platform, feeling the gentle sway as the tower flexibly repulsed the breeze. A few heart-in-the-mouth moments while getting on and descending the wooden ladder, but otherwise there was no hitch.

Many thousands who served in the armed forces were very much more fortunate than their families who were left in the cities or other vulnerable places which were targets for the enemy. I recall that during long periods in the battery operations post, when completely away from it all, I would be distressingly snapped back to reality while watching those terrifying silent V2 rockets zigzagging their way up to reach an altitude required to set the 12-ton projectile, with its warhead of explosive weighing one ton, on the correct trajectory for London. There was absolutely no warning. After the shattering explosion a thunderous roar was heard, this was the noise of its bulky flight tearing through the atmosphere at 3,000 mph, much faster than sound. The number of rockets reaching Britain was one thousand and fifty, killing nearly three thousand and seriously injuring almost seven thousand people. This was Hitler's final fling.

We would also hear in comparative safety the thundering noise of droves of VI (Doodle-Bugs or Buzz bombs) flying low en route to London. This was a jet driven robot bomb controlled by a gyroscope carrying an explosive warhead weighing one ton. Somewhere over the selected target the engine cut... silence... the seemingly long and timorous wait until either distant 'boom' or the close shattering 'bang' would intimate to the listeners that, 'That was not for us!' Perhaps, somewhere not too far away one, two or maybe a family died that never heard the explosion. Of eight thousand of these missiles launched against Britain two thousand three hundred reached the London area, damaging more than one million homes. Hundreds were also destroyed by RAF fighters, rocket and

AA batteries. The total number of civilians killed in Britain by enemy action was almost seventy thousand of which nearly eight thousand were children. London's death toll was thirty thousand.

The following are extracts from some of the letters I received from Audrey during the war period – severely censored!

*November 1943*

*I should think the overdraft will be down to about £25 to £30 by Christmas. That is, of course, without counting anything we may be able to rake in. I shall have to order another load of logs but am hoping the coal will last out until after Christmas. At any rate I am not going to buy anything unless it is essential until it is clear. It will be a great relief to my mind when it is. Everything is so terribly expensive these days that sometimes it seems hopeless. Young Brian is quite an expense as there is always something he is needing. He grows like a weed. His Radio-Malt costs five shillings and fourpence a jar too.*

*As I told you some very cheap boots were £5 5s 0d in London so that is hopeless. As a matter of fact now I shall be very glad if you will give me the money, as a pair of shoes which I asked Lilley and Skinner could they get for me last February have just come in. The girl has phoned me so I shall have to have them and make do with my old boots in any case because the coupons would not run to it. They are a pair of low heeled ones so I am glad.*

*January 1944*

*They have managed to move one of the bombs from Dad's nursery. It was 6 ft 9 ins long and weighed 1½ tons. You can guess how glad they were to get the detonator out of that!*

*February 1944*

*Thank goodness we have had one or two nights free from raids. After last week it is a blessing. I did hear about four hundred houses were damaged on Thursday night at Tottenham.*

*Brian and I had a lovely day in town. It was sunshine to start with too. We had a look at the shops and then met Joy at twelve at the Regent Palace. We queued for lunch but at 12.40 p.m. Joy had to leave and get a sandwich somewhere. It was a shame. Brian and I eventually got in at 12.55. We had quite a nice lunch – soup and roast pork. I had one gin and squash and Brian had no sweet and that came to 11s 5d. Isn't it awful.*

*I had my blood transfusion on Saturday. Except for feeling rather tired and my arm a little painful I have felt no ill-effects. The only sensation I did not like was waiting for my doctor and watching the other people's bottles fill up with blood. That I think is worse than having it done and somehow you feel as if you must watch. One lady behind me nearly passed out. As a matter of fact the nurse had just left the room, I was laying down at the time, and I saw her change colour, so I got up and laid her down. She was so terribly cold too. However, she did not completely pass out.*

*Brian has been saving ship halfpennys and wren farthings for his school, Rodney is too, although I believe I told you. He took a box full this morning it is surprising where they come from. He gets them from his aunties as well. The next lot he is saving for your fund, although this is supposed to be a surprise for when you come home. He is also including threepenny pieces in this too, although when Edna and I were talking about it on Saturday he suggested half-crowns, if you please.*

*June 1944*

*Brian sleeps in the shelter every night now and I go in with him until about 4–5 a.m. when I go upstairs and chance it. It is not very restful under the shelter for me but I cannot bear the thought of leaving him down there alone all night. If anything did happen it would be so quick and I should never reach him.*

*Gladys and Charles (Edna's sister) have lost their pub. In fact they have only the kitchen left. Gladys was shaken up rather badly and has a shoulder badly cut, but they are alive. An uncle of my mother's has been bombed out completely at Eltham.*

*Really we are lucky this side of London. The devastation is simply terrible elsewhere. I think I told you about the one at Hadley Road, but since then we have had one at Ponders End and another at Southgate. I was on the telephone when the Ponders End one went over and the explosion took the thing right out of my hand and the floor simply rocked. Mrs Gibbs's mother living a little nearer to the one at Southgate, was blown right out of bed.*

*June 1944*

*The warning went at twelve o'clock last night and we did not get the all clear until eleven o'clock this morning. Everyone has got to the stage of listening intently every time aircraft are about.*

*Brian goes to school when it is all clear but if it is after ten or three does not go at all. There are only about eight of them going to Miss Ward's bungalow in Ringmer Place, off Bush Hill where Edgar Dipple used to live. She has a good shelter for them there and he is not far from me. If the warning is still on when it is time for him to leave, I go down for him. It is the best we can do and just hope that nothing happens.*

*The part I am not keen on is being in this old house (Elmscott, Bush Hill) all day entirely alone. We have had three warnings this morning and you can hear the explosions going off all around. The trouble is with these rockets they do so much damage, far more than the land mines.*

*The Baker Street one went off about midnight on Saturday. Poor old Sid Crowl, Freddie Cowan, Mollie Boundy and lots of others have lost their houses. There are hundreds damaged. Strangely enough though most of them have been able to salvage most of their furniture, although the glass does such a lot of damage.*

*The one near home fell on Chesterfield Road schools just outside Enfield Lock station. My people have lost some windows and all the locks of the doors came off, but it is not too serious. Poor old Fred Ridgewell has only one room left with a ceiling to it. His wife, daughter and new baby managed to get under the stairs and so saved themselves from injury. They have gone right away but he is there trying to straighten the furniture up and get it into this one room. Arnos Grove, Winchmore Hill and all the surrounding districts are suffering. I would much rather have a good old-fashioned blitz these things are so uncanny.*

*The other side of London is simply shocking. Hilda had to lie flat three times going to get some lunch yesterday so she said she is going to give it up and take some sandwiches with her.*

*One thing I wanted to ask you, would you mind if I decanted a bottle of our port. I think there are about five bottles there. I do not want it for ordinary use but if and when I cannot sleep, it might help a little.*

*July 1944*

*We had a very bad evening yesterday. They were coming down all around us. Without exaggerating I heard at least twenty. Although we are safe, each time one thinks of some poor soul getting it. One which stopped over our houses on Tuesday evening travelled a long way before it exploded and I heard it was Potters Bar. I phoned Phyl and she tells me it went in the spinney near the Chequers Inn. They are all quite well but she feels as I do, more scared of these things than the ordinary raids. It is all so uncanny and one is strung up the whole time listening. George phones her up every morning to see if they are all right.*

*Did I tell you one fell in the Kingsway last Friday? It was an appalling affair. Dick was coming back from lunch when it happened and was some way away fortunately. We are burying the second-in-command B Company today. He was cut to pieces poor chap. Apparently he was waiting for a lift to go to Bush House and some fellows let a party of girls take the first car and he waited for the next – then it happened. Still I suppose we must not let it get us down, but I must say I feel very edgy lately.*

*Mrs Graham and two young schoolboys were caught in the avenue the other day. They all went down flat. Really when you come to think of it there is a funny side to it all. Pity we cannot take a film of it.*

*October 1944*

*I was worried on Friday because I had not been well enough to get up and do the books so as it was raining I hired a car to take me to Ridgemount and back. It was teeming and the only thing I could do because I had to get the books off to the stocktaker. It cost me seven shillings and sixpence unfortunately.*

*We are still being troubled with rockets and bombs. Saturday night Ponders End and Cheshunt got it. Last night there was a rocket somewhere at about 7.30 and at 1.15 a.m. a flying bomb somewhere near. It sounded like Ponders End again.*

*On Saturday night I thought I would watch out of the kitchen window. I saw the searchlights signalling and then move. Suddenly the sky lit up and I saw this wretched thing coming straight for Enfield. As I told you it fell at Ponders End but I must say I moved a bit sharp to get under the shelter. I did not like the direction of it at all.*

*I think I told you there would be about £30 balance in the bank didn't I, dear? Well, I'm afraid I made a mistake it was only £20. Instead of drawing that cheque I am going to pay £2 into your PO account each week for twelve weeks. That will balance it so that I have a little to meet expenses with at the bank. I hope I am making this clear to you. I have had the telephone account in this week which had to be paid straight away. It comes to £6 7s 11d. Your calls came to £3. The other is rental for six months and my calls. Awful blow isn't it? Still it is just as well to do it this way.*

*This week I have had to buy Brian a pair of gloves, five shillings and threepence and one pair of shoes repaired, five shillings and ninepence. That is 11s 0d gone without anything else. These are only essentials.*

*When I went down to Battalion HQ on Saturday, Captain Johns asked me if I had seen the Colonel. Apparently Miss Edwards, the head one at battalion is leaving and he wants me to take her place. If the hours are the same I shall be pleased to do it as it will be just as convenient to go there as to come to Elmscott in fact during the winter months it will be much more pleasant. How long it is likely to last I have no idea, but I will let you know more when I have been definitely approached.*

*November 1944*

*As I told you we are having a pretty hectic time with the other weapons beside the flying bombs. We had two alerts at breakfast time yesterday for flying bombs but they are much better than those other things. Everyone is really strung up. We were sitting by the fire last night when one came over and we nearly shot through the ceiling. Fortunately Brian was sleeping and did not wake. I was really surprised. There was an awful mess between Winchmore Hill and Palmers Green Stations. One caught a train and there were lots of casualties from flying glass. All the shops are in a dreadful state. Bob has been busy this week getting his shop straight again – he is very fed up with it all. Our house simply rocked as you can well imagine and although Brian was terribly frightened at the time he seems to have recovered all right and more or less now takes them as a joke.*

*I feel thankful each morning to find my home is still whole.*

*December 1944*

*I have not heard anything more about the council job so far, but two others in the local paper this week attracted me. One in Enfield, £3 10s 0d, short hours and every other Saturday off and the other with Chamberlain and Willows – £4 – Mondays to Fridays, hours 9–5. Still we shall see.*

*I am going to take the opportunity of staying at Bournemouth for a few days with Edna and Bob. The break will do Brian good, also myself. I think it will mean having these few days without pay but it can't be helped.*

*I had an offer of an appointment with the council today. The wages with war bonus would come to £3 10s 6d, only 6d more than what I am getting and not nearly such good hours. I am enclosing the detail for you to see – please return it, dear. With my job I get fourteen days leave any time I like during the summer and at the council one I must work a year before any leave is granted and it is the third year before twelve days is due.*

*April 1945*

*I have had a shock this week. The doctor's bill arrived and for three visits he has charged me 11 17s 6d. Brian's school fees also had to be paid and now the telephone bill has arrived. This amounts to £7 14s 11d. The trunk calls are nearly £4. I think we shall definitely have to make them three minute calls in future, it will help a little.*

*I am sending a two-unit Board of Trade coupon on to you, dear. This you can change anywhere and if you only manage to get one collar they will give you a one-unit one in exchange. This is all quite legal.*

> *As you say I think there will be some very hard fighting to actually take Berlin but thank goodness the Russians look like being there first. One can hardly grasp that all these horrible things have been going on. The pictures have been terrible haven't they? I have been so afraid of Brian seeing them this last few days. Can you imagine the women carrying out such brutal treatment. I think they must all be insane. When you think we are supposed to be a civilised world today! It seems to be far worse than what happened in the olden days.*

My last two postings were to Brussels and Bad Oeynhausen, near Minden, in Germany. I felt little bitterness towards the German people but I can understand the feelings of all those who suffered mercilessly and horrifically at the hands of the debased and depraved few. Hitler, without doubt, was the greatest war-crazed maniac the world had ever seen, but the incredible truth was that it took the might of almost the rest of the world to suppress him. What a supreme nation Germany might have been if this man had used his mesmeric influence and the talents and will of his people for peaceful motives instead of for war... maybe the whole world would have been in a less deplorable state than it is in the Seventies.

We and other nations must shoulder a large measure of the blame for the eccentric complacency displayed by the majority in the face of the very obvious danger signals showing during the middle and late Thirties.

On 4th May, 1945, the North German Command surrendered to Field Marshall Montgomery, and three days later the German General Staff capitulated to General Eisenhower, and so VE Day was celebrated by millions of people – the agonies over. No more bombing, no more black-out, but to me the whole exercise seemed somehow unfinished. Maybe the outcome was disturbing in its incompleteness.

It is no wonder that many of the people who gave their best years to the last two wars, and especially those who served in both, do not disguise their contempt of the feeble way in which Britain's militant 'enemies of society' at all levels have been regarded as heroes by undiscriminating sections of the public. When one ponders upon the shocking waste of life, the suffering of the maimed, to say nothing of the astronomical cost financially, we are forced to acknowledge the shameful gap which exists between the narrow materialism of present-day international standards and the glowing future which the genius of scientists, humanists and technocrats has put within our grasp.

Finally came the most eventful day of the war – 6th August, 1945 – when the first atomic bomb was dropped on Hiroshima to terminate the conflict with Japan, and three days later another single bomb was unleashed on Nagasaki. The two bombs caused a quarter of a million casualties, and so for good or evil the world entered another precarious phase.

Of course I, like so many others, regret the loss of five years or more of normal life, but the experience of some twenty postings involving all types of interesting assignments other than the duties I was trained for, and the pleasure of meeting and working with characters of all types, helped to compensate for this unpremeditated distraction.

There was something very special about taking leave or even short passes whilst in the services but, when one considers the extreme anticipation and excitement of going home for a period of normality, I recall little of the happenings. However, one of these periods stays foremost in my mind because I have since been frequently reminded of it when passing The Carlton Hotel, at Bognor, and happily recalling our week's stay there with A.J.S. and Jennie in company with friends Bill and Vera Towler. Edward, the young Duke of Kent with his sister, Princess Alexandra, and younger brother, Prince Michael, were then in residence. Only our party and one other family were permitted to stay as guests, the remainder of the hotel having been taken over for the occasion, obviously more than was needed but a necessary precaution undoubtedly for security reasons.

We were amazed at the freedom everybody enjoyed – completely natural and devoid of all fuss. The young prince was then in a pram but we were fascinated watching the confident and disciplined way in which the duke and princess would act when given their lessons – a complete study of concentration, but only for the seconds it took to allow the nanny or tutor to close the doors behind her. A cautious and wily turn of the head established the all clear. The royal pupils would then jump sprightly to life by downing tools and mischievously hopping on to chairs assuming an attitude indicating freedom at last.

Their father, Prince George, received the title Duke of Kent in 1934 when he married Princess Marina of Greece. To the nation's great sorrow the duke was tragically killed in an air crash in 1942.

Another of my visits home presented me with the pleasurable opportunity of meeting and chatting with the glamorous and paragon star, Anna Neagle. The occasion was in connection with the National Savings Campaign and the balcony fronting The George and overlooking the town was an ideal setting for such an undertaking.

When A.J.S. was living at Ridgemount, on the Ridgeway, he acquired a pony and trap which was used frequently for local calls. Naturally he salved his conscience with the belief that the exercise was a great war effort, but I am positive the thrill of clip-clopping to one of the locals and easing up at their destination with an anxious and hopeful 'Whoa Polly', accompanied by the snort, the creaking of strained leather mingled with the crunch of the wheels on gravel was the real motive!

Twice I accompanied A.J.S. to The Jolly Farmer in his proud little outfit, and I detected that increased touch of excitement that encouraged him to revel so much more in the atmosphere of a good old British pub.

# Chapter XXXIV

Released after five years – the Fund for the Children of the Fighting Forces (FCFF) – Ridgemount, Enfield – the Gannons – tennis and the Mottrams – the old bus companies – the Norfolk Hotel, Arundel – out of work

Released from the Services on 11th February, 1946, I like millions of others, was delighted to be reunited with my family, and to return to a normal way of life. We had obviously planned to join Standbrooks again and eventually to control The George, but for reasons unknown to us this was not to be.

The fund for the children of the fighting forces continued until the termination of the war, having investigated and dealt with approximately one thousand five hundred cases over a period of six years. The object initially was really to give the kiddies extra comforts and pleasure, but the need for more necessitous treatment proved greater, and so help was given in the form of clothing or grants. The following original members were still serving on the committee when the fund's activities terminated: Arthur Bridget, Stan Thorpe, Lewis Dixon and Stan Walker. It is quite impossible to mention the names of the many friends, whether in a working capacity or not, who registered expressions of thoughtfulness towards others in so many ways.

A typical example was an occasion organised by Jack Edwards, then the extremely popular entertainments officer for Enfield Council, who organised a boxing tournament at the Enfield stadium in August 1942 as an attraction to the 'stay-at-home-holiday' period in conjunction with the FCFF, the proceeds of which were divided between the Red Cross and St John Ambulance funds and the FCFF.

The following letter is a fine illustration of the courtesy of the treasurer, then well in his seventies, in expressing kindly consideration for the feelings of two youngsters:

*To: Masters Brian Standbrook and Rodney Freeman.*

*March 30, 1944*
*Dear Boys,*

*The chairman and committee have asked me to thank you for your very thoughtful and wonderful effort on behalf of our friend which Brian's father handed to us at our last meeting, it came as a very agreeable surprise and has been entered in our minutes.*

*It was a kindly thought for you two boys to think of the boys and girls of Enfield's fighting men and to work so well on their behalf, and now I am going to ask you to continue your good work and see if you can reach a pound in your next effort.*

*With kind regards and good luck,*
*Yours sincerely,*
*A. E. Bridger,*
*Hon. Treas.*

During the early part of the war, A.J.S. and Jennie moved to a delightful house situated on the west side of the Ridgeway and named Ridgemount. Although the building sported a generous frontage, a passer-by would never conjecture that the grounds at the rear extended to some four and a half acres, and of this over half was laid out in natural and ornamental gardens, lawns fine enough to play a sporting game of bowls on, walks that skirted the spinney containing a fine variety of trees, and long mellow glades flanked with flowering shrubs and climbing plants mingling with the fine, spongy, sprung turf that only years of tender care can fashion. The en-tout-cas tennis court was in a dreamland setting, but all this luxury was so little used mainly, of course, owing to this period of austerity. Such a home required kids or young people and their laughter to evoke its fullest pleasures.

The previous owners of Ridgemount – Arthur and Hilda Gannon – had resided there since the early Thirties and, with their three children, must have enjoyed the outstanding amenities the house and grounds offered. The tennis court, especially, had the privilege of contributing greatly to the success and fame of their daughter Joy in the tennis world. A Wightman Cup player, she married Tony Mottram in the early Fifties. In 1954 Tony won the British Hard Court Championship, whilst Joy lost to Doris Hart, the American star, in the final of the women's singles at the same championship meeting. Tony and Geoff Paish took the men's doubles, and Joy and Doris Hart won the women's doubles. Tony had the great honour of representing Britain in the Davis Cup fifty-six times. Their son Buster – then twenty years old and around 6 ft 4 inches tall – won the British under-21 title when only sixteen, and at seventeen was the youngest player ever to be included in the Davis Cup squad. He already had beaten several of the world's top players. Linda, their daughter, won the Junior Indoor Championship in 1974, has twice won the Cumberland Tournament and already has a victory over Virginia Wade.

Joy's sister Pearl was also a Wimbledon player, having won both the Hurlingham and Cumberland Tournaments, whilst her daughters Cherry and Joy both had the honour of being British Junior Ski Champions. Hilda Gannon's brother, Chris Clark, was the amateur featherweight champion of England in 1901 and 1902 – a great sporting family indeed.

Arthur Gannon was proprietor of the Prince Bus and Coach Company, one of the many efficient and exciting services that served Enfield, and if they were perhaps a trifle unorthodox at times the public was seldom let down; there was certainly never a 'go slow' period, and what hearty, boisterous and responsible characters the majority of the crews were. Some of these buses were known as 'pirates' and well lived up to their name.

Other well-known local transport proprietors were A.T. and W.C. Bennett, who ran the Admiral buses and Redburn's Motor Service, which was started by Thomas Redburn around 1870 with horse-drawn vehicles, and developed by Len and Archie Redburn. (The latter's son, Tom Redburn, is now mine host at The Falcon, in South Street, Enfield). Biss and Sons' buses plied the route from Wormley to the Elephant & Castle, London. Stanley Biss commenced operating immediately after the first world war. Biss Bros. Coaches are operating today in many fields of the travel and leisure business.

Arthur Gannon was the last to sell out to London Transport in 1932, and it was not uncommon to hear him referred to as the 'lone pirate'. The great takeover of Greater London's numerous privately owned bus services commenced in 1929.

Standbrooks had developed considerably as a small private business, and appeared to be substantial and flourishing with the following establishments: The Cambridge, George Inn, Cuffley Hotel, Crooked Billet, Stonehouse Hotel, Norfolk Arms at Arundel, and the Drome Restaurant, Hatfield. There were also two more sites in Enfield which A.J.S. had acquired through James Neilson, and which A.J.S. passed on to Charringtons for prospective development. The Bullsmore, Bullsmore Lane, Enfield and The Gryphon, Grange Park, Enfield.

The Norfolk Hotel at Arundel was purchased towards the end of the war from the well-known and old established Hare family, who had been in possession since 1894. Leased from the Duke of Norfolk, the hotel offers twenty-eight bedrooms, and has a 'free' full on-license. The following tariff then offered: Single room and breakfast 15s 0d (75p). Daily terms £1 4s 0d (£1.20). Inclusive weekly terms from £8 8s 0d (£4.40). Luncheon 4s 0d (20p). Dinner 5s 0d (25p). Normal routine instructions appertaining to the wartime conditions were always displayed, such as 'ration books must be provided if residing in the hotel for five nights or over' and 'visitors are requested to bring their own towels and soap'.

Alf suffered an extremely serious illness prior to his release from the forces, having contracted an infected liver, but he appeared to make a complete recovery and was quickly installed again at The Cambridge after he was demobilised. Being stationed in Enfield through the war years may have been an asset in many ways, but he was never really free of business anxieties. His popularity at all levels, together with an aptitude for being able to indulge in the spirit of hospitable occasions with unruffled endurance and without losing any of his genuine charm was not altogether conducive to an abstemious or temperate life.

A.J.S. must have appreciated his assistance through those tumultuous years.

There was little sign of Audrey and I being invited back into the family business, and so the immediate future took on a bleak aspect. We were now in quite a desperate position, having necessarily surrendered both of my endowment policies, and the total cash available was negligible, moreover, the owner of our rented house would shortly be returning. We were, at this stage, a little bitter, to say the least, but when one reflected on the straits and needs of others we were indeed fortunate. There is little doubt that six years had conditioned people to a new dimension in thinking. Different priorities with a fresh set of values were being introduced.

My first move to link again with the sport and charities I was connected with before the war was to obtain four tankards for presentation to players of the winning rink in the Enfield Standbrook Bowls Tournament, but my enthusiasm was fleetingly annihilated when I handed them over, only to have them given back to me, with the casual information that the committee had decided to proceed with the wartime practice of presenting certificates! Slightly deflated I took them home, but after twenty-five years there was a very happy sequel to this incident! Hopefully in the next volume.

# Chapter XXXV

We take over the Cuffley Hotel – financial adversity – unfortunate war-time policies – the Social Club – Lizzie Ridout leaves The Plough – Alexandra Amateur Boxing Club – professional boxing and the Toby Club amateur promotions – the new restaurant and its misfortunes – wages and prices


Fate rescued us from our precarious position, and cast us into the business again, due entirely to a difference of opinion within the family on a purely domestic issue – a simple request from A.J.S. and Jennie that resulted in widely differing and impassioned views. The outcome was a call from one of my family offering me The Cuffley Hotel as tenants, which of course I had to refuse owing to my financial position, but I was given to understand quite emphatically that money was not involved in the deal! We accepted uneasily, but with an enormous feeling of relief – the main objective was settled, somewhere to live!

The change was arranged for 9th April, 1946. We were taking over from Peggy who had very successfully managed the business on her own during the war period, but suffered the traumatic experience of divorce shortly after Reg had been released from the services.

Following the formal transfer of license at Hatfield, and the rather light-hearted, but involved, change we were speedily conveyed to reality when the final settlement for inventory and stock was agreed, and I was presented with an account for over £1,300! A burdensome problem with which to laugh the evening buoyantly away. Four weeks later our survival looked grim – we had an overdraft in the region of £250 with immediate cash requirement for equipment and improvements plus a tax demand for £200 or more. This left me nonplussed, but I was strongly advised to pay up. What effrontery to demand the tax in advance now. I sent £100 on account and mindfully, in a facetious mood, that somebody must pay for the war! I was determined to alter a policy, pursued fortunately by the few, that had on several occasions infuriated me when the pubs had not sufficient stocks to satisfy the demands of their customers. A licensee of course, is exceptionally vulnerable as compared with other retail trades in which customers are more or less in and out. Obviously the great problem was an attempt to be fair to old-standing or regular customers without causing embarrassment to the not-so-frequent callers and strangers. We all differ, and rightly, in our personal attitude to the dispensing of favours but what annoyed me was the blatant and stupid way in which the cover-up was often attempted. A common instance was the putting of beer in tankards during a mineral and spirit only period, or serving whisky from a ginger ale or ginger wine bottle. There was also the quite common habit of serving a mystery packet of cigarettes held in a bulging fist clenched with palm down and offered to the recipient as if playing 'Tippit'! In allocating the alternate beer and spirit periods I admit it was impossible to be absolutely fair, but we attempted it as did the majority of licensees.

I remember A.J.S. visiting us and having to make do with a ginger ale during a spirits off period, and two customers approaching me saying, 'We'll have one of what your father's got,' – which they did. After the first sip, their expressions laid bare their thoughts. Off they went to A.J.S.

for a check. I never knew what was said, but I could well imagine A.J.S. saying, 'Well, I've go to b— well put up with it,' because they were all smiling.

One instance I recall was so blatantly cheeky that it was amusing. Driving home from Framlingham with Audrey on a scorching hot day, we looked desperately for a pub that had beer on sale, but having no success, agreed to stop at the next one open whatever it was offering. We pulled into a very well-known hostel, a few miles from Epping, displaying the mineral and spirits only sign. There were only two other customers in the bar, one of whom happened to be the manageress of The Crooked Billet. Having been introduced to the licensee, I asked the company to join me in a drink, after which I remarked persuasively, 'Couldn't I do with a nice cool pint of beer – I'm parched.' The landlord replied, 'I'm so sorry, the beer is not on until later tonight,' and to ease his discomfort, I exclaimed, 'For goodness sake, I fully understand, I admire you for sticking to your rules – I'll have a gin and tonic.' Pausing I said, 'Will you join us?' Replying enthusiastically, 'Thank you – be delighted,' he collected a tankard, filled it to the brim, displaying an exciting bubbling head that set my parched tongue attempting to slide along my dry lips! 'Cheerio,' said mine host unconcernedly and drank it himself. If only he had some excuse such as 'doctor's orders' or something, no matter how unconvincing it might have appeared!

Cuffley was a tremendously friendly and social village – light-hearted, carefree, and contented enough for most people to wear a happy or friendly face. Although the village had expanded considerably, now having a population of approximately three thousand, the same spirit prevails today although the population had more than doubled by 1974.

Pubs were still completely traditional then, and the public bar still a prominent feature respected as an important part of the business. How many pub-goers are fully aware of the subtle thinking behind the change which has taken place? Cuffley is a good example of a village with a public bar trade that was then common to all pubs sited outside densely populated towns. Quite a third of the clientele were business directors, professional men or tradesmen, all of whom should theoretically have been in the saloon bar contributing that extra penny per drink to assist in reducing my overdraft! But this economic free-thinking was yet to be established and the customer was then considered a little more important than his money. Unfortunately this outlook is tending to be reversed today, and the infection is contaminating all aspects of life. The scene has changed – the busiest bar is the most expensive bar and, with ever-rising costs, a public bar is just not viable in high cost areas. It appears that the better the standard of living the more immature, diversified and inferior life becomes, to the accompaniment of the general lowering of standards in most services.

Although we had never taken a day and a half off duty in a week, we very much appreciated closing one day a week whilst the beer rationing period lasted. The staff were allowed only one day off duty then, and that a boon for all to be off and on duty together – in fact the whole business efficiency and tempo was much improved!

We existed very meagrely until we were assured that the barrier to solvency had been lowered. We did not run a car, and the extent of our outings was to Enfield by train to visit the flicks or to go really showy and finish up at Finsbury

Park Empire! It was not long before frustration was behind us and a new base built on anticipation.

Now we were more settled the organising and promoting bug was again demanding action, and so we created various types of outings and competitions to suit all ages, and where possible the profits were devoted to charity. The following projects were easily organised owing mainly to the general help and support rendered by the Cuffley people: darts competitions and matches, snooker, billiards and table tennis competitions; cricket and tennis matches; outings to race meetings, boxing, a visit to the Ceremony of the Keys at the Tower of London; circus, dances, whist drives; and as many as sixty would support the Wood Green Operatic Society through the instrumentality of Gordon Parr, who played the lead in many fine shows that were promoted at the Wood Green Empire or the Scala Theatre.

Eventually the Cuffley Hotel Social Club was formed with the object of raising money for charity. The intention was to make donations in kind, relative to the recipients' specific requirements rather than with money. This generated more interest and greater participation by everyone linked with any project. The principle, in general, is still adhered to today, and many local charities now work with the same object.

An outstanding example was our first effort when we arranged a visit of our committee to Dr Barnardo's Home at Ilford. Having been taken on a tour of the Home by the principal we were amazed at the items needed but not forthcoming; for instance there was an extreme lack of equipment in the gymnasium. The committee later decided to supply a vaulting horse and springboard, which were duly presented. Many photographs showing girls in action on the vaulting horse were sent to us and these together with very appreciative letters, were displayed in the bar, to the great pleasure of the customers, especially those who had contributed. The club dedicated the funds for a year to the Halliwick Cripples School at Winchmore Hill, later to be known as the Halliwick School for physically handicapped children.

The school was, and still is, administered by the Church of England Children's Society, and relied very much on local support, not only for the little extras such as the friends from Cuffley were donating, but for building improvements, and the installation of lifts, etc, towards which the people of Enfield gave so much, especially institutions such as the Enfield Rotary Clubs and Round Table.

The committee representing the pub organised no fewer than twenty-eight small promotions in eight months to raise the money for the items we had promised to the Halliwick School, and for a proposed tea party for the children in the Cabin at Cuffley. The ladies' section played the major part in promoting the party, and helped vigorously in acquiring the funds. Every child was given a substantial present. Gordon Parr, with his operatic colleagues, entertained the children, and he also brought along Geoffrey Robinson, the magician, who was well-known to TV viewers. The evening was brought to a close by Gordon and his colleagues rendering, very invigoratingly, 'Bless This House'. The impressively touching atmosphere was amplified by the wooden building which reverberated like a drum. It was a moving moment. Standing next to me was a committee member with tears streaming down her face. It is strange how gladness and sadness can be so infectious. She had me with my throat tightening up, and now I had immediately to say a few words to terminate the proceedings! I clambered on to the stage, bewildered and speechless, finally muttering a series of incoherent thanks. I was immediately reminded how inadequate I was when the matron, Miss Alford, called on one of the children to reply on behalf of Matron and the girls. This she did with a confidence and clarity of speech that had everyone spellbound, saying what a wonderful time they had all had, and how pleased they were with their gifts, also how much they enjoyed the lovely blankets which were so warm and cosy (fifty blankets were presented by the club).

Brian volunteered to accompany the children back to Halliwick and to assist in unloading the invalid chairs. What a dance they led him! – being much about their age he had little chance. When I entered the coach to say goodbye they were all calling to him, 'Brian, can I have my parcel down?' and, 'Brian, can I have my parcel up?'. Feeling embarrassed for him I hopped off smartly before he changed his mind!

This little club had some two hundred members of whom about one hundred and twenty resided at or in the vicinity of Cuffley. Unfortunately, when looking through the list of members one is immediately reminded how twenty-five to nearly thirty years can take its toll of so many of them. A few who helped to establish and made the club successful are still in Cuffley, such as Tim and Jo Stone, Gordon and Mimmie Parr, Sydney and Mirian Becker-Jones, George and Dorothy Boothman, Harold and Rene Meads, and Freddie Shepherd.

One very simple and consistent method of raising money which I introduced was a 101 darts competition, a monthly event with any number of persons entering. The draw was already displayed from the preliminary or first round to the final, ready for the first arrivals to play, and the whole thing was completed in one evening. The names of winner and runner-up were engraved on separate tankards for the recipients' exclusive use, and with an allocation of free beer. This competition ran successfully for more than four years, 1947 to 1951. The tankards recording those happy evenings are in my possession.

Following some of the busiest nights when the atmosphere had been charged with that merry, bubbling and buoyant mood, I would take Kim, the dalmatian, out after completing the routine chores and breathe deeply the cool clean air. Often when walking along Tolmers Road I was reminded of the complete change – although only perhaps 11.20 p.m. Cuffley appeared to be in a drowsy slumber and so complete was the silence that every step taken on the crunchy gravel seemed to me an affront on the absolute stillness, and my thoughts would wander back to the excitement and hubbub of the evening – 'Did it all happen?'

Audrey organised a Christmas Club for the staff and friends wishing to join. There were no rules or regulations. One could pay in any amount at any time, and so with withdrawals – the very essence of simplicity and convenience. All the profits derived from the rate of investment were donated to charity, and the system still continues.

An annual event always enthusiastically supported was the stag party organised by the Cuffley Cricket Club and held at the Cabin. I supplied the bar stock at cost price, organised the bar and its attendant equipment, and was responsible for the system which made the profit that was donated wholly to the cricket club (without taking any cash!). Tim Stone (Cuffley's 'Mr Cricket') arranged the food, and it must be admitted that I never met another person as knowledgeable in his favourite subjects – cricket, food and fishing. Nobody will ever know the depth of his knowledge or ability in any other subject simply because he never mentioned anything else – ever! He was a great friend of Wally Hammond who, living at Cuffley, attended the club's local joke-telling extravaganza. Yes, Tim did have another subject – and a master memory for communicating tales or jokes. It was an astonishing repertoire, but even more wondrous was how he acquired them, because few people ever squeezed in to tell their story before Tim was telling his next!

The beer shortage was eased during the summer months by sending 'Big Bertha' to Devonshire by rail to be replenished with cider. Big Bertha was a large cask holding 54 gallons (hogshead) and on its re-arrival at Cuffley the well-known character, George the Porter, would nip in and call out, 'Big Bertha's in – all hands on deck.' One hot weekend I remember Brian keeping us all supplied from the cask in the off license, using any receptacle he could lay his hands on. He was in such a state he had to put his wellies on. The scene would have been understandable had there been a fire and the only available water was in the cask – it developed into just one great splash-up, with Brian laughing his head off and wallowing in the profits!

In the early days Cuffley was without a hairdresser, and so every two weeks one was engaged to attend at the off license during the evening, and it was not uncommon when 'Next, please' was called to have one person in each bar, about equidistant away, to be waiting at the counter flap like greyhounds when the traps open, and woe betide anyone in the way. There were, of course, periods when few hairdressers could offer the peaceful amenities of a private appointment, television and a pint!

Joe, our very affable and likeable real country type, part-time gardener, very much amused me with a remark in connection with a heap of rubble that we were unable to dispose of. As a final comment I said, 'If we don't succeed next week, dig a hole and bury the lot!' Joe, with a confused look on his friendly face, replied, 'But we'll never get it all in, sir.'

One highlight during our stay at Cuffley was the grand and stately wedding of Princess Elizabeth to HRH Prince Philip on 20th November, 1947. This was a glorious example of British pageantry in its grandest form – but so humbly celebrated with solemnity and sincerity that the outcome of all the pomp and ceremony was simplicity and dignity. Thank God we still have a royal family, and I wish everyone would give a little more thought to the stability that royalty gives this country and the ambassadorial value that it has in the rest of the world. Few people would exchange their responsibilities and freedom for those of the royal family.

The Plough, Cuffley, which has been referred to previously, was still in the possession of dear old Alice (Lizzie) Rideout, having taken over as hosts with her husband William (Bill) in 1914; she was greatly respected locally.

McMullens applied for a full 'on license', in, I believe, 1945, when hitherto they had held only a beer and wine license. Normally Charringtons, through the licensee, would have opposed the application, but I had always felt very strongly regarding these stupid restricted licenses, and in my opinion every 'public on license' should have been automatically changed, or at least given the option of being fully licensed. However, I was one of the first, if not the first, to sign Lizzie's petition.

Proof of the congenial village spirit that existed then was verified when Lizzie gave her farewell party when leaving The Plough in December 1950 after thirty-six years of true village inn service. All her friends were invited, who with their friends, accounted for some half of my customers. Lizzie had laid on eighteen gallons (kilderkin) of Burton for the boys, and when the fun was under way, one of the lads thought how nice it would be to have a little music, probably with a sneaking mental picture of a large nearby public bar sporting a very lonely piano. It must have been so, because about 9 p.m. hefty Lew Baker, accompanied by some other powerful boys, said, 'Can we borrow your piano, Stan?' their hands all ready for the first lift. I said, 'You're wasting time,' and helped them load it on the lorry!

It was always a pleasure – and so easy – to organise a party for almost anything at Cuffley, and a pleasure too for me to browse through my scribbled notebook recording one hundred and twenty-five outings, competitions, matches, etc. For instance there was an outing to Ascot to see the Gold Cup race on 17th June, 1948, the cost of which was £1 5s 0d per head, and this included coach, buffet lunch, drinks and food on arriving back to Cuffley. The sad but inevitable story is that to my knowledge at least half of the party are no longer with us. Charles Fisher, an officer in the fire service, very sadly lost his life in the underground fire at Covent Garden not long after this outing; we are happy to remain in contact with Billy, his widow.

Eric Anderton, a loveable character, who had the honour of being the Mayor of Wood Green on three occasions, enjoyed his weekly riding session, when he would accompany the riding master, Don Lyne, (whose family name was a by-word in Enfield) on a ride from The Fallow Buck to Cuffley. Eric, a keen all-round sportsman, was one of the instigators in the reformation of the old Alexandra Boxing Club at a meeting held on 5th November, 1929, at The Alexandra pub in Commerce Road, Wood Green, when the licensee Charlie Burry was in the chair. The committee decided to name the new venture the 'Alexandra Amateur Boxing Club'. At a later meeting that year Eric was elected president and held that distinction until he died in 1959.

The popularity of this club in the Thirties is emphasised by the enormous amount of income derived from their open shows. For instance, the show promoted in February, 1933, benefited the club by near £52 – representing today (1974) something in the region of between £400 and £500. In 1940 the club ceased to function and it was not until 8th July, 1949, that a meeting was held, with Eric as chairman, to reform the club once more.

When the boxers had finally arranged their new training quarters, which opened in August at the Alexandra Palace, the Cuffley contingent supported the exercise with great enthusiasm, afterwards attending all promotions including the annual dinner. As a gesture of their ardour, boxing gloves were presented to the club. The following names were the original patrons from Cuffley: George Boothman, Tim Stone, Sydney Becker-Jones, Bill Grace, Cyril Madsen, Norman Edgerton, John Burgess, Horace Drew, Bill Jones and George Goodman. It is a pleasing thought that the last-named later had the honour of becoming their president, following the sad passing of the well-known sportsman Jack Randall, who had succeeded Eric Anderton. Jack organised an enjoyable evening for our Cuffley Club at the Cavendish Club in Whittington Road, Wood Green which helped to swell our charity fund. I was invited to serve on the committee as a co-opted member, but as much as I would have liked it, time would not permit.

We seldom missed the monthly boxing show promoted by Eddie Mallett at Watford Town Hall for these evenings were always entertaining and convivial. Audrey would issue the party of ten with a tasty parcel of eats, and a little bottle of pick-me-up each. On one of these occasions a well-known local nurseryman was introduced to boxing, and in between the bouts his head was turning from side to side, looking inquisitively pensive at the contestants receiving attention from their seconds, and finally at the end of a round he glanced at one corner as the second was removing his boxer's gum shield, then at the opposite corner where a similar operation was being carried out, then he nudged me, and excitedly remarked, 'Look, look, they've all got false teeth!'

I still retain fifteen programmes of the many major boxing promotions I and our party of friends attended between 1946 and 1950. These events included the following boxers: Bruce Woodcock and Gus Lesnevich, as well as Nesse Anderson, Joe Baksi, Lee Oma, Jack Gardner, and the contest for the world heavyweight crown with Lee Savold when Bruce retired with a badly cut eye in the fourth round. In addition to the fight between Freddie Mills and Joe Baksi, we saw Lloyd Marshall, Pol Goffaux and Joey Maxim; and Rinty Monaghan v. Dado Marino (Rinty was beaten on a foul in the ninth round, but later won the re-match on points). Rinty retired as the undefeated world, empire and British champion in 1949 after being held to a draw by Terry Allen. Many other notable boxers were contestants on these programmes including: Eric Boon, Arthur Danahar, Randolph Turpin, Don Cockell, Johnny Williams, Jackie Turpin, Ernie Roderick, Danny O'Sullivan, Eddie Thomas, Len Fowler and Jim Webster.

The best amateur boxing shows I ever attended were promoted by Charringtons Brewery at the Toby Club, Mile End. The atmosphere was always vibrant with eager anticipation, perhaps in a lesser degree but similar to that which existed at York Hall before its closure in 1974. On one of these occasions I suffered the most uncomfortable evening ever, regardless of the fine entertainment. The hall that evening was very crowded, our party sitting next to the ring from the corner down. I had just remarked, 'Somebody's going to have that bucket in their lap if it's not moved.' It had been left inadvertently in the ring, and within seconds one of the contestants slipped, and the complete contents of icy water were kicked over straight into my lap! After a short while discomfort was eased by the water attaining body temperature, unless, of course, any movement was attempted. On leaving I found my clothes still moist enough to make me acquire a peculiar Michael Crawford walk that, in the eyes of an onlooker, made it anybody's guess as to my complaint. Meeting the old, large seven-seater car at the entrance I patiently waited at its rear for our party to arrive; the freezing mist reminding me of my utter discomfort. Whilst muttering repeatedly to myself, 'Come on, you boys,' I suddenly realised one leg was frozen and the other fiery hot. Cautiously I peeped at the hot one. Half my trouser leg had gone – just tatters and black oil! I had no idea the engine had been running!

Chatting with Eric Anderton about the annual function of the Alexandra Boxing Club, I suggested the Cambridge as a possible venue; hitherto the dinner had been held at the rear of a restaurant and shop which was devoid of all the necessary atmosphere. The next function was arranged at the Cambridge and continued there for the next twenty-five years. The first one was a great success, with only myself wishing I hadn't suggested the change! I had been seated but a few seconds when a waitress knocked over a tall vase of flowers, the end of which nestled on the edge of the table, cascading the whole contents into my lap. Agreed, it was not two gallons as before, but half a pint is more than enough to have one wriggling about in dubious postures! The waitress was extremely apologetic, but I comforted her with a jocular remark and a smile. The first course was very thick tomato soup and as it was served to the guest opposite I thought, 'That'll warm me up,' and it did just that, but not quite in the way I anticipated – the waitress performed a pretty little peculiar step and jettisoned the lot all over my back! Another comforting remark and a slightly confused smile to the poor girl. It was so embarrassing for both of us – what with her rubbing me down in the middle of the hall – I had to comfort her to comfort myself.

Having paid seventy-five per cent of our loan back to A.J.S. I was very kindly released from any further commitment, and this was indeed a pleasing tonic. Shortly afterwards I purchased my first new car, an Austin Eight Saloon, the cost of which was £280 plus £78 10s 6d purchase tax. The increased volume of catering and other commitments made some means of transport imperative, but to obtain a supplement to my sparse petrol allowance I had finally to contact our member of parliament, C.W. Dumpleton. The result was a supplement of five gallons per month, but I could not drive the car outside a ten mile radius of Cuffley! When Brian moved from Hertford Grammar School to Framlingham College, in Suffolk, I immediately sold the car and acquired an 8 hp van which was unrestricted in movement, and the red petrol was very much easier to come by!

We always found tremendous excitement in visiting Brian, but a determined effort was necessary to secure the whole day off, especially since the visit took place on a Sunday. We would work until midnight or later on the Saturday in preparation for an early start – pewter all cleaned, cellar work completed and cash organised for the following day. Leaving home around 7.30 a.m. we would arrive some time before 10 a.m. Brian had to be back in time to attend the evening service, after which we would make our way home via Witham, stopping at The Spread Eagle where we always enjoyed a well-presented snack and a drink in company with the hosts, our old Enfield friends Frank and Barbara Evans. What an awful controversial subject schooling is today, but the average Britisher, I am sure, is still trying hard to hang on to the well-frayed rope that represents freedom. If any family (whether or not they suffer any hardship thereby or give up certain pleasures as a result) choose to send their children to attend any school other than the state system, they should proudly do so.

Adjoining The Cuffley Hotel were two semi-detached wooden bungalows, known as East Kilve and West Kilve, which came on to the market when my enthusiasm for expansion was perhaps too impassioned. My imagination ran riot and I had a vision of a country cottage-type restaurant featuring the long verandah reglazed with leaded lights, with an inside theme involving masses of wrought iron and copper, soft concealed lighting, and candelabra on all tables. The latter we had already purchased from various antique shops at ridiculously low prices, but the project was not to be realised, and the candelabra and other equipment all still in store after nearly thirty years!

The wonderful character who represented the estate agents responsible for negotiating the sale was a typical Dickens type – I always referred to him as Mr Snodgrass. He abounded in all the old-fashioned gentlemanly characteristics; his light small-checked suit with bowler hat was reminiscent of that era and the lined but young, windswept-looking face sported a rather protruding, high-boned nose, a degree more weather beaten than the rest, which amplified his friendly, keen very blue eyes. His speech was gruff and haughty, but always touched with humour, and when expletives were used they appeared at just the right time with exactly the correct emphasis. Even his drinking ethics were amusing, but one feature that identified Joe Chamberlain was his deliberate, unhurried walk – so that once he had commenced to cross the road he had all other moving things conforming to his consistently timeless and dreamy gait.

I was under the impression, perhaps vaguely, that both properties would be sold with vacant possession – the occupants in the one next to the pub were supposed to be moving to a place on the Thames. I called to see them regarding the date, and was amazed to hear the two elderly sisters say almost simultaneously, 'We have never thought of moving anywhere!' My dreams were shattered! Half-heartedly I decided to develop the corner property only, and having been informed that catering had previously been carried out at East Kilve I confidently applied to the Hatfield council for the property's 'change of use', but again the project was halted by their refusal to this request.

I was in a fine predicament now, with a total mortgage of £1,625, maintenance of both properties and rates to find, with only the rent of £1 8s 8d a week from West Kilve to help with the outgoings! Eventually I did manage to obtain permission to open as a restaurant, but not without problems – the Central Land Board required a £200 fee for the change of use! I think this was my first experience of the post-war bureaucracy that was later to be a natural way of life. I was almost convulsed when a youngster dressed like a little Lord Fauntleroy arrogantly climbed out of a sizeable new car to instruct me (dressed in a smock and top boots) overbearingly on the requirements of this new Cromwellian Act – all I wanted to say to him was, 'Why don't you get yourself to — work!' I did manage to spread the payment over five years which saved my bank overdraft from extra embarrassment, and with a little private borrowing we managed to carry out the necessary alterations and attain the equipment and furnishings. Having overcome most of the obstacles, and with the potential for evening catering looking bright, we received a letter from the council stating that complaints had been lodged by the next door occupants regarding excessive noise from the kitchen, resulting in an order to close down the evening meals – in fact, there was to be no more catering after 6 p.m.!

What long days they were for Audrey when on duty in the restaurant as cook. Apart from the usual morning work in the pub, the bar in the evening, the task of catering for about thirty-five luncheons in a small inadequate kitchen, followed by preparation for the afternoon teas with home-made cakes, etc, there was all the clerical work for both businesses.

I was very fortunate in being helped financially by two property transactions, for which the initial outlay was only £290 plus mortgages for £2,600 odd. The larger property was sold, producing a profit of £500 which was invested in the restaurant. The two properties referred to would today be valued at something in the region of £45,000 to £50,000 (1974).

The restaurant was named as the result of a visit with a party to see the Ceremony of the Keys at the Tower of London, after which we adjourned to the bar to meet the Yeoman Warders. I mentioned the new restaurant, so far unnamed, and asked them to put forward a name that represented part of the Tower. Numerous titles were suggested by the Yeomen and I settled for Lanthorne Restaurant. The Lanthorne Tower was so named because in bygone days the small turret arising from the roof housed a lantern or flare which after sundown would help to guide the ships up the Thames. Originally built in the thirteenth century by Henry III, when it formed part of the royal residence, in the time of Henry VIII it comprised the King's bedchamber and privy closet.

After realising the project could never be developed as a restaurant in the foreseeable future I sold the business to a friend. I had to keep West Kilve – only because nobody would buy it!

A.J.S. was still in possession of the land in Station Road that ran from the pub to the old Cabin, except of course the 100 feet he had already sold to Charringtons at the original purchase price and which is now the car park. The whole measured 260 feet with a depth of 160 feet. I thought it was almost criminal that this land was just growing wild and not producing, and so I developed a bright idea to cultivate it. One of our farming customers was soon down with a small plough, but preparing it was far from the easy job I thought it would be. When the process was completed I engaged three German prisoners of war, who were let out to farmers at a very reasonable rate of pay, and it was not long before the land was planted with all types of vegetables. The whole scheme was a failure. Everything appeared to mature at once, and we hadn't time to attend to the land's many requirements, and so we would tell the customers to help themselves if they were capable of spotting the cabbages or other vegetables that were interwoven with the many other inedible growths.

There was another piece of land in Station Road, owned by A.J.S., situated directly opposite Tolmers Road, having a frontage of 158 feet and a depth of 135 feet. There was also a plot in Tolmers Road, joining my property and the pub site, with a frontage of 60 feet with a depth of 65 feet. This was priced at £650 and the land on Station Road was £40 per foot – this was in 1948.

In 1949 George and Phyllis left The White Horse, Potters Bar to take over The Midland Arms, at Hendon – a large pub with a hall on the first floor, both the whole premises and business having been badly neglected. That change could have been a record for a pub transformation, not only in refurbishing, but also in increase and change of clientele.

From 1946 to 1950 there was no significant change in the cost of living.

As it has always been, and will continue to be, the index of purchasing power can only be related to wages, and within this period wages were little improved upon the rates applicable to the pre-war era. On average I think it is fair to mention that the licensed trade and retail trade in general, were somewhat lagging behind most other areas of employment. As an example of our wages in 1950, a married couple living and sleeping in would receive £7 a week joint. A barman was paid £3 10s 0d and a barmaid £2

15s 0d to £3. Audrey and I allowed ourselves £8 a week joint (about 1s 0d per hour) plus £2 expenses. An example taken from the building trade is as follows:

Fixing a 25 gallon hot water tank, including materials, labour and builder's profit was £8 9s 1d; the labour quoted was six hours at 3s 0d an hour (tradesman) and six hours at 2s 5d an hour (mate). Our bar prices were as follows: bitter beer, pint 1s 3d (6.25p), bottle of pale ale 10d (4.16p), and whisky 1s 10d (9.17p). A bottle of whisky retailed at £1 13s 4d (166.7p). One ton of coal was £4 13s 8d. Petrol was 2s 1d (10.41p).

# Chapter XXXVI

Nationalisation and rationing – A.J.S. and the Inland Revenue – the aftermath of war – back to The George – the decline of pubs followed by fresh enthusiasm – Enfield Horse Society and the Four in Hand – boxing promotions – Festival of Britain 1951 and the Great Exhibition 1851 – the hall re-opens – menus – wages and profit margins

The year 1948 witnessed the termination of the extremely efficient North-Met Electricity Board which gave way to nationalisation, as did also the railways of Britain. On a brighter note, bread rationing ended in the same year. The next year clothes rationing was concluded, but the gas service and industry was nationalised. 1950 was brightened by the ending of the points rationing system and we also said goodbye to petrol and soap rationing.

During the early years of our spell at Cuffley, there appeared obvious signs that something was amiss with the Standbrook set-up; many licensed houses were suffering from a form of sickness following the many years of war-time trading, in which period the easy, non-competitive attitude applying to every facet of the licensed trade (including redecorating and refurbishing) had not been attended to, simply because it had been impossible to do so. It was that period during the years after the war that were so important in coping with change and planning the future. A.J.S. was extremely unfortunate at this look-ahead period in facing near bankruptcy. The little knowledge I had of the financial upset was that the accountant acting for A.J.S. had lost a battle with the Inland Revenue. There was something radically wrong, because the amount involved was very substantial even by today's standards – a mystery that will always remain unsolved.

The whole affair was a tremendous shock to A.J.S. and Jennie, and they immediately commenced raising whatever money they could. The Norfolk Hotel was sold, as well as The Crooked Billet and the Drome Restaurant, together with the land at Cuffley adjoining the hotel, practically all the stocks and shares A.J.S. was holding and, finally, their house on the Ridgeway. Without the latter the amount raised must have been something over £50,000; and in addition to this there was the burden of each business paying alternately £100 per month extra to the Inland Revenue.

The sale of Ridgemount was due entirely to the excessive cost of upkeep of the house and grounds. I did my utmost to persuade A.J.S. to hold the property, mainly because the ecclesiastical leaseholds were being converted to freeholds, and for a comparatively infinitesimal amount of money, but under the prevailing circumstances they were adamant. Everybody does what is thought to be right at the time. This lovely house, with its delightful grounds was sold in 1948 by Maples in conjunction with James Neilson for the ludicrous price of £5,000 inclusive of curtains, many of the carpets, and a full-size billiard table with the accessories. Tommy and Olive Knight who were close friends and neighbours to A.J.S. and Jennie in Broadwalk, purchased Ridgemount in the early Fifties and later acquired the freehold. The land was sold to A. Marston & Co, who developed the new estate of ten ranch style bungalows accessible only by the new road at the side of Ridgemount named Ridgemount Gardens. The initial selling price of these bungalows was from £6,500 but by 1974 the price had multiplied six or seven times. Ridgemount survived the development and is now owned by a well-known member of an old-established local family, the optician Gordon Thomas, who has resided there with his wife Gladys since 1961.

It is quite natural for the family to use the word 'if' when diagnosing these Standbrook misfortunes... 'if' this had or hadn't happened; and attribute our ups and downs to 'fate'. Whether the cause be one's own mistakes or somebody else's, the past is irretrievable and so the next move or decision follows the immediate situation making the word 'if' almost meaningless. Everybody's life was changed at the outbreak of the war and during the six year aftermath that followed, until normal routine was resumed (if it ever was!).

My thoughts wander to the many complications which arose within the family directly following the cessation of hostilities. My sister Peggy and her husband Reg Handisyde separated and were finally divorced; the two daughters Shirley and Jennifer remaining with their mother. Peggy later married Harry Greaves and in 1947 they moved to Arundel where they managed The Norfolk Hotel. Later, when the hotel was sold in April 1949, they took over The Stonehouse Hotel having a joint license with A.J.S. Billy their son was born there in June 1949. Reg Handisyde married Eve Muldoon, who had tragically lost her husband Reg whilst he was serving with the RAF. The Muldoon family (hairdressers in Church Street) were well-known and respected in Enfield. Reg and Eve later became the very popular hosts at the charming and quaint little thatched inn called The Bell at Cottered, Hertfordshire.

Brother Alf and his wife Edna also separated, their marriage ending in the inevitable divorce. Their daughter, Jeanne, stayed with her father. Alf later married Betty Hawkins which union produced another daughter, Caroline, but again after a few years that marriage broke up, ending finally in divorce.

Edna later married William (Bill) Garner and they are currently living at Wasperton, Warwickshire. Edna's daughter, Jeanne, is living with them.

Bill, one of the best-known men in the motor production industry commenced his career in 1937 with the Riley Car Company, and following progressive spells with David Brown, Daimlers, British Oxygen, he finally joined Rootes in 1951 becoming managing director at Linwood in 1964. His final appointment was to their Automobile Products Group Board as director of manufacturing activities. Retiring in June 1977 the family will be moving to Bournemouth.

Although quite happy at Cuffley we both felt the urge to expand either to make some extensive alterations at the Cuffley pub or to seek larger premises offering catering and banquet facilities (this is the point where I should have visited a psychiatrist!). I was disillusioned about the former suggestion, having made numerous attempts to implement structural alterations which would conform to the original plan drawn up in 1936, in addition to the extension of the dining room to accommodate a restaurant and small banqueting hall. The inevitable response from the brewers, one so familiar today, was, 'Sorry, no more money available, the allocation has been halved.'

The brewers have always been the economic chopping block for most sections of society, but I think it should be remembered that the profit margin relative to output and invested capital had always been comparatively low. This was reflected in most licensed houses by minimal and competitive prices which, in turn, resulted in low rents and inadequate wage rates which have never really been in step with reality. The non-political reason for this is mainly the unreasonable level of excise duty and general taxation levied against the licensed trade.

I regard this present period as the embryo stage of new thinking in regard to pubs and the start of a more realistic attitude.

A.J.S. and Jennie had been through a rather stormy period, but A.J.S. had certainly not lost any of his vigour and enthusiasm for business, nor had it affected his sense of humour, but shock and worry had unquestionably taken its toll upon his health. The Stonehouse Hotel, too, had been a source of concern, but this was rectified when Peggy and Harry Greaves took control following the sale of The Norfolk Hotel at Arundel.

The George was also suffering the aftermath of the war years and late in 1950 A.J.S. offered the management as a proposition to Audrey and I, but we were determined to stay independent. However, the suggestion was again referred to and almost mirthfully I said, 'Yes, if I may retain The Cuffley Hotel!' A.J.S. agreed, provided permission was obtained from Charringtons. This, of course, was by no means certain, since the unusual circumstances could hardly be conceived in which a licensee installed a manager in his own pub whilst he himself went as manager for another licensee. The exercise would have been simplified had Standbrooks then been a company. However, the proposition was favourably considered by the brewery, and immediate arrangements were made for the change.

Although rationing and the general shortage of materials and commodities continued until the early Fifties and the majority of people accepted this as a normality in family life after ten years, it was not until Audrey and myself were reinstated at The George in May 1951, that we fully comprehended what deterioration those long years could inflict upon property, general equipment, and everything else applicable to the business. The mammoth task of reorganising and redecorating, with all that they implied, was easy enough, the real challenge came in achieving the operation when adequate cash was not available.

We were so engrossed in our efforts to become re-established that our first off-duty period came after eating, sleeping and working rough for something over four weeks. Then we were relieved by A.J.S. one evening from 6 p.m. until 9.30 p.m. Many licensees have endured this ordeal and worse, and they will understand and appreciate our feelings when we drove into the country feeling like a couple of school kids released after having been deprived of all their pleasures. We were completely satisfied with simply relaxing and sitting amongst the cows listening to their mooing and moans. Strange how such opposite occupations may be equally enjoyed!

In many ways this period appeared merely an extension of the pre-war era, especially in so far as pubs were concerned. The times had not yet brought massive spending by the younger generation, therefore concern for the individual customer, and the importance of the licensee having consideration for his patrons appeared more significant then than now. For this reason The Cuffley Hotel was really not suited to management. My intention was to create an atmosphere of goodwill between The George and The Cuffley Hotel. But all my ideas seemed to fade in face of the pressures of The George. During the first few weeks the manager brought all the necessary information to The George for Audrey to complete the weekly balance sheet and not once did we visit The Cuffley during that period – it certainly appears very much more wrong now than it did then!

Enfield Amateur Boxing Club, of which A.J.S. was then president, helped to bring a little glory to Enfield when the club boxed a strong team of Frenchmen from Le Havre in a special Festival of Sport International match before a crowd of more than two thousand at Enfield Stadium. Enfield won eight of the nine bouts. Madame Perier, wife of the visiting president, Dr François Perier, presented the prizes. The Le Havre Club is the oldest boxing club in France, having been founded in 1872. Johnny Wright of The Fallow Buck, boxed a special four-round contest in which he outpointed Pat Dempsey, from Battersea. A function was held the following evening in honour of the Le Havre Club at The Cambridge Hotel.

The first Enfield Horse Show was promoted in 1948 in the delightful grounds of Forty Hall, and a more suitable setting to proclaim and foster the horsey atmosphere would be difficult to find. Mr and Mrs Derek Parker Bowles were then in residence at Forty Hall, he having inherited the estate from his uncle, the late Sir Henry Ferryman Bowles, who died in 1944.

In 1951 the Enfield and District Horse Society added a special feature to their programme by advertising the show in a novel way when a coach and four was engaged to tour Enfield, displaying all the pride and picturesqueness of what was once the major form of travel in the less pretentious past.

The passengers, all of whom were members of the society, added joviality to this elegant Dickensian scene attired in colourful period costumes. After a drive to the town to keep the arranged appointment at The George, a prolonged tantara on the post-horn stimulatingly and almost arrogantly signalled the arrival of the four-in-hand which came clattering up to the inn among the thousand and more onlookers. To add a touch of reality to the scene several customers had donned rustic garments and, with clay pipes, were sitting at tables in front of The George.

A.J.S. was unwell during this period and requested me to obtain the appropriate attire of an affluent innkeeper. Physically I little fitted the role and would have been better qualified to have been seen emerging from number one trap among the greyhounds. I ordered the clothes slightly larger than required to allow for stuffing the odd cushion here and there. However, A.J.S. gave in to my reasoning after he had improved sufficiently to play the role and so my lush guvnor's outfit was exchanged for a potman's stately apparel! The garments in fact would not have been amiss at any royal occasion. 'Strange old type of potman they had in those days,' I thought (coloured breeches and waistcoat, white shirt with puffed sleeves, and white stockings with buckle shoes) as I strutted out carrying a large copper tray full with old pint pewter pots of frothy beer. A.J.S. was in his glory, dressed in his comely mine host outfit, and very relaxed with his foot resting on the coach step. I very courteously offered the tray of drinks from which he took one with boyish delight and displaying a disarming smile, he raised his glass, said, *'tiddleypush,'* and then to the guests on the coach, 'good health to you all.' As I walked away he called, 'Wait, boy,' and fumbled in his pocket for a penny, which he tossed to me. This, of course, started a cascade of copper coins from the coach, which compelled me to be on my hands and knees lustfully scooping them up. The whole day was a great success. The only incident which went amusingly wrong occurred when Harry Neville, one of the old-timers who donned the period clothes, opened up a piece of upholstered furniture at home and used the stuffing for his beard and whiskers. Mary, his wife, did flay him for that!

The chairman of the Enfield Horse Society, E.G. Sims, arranged a small dinner party at The Cuffley Hotel in October, 1951 and we thought the following account quoting these enormous prices was beginning to get out of hand!

|  | £ | s | d |
|---|---|---|---|
| Seven dinners @ 10s 6d | 3 | 13 | 6 |
| Wine |  | 17 | 0 |
| Sherries |  | 17 | 6 |
| Sundry drinks | 1 | 2 | 8 |
|  | £6 | 10s | 8d |

The charming letter we received in return enclosing an extra 15s 0d for staff nullified our fears of pricing ourselves out of business!

Although I did not attend so many sporting events in 1951 I had parties of up to thirty attending the boxing promotions at Watford Town Hall, and a few shows staged by Jack Solomon presenting many well-known boxers such as Jack Gardner, Don Cockell, Jo Weiden, Johnny Williams, Wally Thom, Dave Sands, Bruce Woodcock, Freddie Mills, George Walker, Yolande Pompee and Arthur Howard, when as an amateur he boxed for Great Britain against America.

The greatest contest was the world middleweight championship bout between the holder, 'Sugar' Ray Robinson and Randolph Turpin, the British and European champion. Turpin gave an almost perfect display of skill, stamina and aggression to beat one of the greatest exponents of the 'noble art' that ever lived, and to take the crown from him. Robinson, a gangling 6 feet of boxing machinery, was undefeated as an amateur in one hundred and twenty-five contests – winning half of them inside the distance. He also took the Golden Gloves featherweight and lightweight titles. Turpin held the title only for a little over two months, being beaten by Robinson on points in the return match in New York.

The highlight of 1951, and the first real sign of returning to normal, was the opening of the Festival of Britain. At the least it was a projection of enterprise and goodwill that the poor old country badly needed. The official opening was made by King George on 3rd May from the steps of St Paul's Cathedral, following a service of dedication attended by members of the royal family and leading dignitaries of the time. The opening ceremony was broadcast to the Commonwealth and the rest of the world. The enterprise was commenced in 1949 by reclaiming 4½ acres beside the river Thames, the area being laid out as gardens as a memorial to the thousands of Londoners killed in the raids on the capital during the Second World War. The Royal Festival Hall is no doubt the finest of its kind in Britain, seating 3,172 persons and costing 2½ million pounds.

The opening was made exactly one hundred years after the Great Exhibition of 1851 in Hyde Park, when Queen Victoria declared open the amazing Crystal Palace. That enterprise had been promoted to stimulate competitive inventive genius in industry, sculpture and fine arts. The extraordinary building was constructed without bricks or mortar and was completed in seven months. (It is unlikely that a small bungalow would be completed today in that time.) Prince Albert was chairman of the commission for this great work. The Lord Mayor of London invited nearly all the mayors of cities, boroughs and towns of the United Kingdom to a banquet at the Mansion House to meet the prince and to hear the royal consort explain the proposed undertaking. Although competing with the great Brunel, and some two hundred and fifty other architects, Joseph Paxton (later Sir Joseph), was commissioned to build his enormous glass Crystal Palace. Constructed completely of iron and glass the site covered was approximately twenty acres, with a reputed length of 1,851 feet and 456 feet wide in the broadest part. It was erected completely in glass and iron of which latter there were 9,642 tons, the whole glass area covering the site being some twenty-five acres. The transept had a semi-circular glass roof one hundred and eighty feet high, giving ample room to enclose the trees around which the structure was built. The stately opening witnessed, up until noon, the colourful arrival of 4,550 state carriages, broughams, hackneys, post chaises and every other type of carriage.

The exhibition was open for one hundred and forty-four days, admitting 6,170,000 or an average of 43,536 per day, equivalent to one third of the population of Britain in that year. Between the years 1852 and 1854 this huge glass construction was taken to pieces and rebuilt on a selected three hundred acre site at Sydenham, SE London and again opened by Queen Victoria. Unfortunately this elegant edifice was completely destroyed by fire on 1st December, 1936; the whole structure was ablaze from end to end within thirty minutes.

We found the whole exercise very tough for the rest of the year, and in what little time we managed to have off duty we visited The Cuffley Hotel. The trade was then still very personal and, unlike today, there was very little successful or indiscriminate money about. By the end of the year it was obvious that all was not well with the business, and that the very perception of the Cuffley clientele, and expectations of trade in general did not make the pub amenable to management.

I would like to record also, in defence of management and staff in general, that the rate of pay was still very low and probably the lowest of any comparable trade in Britain if the number of hours worked were considered! The profit margin in a pub taking some £15,000 per annum was such that to award a rise in wages of one pound per head of the staff employed would have meant the difference between returning or not returning a profit on the annual audit! Only during the last three years have wages in the licensed trade shown signs of being comparable with the job being accomplished.

September 14th saw the hall of The George in operation again following its almost complete closure in 1941. The first booking was a luncheon party for only twenty-five persons, and one may well say, 'What a dull and uninteresting operation!' but to me then it was an important occasion which demanded all the thought and care that one would apply to the promotion of a regal banquet. How very stupid it all appears now, to care so much to gain so little! But most grades of people were still in the era of unknowingly working for far too little, but strangely and knowingly they were working far more competently! The menu on this occasion consisted of five courses and coffee, for which the cost was 10s 6d (52½p).

The Enfield Round Table and the Ladies' Circle arranged their meetings at The George and the charge for their three course meal and coffee was 5s 0d (25p) plus 2½p gratuities. The following period up until Christmas proved that the premises were in great demand, because we catered for no fewer than seventy varied bookings.

The smash and grab for wages, taxes and profits had yet to be conceived, as the following examples will establish. Our joint wages were then £12 10s 0d per week from which our gross deductions were £1 1s 0d. A married couple living and sleeping on the premises would receive a joint wage of £10 per week and their total deductions would only be about 12s 6d (62½p) which represents approximately six per cent of the gross wage. Today the equivalent wage would be in the region of £40, but the average deductions some £6 which is fifteen per cent of the gross earnings. The gross wage for the twenty staff employed then was between £75 and £80 per week which was excluding staff engaged for functions and the PAYE deducted rarely exceeded £3, which together with the health and unemployment stamps, say £5 5s 0d, amounted to around ten per cent. Today the comparable wages would be £350, involving deductions of about £53, which represents some fifteen per cent of the gross wages.

Percentage levels on stocks during the Fifties were considerably more varied than today, and this was understandably attributable to the various bars operating different prices and the volume of trade in the respective bars fluctuating from one house to another.

The George operated four prices until 1962 when owing to an alteration structurally, it was reduced to three. Finally, following further extensive alterations in 1970, and like so many houses, the bars offered only one price. That, obviously, is a case of 'God bless the licensee' and 'Lord help the customer'!

The subject is extremely controversial, but to be concisely explicit, The George would, as would most town pubs, lose heavily if the situation was reversed and all drinks were sold at the real public bar prices! I can well imagine readers thinking, 'Why not a happy medium?' – I would – but so many perplexing queries arise from the host of varying circumstances applying to every house that the complications would be endless.

In this era The George's monthly stocktaking centred around twenty-nine per cent on liquor sales, but if the sale of cigarettes were included the percentage would be considerably lower. Stock control in a pub employing a large staff, regardless of how efficiently the proprietor or manager was promoting the business from the customer's point of view, is the only criterion as to the viability of the business. The Crooked Billet was a typical example of this; although the business had to be sold, it was doomed to failure through the drop in takings and the extremely low stock results of only twenty per cent.

# Chapter XXXVII

Walk across Wales – we vacate the Cuffley Hotel – presentation fifty years Neilsons and reunion of staff – George and Phyllis take The New Venture, Hemel Hempstead – The Midland Arms, Hendon, managed by John and Eileen (daughter and son-in-law) – The Bottle & Glass near Aylesbury – words synonymous 'Ale House' and 'Public House' – the Elizabethan 1953 Dinner Club – Seckford Hall, Woodbridge


One of my most colourful and enjoyable memories was a walk across Wales with Brian. We started the walk on 20th April, 1952 from Corwen where we stayed overnight at a small hotel called The Crown Hotel (bed and breakfast) 12s 6d (62½p). The proprietor Mr Horrocks, had arranged to drive my car to Caernarvon early morning and leave it at the well-known Red garages where I would collect it at the termination of the walk. He waved goodbye as he drove off in teaming rain, and surely thinking, as he saw Brian and I forlornly standing there with army gas capes on, little flat caps perched on our heads, sagging under the weight of heavy packs, with knobbly walking sticks dangling at ease – 'There's a right couple of Charlies!' If he wasn't, I was – when I turned to Brian and said, 'I'll stop him and we'll drive to Betws-y-Coed and start walking from there.' No luck, his mind was made up!

We trudged along in the rain for about six miles when the weather, thankfully, brightened. We arrived at an isolated hotel named The Saracens at Carrigydrudian having walked about eleven miles – we gulped down a

Guinness each and devoured a lunch in a way that I witnessed our Dalmatian dog gollop a pound of sausages he had stolen from the butchers! On to Betws-y-Coed stopping for tea at The Voelas Arms, Pentrefoelas en route; off came our shoes under the table (gigantic blisters on my feet). Brian appeared dejected when I enquired if they could accommodate us for the night and more so when the young lady said, 'yes'. However, I managed to painfully struggle into my shoes and attempt the last five miles, having covered nearly twenty. Driving rain hit us again when up in the hills and we found shelter in the porch of a little chapel. Whilst changing our socks (well primed with boracic powder) and studying my blistered and bleeding feet I said, with a modicum of venom, 'We must be b— barmy!' Although downhill, I know not how I managed the last mile – the only callous comfort I found was when Brian at last admitted suffering blisters! We arrived at The Craig-y-dderwen Hotel, Betws-y-Coed at dusk (17s 0d [85p]) inclusive of bed, breakfast, dinner and early morning tea, and was comforted by the knowledge that a doctor resided next door.

I was amazed the following morning at being able to wear shoes let alone walk. Treating our feet with respect we only covered about twelve miles that day arriving at Doinyddelen early afternoon, and finding accommodation at Elen's Castle Hotel (dinner, bed and breakfast, 18s 6d [92½p]) which had not yet opened for the season. How kind were the owners, Mr and Mrs Valentine: in their efforts to make us comfortable they cleared one of their own family bedrooms for us. A typical example of Welsh hospitality. Next morning we were warned not to proceed on the course over the hills we had planned on the ordnance survey map, as we would surely get lost. What better invitation could Brian have – a chance to get lost! Off we went and within one hour we hadn't a clue where we were – even the lake marked on the map had seemingly disappeared.

We agreed a direction and made our way across swamps for about three miles; certainly a relief having our feet in water for nearly two hours. About centre of this desolate area we came across an RAF fighter plane that had crashed.

After many exciting and amusing incidents we arrived at The Peny-pas Hotel which is directly opposite the common starting point for climbing Snowdon, known as the 'Pyg Track'. We appeared to be the only two for lunch and were given places at a large oval table capable of seating about ten climbers. Having voraciously enjoyed our meal, I enquired the direction for the easiest route up the mountain – the lady looked at our dress and our footwear and remarked, 'You are a little late, and you're not going up like that!' looking again at our shoes. I thought it precarious as the top of the mountain was in cloud and time was not on our side. 'Brian, we'll make an early start in the morning,' I said (we had already covered the long, arduous walk over the hills). 'But you promised if your feet were all right,' he said. We made our way to the 'Pyg Track'.

We only met one person and she was descending, and she mentioned her being the last person on the mountain and warned us regarding the missing or destroyed cairns (pyramids of stone markers to keep inexperienced climbers like us from getting lost). Somewhere about half way up we lost the cairns, and found ourselves looking down a sheer drop of about a thousand feet.

The sun was now setting well down the other side of the mountain causing the gigantic abyss to assume a mysterious and almost offensive appearance; the gloomy spectacle was amplified by a swirling mist descending from the top and developing long feathery tentacles that creepingly appeared to be feeling their way down – a perfect setting for a scene of fantasy. I didn't like it at all and suggested retracing our steps, but I lost again in the face of Brian's enthusiasm. Eventually we found ourselves entering the cold heavy mist; and appeared to have left the rocks behind finding ourselves on a steep slope with a loose shale surface. Visibility was now almost nil, and Brian nowhere to be seen nor heard – I shouted for him to come back but no answer, was near to panic and was about to shout again when I heard a distant voice call, 'I'm at the top!' Scrambling up in the direction of his voice I found him standing at the side of the railway line. I was just thinking how lucky we had been, and how thankful I was, when I heard a muffled vibrating noise, but before I could even imagine what it was or from which direction it came, a great shadowy monster loomed out of the mist – it was the train! Who, but the devil, would expect to see a train at the top of Snowdon on a day like it was, and with deep snow all around. My memory is hazy as to my reaction but Brian insists that I flung myself off the track saying, 'B— hell, what's that?' We followed the line for about two hundred yards and found we were at the top where a fleeting break in the cloud gave us a wonderful sunbathed panoramic view of the west side of the mountain. It was difficult to believe we were standing there with our eyelashes frozen.

The only sensible choice of getting down through the mist without losing our bearings was by following the railway track. After about four miles and an hour and a half of hopping in small and jumping in large strides enabling us to tread on the wooden sleepers, we arrived at Llanberis feeling and walking like clockwork toys! We stayed that night at The Padarn Villa Hotel (bed and breakfast, £3) and I was never more thankful than when we were booked in, freshened up and with a pint of glorious beer to relax our system.

We walked to Caernarvon the following morning where we collected the car and drove straight up to Llandudno for a little more walking.

Regretfully we gave up The Cuffley Hotel in 1952 with, of course, very mixed feelings, but there seemed little alternative as it was quite impossible for us to make the business viable again whilst we were so busy restoring The George to its pre-war scale of service. Arrangements were made through Vivian Bates and Leslie Buzzard of Johnson & Co, in conjunction with Charringtons, to change on 30th June, 1952, the license being transferred at 10.30 a.m. that day at the Hatfield Court House.

Two weeks before we left The Cuffley Hotel I arranged a cricket XI to play the Cuffley Club on behalf of Halliwick School for the physically handicapped. The game raised over £40 and it was typical of the Cuffley residents, especially the ladies, that they should make the whole promotion worthy of the cause by their enthusiasm and kindliness of purpose.

GRAND EFFORT

Approximately £40 was raised as a result of the match between Cuffley CC and a Cuffley Hotel Social Club side got together by Mr 'Stan' Standbrook, of The George Hotel, Enfield.

Proceeds go to Halliwick Cripples' School, which has already received (as equipment for a special rest room) a portable radio set, a large Wilton carpet, four

Lloyd loom chairs and two writing tables as a result of the Social Club's benefactions.

The following is the last letter from Matron of Halliwick School concerning Cuffley.

### HALLIWICK CRIPPLES' SCHOOL

*Bush Hill Road,*
*Winchmore Hill, N21*
*8th July, 1952*

*Dear Mr Standbrook,*

*I would like you to know how very pleased we all are with the chairs, tables and carpet which you and your friends have so kindly given us. They have been put into the dormitory which is used by the older girls, and they have made the room so very comfortable and the girls are very thrilled with them.*

*Would you please convey our best wishes to all the people at Cuffley who subscribed towards this really wonderful gift.*

*Yours very sincerely,*
*K.E. Alford*
*Matron*

For the last time I organised the bar, with all profits going to the Cuffley Cricket Club funds. I must record that the appreciation of the club, expressed through Jack Ball and Bill Morris, was truly magnificent.

Brian promoted his first charity supper dance at The George at the age of sixteen whilst on holiday from Framlingham College. As a result £16 was donated to Halliwick.

The first function of the Enfield Horse Society was held on 2nd May, 1952 at The George. Audrey and I, with some friends, supported it, and eighty guests attended. The menu consisted of:

> Smoked Salmon
> Sole Bonne Femme
>
> Chicken and Gammon
>
> Gateaux and Cream
> Cheese
> Coffee

The charge for this was 12s 6d (62½p), and how ridiculously cheap it appears, but ten guests would have meant 'Bang goes a week's wages'!

One of the nicest little gatherings I had the pleasure to attend was arranged by H.W. (Bill) Neilson at the Granville Restaurant (now The Norfolk) to honour and make the attendant presentations to Ben Liffen in celebration of his very loyal fifty years service with the firm of James Neilson. How strange fate may be – on arriving at Enfield town he almost boarded the next train back to London, but something compelled him to toss a coin, which resulted in him keeping his interview with Webb & Neilson, the auctioneers and surveyors, and so he stayed to keep this golden appointment. James Neilson had arrived the year prior to Ben to join forces with W. Webb, arriving with a £5 note in his pocket and a typewriter tucked under his arm.

The occasion was attended by past and present members of the staff, and several very close professional associates. Bill Neilson personally presented Ben with a Longines gold wrist watch, and Jack Pulling handed him a briefcase and gold cuff links on behalf of those attending.

James Neilson's two other sons were also present – Bob (no man ever drank a drink more joyously) and John, our well-known local chartered architect.

Brother George at 6 p.m. on Christmas Eve, 1952, unlocked the doors to the public bar of the first of the new licensed houses in the new town of Hemel Hempstead – the new venture, a Benskins enterprise. It stands prominently on one side of Queen's Square, which was named with the consent of Her Majesty, Elizabeth II, who had recently laid the foundation stone of the church of St Barnabas, which stands in the corner of the square.

George continued holding the license of The Midland Arms, at Hendon and was fortunate in having his daughter Eileen and her husband John to take over, the couple having married on 14th October. A more refreshing pair it would be difficult to find, and I have yet to learn the doubtful tactics used by George to inveigle John Gomersall into the pub business when he seemed so far removed from a licensee's life of incarceration. But John succeeded without changing, and can truthfully say, 'I did it my way', so much so that he speaks of writing a book entitled *How Not to Run a Pub*.

They are now hosts of The Bottle and Glass at Gibraltar near Aylesbury, a little thatched inn that must be credited as being one of the truest examples of a typical olde worlde British victualling tavern. The whole place is impregnated with the happy-go-lucky atmosphere of Eileen and John's easy-going lightheartedness that appears to create a harmony reciprocal to the staff, patrons and building.

The general expression 'public house' is the widely used term for any establishment that is open to the public for consuming alcohol apart from its many other attendant outlets and in many cases the name jars and seems quite discordant when referring to a mellow country inn. The following is a version of the thinking in the latter half of the eighteenth century in context with licensed premises.

### *Ale-House – Public-House*

Nothing is more common, than the general use of these terms, to express one and the same things, but, with great impropriety; though every *ale-house* is, undoubtedly, a *public-house* it does not follow, that every *public-house* is an *ale-house*.

*Public-house*, is a more extensive impression, implying a house, open for the entertainment of the public; where, *ale-house* is more limited, denoting a particular species of *public-house*, that which is appropriated to the sale of beer, thus, taverns, coffee-houses, etc. are *public-houses* but not *ale-houses*.

Gentlemen frequent many public houses without any sort of disgrace; but, it always lessens their character to be seen in an *ale-house*.

*The Signification of Words Esteemed Synonymous in the English Language Investigated* 1766
No. 226, page 23

One morning in October, when Bill Neilson was lunching with Audrey and I, he suggested organising a few friends to dine and wine together, for the absolute joy of reflecting and deliberating on the unusual and less known foods and wines. This, so far as price was concerned, came well within the realms of normal thinking, and plans were laid for a rather casual dinner meeting. On Monday, 17th November, the following friends attended this very informal affair: Bill Neilson, Bernard Pearce, Leslie Patton, Roy Firmin, Stan Farmer, Fred Adcock, Tony Cox, John Sell, Pat Watson, Ted Eustance, Lenn Cann, E. Edward, with myself as chairman. This numbered thirteen, and with the old fateful Thirteen Club well in mind I refused to let the meal be served until another person was found to join us.

I toured the bars without success, paraded outside The George hoping to find a person immediately free of any commitments, but it was not until I spotted Reg Lunnon in his white smock taking his break from the busy cafe he was running nearby that my hopes were fulfilled. I explained the situation, so that just after 9 p.m. we were in the process of eating. What stuff and nonsense superstition is! But I think everyone, under given circumstances and no matter how insignificant the issue, at times yields to these primitive myths. The following menu with the respective wines was served for one guinea inclusive – equivalent today (1974) to one single measure of the 1904 brandy!

Antipasto, Hors d'oeuvres

Chicken à la Reine
Fillet Sole Thermidor
(Hock 1945 – Liebfraumilch)
Sirloin Steak Bracontere
Asparagus Tips
Buttered Sprouts
French Fried Potatoes
(Pommard 1947)
Beignets de Gibier à la Diane

Biscuits, Cheese and Butter
Coffee
(Heines 1904 Brandy)

The next dinner was held on 17th December, 1952, and I venture to quote the following information to help clarify the memory of those members whether now active in the club or not, which may be blurred after the last twenty-two confusing years! Twenty-five potential members gathered for this meeting, and the following names are in addition to those attending the first function: Phillip Nicholas, Bob Ascroft, Herbie Ellison, Bob Vernum, Mick Castell, Pat Sullivan, Guy Arnold, John Lindell, Dr George Stephen, Ernie Carter, Leslie Beer, Leslie Hounslow, Charles Heast, J. Stevenson. The following report was by the *Enfield Gazette* under 'Townsmen's Notes': (Leo Eastwick).

Next Christmas, no difficulty should be experienced in choosing the most delectable of festive fare. By then there will have been founded an association of Enfield Gourmets, whose expert advice and example might well be followed. They have already met informally, that is, as a dinner club without a name, and at the next meeting will seek to be established under a title.

Venue is The George Hotel, The Town, where, presided over by the inn's host, Mr Stanley Standbrook, twenty-five connoisseurs from the town's various walks of life sat down last Wednesday to Grapefruit Maraschino; Consomme Julienne; Halibut (White Burgundy – Meursault 1946); Roast Chicken – Georgian style, Game Chips, Buttered Sprouts, Asparagus Tips, Roast Potatoes (Claret – St Julien); American fruit Ice Gateaux; Cheeses and Biscuits; Coffee; Creme de Cacao, Van de Hum, and Borvili Cherry Brandy Liqueurs.

## Chef Toasted

At the end of the feast came calls for the Chef who, appearing in the insignia of his craft, bowed in response to the company's toast of appreciation. There were tributes to 'Madam' too. However, on the next occasion when these epicures who value good things to eat and drink foregather the emphasis will be on talking – about the club. And to ensure proper time for discussion, the main dish is likely to be simple 'steak pud', partaken perhaps in the flickering glow of candles in bottles and stimulated by quaffs from flagons of rich old ale.

The agenda will be concerned with such matters as defining the club's aims and objects, forming a committee and deciding upon a name. No problem is anticipated, except perhaps in the choice of a title, suggestions for which have so far included: Enfield Gourmets' Dinner Club; Elizabethan Dinner Club; Elizabethan 53 Dinner Club.

## Membership

The figure 53 is quite important, for besides identification with Coronation Year it is also the proposed limit to the number of members. The general idea is that the gourmets should meet at The George once a month, probably on a Wednesday night, each taking a turn at prescribing the main dish, so that the menu might be headed for example, 'Mr J. Brown's Menu'. Annual subscription suggested is 5s 0d. Each dinner will cost a guinea. Any surplus – of money, not food and wine – will go to charity.

So *next* Christmas...

When visiting Brian at Framlingham we would occasionally stay at Seckford Hall, Woodbridge in Suffolk to take Brian there to have tea. This enchanting old country house offers all the fascinating charm and grace of mellow Tudor England. It was built in 1530 by Sir Thomas Seckford, one of the great families of Suffolk. One of the Seckfords was master of the court of requests to Elizabeth I and the Queen is reputed to have held court there. The tariff during the early Fifties was ten to eleven guineas per week plus a little extra for a private bathroom. Another large room with a fine old four-poster bed and adjoining bathroom was available at thirteen guineas per week. These rates included early morning tea together with a newspaper, mid-morning tea or coffee and afternoon tea, apart from the normal full board. This delightfully romantic house was purchased by Harold and Lenna Bunn in 1951 and transformed over the years into the captivating hotel it is now. Before this new venture Harold was living in Enfield, and it was his custom to break his journey home from business to have a quickie at The George.

Michael and Christine Bunn became the resident proprietors following the death of Harold in 1965. His wife Lenna continued to reside at the hotel, handing most of the administration and superintendence over to her son and daughter-in-law.

I purchased a new Vauxhall Velox in 1951 and in relation to most other commodities the cost appears to be significantly high at £808. At this period cars were extremely difficult to obtain, and invariably without choice of colour. I ordered a Standard Vanguard in 1948, when the nearest delivery date was four years. I also have a letter from Grays of Hatfield dated November, 1950, regarding the delivery of Morris cars saying, 'We do not anticipate being able to supply under four years.'

The Enfield Amateur Boxing Club made The George their headquarters for meetings in 1952 and I was delighted and honoured to be invited to serve on the committee, especially as A.J.S. was president. In view of his ailing health it allowed me to relieve him of some of his duties.

It was a sad day for the royal family and for the people when King George VI passed away on 6th February, 1952, at Sandringham, where he had been born fifty-six years earlier. Princess Elizabeth, now Queen Elizabeth II, with the Duke of Edinburgh, flew home from Kenya the following day.

This was the year that mythically started the excuses for the world's worsening weather; Britain exploded her first atomic weapon in the Monte Bello Islands, off NW Australia, and America exploded a hydrogen bomb in mid-Pacific.

# Chapter XXXVIII

Charity accounts checked by Scotland Yard – catering and the 53 Club – menus and prices – Enfield and District Horse Society – chess – Coronation Trophy – coronation of Elizabeth II – Enfield ABC first amateur boxing championship

'Why me?' was my indignant response when I was requested by the police to submit a balance sheet and proof of expenditure, following a function I promoted on behalf of Halliwick School on 9th January, 1953. There was little doubt that Scotland Yard had good reason to believe that there was a high percentage of malpractice in connection with the handling of charity money at this period. I presumed this was a random check, possibly selected from those licensees who had made an application for an extension of the license for a special occasion. Everything relating to the event had been meticulously finalised and immediately sent to Scotland Yard resulting in the two following letters:

HALLIWICK CRIPPLES' SCHOOL
Administered by
CHURCH OF ENGLAND CHILDREN'S SOCIETY
Bush Hill Road, Winchmore Hill, N21
Telephone: Laburnum 2442

Matron: Miss K.E. Alford, SRN, SCM

*22nd January, 1953*

*Dear Mr Standbrook,*

*As promised I am sending you our receipt for £18 7s 6d. I am so sorry that, after all your hard work, you should have had all this trouble, and I do hope that everything will run smoothly now.*

*Yours sincerely,*
*K.E. Alford,*
*Matron*

*New Scotland Yard*
*London SW1*

*Sir,*
*I am directed by the Commissioner to thank you for the sight of the accounts relating to the dance held on 9th January in aid of Halliwick Cripples' School. The accounts and the receipt issued by the School are returned herewith.*

*I am, Sir,*
*Your obedient Servant,*
*A. Ellis,*
*for Assistant Commissioner*

1953 was possibly the first year the catering and other facilities had really been exploited at The George and in which the premises became a centre for meetings, and luncheon parties, whenever possible the accommodation was free of charge for charitable organisations and benevolent associations, also in many cases for sporting activities. I remember once having seven meetings in one evening, the seventh which was through a misunderstanding I accommodated down in the bottle beer cellar, and of course, at no charge. I was never happier than when in these lively situations, which created the atmosphere, trust and goodwill of all concerned; but the present times, alas, extinguish the thought of running or building a business on these benevolent lines because the pound plus of flesh that appears so necessary today must logically be passed on.

Although the proposed dining club had been launched with much enthusiasm, it was not until 3rd February, 1953 when a rather light-hearted, but expressive, meeting was attended by some eight or nine members, that the club was established. Bill Neilson, in one of his waggish demonstrative moods following his three large helpings of real old-fashioned steak and kidney pudding and a little red wine, had the meeting in full submission with Roy Firmin unresistingly taking the chair, Mick Castell peaceably taking over as treasurer, and myself as the temporary secretary, and so being coronation year a suitable regal title was evolved, and finalised by Bill Neilson when he proposed the name 'Elizabethan 53 Dinner Club'. The cost of the meal for future functions, including two wines and a liqueur, was agreed at one guinea (£1.05). The fee for membership was 10s 6d (52½p) and the number of members limited to fifty-three. This meeting terminated with the treasurer receiving £1 12s 0d (£1.60) a profit on the evening and the club's first money.

The next dinner was held on 3rd March with Roy Firmin as chairman, the other officers were also elected as they were at the previous meeting, and the recommendations regarding name etc., were unanimously agreed: the club was officially launched and proof of the club's progress was the test of time, the members celebrated the one hundredth dinner in 1969 when our speaker was Ross McWhirter and the twenty-first anniversary year in 1964, the speaker being the Earl of Arram. The last function was the one hundred and thirty-third. I am proud to say that I have attended every one except two, this was due to being out of the country when visiting Brian in New Zealand.

The following function held on 5th May was the club's first guest evening, the chairman being John Sell. Bernard Pearce who had been astutely, if not spuriously, spirited into being the club's new secretary proposed the toast of the guests and was responded to by Aubrey Lindell. Bob Sykes proposed the chairman and the club. After twenty-two years there has been little change in the format, but a significant alteration in the costing. The following was reported in the local paper:

### ALL THIS – AND PEAR HELENE

It began well enough with the hors d'oeuvres – merely eclairs filled with prawns, chicken and anchovy, covered with sauce and glazed with aspic jelly.

But skipping lightly over the creme Egyptienne the gastronomers really began to take things seriously with the trout Meuniere – rainbow trout fried in butter and garnished with lemon and chopped parsley... the prelude to...

Chicken Maryland (fried fillet garnished with banana fritter, cauliflower dressed with chopped eggs, parsley and rich brown butter.)

Pause for sorbet and Maraschino before scrambled egg, garnished with chicken's liver fried in butter, and surrounded by Madeira sauce, parsley and chopped tomato.

And so to Pear Helene, and that...!

It was nearly two hours later that the Elizabethan Dining Club thanked chef Murphy and left The George Hotel to dream of next gastronomical extravaganza in September.

The chef's basic wage was then £9 10s 0d per week. The total gross wages for our twenty-two staff, and including the casual staff for the week were £96 13s 9d and the gross takings were £800 – approx twelve per cent – how very detached from our present wasteful and inflationary world! The incredibly low payment for casual work was 50p per session which was from 7 p.m. until 10.30 p.m. plus the clearing up time – approximately 12½p an hour.

All prices kept steady during the year, the outrageous price increases were still a long way off, in thirty-three years the price of a bottle of whisky had increased from 12s 6d (62½p) of which the excise duty payable was £8 5s 2d in 1920 to only £1 13s 4d (£1.67) duty payable £1 4s 7d (£1.23). A half pint bottle of Pale Ale in the saloon bars was 11d (approximately 4.6p) and a Guinness was 1s 3d (6.25p).

I was delighted when the Enfield Rotary Club decided to hold their luncheon meetings at The George – their presence always imparted a feeling of our being in touch with the whole of Enfield. The cost of the meal then for the three course lunch and coffee was 5s 0d (25p) plus 6d gratuities.

During 1953 we catered for three hundred and twenty-one various bookings; so many of these functions represented well-known clubs or associations, many worthy of mentioning in detail, especially some of the characters involved, but needless to say time nor room will permit. The Enfield Horse Society had their second annual function at The George, mustering ninety-six guests among whom were many well-known personalities. The cost of the five course meal, plus coffee was 12s 6d (62½p) inclusive. The Enfield Boxing Club held their annual function for the first time at The George as did the *Enfield Gazette & Observer*.

I chuckle when I think of how a large Dover sole was always offered as alternative main course if the guest was a non-meat eater, or any other reason – at the NUT function three were substituted within a 10s 6d per head menu!

The Enfield and District Horse Society had their annual show at Forty Hall on 22nd August and the following extremely capable collection of local personalities were involved in the Society's promotion. Derek Parker Bowles (president), Major Faudel-Phillips (patron), E.G. Sims (chairman), Tommy Dufton (vice chairman), D.T. Evans (secretary), Norman Wootton (treasurer), Raymond Brooke-Ward assisted by Anna Murrell (commentators), Myrna Sims (asst. show secretary), Michael Thomas and R.H. Fidler (medical officers), Houston Andrew and B.A. MacGuire (veterinary surgeons). On the general council were A. Ailes, Stanley Baldwin, Leslie Beer, Karl Ledsham Darter, J.E. Day, George Dunton, Reg Epps, Denton and Leslie Everett, Len Fish, Will Fountain, Sydney Hayball, Bill Latham, Don Lyne, D. Mahony, Col. S.A. Medcalf,

D.R. Morgan, Douglas Mould, Harold Townsend, R. Wadham, C. Wilson, C. Wiseman, Bill Wright, D.W. Wylie. I also had the honour of serving with them.

The value of the prizes then were very different from today; the open jumping competition only offered £12 first prize.

The Enfield Chess Club made The George their headquarters in 1951. The game where time ceases to exist, and the game, assuming the players are within a given category, provides the same enjoyment both to beginners or experts. This pastime is of great antiquity, being introduced into Spain by the Arabs at the period of their conquests during the eighth century, and later established through Europe during the Crusades. The first book about chess was published in England by William Caxton in 1475.

The Standbrook Coronation Trophy was presented to the club in 1953 for open competition to all persons residing in Enfield. The first winner was the match Captain of the club H. (Guy) Arnold. The cup has been won by many talented players including William R. Hartston who won it twice, in 1963 and 1966 and became the British Champion in 1974. Another cup was introduced for competition among the Enfield senior schoolboys – this was also won by William in 1962.

In 1958 special replicas were presented with the trophies by Audrey at the annual general meeting; these were mounted on a base made from the wood of the old cedar tree which has been previously referred to. The winner was the club's secretary, Hector Lawrence, who still continues to promote the club; the other finalist was Julius H. Hankansson, the club's president.

On Tuesday 2nd June, 1953 the people of Britain witnessed another great spectacle featuring British

Pageantry at its zenith: the Coronation of Elizabeth II and the continuance of such an exciting, rumbustiously dramatic and yet colourful royal family that undoubtedly will never be surpassed – nearly one thousand years of British monarchy; since King Edgar was crowned in Bath cathedral in AD 973, and almost four hundred years later Elizabeth I was crowned on the same throne and in the same abbey; probably the most colourful, vibrant, dutiful, and inherently noble queen that glorified England through those momentous and turbulent times. Now Elizabeth II with her husband Prince Philip and the children Charles, Prince of Wales, Princess Anne, Prince Andrew and Prince Edward (born respectively 1946, 1950, 1960, 1964), all fulfilling their roles with humble dignity.

The 1953 celebrations continued for a week, and all licensed premises were automatically given an extension of licensing hours until midnight from Tuesday until the Saturday, and on Coronation day the pubs were open all day. We also had an organised function in the hall during the evening for which the ticket charge was one guinea. I am positive that all licensees, and their customers were relieved and happy to return to normal routine on the Sunday.

The Enfield Amateur Boxing Club opened their new gymnasium early in the year. This was housed in the old stables come garage at the rear of The George. Jake Tuli, the British Empire flyweight champion was the guest of the evening. He attained the championship by stopping Teddy Gardner (who took the title from Terry Allen) in the twelfth round, and lost the title to Dai Dower on points over fifteen rounds in 1954.

The club first evolved in 1946 as the Eastern Enfield Amateur Boxing Club, having their training quarters at the Decontamination Centre, Scotland Green Road.

The enthusiasm and dedication was so decisive that in 1947 the club expanded and was renamed the Enfield Amateur Boxing Club and A.J.S. became their president. The following are some of the officials representing the club in those early years. Harry Bone, the first chairman, was followed by Ivor Seager who consolidated the club with his quiet but forceful way of getting everything organised in a comparatively unnoticeable manner. In 1954 another extremely dedicated sportsman named Jack Nichols was installed in the chair. Les Osborn was superseded by Mick Rowlands as secretary and was later followed by Jack Sibley. Willy Willmott followed George Watson as treasurer. Bill Mandrell and Harry Bone were made life vice presidents for their devoted service to the club and amateur boxing. The most important and exacting office in any amateur boxing club is that of competition secretary; this duty was carried out by George Ewer and Bill Cox. The ABA and professional instructors were Jackie Colbourne, Jim Riddle, Charlie Whitham, Johnny Wright, Jimmy Cole, Len Jackson, Topper Brown and G. Rafferty. Jack Hayday who was the licensee of The Railway Tavern, Enfield Lock, was the popular MC. The doctors, without whom the show cannot be staged were Doctors Barnes, George Stephens and Michael Thomas. Apart from being committee members, the following personnel served the club faithfully in various roles: Ted Pursey, Dick Hamstead, Joe Lewis, Paddy Rogers, Charlie Tew, Arthur Kemp, Bill Pearson, George Lobb, Lenny Woodcock, Sydney Heffer, Frank Ashman, Tony and Bill Martin,

George Freeman, Alf Southall and Messrs. Briggs, Forster, Wright and Cannon.

The club's patron was Col. (Jack) Crosby, OBE, MC, Deputy Lieutenant of Middlesex, one of Enfield's greatest organisers and characters.

The club was repaid with honour where in 1952 young Finnegan became an all England schoolboy champion. The following year G. Bright repeated this great honour. Both the boys were under the guidance of Johnny Wright and Len Woodcock. Among the many youngsters who brought credit to the club were P.A. Tineley – runner-up Southern England Schoolboy Championship, later winning the Army Cadet Championships three times consecutively. Frankie Green was another junior, who (not quite making the top) brought many honours to the club. His parents were also extremely keen supporters and were members of the committee for several years.

Arthur Kemp passed his timekeeper's examination in 1952 with marks of ninety-five per cent and in 1974 is still continuing the good work with the club. He is also an ABA official, and I would like to extend my appreciation to these 'gentlemen of sport' who keep amateur boxing one of the cleanest of all sports.

I was co-opted on to the committee in 1952 when the proposed new gymnasium at The George was under discussion, and during the following fifteen years I learned to respect the officers and committee who gave so much of their time and energy to the sport that keeps so many youngsters healthily disciplined.

The Enfield council's coronation week began on Saturday 3rd May with an open air boxing tournament promoted by the Enfield Club in association with the Enfield UDC at Ponders End recreation ground. Although the programme presented a fine evening's boxing the attendance was severely reduced by the cold and threatening weather, resulting in a substantial loss to the club. Cr. Archie Tatman presented the prizes. A.J.S. was not in attendance due to his decline in health. Jake Tuli and Alex Buxton attended and both enjoyed a lively evening's boxing.

The first Amateur Boxing Championships were held in 1867, but without any controlling body – obviously a hit and miss operation, but a healthy start for a sport that demands serious control. Only three weights were contested for – light, middle and heavy. The ABA commenced its long nurturing of better sportsmanship through the precepts of amateurism when Mr R. Frost-Smith convened the first meeting on 21st January, 1880 when the principals met, representing four boxing clubs, three athletic clubs and one rowing club. The first championships were held on 18th April, 1881 in St James Hall, Piccadilly (now the site of the Piccadilly Hotel). Silver cups valued at ten guineas were presented to the winners of four weights only; feather, light, middle and heavy. The oldest club belonging to the association is the Belsize ABC which was founded in 1881 and affiliated in 1882 and is still thriving today (1974).

# Chapter XXXIX

Framlingham College and Princess Alice – husband and wife relationship in the trade – dramatical happenings in and from the trade – an attempt to solve an important factor still unsolved – Christmas – menus and prices

Brian was still at Framlingham College, and on 25th July we attended speech day, when both Audrey and I remarked on the quality and delivery of the speech made by Princess Alice, especially considering her advancing years. Twenty-two years later my grandson Jonathan arrived home from Framlingham at half-term, and immediately quoted Princess Alice, saying how remarkable she was in making her speech at ninety-two years of age!

No matter how complete the licensee, he is incomplete without a comparable and understanding partner; this union or relationship, whether in the capacity of entertaining or back stage, is as essential as water is to swimming. I was reminded of this when Audrey underwent a major operation, suffering seven weeks in the local cottage hospital. There cannot be and never will be a busier life than promoting a large licensed catering house, especially if offering a hall with all its attendant functions and extended licensing hours, particularly without a partner, and a secretary. (The latter duties then were invariably undertaken by the wife of the licensee.) This loss of companionship was most noticeable when the last chores were completed at the end of the evening session, the final door bolted and locked, then back to an empty office offering little but silence, in such cold contrast to when the bars were alive and buzzing with the warmth of people! This is the time, when, like most licensees, we would relax and chat over a final drink – not because the drink was so important, it appears at the time the only natural way of unwinding the system, following the trials, pleasures and the harassment of the day's incidents; indeed without this relevant company who wants to drink? This may sound a little naïve to many, especially those outside of the trade, for one needs to experience to know the pulsating stimulus relative to the passion, sadness and the kindness, in fact every facet that helps to characterise the personalities of human beings.

During this period two incidents occurred which time alone tends to make amusing, and in both cases involve our very likeable chef. Most of his impulsiveness was accelerated solely by his desire to please. I was not on the spot when the first incident happened, but arrived on the scene when everyone was crawling about on hands and knees, some hanging on the stairs, and the chef attempting to climb on the service hotplate. I blurted out, 'What in heaven's sake is going on?' 'Dropped the fish course,' was his dejected answer. 'We'll have to tell them the fish course is off,' I said, and he replied, 'No. I'll save 'em.' Eighty poached fillets of sole, the majority down the back of the old-fashioned cast iron cupboard, and others scattered generally around! Eventually all were gathered except a few that could not be reached – so chef heroically climbed on top of the very hot cupboard and instantly performed the most fanatical dance on his knees – we couldn't get him off immediately as he wouldn't stay still long enough for anyone to grasp him! At the commencement of chef's mishap, Rose, our head waitress, was attempting to retrieve the same fillets with a stick by leaning over the edge of the hotplate when another waitress lifted one of the heavy weights that kept the meat covers suspended which released the heavy galvanised contraption with a metallic crunch, which crashed right on her head.

Poor Rose. We were certainly in an awful predicament now – chef still burning up on the hotplate, Rose laid out on the floor, and the fish still to be served – the priorities fell into place with chef being pulled off the hot top, his knees not burned sufficiently to stop him dashing into the kitchen to make more sauce, whilst others were washing the fish under the hot tap; two more were bringing Rose round with a brandy and so back to the turmoil. But, the show went on and without a complaint!

The other incident happened on one of those rare occasions when I had arranged with chef to have an evening meal, insisting I had only ten minutes to spare and would be there at precisely 7.50 p.m., but this was one time when he slipped up! Promptness to the extreme – for when I arrived at the end of the passage, there he was crouching low, his head peeping around the kitchen door, and my meal already clutched in his hands like a rugby ball (his thoughts must have been, 'I'll give him an example of keeping time!') Immediately he knew I had seen him he made a furious leap forward, at the end of which he fell flat on his face – eggs and bacon splattered everywhere. The scene only lasted for a split second, because he was up and in the kitchen before I realised that was, or had been, my meal! I stopped him before he had anything cooking and returned to the office for a quick snack of bread and cheese, and to show my appreciation for his endeavour, I sent him a nice drink for his excellent timing.

I must relate one other episode whilst chef White was in our employ; an occasion when I was entirely to blame. The calamity happened at a function when serving the sweet which, apart from other trimmings, included hot maple syrup being poured over the ice cream and known as 'Chocolate Surprise'. Being short of maple syrup I instructed chef to mix some ordinary syrup with it; he didn't exactly refuse, but he certainly showed signs of not being fully in agreement. However, with a dubious expression and a little bewilderment the mix went on, and was eventually poured over the chocolate ice cream. Looking perfectly normal, the waitresses commenced service. After some two minutes a deathly hush descended on the hall, followed by peculiar inarticulate noises, interrupted with laughter and moans; then the head waitress appeared: 'Oooh Mr Stan they're all having trouble with the sweet – some are pulling it out of their mouths like spearmint – it's all stuck between their glass and spoon – whatever's happened?'

Then another waitress arrived saying, 'I've got two of mine with their dentures stuck together' and yet another, 'It's stuck to everything, they can't get it out of their mouths'. 'Tis a fine old joke now, but then I felt dreadful... and had thoughts of one of the guests choking to death having swallowed his teeth! The mixture had turned into a liquid toffee, solidifying on contact with the ice cream, turning this somewhat delicate sauce into something akin to wet dough mixed with Bostick! The guests appeared to take the incident lightheartedly, but that was from those I met at the bar after the dinner, who thought the episode rather amusing, all of whom presumably sported their own teeth.

One of the most intelligent and wise moves ever made by a brewery was in this year 1953 when Charringtons sent a circular letter to their tenants requesting them to place all waste beers (generally known as ullage) such as the morning and evening 'pull up' (loading and clearing the beer pipes), also the pint or so from the end of a cask, even the drippings from the bottles – these were all mixed together and placed into an empty ale tub termed the spillage cask; this was marked with a special label and sent back to the brewery where it was analysed, tested for gravity, measured and full credit allowed. There was also an allowance for the complete thick ends or bottoms of casks; this was sent back in another cask, the ends of which were painted red. Hygiene and perfect draught beer were the obvious objectives, but alas, the scheme was discontinued after a long run, but for what reason I know not. Perhaps a mite more liaison and confidence in their well meaning tenants could have subdued the rapid growth of keg beer? The problem has never really been solved, and I knew of one country pub that sold beer tasting like a cocktail of minerals following a very hot weekend! Thank goodness cases like this were extremely isolated. However, I appreciated a brave attempt to solve one of the most controversial and major problems relative to the pub trade.

The Coronation was commemorated by launching the nips of strong ale which was named Royal Toby – a delightful beer with a high enough gravity to make the average person comfortably mellow after consuming four. Many people were sorry to see this beer phased from the market nearly twenty years later.

This year (1953) Charringtons launched their export bottled Toby lager on to the home market; the wholesale price was 60p per dozen, retailing at 1s 6d (7½p). The demand for lager beer at this period was apparent, but the public were very wary of the home product after being so familiar with the great foreign brews such as Carlsberg, who were exporting their beer from Copenhagen to the British Isles in 1869. Today the home brewed lagers have made enormous strides in their presentation and product. Charringtons also marketed for the first time in Great Britain one of the world's most renowned mineral waters after entering into an agreement with Canada Dry International.

At the annual general meeting of the Enfield (Standbrook) Bowls Tournament the secretary – Bert Hird – made a glowing tribute to the late chairman and a founder member, Charles Maunder, who has been referred to earlier.

A happy moment for children and the sweet toothed, but hardly for their teeth, when the announcement was made that sweet rationing was to be discontinued.

The flat rate for the car tax was raised from £10 to £12 10s 0d.

Everest, the world's highest and most elusive mountain, was conquered this year (1953) following the numerous attempts made since the initial climb was undertaken in 1922. The expedition was led by Col. H.C.J.H. Hunt, CBE, DSO and the summit was reached by Edmund Hillary (created KBE of New Zealand) and Sherpa Tensing Norgay.

In November the Queen and Prince Philip undertook the most comprehensive and arduous tour of the Commonwealth possibly ever staged; six months of travel with a schedule vast and intense enough to tax the system of any human being physically and mentally. This period certainly appeared to have a sense of purpose; the foundations were laid for a seemingly new era, but the fabric of the building never really bonded – always setbacks with far too many people in all walks of life who were ready to slow the development by words or actions.

The bank rate was reduced from four per cent to three and a half per cent, but houses were not easily sold at the comparatively low prices then offered. For example – a three bedroomed semi-detached house would be priced at between £1,600 and £3,500 or quite a luxury house for around £6,000! Who was responsible for the extreme change of tactics and the crazy changes of values and world currencies? Is not the basic cure for the greater part of this nonsense a maximum world bank rate of say eight per cent or even lower?

This was the second year the Western Enfield Samaritan Christmas tree was erected outside The George – for which the lighting is connected to The George supply. The occasion is always attended by the Mayor and Mayoress (then the chairman of the council) who officially speaks at the opening ceremony, after which all concerned are victualled in The George. Many thousands of pounds have been gathered for the old people's parcels by a few dedicated collectors who man the Christmas tree.

Due to the present (1975) inflation crisis the borough decided not to send the annual one thousand Christmas parcels to the old people. At a recent meeting of the Sportsman's 68 Club the committee, having seen the report in the local paper, immediately agreed to donate sufficient money to cover the cost of one hundred of these parcels. The chairman of the Samaritans, Alan Garrett, who is a member of the Elizabethan 53 Club, very kindly accepted the responsibility of this undertaking, and so an additional chore for his willing helpers who delight in spreading a little more Christmas cheer.

The menu offered for the 1954 Christmas lunch was as follows: Fresh soup, roast turkey and gammon, stuffing, chipolata sausage, peas, brussels sprouts, roast potatoes. Christmas pudding served with mince pie and brandy sauce. Cheese and coffee. We served one hundred and seven of these luncheons at midday Christmas Eve at 10s 6d (52½p) per head. The price of turkeys was between 4s 6d (22½p) and 5s 0d (25p) per pound. The waitresses were paid 12s 6d (62½p) per session. Following the midday and evening session I made notes for the following year. I quote 'Very short of glasses, so many stolen and broken, only six liqueur glasses left – the extra glasses in use must in future be all cheap types. 'Twas ever thus!'

# Chapter XL

Brewsters Sessions 1954 – a break-in and a gold cup – Brian overturns my car – the Trades Council Function and Edgar Lee – 'unionism' and the 'others' – Enfield's fine record – 53 Club – presentation of gavel and block – functions held during 1954 and the inadequate amenities

I am certain many would agree that during the period William Skinner was the chairman of the Enfield magistrates court (1949–1965) the atmosphere, courtesy and diplomacy would be almost impossible to eclipse. However, the 1954 Brewster Sessions (renewal of justices licenses) saw W.S. a little disconcerted when the 1949–59 highly disciplined, but equitable Chief Supt. Jim (Chic) Henderson (who was responsible for Enfield police) gave his report stating that on the whole licensed premises in the Enfield area had been well-conducted and there were no objections to any of the licenses being renewed. There had been thirty-one cases of persons being drunk and incapable, of whom only twenty were local, and sixteen cases of drunkenness with aggravation, thirteen being local, four cases of driving under the influence of drink, of which three were local persons. Two licensees were fined for allowing their premises to be used for betting. Considering the population of approximately one hundred and thirty thousand, also the vast area of Enfield, the result was creditable, but the irony of the conclusion was that the remainder of the division, which included Tottenham,

Edmonton, Wood Green and Southgate had a clean sheet! The chairman in his summing up said, 'We do thank the police for their vigilance here,' and added, 'and the fact that there were these prosecutions may be a compliment to the police.' Ninety-six licenses in all were renewed, made up of fifty-nine full victuallers, six beer only, and thirty-one off licenses.

The health of A.J.S. was now declining, so much so that he had been admitted to St Bartholomew's Hospital, and after William Skinner announced the transfer of license from A.J.S. to A.J.S. and myself, he added, 'Would you convey the Bench's good wishes to your father,' proving a little of his thoughtfulness and warmth that characterised W.S. so much.

The Good Friday of 1954 proved anything but good. At opening up time at 5.15 p.m. I found the office door bolted on the inside and the lounge bar entrance doors open. There were no signs of a forced entry and we assumed that the well-known trick of hiding in the toilet was adopted. This had been attempted many times at The George; in fact on one occasion Audrey disturbed a rather frightening-looking person who was about to plunder the bar, which led to an identity parade after a similar attempt when he was caught and arrested – a case where identification was unmistakable.

It has always been common practice to check all toilets after closing the bars; should a person be found it was invariably in the loo, sitting composed and comfortable, waiting for the silence that would indicate all was clear. Should he be discovered he would probably introduce a period of amateur dramatics with his hand on his stomach and a series of grunts and groans – maybe he would have the effrontery to blame the licensee for his condition and predicament, saying the beer or the food was infected.

I am convinced this operation was conducted by somebody who was familiar with the layout and routine of The George because of the meticulous way they emptied the change tills which carried between £30 and £40 of silver in five glass tubes, each holding anything up to eighty coins; two with half crowns, two with florins and one with shillings; every time the note drawer was pulled open ten shillings worth of silver would issue from the tubes, accompanied by a clamorous bell. The three machines were replaced in the cupboard that had been prized open, each one having its glass tubes in their requisite places.

My first shattering thought when I found the door of the office bolted was, 'Great Scott! They've taken the gold cup!' Fortunately this well-known and valued trophy was still intact, locked in the bottom draw of the steel filing cabinet. The Gomm cup was presented in 1912 for two rink (now referred to as 'fours') representation from clubs in the county of Middlesex. The trophy was insured for £1,500. The cup had been won by the Enfield Town Bowling Club in 1952 and loaned to me for public display in the lounge bar where it was exhibited in the centre of the display cabinet. The club, together with the General Accident Insurance Co., and myself must have had a more trusting and confident viewpoint towards the general public then, because today, under similar conditions and with identical precautions taken, I would rather insure a snowball in hell! (This cup was also won by the bowling section of the Bush Hill Park Social Club in 1922, 1932 and 1969.)

The Old Star at Wormley changed hands on 8th September; the new hosts were Mr and Mrs Harry Bone, newcomers to the licensed trade. Harry, who played a great part in the early development of the Enfield Amateur Boxing Club, was an ex-police boxing champion. Up until the mid-Sixties I would encourage any couple to enter the licensed or pub business and would enthusiastically assist them to fulfil their ambitions, but I cannot be certain whether at this period my attitude changed or the trade was failing in its objective. I am now very apprehensive when couples suggest leaving excellent jobs to become licensees. Perhaps seeing so many changes, and the complexities that have evolved from the rapid growth of breweries, has given me doubts in place of the understanding that existed. One thing is positive – there is no room in the pub business for half-way licensees, regardless of the methods of promotion; whether it be a tiny back street business or a prestige licensed catering hotel, the host must love it or loathe it – no shades of grey, just white or black.

The possibility of Charringtons acquiring the Kemp Town Brewery at Brighton was being considered as far back as 1930, but it was not until late 1954 that the take over was finally completed.

Brian, having completed a course of driving instruction consisting of eight one hour lessons at a cost of six guineas, passed his driving test on 5th May, 1954. He then began to establish an artless and passionate interest in my new Ford Zephyr Mk 1 car; he had driven it on several occasions, but not solo – being fully aware that the request to borrow the car was imminent, I said, 'Yes' almost enthusiastically when asked. There was little petrol in the tank and still less money in his pocket, so I was assured of him not flitting to the coast or elsewhere should he be in one of the adventurous moods that he was so capable of adopting, and so he promised to be home for lunch. My parting words were, 'Do be careful, and you know the car has been sold.' Well, he took little notice of the remark because shortly afterwards he turned the car upside down!

The following few hours were a nightmare. I was positive he had met with an accident, although the police had done everything possible, including contacting the hospitals, without results; it was not until 4.30 p.m. that we received a call stating Brian had been involved in an accident with two passengers, but all had escaped with minor injuries. Apparently he had met two of our old staff, Bert and Ann Watkins, in The Duke of Abercorn and in course of conversation they stated they had never seen The Cuffley Hotel. This was an excellent excuse for Brian to take them back to where they were working at Potters Bar and drop in for a quickie en route. Leaving the pub they made their way along the Ridgeway, at the end of which are a series of dips and turns, presenting a particularly surprising bend to begin with. Not being really experienced with the speed of a large fairly high-powered car he drove into the bend too fast – a gallant attempt to brake and half skid the car round was apparent by the continuous skid marks left on the road, but the car mounted the verge and plunged broadside over the edge, dropping about seven feet, landing upside down. How the car landed in this one clear space, missing the numerous trees was a miracle. Brian managed to scramble through the offside front door window, but before doing so said to Bert and Ann, 'Out quickly, and get the car back on the road – what will Father say?' He managed to pull Ann through the open nearside front door window. Her husband bore no similarity to his streamlined wife, in fact, he sported quite a massive middle for a short person, and was finding the exercise somewhat painful, squeezing his widest part through the same space. After all concerned realised the position was hopeless, and petrol was pouring on to the floor he was ordered to reverse and squeeze back – in her desperate attempt to help him on his way, Ann put her foot in his face, saying, 'Get back you silly bugger.' After battering the door lock Brian succeeded in opening it sufficiently for Bert to painfully squeeze through – poor chap, his injuries were probably more severe from this episode than when the car somersaulted! Ann had six stitches in her head, but apart from a severe shaking and shock they were all extremely lucky in suffering nothing worse than a few bruises. This was the third occasion one of the family had been in this type of accident. Phyllis, my sister-in-law, turned her car over and suffered a severely lacerated arm when visiting the evacuated children during the war.

Whilst awaiting delivery of a new Standard Vanguard, I was lightheartedly conned into buying a 1937 semiautomatic or fluid flywheel Daimler for which I paid £150 – it had that rare vintage smell, a cocktail of petrol, oil, leather tinged with the aroma from a well-kept stable. Brian thought the contraption was priceless and learned and loved the many chaotic and confusing antics the car produced.

The competition in catering was then quite fierce; not that one could afford to trim the profits, it was just a natural built-in pub operation relative to the prevailing period. Most establishments promoted food as an attraction for the general trade; today no department could afford to support this pleasant amenity. The following is an example of a meal served to a well-known wandering cricket team promoted by Dicky Dale and known as Dales XI – all this for 10s 6d (52½p).

Cream Chicken Soup
Sole Bonne Femme

Saddle of Southdown Lamb
Redcurrant Jelly, Roast and Creamed Potatoes
Cauliflower

Apple Pie and Ice Cream
Cheese Board
Coffee

Friday 9th April 1954 may have signified a page of modern history being written at The George when for probably the first time, a representative of the Enfield Manufacturers' Association attended a dinner at the local Trades Council and spoke on behalf of his colleagues. The occasion was the inaugural function of the Enfield Trades (1953) Council, and the visitor was the very highly respected Edgar Lee of Belling and Lee, president of the Enfield District Manufacturers' Association.

The chairman of the Trades Council, T. McNamara, introduced Edgar Lee saying, 'This is a unique occasion, one which brings into amity warring parties of the past,' and, 'Trade Unionists who had found in him a willingness to work together, which is wholly admirable.' Replying on behalf of one hundred and seven industrial firms Edgar Lee said, 'I cannot look on ourselves as two sides of industry – I feel we sink or swim together – I don't regard myself as an employer; we are all employed by the great public of the world, and we are elected by the lady with the shopping basket.'

Another of the speakers – Archie Tatman – the chairman of the district council (this was the last year of Enfield as a

UDC) said, 'Relations between the trade unions and industry in Enfield would bear comparison anywhere in the whole of Britain, and the relations between employers and workpeople is much admired and could be copied throughout the country.'

Another guest representing the TUCC, (Tom O'Brien, MP), who had been chairman of the TUCC the previous year, told the gathering, 'The Trade Union movement today is one of the greatest institutions of the realm,' and, 'our system of collective bargaining is a first-class example to the world, and has been built up through years of co-operation between the two parties of industry.' Referring to Edgar Lee he said, 'Here is a gentleman who typifies the understanding that exists between us today, and which I hope will continue to develop between industry and the TUC movement as a whole.'

The reply for the guests was made by Ernest Davies, MP for Enfield East.

One of the exceptions to the controversial changes that have taken place in Enfield since 1954 that I am positive would be generally supported by the populace is the fine record that the town has enjoyed in relationship to all parties concerned in the industrial province of greater Enfield.

By whom and when did this prevailing line of demarcation start between the warring parties of unionism and 'the others' whoever they may be? Although my job has afforded me every opportunity of meeting the much projected militant, the anti-social mortal that is only content when agitating, I am happy to report very little of my time has been wasted with them. The erosion of our free society could be lessened if we could export these anti-British persons to the country where their ideals prevail, or exchange them for persons seeking their own personal freedom. Those that prefer to sing the 'Red Flag' rather than their own country's national anthem should also be offered the opportunity of joining their comrades, and be released from the mean and lamentable life they stress this country offers them – the money would easily be found for their fares and compensation. I abhor all forms of extremity in any political denomination, not because of the brand of politics, but the application of fabricated and shallow thinking.

Unfortunately the expression, free society, is so little understood today, with its meaning only relative to our laws. Maybe the significance of the words 'free society' should be the operative ones when forming any new law, enforcement or regulation.

One of the great mysteries still requiring explanation is the embryonic dimension called 'time'. In many ways this fourth dimension controls our planet and the universe – a million years is so infinitesimal in nature's noticeable course of change, and yet in a decade humans can, and do, change our whole projection of thinking and environmental living. Maybe on reflection and in comparison this is the paramount cause of the many failures in this supposedly civilised world.

I wonder now when looking back to 1954 how asinine was the general enthusiasm for doing so much for so little, when the present offers exactly the reverse.

The ninth dinner of the Elizabethan 53 Dinner Club was held on Wednesday 31st March; at this function the gavel and block was presented to the chairman, Mick Castell. The following account is an extract from the Enfield Gazette and Observer as reported by Leo Eastwick:

GASTRONOMERS' GAVEL

Excercises in 'gastronomic education', horrifying as it may sound, is the expression by which the Elizabethan 1953 Dining Club seeks to justify its periodical experiments in the art of good eating and drinking.

Chairman Mr A.W.F Castell, his palate fresh from the delicate savour of poached trout, to say nothing of the excellent Graves which went with it, used this discouraging term for what was a wholly delightful experience when members and their guests attended last week's meeting at The George Hotel headquarters.

*Liberal Lines*

The education proceeded on very liberal lines through seven courses and by the time the gorgonzola and very old tawny port had been reached by way of steak, mushrooms and the full-blooded Nuits St George 1947 the pupils had been edified to a point which temporarily saturated the enthusiasm of even so zealous a member as the highly capable secretary, Mr H.G. Arnold.

The evening was made memorable by the following imaginative touch supplied by the licensee Mr S.W. (Stan) Standbrook to whom the Elizabethan club owes its origin.

*Two Reigns Linked*

As a traditionalist who deplores the decline of Enfield's County Town atmosphere Mr Standbrook searched for a link to unite the two Elizabethan reigns, and found it in the ancient Palace of the great

Queen which stood opposite the Market Place until its destruction in 1928.

Its demolition was a sad blow to Mr Standbrook, who was at the time articled as an architect to the late Mr James Neilson, and who had a hand in the preparation of the Tudor Room in Gentleman's Row, where the magnificent panelling and ceiling were re-erected.

### Chopping Block

While making enquiries as to the existence of any remaining timber from the old building Mr Standbrook was astonished to learn that his friend Bob Vernum possessed a piece of one of the huge oak beams which had done duty as a chopping block for nearly thirty years in the garden of his Fyfield Road home. The oak was readily placed at Mr Standbrook's disposal.

Further search brought to light a plank of timber from the great cedar tree which stood in the grounds and which had been planted by Dr Robert Uvedale, to whom the Palace was let in 1660.

### Gavel of Own Design

Mr Standbrook's object was to make a chairman's gavel for the use of the Elizabethan Club. Application to three museums and a national newspaper failed to reveal an authentic model of the period, and the fine piece of oak was fashioned into a gavel and block to the donor's own simple and appropriate design with a base of the cedarwood.

As a symbolic refinement the four sides of the base were decorated with two shilling pieces of the reign of

Elizabeth II with two similar coins of Elizabeth I, the latter unearthed by Mr Standbrook in St Albans. He made the presentation to Mr Castell at the last meeting.

The response on behalf of the guests was effectively carried out jointly by Tim Stone and Geoffrey Arnold. The club's first AGM held on 13th May was in the competent hands of Bernard Pearce, but he was not sufficiently persuasive to reverse the decision regarding a night for the ladies, as the following report declares:

### DINNER CLUB STAYS 'MEN ONLY'

Members of Enfield's Elizabethan 1953 Dinner Club, at their annual general meeting, decided against inviting ladies to their functions.

The meeting, together with a member's dinner, was held at The George Hotel with Mr Bernard Pearce in the chair.

Mr A.W. Castell and Mr H.G. Arnold were re-elected hon. treasurer and hon. secretary respectively.

The cash statement showed a small sum in hand, and it was unanimously agreed that £5 should be donated to both the Eastern and Western Enfield Samaritan Associations.

Opinion was divided over ladies' nights, but eventually the vote of the 'misogynists' was too strong, and 1955 is the earliest occasion on which ladies can now hope to dine with the club in the event of this year's decision being reversed at the next general meeting.

Mr C. Heast was elected chairman of the next dinner, which will be held in September.

Charles Heast, now happily settled with his family in New Zealand, was chairman for the club's next function held on 20th October, 1954 and I hope this occasion is held dear in his memory, especially when comparing the inclusive cost of one guinea (£1.05) for the following menu and wines with today's muddles and complex prices and now the addition of VAT which is added to any other service charge apart from the basic cost. Even with the existing immoderate and mis-computed affluence now prevailing; consternation mingled with rebellious thought appears legitimate! The cost of the meals was kept minimal and stable by entering the wines and invariably the liqueurs at cost or off sales price-indeed this continued until the late Sixties.

>

Iced Honeydew Melon and Spice with
White Wine Sauce
Hotch Potch Soup
Poached Dublin Bay Prawns
Tartare Sauce

Baked Haunch of Royal Venison and Wine Gravy
Redcurrant Jelly
French Beans, Brussels Sprouts, Baked Potatoes

Baked Apple Dumplings and Custard Sauce
Camembert and Cheddar Cheese
Biscuits and Butter
Coffee
Burgundy Nuits St George 1947
Claret Chateau Leoville-Barton 1947
Bisquit Dubouche VSOP or Kummel

The toast of the chairman and the club was proposed by Tony Cox, and the guests by Phillip Nicholas, to which Maurice Hill replied (the agent to Iain MacLeod). A barrister, Frederick Mattar, who was a guest of Bob Sykes, was our first speaker. Although impromptu he had the attention of the gathering when he gave a casual and applicable talk quoted as 'Between the two Queens' (Elizabeth I and Elizabeth II).

The last function of the club for 1954 was held on the 14th December when our first speaker proper – Jim Manning – spoke on 'Food and Sport'. The chairman on this occasion was Willy Willmott, the toast of the club was proposed by Len Keighley and the vote of thanks to the speaker was undertaken by Bill Neilson.

The Enfield Hundred Historical Society held their first annual dinner at The George on 21st January, 1954 and at this function I was delighted to present a gavel and block made from the wood of the old palace – and Uvedale's cedar tree to Godfrey Groves who received it on behalf of the society.

Pieces of the cedar tree have been given to many friends residing overseas, and one such recipient was Felicia Romero who was thrilled to take a piece home with her to Philadelphia this year. Pieces have found their way to numerous countries including Africa, New Zealand, Australia and Alaska. When cut or sawn the cedar wood quickly confirms its authenticity by the distinctive and captivating aromatic smell.

The following list of functions held in 1954 (apart from those already mentioned) is being quoted only for the record, as it would not be practical to mention all in detail: Master Barbers Association, Sangamo Western Apprentices, *Enfield Gazette and Observer*, Ediswans-Cosmos Foreman's

Association also Ladies' Night, Astral Engineering Co., Enfield and District Manufacturers' Association, Sunnyside Tennis Club, Elms Athletic Club, United Friendly Social Club, Enfield and Edmonton Taxes Social Club, Ponders End Piscatorial Society, The Catenian Association, Enfield and District Horse Society, North Enfield Cricket Club, Enfield Scouts Reunion, Enfield Post Office, Enfield Chess Club, Bellings Football Club also Social Club, Conservative Association Chase Ward, Enfield Doctors Ethical, Royal Small Arms, Enfield Old Grammarians Football Club, Enfield Chase Tennis Club, St Stephen's Church Choir, Chase Secondary Modern Boys' School, Reg. Varney, family and staff, Pearl Insurance Co., Doric Social Club, Prudential Assurance, Industrial Life Officers, Price Bakers, Enfield Swimming Club, Bury Lodge Bowling Club, Botany Bay Cricket Club, Carlton Tennis Club, Enfield Camera Club, Enfield Cricket Club Tennis section, Durants Park Bowls Club, St Paul's Choir, Enfield Boxing Club, Doric Social Club, Ruberoid Social Club, Royal Air Force Association, Enfield Standbrook Bowls Tournament.

There were also numerous other functions such as weddings, dances, charity promotions, Rotary and Round Table, luncheon parties, flower shows and meetings. Perhaps we failed to realise in our enthusiasm and non-stop work that it was all magnified by the fact that The George had never shaken hands with reality. This situation probably existed in over half of the licensed catering establishments, and in many cases this applied to the non-catering pub, but in most instances improvements to bars were dealt with by the brewers much more approvingly, mainly attributable to lower cost and the profit gained by the increased sale of liquor.

The first floor containing the hall, club room and kitchens was still original, antiquated and lacking numerous modern facilities, and it was only the extreme effort and enthusiasm of everybody, especially our staff, that created an atmosphere of goodwill, homeliness and courtesy that made the many inconveniences unimportant.

The following are extracts from four of the numerous letters received during the year, making it all worthwhile.

*Chase Secondary Modern Boys' School*
*Trinity Street*
*Enfield*
*15th February, 1954*

*Dear Sir,*

*Re: Dinner Dance Friday 12th February, 1954.*

*I should like to express my personal satisfaction and thanks, and that of the staff of the school for your good service and good meal on the occasion of the above function.*

*I understand that Mr Oliver has already suggested a date for 1955, for this he will doubtless have full support from the staff.*

*Yours sincerely,*
*R. W. Taylor*
*Headmaster*

*Carlton Tennis Club*
*343 Carterhatch Lane*
*Enfield*
*Middlesex*
*23rd November, 1954*

*Dear Mr Standbrook,*

*I should like to take this opportunity of thanking you and your staff for all you did to make our Dinner and Dance such a success. The verdict of everyone was that it was the best yet and you were responsible, in no small way for that opinion...*

*Yours sincerely,*
*Vera E. M. Jarvis*
*Hon. Sec.*

*42 Woodland Way*
*Winchmore Hill N21*

*Dear Mr and Mrs Standbrook,*

*Once again on behalf of myself and my wife, I would like to express our very sincere thanks for the wonderful reception you gave us on Saturday.*

*We thought, and so did everyone else present, that the food and wines were excellent and that the whole banquet was carried out properly. We are more than pleased that we took Stan's advice to have a sit down meal and a band. The table decorations looked lovely and we owe Mrs Standbrook especial thanks for that.*

*It is our hope that Mrs Standbrook will soon recover from her operation and have a very speedy recovery to good health.*

*Yours very truly,*
*Cyril V. White*

*137 Kenilworth Crescent*
*Enfield*
*Middlesex*
*14th April, 1954*

*Dear Mr Standbrook,*

*May we again express to you our sincere thanks for all the arrangements you made, including the most excellent refreshments, which so greatly added to the success of the evening. We shall always retain very happy memories of a most enjoyable party at The George.*

*Yours sincerely,*
*D. Turpin*

# Chapter XLI

Function at House of Commons – 127th Anniversary Festival LVBI – royal patronage for one hundred and fifty years – Enfield Conservative Party and the Rt. Hon. Iain Macleod (Eve Macleod, later Baroness of Borve) – The League of Hospital Friends – Britain and charity – professional boxing – the Cooper twins – Alfred James Standbrook – his demise and tributes

Another gavel and block (made from the old Cedar and Oak) was presented to the Rt. Hon. Iain Macleod, then Minister of Health, MP for Enfield West, who received it on behalf of the Enfield Conservative Association, at a function held at the House of Commons in honour of the Rt. Hon. Sir Winston Churchill in 1954, the year of his eightieth birthday. Iain with his wife Eve, together with Jim Manning (prospective candidate for Enfield East) and his wife were the joint hosts of the evening. The chairman for the dinner was County Ald. Graham Rowlandson (later Sir Graham). The guest of honour was Sir Edward Boyle who was then the parliamentary secretary to the Ministry of Supply. An extremely pleasant and mellow evening that completely blended with the atmosphere of what is probably the greatest democratic and historical institution in the world.

Unfortunately parliament today does appear to be veering away from the great characters of yesterday; this could be attributed, not only in Britain, to the world's decline from individualism, and being replaced by a confusing and deceitful form of collectivism, which in turn feeds the minority extremist groups that discard human principles as simply as breakers discard sand on the seashore! All credit to the losers that find the heart and courage to uphold their principles. My answer would be, 'Tis better to lose the battle in good faith than to be the victor in bad.'

The 127th Anniversary Festival of the Licensed Victuallers Benevolent Institution was held on 10th November 1954 at the Connaught Rooms, under the presidency of Mr E.R. Chadwyck-Healey, MC, then the chairman of Charrington & Co. The toast list included Edward Markham (chairman of the institution), Tom O'Brien, MP, Sir Ian Fraser, CH, CBE, MP (director of Charringtons), Albert Dyer, MBE, Brian Johnston, MC.

The evening was a great one and certainly a striking credit to the trade. How stable and forward looking the vast and complicated licensed business has been since 1827 when the first six acres of land were purchased so that almshouses could be erected and the aged or infirm members of the trade pass their latter years proudly in respect and peace. The following year the institution was honoured and rewarded for its hard and distinguished work when HRH the Duke of Sussex (uncle of the late Queen Victoria) became the first patron, and through those one hundred and twenty-seven years royalty has continued to patronise this resolute and charitable section of the trade. In 1877 HRH the Prince of Wales presided at the Jubilee Festival Dinner held at Willis's Rooms; HRH the Duke of York (HM King George V) presided at the seventieth Festival Dinner held at the Hotel Cecil. The 92nd Dinner held in 1919 was presided over by HRH the Prince of Wales (HM King Edward VIII) to celebrate the 'peace' following the 1914–1918 war and was held at the Connaught Rooms. The centenary celebrations held in 1927 were presided over by HRH the Duke of York (HM King George VI) and held at the same venue. The late Duke of Kent presided at the 108th anniversary in 1935; this function continued to be held in the Grand Hall, Connaught Rooms. HRH the Duke of Edinburgh became the patron in succession to his late father-in-law King George VI in 1952.

The town ward of the Enfield Conservative Association, held its annual function in February 1954. The attitude then of the organisers was exceedingly charming in projecting a village establishment priceless in character, and dignified in its expediency, but not quite the adventurous stimulus necessary when dealing with one of Britain's most distinguished and impressive members of parliament, namely, the Rt. Hon. Iain MacLeod referred to earlier, then Minister of Health. The menu for this function was very ordinary and cost wise it was impossible to improve, but my words were heeded later, and the promotion hereafter gathered momentum and completely fulfilled its obligations. Eve MacLeod proposed the Queen and also responded to the toast of 'The Ladies' which was given by County Ald. Graham Rowlandson (Later Sir Graham).

I am certain the majority of people then were not basically politically minded, but today most of us are literally driven to political thinking by extremists, and a way out type that confuses normal considerate persons, but I must reiterate my complete confidence in Iain MacLeod's precise clear, sharp, and direct thinking, so positive, that in normal careless conversation there were no wasted words, no long unnecessary phrases, every word clipped to stress the level of importance he wished to attach to it; his eyes flashed with his mood of speech to the extent of unlocking his thoughts. He generated a warm confidence that was almost commanding, and yet, no matter how formal or prim his mood, humour was always close to the surface, and when that appeared it automatically fused into the company or audience; an ordinary mortal endowed with brilliance. How basically true, and in every respect was his following quote: 'Everyone should have an equal opportunity to prove themselves unequal.'

No man ever had a more dedicated or suitable partner than his wife Eve (now Baroness MacLeod of Borve); with her flair for creating, and getting things done – no shilly-shallying; bearing a great similarity to her husband in directness of speech, and get-on-with-the-job attitude, especially when related to her numerous charitable and other dedicated objectives but, above all, her foremost quality was the extreme courage and bravery displayed in the years after her collapse with meningitis and polio on 28th June, 1952. The strain from then on for both herself and her husband must have been appalling, especially as Iain was the new Minister of Health necessitating him being at the House of Commons almost every evening and visiting the hospital during the afternoon plus caring for two children. I will always remember when later on Eve was in the wheelchair how the look in her eyes would say, 'I could do it better on my own,' when three of us would be manoeuvring the chair up the extremely awkward staircase at The George. Very often Sir Graham Rowlandson, also in a wheelchair would attend the same gathering.

Eve disliked help when she thought she was capable of managing herself.

The only way that I succeeded was to accompany her to her car whilst in conversation, and being certain my actions were showing courtesy rather than direct help – I knew that if Eve thought that I thought she needed help I would have soon known!

I had the privilege of occasionally driving Eve home to Ladykirk on the Ridgeway, Enfield, in fact it was next door but one to Ridgemount. The homely atmosphere on entering was immediately apparent and magnified by the casual informal attitude that would make any guest think, 'I'm at home too.' The one significant difference to any normal home was the pile of parliamentary, and (I assume) law books piled on the settee, leaving Iain little space for comfort.

Following a whist drive Audrey had organised on behalf of the Enfield and Cheshunt League of Hospital Friends, she was invited by Eve MacLeod to serve on the committee. A very happy association followed in which the facilities of The George were at the disposal of the League.

The inaugural meeting was held in 1953 at Ladykirk the home of the founders Iain and Eve Macleod, this was followed by a public meeting at the Enfield grammar school, which was chaired by Archie Tatman and attended by four hundred and fifty persons. The national chairman and founder of the league in 1948, Percy Wetenhall, OBE, addressed the meeting. The present national chairman is Eve MacLeod (Baroness MacLeod of Borve, JP).

The Officers elected were as follows: president – chairman of Enfield UDC, Archie Tatman; vice president – chairman Cheshunt UDC, Margery Heyter; chairman – Archie Tatman; secretary – Freda Frank; treasurer – Harry Heafield (still in office) and some of the early members all of whom gave so much time and effort to build the character which the league proudly bears today – Eve MacLeod, Derek and Joan Stocking, Dorothy Dixon, Sue

Turner, Elsie Wilson, Ida McLintoc, Miss Grant, Margery Miles, Edna Maxwell, Pris James, Clarence Fishpool, Jack Edwards, Mr Peachell, Mesdames Rowland, Denis, Phyper, Froom, Edlin, Miss Eyres and Messrs Hardy, Barnard, Grubb, Hicks, Platten and Spicer, plus many others who contributed to this charitable effort.

In 1948 there were many guilds formed to help hospitals, but these were psychologically driven underground when the government stated the new health service was self supporting and it would not be necessary to apply voluntary or monetary help in any way! What utter nonsense! Take away the amenities supplied by the League of Hospital Friends over these twenty-odd years, and the hospitals would be as barren as prisons; just think of the little extra comforts that have been introduced for the patients and the visitors – privacy screens, tele-trolleys, surgical equipment, various furnishings, canteens, and chapels, etc., all of which has cost millions of pounds and has been collected in general from the ordinary kindly public; added to this there is the voluntary working force applicable to manning the canteens and other services. In my opinion, never has dedication and enthusiasm for a more worthy and versatile charitable cause been more important.

I believe every hospital in England and Wales is blessed with a League of Hospital Friends, but only eight in Scotland are affiliated to the National League.

Although a charity that differs from those quoted above, the Enfield Preservation Society is an important plus for all the residents of the Enfield Borough. My sincere thoughts and praise on behalf of all who appreciate the Society's formidable growth since the early meetings that were held at the George Inn.

Enfield residents are fortunate in having such a dedicated, professional and hard-working party of officers who have, and are, and will, battle for any matter that, historical building-wise, road-wise or otherwise does not benefit Enfield. Kind and special thoughts are due to the working parties which help in various projects such as keeping the New River tidy and clean.

The Society's Museum is based at Forty Hall and will include the 1911 Catalogue of the Meux Theobalds Sale which I gave to the Society; also three framed plaques of the plaster motive of the ceiling of the old Elizabethan Palace.

Members enjoy arranged outings to historical places; interesting walks; also meetings with speakers such as David Pam, Graham Dalling, the late and present historical officers to the Borough of Enfield, both of whom have produced fascinating reading in books on Enfield's history.

The Society has approximately 2,200 members.

''Tis pleasant to belong.'

The following is a message from the Minister of Health, Mr Iain Macleod, MP, for the formation of the Enfield and Cheshunt League of Hospital Friends on 12th March, 1954:

> By Subsection 1 of Section 6 of the National Health Service Act all hospitals in the country are owned by the Minister. But although I hold that office I also believe that in the true sense the hospitals should belong to the people of the country. I believe that they should feel that the hospital where they or their family have been treated is 'their' hospital and not mine. And so I have tried ever since I became Minister to encourage the growth of voluntary effort in the hospitals. I want to see every hospital group

with its own League of Friends. I believe that such a body brings the hospitals nearer to the people, and the people nearer to the hospitals.

Fine work has been done by individuals and by different voluntary organisations. But the time has come to knit all these strands together into one body which will dedicate itself to the service of the sick in our local hospitals.

Here is a fine opportunity for service and rich reward. However small the contribution of time or money or service that you can make, be sure it will be warmly welcomed.

We need a League of Friends in our towns for our hospitals. It is now being formed. I hope you and your family will join.

Iain Macleod

The amount of money collected on behalf of charity (or rather to help others) in the British Isles is incalculable – pubs alone probably raise between £15 and £20 million a year, and one seldom, if ever, hears a national word of thanks uttered by any government source; all I ever see are reports of niggardly legislation to stop trifling little raffles and the like! If only those responsible would do something more useful like using the same enthusiasm to stamp out violence and thuggery and the numerous other anti-social ruthless acts.

The year 1954 had been far too busy and involved for me to attend many sporting events, but I have one programme of a Jack Solomon's Boxing promotion at Harringay Arena on 14th September, 1954, that any promoter would be delighted to stage today. The main bout was for the Middleweight Championship of GB, and the BE when Johnny Sullivan beat Gordon Hazel; this was unfortunately over in the first round. The other contests were as follows: Dai Dower beat Hillaire Gaviano in a flyweight contest. The following month he outpointed Jake Tuli to become the empire flyweight champion. Sammy McCarthy (British featherweight champion) beat Joe Woussen. Ron Barton in a lightweight contest beat Brian Anders. (He retired in 1956, an undefeated champion), Johnny Williams (British and empire champion in 1952) beat Jack Hobbs. Last but by no means least the Cooper twins, Henry and George (hereinafter Jim) made their professional debut after being amateur stars. For Henry the beginning of a colourful road to fame, and a future sportsman to be admired by all, boxing enthusiasts or not. Jim, when only seventeen, suffered a badly broken hand, but he was considered by many during those early years to be a finer prospect with greater punching power. The two contests were of six rounds duration in which Henry at 13 st 2½ lbs knocked out Harry Painter in the first round whilst Jim at 13 st 6 lbs won on a points decision over Dick Richardson.

This year was important to the athletic world, when Roger Bannister burst the barrier of the four minute mile when he clocked 3 minutes 59.4 seconds at the Iffley Road Track, Oxford.

Almost a decade after the war terminated all food rationing ended, and the bank rate dropped from three and a half per cent to three per cent. From today's viewpoint it is confusing to simply attempt to understand how building societies were then thriving when offering the investor only two and three quarter per cent, but everything money-wise was relevant and without inflation!

The health of A.J.S. had deteriorated drastically early 1954, but although his suffering must have been intense, he amazingly kept his sense of humour, projecting the type of wit, the old style, which is seldom used today, at least not professionally. He had an inbuilt comedy laboratory tucked somewhere in his non-academic brain, that would be instantly activated should any action or oral phrase intimate the minutest suggestion for a comical remark or crazy answer.

While recuperating at Frinton with Jennie, following a particularly bad spell, A.J.S. was taken seriously ill and rushed home to Hathaway, 54 Broadwalk, Winchmore Hill on 26th July. Fortunately my sister Peggy was away with them at the time, and her presence must have been a great comfort to Father, also a moral boost to Mother on the journey home by ambulance.

When I visited Father that evening it was fairly obvious the end was near – there was little anybody could do except to comfort Mother. Peacefully the following day Father passed away; his death due to chronic bronchitis and many complicated diseases of certain organs which in my opinion associated themselves with the hard, hazardous and excitable life of a licensee who lived his part generously and to the full – there were some hard years during the period in the trade from 1908. He was in his sixty-ninth year.

The funeral took place on the following Friday at the Enfield crematorium. The cortege stopped awhile at The George when many friends, customers and staff paid their last respects. The chapel was far too small to contain the mourners, and the service was relayed to those outside.

It was a traumatic experience for the family, running the three businesses, especially The George – everything has to function normally as if nothing had happened, and a pub is not a place where misery is sold or encouraged, but my God, it is a test when tragedy strikes and grief will only be partly submerged awaiting to surface at the slightest incident. However, the customers ease the burden by their thoughtfulness, tact and kindness.

And so the family, together with an innumerable number of friends lost a character that only a miracle could replace.

The two following reports so aptly portray his disposition and humble personality. Extracted from the *Enfield Gazette and Observer* and written by the Editor, Charles Maunder:

### NICE WORDS ABOUT AN ENFIELD TOWNSMAN

In a daily newspaper, I read that Mr A.J. Standbrook, chairman of the Northern Suburban Licensed Victuallers' Association, has accepted a unanimous invitation to preside at the first annual festival of the association since pre-war days. These annual festivals, let me add, produce large sums for financing charitable institutions, and in anything of this kind Alf Standbrook takes his place (again let me add) very modestly in the forefront of all such endeavours with which he becomes associated. Quite a number of Enfield townsmen have first-hand acquaintance with the hospitality dispensed by Mr and Mrs Standbrook at their home in the midst of a beautiful garden at Ridgemount, The Ridgeway, Enfield. Members of a local church as well as sportsmen will bear witness to that.

President Standbrook must surely have blushed while he listened to the speeches which preceded his election as president of the association's annual festival. Said Mr A.H. Janes '...It was most appropriate that one of London's largest and most enterprising associations should have as its president a man from the retail section of the trade, who had given valuable assistance for many years in the safeguarding of its vital interests, and who had won esteem and affection, not only from his fellow traders in that area, but also from licensees in many other districts. He was one of the most genial, as well as one of the most conscientious chairmen in London, and there was no doubt that he would also be remembered as one of the most popular presidents...'

That, I think I hear someone say, is the voice of the trade speaking. Maybe it is, but many Enfield people who know nothing about the trade will probably feel inclined to murmur 'Hear hear' to that obviously sincere tribute. Other speakers in like vein followed Mr Janes, but consideration for the feelings of 'A.J.S.' of Enfield puts a curb on my pen.

Extracted from the *Toby Times* the monthly magazine published by Charrington & Co. Dated July 1949:

No licensee in the London area is better known or more respected than Mr Alfred James Standbrook, whose triple responsibility is The George, Enfield Town; The Cambridge, Palmers Green; and The Stonehouse Hotel, Hatfield.

Mr Standbrook says himself he is a lucky man, for he has his family and a loyal staff to help him. His eldest son, Mr A.J. Standbrook Jnr, is his general assistant, as well as manager of The Cambridge. At

The Stonehouse Hotel, with her husband is his daughter Mrs 'Peggy' Greaves, and at The George, Enfield – Mr and Mrs 'Bill' Gwynn.

Another son, Mr Stanley W. Standbrook, is licensee of The Cuffley Hotel, Cuffley, Herts. having taken over the tenancy when he came out of the services.

Mr Standbrook has held a license since 1907, and his association with Charrington's extends for nearly thirty years, having begun when the Anchor Brewery took over The George from Savill's.

Known throughout the trade as 'Alf', Mr Standbrook was for eight years Chairman of the Northern Suburban Licensed Victuallers' and Beersellers' Association. An ardent sportsman, he is President of the Enfield Amateur Boxing Club, and donor of the Standbrook Cup to the Enfield Hospital Bowls Competition, of which he is also President. From 1899 to 1903 he was Boy Billiards Champion of England.

Mr Standbrook and his wife, Jennie, have been married forty-four years. On behalf of all its readers, *Toby Times* wishes this devoted and popular couple many happy years to come.

*Craigard*
*36 Esplanade*
*Frinton-on-Sea*
*Essex CO13 9HZ*
*21st July, 1976*

*Dear Stan,*
*Your father who worked at The Castle eloped with your mother much to the disgust of my uncle Fred (your*

*grandfather). I well remember him coming round to see my father and actually crying and begging my father to see if he could help him to stop the marriage – my father said he would not interfere. Love always wins and I think this was a very happy marriage and your father Alf was a great man – one of the kindest men I have ever met and what a different place the world would be if people had the same character. Your grandfather (Fred Pluck) later joined the Union Literage Co. and I believe he invented the concrete barge. He was a clever man.*

*Must now close and look forward to seeing you later in the year.*

*Yours as ever,*
*Tom*

To the reader:

It is possible you will derive some enjoyment from reading this book; perhaps, understandably you may skip many pages that to your goodself have been of no interest or to your liking; it is possible you will have continued reading for the sake of saying truthfully, 'I have read it completely!' Could be you may think the composition or material is somewhat weak and simple making the reading less interesting, or you may think I had the material to have created a more exciting, elative or perhaps amusing production; maybe some subjects could have been produced more controversially, which of course added to a meagre quota of imagination and perhaps a modicum of exaggeration obviously must project more impressive and exciting reading; but the degree of parity between labouring for love or for reward creates a significant psychological approach which has encouraged me to have programmed a course of conviction and ideology.

On behalf of charity I sincerely wish to express my thanks and gratitude to you for purchasing this book, and with complete humility I would very kindly request you to accept my best wishes for your future health and happiness.

Stan Standbrook<br>
and all my family

# Epilogue

The reader will wonder why this book was not published by the intended date of 1974. The answer is that I failed to promote the issue by having the book printed and distributed in Enfield, having been hoping to sell two thousand copies locally and raising the maximum money for charity – the result was a complete failure. The final effort arrived with the encouraging help of Minerva Press through their normal routine of publishing.

Due to circumstances now prevailing (1997) with my dear wife Audrey (born 1907) now blind and needing constant attention, and myself (born 1909) now leaves me little time to continue with the second volume that covers 1955 to 1974. The first chapter is now being typed. We thank Cheshire Care for the carers' kindness and love shown to Audrey during their early morning and late evening visits, and also the very kind support from Poole Social Services.

We took over the license of The Cambridge in 1962, when my popular and much respected brother Alf died; unfortunately, the enterprise met with many controversial aspects. Following a period of management we took over ourselves, and put the George under management.

Our son Brian, now (1954) home from boarding school in Framlingham, took the Westminster Catering College course followed by two years' national service in the Army

Catering Corps, obtaining the rank of Lieutenant and meeting Graham Kerr (television's 'Galloping Gourmet'). Following his release, Brian married Wendy Fowles, and took the license with myself of the King George in Barnet. There was a great surprise when they eventually decided to go to New Zealand following interviews with New Zealand House in London. We took them to RAF Lynham on 8th November 1959 and they flew to New Zealand the next day. They were posted to Auckland, resulting in a very pleasant surprise – Brian met his boss, Sqn Ldr Graham Kerr, later to be his second in command (Catering).

Audrey and I visited them early in 1963, disembarking from the *Rieahine* at Wellington, and we were met by Brian, with a charming bouquet of flowers for Audrey from Graham Kerr – how kind of him. Graham later joined us at the hotel. We went by air to Auckland the following day.

Wendy returned to England in 1965 with the three children Jonathan, Sarah and Timothy – a happy, boisterous and full of fun trio.

My first enthusiastic effort charity-wise was in 1928. We promoted a supper dance at the George, the proceeds going to the Enfield War Memorial Hospital, and so comparatively silly when set against 1997 prices: tickets were five shillings (25p) including buffet. I remember having a small aquarium filled with beans and a prize for guessing the number therein – amazingly and embarrassingly, Jennie (Mother) guessed the exact number which was 2248! So pleased to know the recorder was not one of the family! The hospital benefited by some £12-odd, equivalent to about £250 in 1997. Our thanks to all who made the promotion possible.

Our very special and sincere thanks go to the Enfield Bowlers who participated in the Enfield Standbrook

Charity Bowls Tournament (chapter 27, page 315) especially as they lost their HQ when we vacated the George in 1978. The competition successfully carried on until the Bush Hill Park Tennis, Bowls and Social Club kindly offered their ideal facilities at the new HQ, fittingly where the first finals had been staged forty-two years earlier. My thoughts are comforted by the enthusiasm of the present and past presidents, officers and committee members that have promoted the competition with so much dedication; also to all the clubs and bowlers for their wonderful support. This also includes the Ladies' Charity Competition which commenced in 1974, commemorating our fifty years at the George, and not forgetting the many behind the scenes supporters who help with the raffles, catering and so on, who are often taken for granted.

The first charity function at The Cambridge was the Licensed Victuallers' Supper Dance, organised by Doreen Fairlie and Irene Holdsworth in 1963, which raised £133. Peter Baker of Spurs had my football signed by the team; the ball was auctioned. I presented a tankard on behalf of Jennie to Mr Knee (in place of Mr Wigan of Charringtons).

Our grateful thanks to the three mayors and all supporting an important landmark in Enfield's history on 10th March, 1965: the integration of the three boroughs of Enfield, Edmonton and Southgate. Enfield's mayor, Alderman Ernest Mackenzie JP (Chairman), Edmonton's, Alderman Cyril Lacey JP and Southgate's Councillor Harry Farbey were each promised £80 for their chosen charities. The mayor and mayoress with Audrey and myself received the guests. Mrs Iain MacLeod (later Baroness MacLeod of Borve) proposed the borough of Enfield, with response by the mayor of Enfield. The borough of Edmonton was proposed by Alderman Thomas Joyce OBE with response by the Mayor of Edmonton; the borough of Southgate was proposed by Wm. Skinner OBE, DL, JP, – response by the Mayor of Southgate. Charity and friends were proposed by SWS. and replied to by Dennis Apps. The evening produced £80 for each mayor plus £42 which the mayor of Enfield donated to the Enfield & Cheshunt Hospital League of Friends.

A generous thanks must also go to all supporting the Sportsman's Night on 17th May 1966, and to Joe Mercer, the chairman of the Licensed Victuallers National Homes, for whom £425 was raised. The following guests attended: Alan Rudkin, Teddy Broadribb, Arthur Danahar, Alf Mancini, Tony Mancini, Johnny Williams and Johnny Wright. Len Harvey was unwell, but sent his Lonsdale belt and world trophy, and also in attendance was Kid Lewis. Two other Lonsdale belts were on show, belonging to Alan Rudkin and Pat O'Keefe – the latter kindly loaned by his nephew Bill Stratton. Henry Cooper would have been with us, but he was boxing Cassius Clay (later Muhammad Ali) on the following Saturday at the Arsenal football ground, but we had boxing gloves signed by Henry and Ali which were auctioned (presented by R. Stewardson), also a cricket bat from Fred Titmus, signed by him and the England and Australian Test teams and used by him in the match, and a football signed by the Spurs team. Teddy Waltham compered the boxing films – some going back to the First World War and early Twenties. Pat O'Keefe had the great honour of having tea with our Gracious Lady the Queen Mother in his bungalow at the LV Homes at Denham when 144 new homes were officially opened. This year, 1997, my sister-in-law Phyllis, also in the homes, had the honour of having tea with Prince Philip and was amazed at his informality and amusing chat, as if with a customer when in business. I myself have also attended three functions when the Prince has been the honoured guest, and enjoyed his lively speeches. He was president and patron of the LV Homes.

A meeting was called on 6th March, 1967 to explore the possibility of The Cambridge and the George raising money for local charities; this was followed up with another meeting held on 18th April, resulting in them being named the Cambridge and George Charity Association with Jim Pines OBE, JP as chairman. Four promotions followed including a fashion show, expertly projected by Winnie Hammond, the proprietor of Irene's dress shop. The last promotion, held on 6th November, 1967, was the important and unique function when Tottenham Hotspur won the coveted FA Cup and Enfield the Amateur Cup. Both cups were with us overnight – maybe the only time the two cups had been together. We had the great pleasure of promoting a Cup Winners' Night for charity, and we appreciate and sincerely thank both clubs and teams and all concerned with supporting and making the evening unforgettable. Both teams were led in by their captains with their cups, to a great and enthusiastic welcome. The chairman, Jim Pines, proposed the toast, to the Queen and guests – the latter was replied to by Dave Mackay (Spurs) and Tommy Lawrence (manager of Enfield AFC). Football was proposed by Dick Butt (president of EFC) and replied to by Eddie Bailey (assistant manager of Spurs). Charity was proposed by the president – SWS and replied to by Dennis Apps. Tim Holland, with Ron Whitbread, represented Charringtons – Tim said a few words and presented a bottle of Asti Gancia to each player and a magnum of champagne for auction. Cliff Jones brought his uncle Bryn Jones who had been transferred to Arsenal in

1936 for a record £14,000. Both cups had a loving clean next morning.

The children from Halliwick School for Physically Handicapped Children enjoyed a tea party at The Cambridge in 1967 – an entertainer and his dog greatly amused them and it was a tonic to everyone to see their happy concentrating faces being so attentive. They thoroughly enjoyed all the treats and goodies with which the keen and thoughtful Cambridge staff and members so enthusiastically attended to the children's wants so kindly. Our thanks to all concerned in making the party such a happy occasion.

Another very successful outing for the children and staff was a day on the Thames on a chartered boat. I saw the party off at 8.30 a.m. – everything was laid on, including a chicken lunch and various drinks.

Two letters of appreciation were received from the school – one from the Headmaster and one from the Matron.

Following requests to change the name of the CGCA, at first, very much against my wishes, a meeting was called, the intention being to change to a name projecting a sporting aspect. The outcome was the Sportsmans' 68 Dinner Club. The result was encouraging and finally settled with a very dedicated band of enthusiastic officers and committee members, while their ladies formed their own committee enhancing and promoting many money-raising events. I designed the logo and menus, which were completed by an artist.

Taking 'the George' out of the original name was not very kindly accepted by Brian – had I been in his place I would have been extremely annoyed.

The first promotion under the new name was held on 3rd April, 1968, a sporting function honouring Johnny Pritchet and Alan Rudkin (British middleweight and bantamweight boxing champions). The Club was proposed by John Saggs with response by the chairman, Jim Pines. Reg Gutteridge was our guest speaker. I had the privilege of proposing the speaker and guests and the pleasure of making the presentation to Johnny and Alan of a candelabrum. Teddy Waltham (secretary to the BBBC) replied. He was the National Amateur Schoolboy Boxing Champion and had refereed more professional world title bouts than anyone else. 'The Last Bell' was announced by Reg Varny. Many other well-known sportsmen attended. A very warm thanks to all for making this a pleasant and successful evening for charity.

Fred Titmus (England and Middlesex wicketkeeper) together with Ron Jones (Captain of the British Olympic Team) were honoured on 11th December, 1968. The Club was proposed by Jim Curran and replied to by Jim Pines. The speaker was the very much in demand Arthur Dickson-Wright MS, FRCS, proposed by Dr Brian Curtin and replied to by Leslie Golding. I had the honour, as president, of making the presentation to both, and, according to my diary, 'their replies were very complimentary'. Also, I quote, 'Reg Gutteridge was excellent announcing "The Last Bell"'. My guests were Norman Easley, Linley Armitage, Jack Ashton, Alderman Bill Cook, Malcolm Blackmore, George Sewell, Charlie Ward (who boxed on my grandfather's promotion), Alan Fairbairn, John Amiss, Ron Parker, Derek Morris, David Walton and Tim Stone; also in attendance were Johnny Pritchet, Alan Rudkin, Dick Sterne, John Murray and Cliff Jones. Quote from diary: 'Dickson-Wright made the

"Draw". Reg Gutteridge won first prize and Mike England the Turkey.'

The Club honoured Alan and Cathy Rudkin on 30th April, 1969. Alan had just returned from Australia where he had challenged Lionel Rose for the bantamweight championship of the world, losing by an extremely low margin – his second attempt at the title. A very entertaining evening followed; the guests were received by Alan and Cathy, together with Teddy and Kitty. Jim Pines, our chairman as with every function, said grace and proposed the toast to the Queen. John Saggs proposed the welcome to Cathy and Alan and the other guests and was replied to by Jock Oram. Teddy Waltham's toast to Alan was replied to with much appreciation.

'The Last Round' was announced by the very likeable Harry Carpenter, the BBC commentator; Teddy Waltham auctioned a letter to the Club from Sugar Ray Robinson which I had obtained from him at the Hilton Hotel; Harry auctioned the signed boxing gloves and Cliff Jones a football signed by the Spurs, Arsenal, West Ham and Chelsea teams. We had a three-tier cake made, the top representing a boxing ring with ropes and boxers. Alan and Cathy cut it at 11.45 p.m. and all 160 were served with a piece. The presentation was made by the president – cut glass decanter and six glasses. Also in attendance were Allan Clarke (TV commentator), Brian McCaffry (boxing commentator) and Johnny Pritchet, to whom the chairman made a presentation. My guests were Ron and Margaret Parker, Jim and Ena Folkes, Len and Mrs Mancini, Jim Crame and Superintendant Whyte of the CID. Thanks to all for raising £250.

A great evening was enjoyed by 177 attending a sportsmen's promotion on 13th October, 1969, raising £203 for charity and honouring Dave Mackay for his nine unforgettable years with Spurs in which he won three FA Cup winner's medals, the League and Cup double and also the first British success in Europe, beating Athletico Madrid 5–1 at Rotterdam in 1963. Dave captained Scotland internationally, and was Footballer of the Year.

Cliff Jones was also honoured – a great friend of Dave and always a delight to watch with his outstanding and unusual style. He was also a keen supporter of our Club's charity efforts.

The guest of the evening was his cousin, Ken Jones, a sports journalist. The Club was proposed by Ray Williams and responded to by the chairman. The guests were proposed by Dr Brian Curtin, and replied to by Bill Cook, mayor of Enfield. Presentations to the honoured guests were made by Jim Pines OBE, JP and replied to by Dave and Cliff. The 'Final Whistle' was announced by Ken Jones. Many other well-known sportsmen and personalities attended. My guests were Alan Rudkin, Johnny Pritchet, Bill Cook and Alan Young.

1 must thank Dennis Grill (through Fred Forrest) for introducing Michael Bonallack whom the Club honoured on 19th February, 1970. Michael was British Amateur Golf Champion in 1961, '65, '68 and '69, the English title holder in 1962, '63, '65, '67 and '68 and Boy Champion in 1952, plus many other honours.

His wife Angela also has a tremendous golfing record, winning the English Amateur Championship in 1958 and '63, and being runner-up in 1960 and '62; she was also Champion of Sweden and of Germany in 1955 and of Scandinavia in 1956 and Portugal 1957, and she played for England from 1956 to 1968. Michael's sister Sally has also captured the English title.

The Club was proposed by Richard Harris and replied to by Jim Pines. The guests were proposed by John Saggs (now the president) and replied to by the mayor, Alderman W. Cook. The president made the presentation to Michael, who enthusiastically replied. 'The 19th Hole' was announced by Jack Stratton (golf correspondent for the *Sun*). The artiste was Harold Blackburn, by kind permission of Sadlers Wells. We received a kind letter from Michael – a very charming person.

Henry and Albina Cooper were the guests of the evening when the Club honoured Reg and Connie Gutteridge on 13th May, 1970. Reg's family is steeped in boxing, from the opening of the National Sporting Club in 1891. His grandfather was the first boxer to step in the ring, winning the first bout, and then as the Club's chief second stayed until the Club closed in 1937 very much in debt.

Dick Gutteridge, father of Reg, and his twin brother Jack were famous full-time instructors; most well-known boxers of that period were trained or seconded by the twins. Reg was a successful amateur boxer, winning many titles. He joined the *Evening News* in 1938 and eventually became one of the most authoritative boxing correspondents in the world.

My diary is sometimes confusing – maybe the reader will make more sense of the following entry. 'Our guests to be honoured, Reg and Connie, arrived with George Bass at 8 p.m. (Dinner set for 7.30 p.m.) The mayor and mayoress (Bill and Jean Cook) waited till after the reception then were announced with Reg and Connie G. and Henry and Albina Cooper with whom Audrey and I had received the guests after the members and their ladies were assembled.'

The welcome to Reg and Connie was proposed by John Saggs (president) with a response by the mayor, Alderman

W. Cook. Reg was proposed by John Bromley, executive producer of London Weekend Television.) The response by Reg was, as always, interesting and lively. The presentation was made by the president. Our thanks to all for making this promotion so enjoyable, especially to Connie for her help on the ladies' committee. The money raised would help the Club to present a new ambulance to the Red Cross.

I must pay my respects and many thanks to the London Ex-Boxers' Association (LEBA) for their interest and help in any sporting event when charity is the goal, apart from their own continuous efforts for charity and to help others. Jack Powell, their president, who sadly passed away in 1996 aged eighty, together with his wife Mary were the most dedicated couple, never to be surpassed. Jack boxed Freddie Mills twice – one was a draw and in the other Jack retired with a cut eye. Mary is a councillor and continues as secretary for LEBA, apart from managing her own business. Their catchphrase: 'It's nice to belong'.

Never in my wildest thoughts did I think Larry Gains would on occasions be my guest at charity functions (see p. 278). Another contest between Eric Boon and Arthur Danahar, was an exciting classic; they were also my guests – together as friends (p. 476).

One treasured memory was spending an evening with Tommy Farr when attending a dinner boxing promotion at the Hilton Hotel in the early Seventies. Tommy took a bow when introduced by the toastmaster (see p. 339). On that night in 1937, together with a friend Lesley Pratt, we arranged to sleep in our lounge at the George and listen to the contest on the radio at 3 a.m., broadcast from America. We switched on and tuned in to hear the announcement and the bell for the first round, then distortion and silence. Not one of my favourite memories.

The committee and members, and also everyone involved, no matter how small their contribution, were pleasingly repaid when a revolving cedar summer house was presented to the Halliwick School for Physically Handicapped Children. The letter from Matron moistens ones eyes and prepares one for greater efforts.

August 1970 saw another presentation that the above efforts made possible when the Club purchased an ambulance for Mrs Dorothy Dixon MBE, divisional director of the Red Cross. I was unable to attend, but received a very kind letter from her. Dorothy collected me from hospital following my knee operation in the new ambulance and provided a stool to rest my leg on – a kindness so very much appreciated.

We very much recall the happy evenings when the Edmonton Pensioners' Club had their supper dance evenings at the Cambridge – with very special arrangements regarding the meal and so on – a tonic to watch such a happy gathering of delightful people. Our very sincere thanks for inviting Audrey and myself to your last evening prior to vacating The Cambridge and presenting us with the engraved rose bowl which has pride of place in our entrance hall – a happy memory.

The following names were honoured during the period 1970 until 1974, when we vacated The Cambridge on 4th April, and for the varied money-making events: Alan Gilzean (guest: Pat Jennings), Frank McLintock and Teddy Waltham (guest: Peter Wilson).

Among other sportsmen honoured were: George Armstrong, Bob Wilson (Arsenal), John Stacey, Bill Nicholson OBE (Spurs), Leslie Compton, Steve Perryman and John Pratt (Spurs), Terry Downs, (Enfield Harriers), Sebastian Coe, Pat Jennings (Spurs) and, as guest of the evening, Harry Carpenter.

The many other ways of raising money were continued including old time music hall performances, flower shows, fashion shows and the Tramps Ball The Race Nights (films) were held at the Firs Hall, Winchmore Hill(due to numbers and space) and, and the cash raised mainly came from the Tote which was run by the Lake family (Leslie was a committee member). When the numbers exceeded the capacity of The Cambridge, the sporting promotions were mainly held at the Regal Suite, Edmonton, and were organised by Jim Curran.

The Sportsmans' 68 Dinner Club arranged a farewell evening for Audrey and myself on 30th March, 1974, prior to vacating The Cambridge on 4th April; 190 attended. Audrey was presented with an elegant porcelain figurine and for me an engraved silver letter opener which I have used today (16th October 1997) and almost every day since. My diary records, 'Everyone was so generous and kind'. My guests were Dorothy Dixon, Sister Truman, Teddy and Kitty Waltham, Jim and May Pines, Jim and Ena Folkes, Chris and Joan Wilkins, Jack and Margaret Oram, Dennis and Kate Apps and Kirk and Susan McBride (Principal of the Whitewebbs Old Peoples Home).

Our last night with the customers on 1st April was attended by some two hundred in the banqueting hall where a free bar and buffet was offered. The presentation to us was made by Dennis Grill and his son David on the stage – a very lovely inscribed fruit bowl from staff and friends. My diary records, 'I replied and to my surprise was relaxed and spoke for about thirty minutes – sure this was because the audience was so very attentive'. Teddy and Kitty

Waltham gave us a Wedgwood table lighter, Frank and Poppy gave us six gold-plated spoons, which we have used almost every day since, and David and Linda Taylor (our local baker) gave us a huge cake which we later cut. Harry Cushing and Ray Wilkins rounded off the evening with their thanks and very kind remarks on behalf of a very charming gathering of friends – an evening to remember.

The following day we attended the staff party. Brian arranged the George staff to relieve the Cambridge staff to enjoy a buffet and free bar in the hall. Brian said a few kind and appropriate words to which I replied. What a strange, empty and sorrowful feeling we had when seeing the customers out for the last time. We had a final drink with the George's staff, and offered our thanks to Brian and his staff for their efficient way they operated the bars.

The changeover on 4th April, 1974, was sad, but was eased by the prevailing circumstances, and it was forty-one years since A.J.S. obtained the full license.

The same year, 1974, we celebrated the family's fifty years at the George and vacated the premises with much sorrow under circumstances we found impossible to cope with. We had planned a new restaurant with a Saladaire and self or waitress service, and even purchased £800 worth of Poole pottery before present prevailing circumstances altered our arrangements.

We thank Charringtons for the kind, considerate and helpful way their directors, managers and staff made our family's fifty-four years so memorable.

I complete this epilogue with thoughts of the Enfield and Cheshunt League of Hospital Friends and the amazing benefits brought about by the officers, committee, members and helpers who have given their services, equipment and care to the Chase Farm Hospital so freely and thoughtfully – such a tonic to know there are many, many who will do and care so much for others without reward but that will be manifest and comforting to one's inner thoughts.

A special thanks to our son Brian for his help, especially his catering expertise.

The following letters fuel enthusiasm for all endeavours to help charities that are promoted by those that give their time and effort so freely, without reward.

*Halliwick School for Physically*
*Handicapped Children*
*Bush Hill Road*
*Winchmore Hill N21*
*Telephone Laburnum 2442*
*12th July, 1969*

*Dear Mr & Mrs Standbrook,*

*The children had a wonderful day on Monday last. The trip on the river was delightful and they thoroughly enjoyed their lunch. The pleasant day was rounded off by a very nice meal at Windsor before the ride home.*

*Thank you so much for arranging the Concert and Supper that made this treat possible. I do appreciate the amount of work and time involved. Would you please extend my sincere thanks to your Patrons who take such an interest in the children in our care.*

*I would like to add that everything ran so smoothly and well on Monday, that the staff felt that it was one of the nicest outings that the children had had.*

*With renewed thanks and best wishes,*

*Yours sincerely,*
*M. King, Matron*

*Halliwick School for Physically*
*Handicapped Children*
*Bush Hill Road*
*Winchmore Hill N21*
*19th July, 1969*

*Dear Committee and Members*

*I am writing to express our sincere thanks to you all for so kindly providing the girls of this School with yesterday's outing on the Thames.*

*I have been on countless outings with handicapped children during the many years I have been dealing with them, but it is a long time since I have experienced such a perfect day as we had yesterday. Everything, including the weather, was just right.*

*I feel sure that some of the girls will also be wanting to write to you, and I will forward their letters later.*

*With my very best wishes to your Club and renewed thanks,*

*Yours sincerely,*
*S.G. Hughes, Headmaster*

*40 Marsden Road*
*Edmonton N9*
*22nd December, 1969*

*Dear Sir,*

*The gift of so many good things for Xmas that you sent to me today (on Mrs Dixon giving you my name) is beyond my ability to find words to thank you. My dear wife was also near to tears. I suppose it is not surprising for us to feel like that at our age; we are both eighty-nine and our friends tell us we look so well they cannot believe it, but we begin to feel it at times. My dear wife is unfortunately a registered blind person of this borough so cannot write her thanks, so we do thank you very much and trust you and yours will have good health and an enjoyable Xmas.*

*Yours sincerely,*
*R.H. Kingston*

*Bridge House*
*1 Forty Hill*
*Enfield*
*Middlesex*

*To Mr Standbrook*

*On behalf of the Residents of the above Home, I wish to thank you for the lovely presents which you gave us, also the various items which you gave to make our Xmas a Happy one.*

*Yours faithfully,*
*F. Green*
*M. Nevill*

Evening News
*Harmsworth Publications Ltd*
*Carmelite House*
*London EC4*
*14th May, 1970*

*Dear Mr Standbrook*

*Thank you for making me so welcome last night. It was a thoroughly enjoyable evening and I think you are to be congratulated, if I may say so, on arranging such a happy gathering.*

*Yours sincerely,*
*T. Iain Mackie*
*Sports Editor*

*London Borough of Enfield*
*Mayor's Parlour*
*Civic Centre, Enfield*
*Middlesex 01 363 5311*
*Mayor – Alderman W. H. Cook*
*14th May, 1970*

*Dear Stan,*

*I would like to tell you, once again, how very much Jean and I enjoyed the Sportsmans' 68 Dinner last night. We had a really wonderful time and were delighted to have the opportunity of meeting some of the colourful sports personalities present. You certainly succeeded in getting a fine gathering, and we congratulate you upon the success of the evening.*

*It has been a great pleasure to us both to meet you and Audrey on so many occasions during our term of office, and we should like to thank you for the many happy evenings spent in your convivial company.*

*With renewed thanks and all good wishes to you both,*

*Yours sincerely,*
*W.H. Cook, Mayor*

*Sports Writers' Association*
*of Great Britain*
*Evening News*
*Harmsworth House*
*London EC4*
*22nd May, 1970*

*Dear Stan,*

*Our belated, but none the less sincere thanks for a tremendous evening. Please thank everybody of the 68 Club and we were really honoured with the presentation and by the company present.*

*Regards,*
*Yours sincerely,*
*Reg Gutteridge*
*Chairman*